birthday 1997
Joan & Richard

Chesapeake Bay Schooners

Quentin Snediker & Ann Jensen

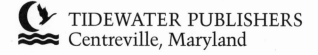
TIDEWATER PUBLISHERS
Centreville, Maryland

Library of Congress Cataloging-in-Publication Data
Snediker, Quentin
    Chesapeake Bay Schooners / Quentin Snediker and Ann Jensen. — 1st
  ed.
        p.   cm.
    Includes bibliographical references and index.
    ISBN 0-87033-435-2
    1. Schooners—Chesapeake Bay (Md. and Va.)   I. Jensen, Ann,
    II. Title.
VM311.F7S66   1992
387.2'24'0975518—dc20   92-25237
                                                              CIP

Manufactured in the United States of America
First edition

Contents

Preface

Chesapeake Bay schooners have seldom been more than a foot-note in chronicles of maritime America. Yet, for nearly two centuries, schooners were the most common vessel type in the American merchant fleet, serving on the Bay and in a vigorous coastwise trade. With the schooner fleets of the North, they dominated the American merchant marine, making it one of the largest and most efficient fleets of domestic carriers in the world.

Among the vessels making up the American merchant fleet of the eighteenth and nineteenth centuries, schooners were the most prosperous of the commercial vessels for those who owned and operated them. The schooner's distinct advantages were recognized early. In the hands of shipwrights on the Chesapeake Bay and in New England, the schooner developed into a vessel having a distinctly regional, and then a national, identity.

The sharp-built Virginia pilot schooner and the famed Baltimore clipper have taken precedence in accounts of the maritime heritage of the Bay, overshadowing the less colorful merchant schooners. The story of the merchant schooner on the Chesapeake Bay never has been told fully. There were, after all, few tales of derring-do with which these hardy vessels could stir the imagination. Unlike their cousins, the oceangoing packets, deepwater schooners, and clippers, Bay freight schooners seldom traveled great distances into alien environments—to China for opium and tea, to Africa for slaves, or on the Atlantic as pirates and privateers.

There aren't many tales of those schooners that regularly braved the contrary winds and tides to go coastwise along treacherous stretches of the Atlantic seaboard. And there are fewer still of the majority of Bay schooners that never sailed beyond the Virginia capes to venture offshore.

Relatively little is known of those vessels that were the workhorses of the Bay; yet they played a significant role in the settlement and economic growth of tidewater Virginia and Maryland, a role much the same as that of the wagon trains and railroads in opening the West. Much of the drama of the Chesapeake Bay schooner is lost to historians because it survived, when it did, only in the memories of Bay watermen and in the stories told by one generation to the next and the next. But now we have come to the last and when they are gone, the memories are gone.

Those who sailed in schooners on the Bay left little in the way of writing to aid historians in recreating the age of working sail on the Chesapeake. Few records survive, especially those used daily, such as schooner logs, account books, journals, correspondence, and later photographs. These were workboats, and the men who sailed them gave no thought to saving their day-to-day records for posterity.

If written records survived, it was pure chance. They were stowed away and forgotten in the bottom of a sea chest, perhaps, or in an attic corner. Some, like several account books for freight and packet schooners owned by the Sands family in Annapolis, survived in the family for more than a hundred years because they were recycled as scrapbooks, with newspaper clippings, poems, pictures, and stories from *Harper's Weekly* neatly pasted over freight lists and orders for supplies going back to the early 1800s.

As for the schooners themselves, most were worked hard, and, if they were not sunk or run down by other vessels or destroyed in some other way, they simply wore out and were abandoned. Seldom did any but the men who sailed them note their passing; yet far more people's lives and livelihoods depended on Bay freight schooners, pungies, and rams than on the famed Baltimore clippers, immortalized in paintings and in ship models, whose exploits are generally known in detail. While the clipper schooners were building their reputations on the high seas during the Revolution and the War of 1812, hundreds of anonymous freight schooners kept the armies and the civilian populations supplied. They continued in that role up into the twentieth century.

In 1965, Kenneth Brooks, Jr., wrote of the fictional schooner *Albatross*, " . . . I imagine she had the same problems of earning her living all her life . . . She came along, fresh and new, about the time steam was showing its muscle on the Bay, and she fought all her life against the steamboats, and in the end, when the trucks and good roads were slowly strangling the steamboats, she was still out there fighting and holding her own . . . most of the men who sailed the Bay, both in steam and under canvas, didn't realize that progress was stalking them from over the hills as the state improved its highways and General Motors and Freuhauf improved their trucks and trailers . . . but when it came, the Depression came to all of them, all at once. And when things got better, the boats were gone and the trucks had stepped

in to fill the gap."[1] The *Albatross* may have been a fiction, but her fate was true to that of her real-life counterparts.

But what were they like, these schooners that filled the rivers and harbors of the Chesapeake Bay a century ago? Where did they come from? Who built them? Owned them? Sailed them? How were they rigged? How were they employed? What of the forces that created and then destroyed them?

The following is our effort to answer those questions and in so doing, to do what no other book has done, which is to chronicle the entire history of these remarkable Bay craft from their European origins to the last survivors. It is not meant to replace the works of naval architect Howard I. Chapelle or Bay historians such as Robert H. Burgess or M. V. Brewington. Indeed, we have depended upon them and other researchers who have gone before to guide us through the maze of history and keep us on course in more recent times and current endeavors.

Long before anybody else put a historic value on vessels such as the schooners that worked the Chesapeake Bay, men like Howard Chapelle, Eric Steinlein, Robert Burgess, and John Earle were studying and documenting them. Until recently, the work of Howard Chapelle on eighteenth and nineteenth century schooners was the one best source, and therefore we have relied on him in numerous instances, realizing that he expanded upon early data and often created missing details based on his own conclusions.

We have used early material from a variety of sources to provide a perspective from which to view the final incarnation of the schooner on the Chesapeake Bay in the nineteenth and twentieth century centerboarder. We explored private and public libraries, photo and plans collections, and archives in search of as much primary source material as possible. In several instances, we have introduced heretofore unpublished material, such as the early nineteenth century correspondence between Annapolis merchants Henry Maynadier and Joseph Sands and that between Captain Charles Gordon and the secretary of the navy during the War of 1812. Our research also uncovered vessel lists and unpublished notes of Howard I. Chapelle, M. V. and Dorothy Brewington, John Earle, and others held in archives from Newport News, Virginia, to Mystic, Connecticut. Wherever possible, we have gone back to memoirs and contemporary records, and newspaper and magazine accounts.

Already most who built and sailed these vessels are lost to us and as time takes us further and further away from the days of Chesapeake Bay schooners, there will be fewer and fewer people who have any direct knowledge of them. In telling the story of the Chesapeake Bay freight schooners, we made every effort to let those speak who knew and sailed them.

We talked to men like C. Calvert Evans, Harry B. Porter, William Stevens, and Woodrow Aaron, men who lived their lives on the Chesapeake, working the schooners, loving and nursing them, cursing and fighting them, boy to man, 'til one or the other, schooner or skipper, gave out.

We owe a tremendous debt to those who shared their time, their memories, their knowledge, and their cherished collections of photographs with us. Their contributions, as you will see, were immeasurable. We especially thank Frank Moorshead, Jr., who allowed us to use his extensive collection of photos, and Woodrow Aaron, Earl Brannock, Shirley Brannock, Ned Brownlee, Robert H. Burgess, John Dubois, John Earle, C. Calvert Evans, Mary Jackson, Jack King, Joseph Liener, James E. Marvil, M.D., A. Pierce Middleton, Wade Murphy, Lynn D. Perry, Harry Benton Porter, Jim Richardson, Jerry Smith, Muffet Staley, William Seaford Stevens, Robert F. Sumrall, Lester Trott, Arthur L. Van Name, Jr., M.D., John Ward, Sr., Mame Warren, M. E. Warren, and Charles W. Wittholz.

There were still others whose names will show up in endnotes and throughout the text and many who are not named but who aided us tremendously in our search. We also are grateful for the assistance of the staffs and volunteers of the libraries, archives, historical societies, and museums included in the Bibliography.

Key to Photo Credits

MdHR	Maryland Hall of Records
MSA	Maryland State Archives

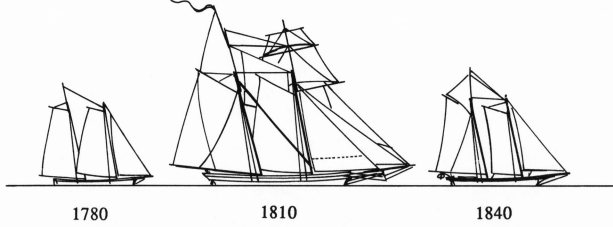

1780   1810   1840

Chesapeake Bay Schooners

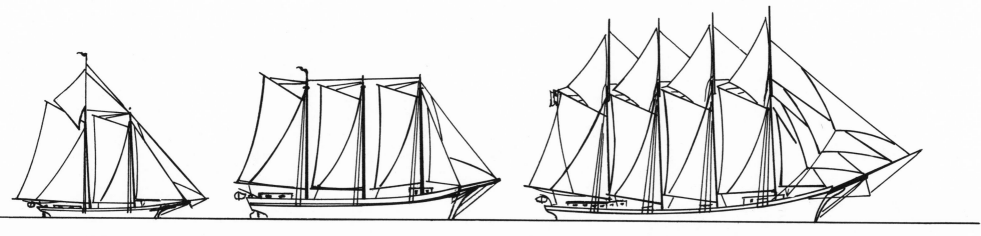

1870   1890   1920

One

The *Fannie Insley:* A Good Boat

In 1918, the *Fannie Insley* was one of two hundred or more schooners still hauling freight from one end of the Chesapeake Bay to the other. For many watermen, sailing freight schooners was the only way of life they knew. Some could even remember how it was when every harbor was full of two-masters like the *Fannie*, with more coming off the stocks in yards all over the Bay.

In 1918, a man who had a good boat could still make a living with it and could keep his family fed and clothed. And for a time yet, men who worked the Bay under sail could ignore the growing number of aging schooners being run into marshes and quiet backwaters and abandoned. It was a hard life running a schooner, but it was a good life.

For Raymond Evans, who came from Elliott Island on Maryland's Eastern Shore, the *Fannie Insley* was a good boat. He bought her in 1918, in partnership with two other Elliot's Island men, Alonzo and Albury Moore. Raymond Evans was her captain and soon after he and the Moores bought the *Fannie*, he moved to Cambridge with his young wife and their two children, Calvert, five, and Dorothy, seven. It was simple enough when you had a good boat like the *Fannie*. He loaded his family and their furniture aboard the schooner and sailed up the Choptank to their new house in Cambridge.[1]

The *Fannie* was built on Church Creek, off the Little Choptank River below Cambridge, Maryland. She was ordered by a brash, young Hooper Island man by the name of John Wesley Brannock in 1883. He paid $1,800 for her and worked her in the pineapple trade between the Bahamas and Baltimore. A good boat like the *Fannie* could make three trips a season and earn more than $1,000 a trip.[2]

By the turn of the century, Captain Brannock and the *Fannie* were out of the pineapple trade. Brannock sold the schooner, and the *Fannie* went to freighting grain and tomatoes on the Bay and hauling lumber up from the Carolinas. She was doing that when Raymond Evans and the Moore brothers bought her.

The *Fannie* was well-built and a sharp sailer. At 78 feet, she was about average for schooners in the Bay trade. When she was running light, she would draw 5 feet; loaded, 8. That was about average too. Loaded, she could carry 120 tons of oyster shell or the equivalent in coal or grain and

The *Fannie Insley* had a fair wind when fourteen-year-old Calvert Evans crawled out on her bowsprit to get this shot. She was sailing "with a bone in her teeth," which was a good way of describing this head-on view with white water curling up on either side of the schooner's cutwater. Calvert and his father, Raymond Evans, were southbound in Tangier Sound with a load of phosphate rock for the fertilizer plants. The *Fannie*'s windlass machinery on the foredeck glistens with the spray thrown up by her plunging bow. The sheen of the water emphasizes the clean, unbroken line of her deck, which allowed plenty of room for working or carrying deck cargo. She carried a gas-powered pump on her deck to the starboard, just forward of the cabin trunk. The 59-ton, 78-foot *Fannie Insley* was built in 1883 by J. W. Brooks at Church Creek, Maryland. (C. Calvert Evans)

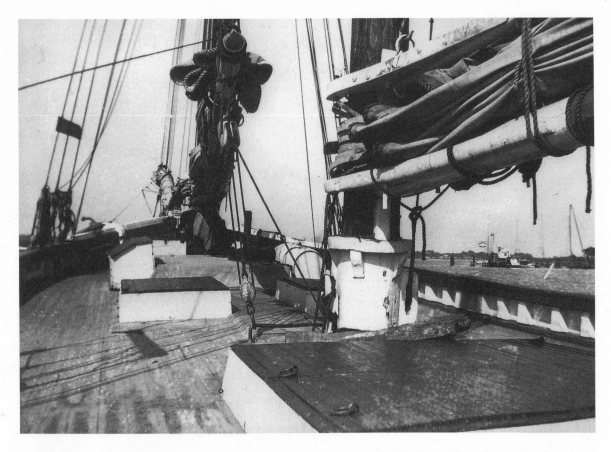

These Bay schooners were working vessels, built for rough usage. Here, we are looking forward from the main hatch on the *Smith K. Martin*. Much of her structural strength lay in features such as the heavy raised plank, called the "king plank," running down the center of her deck. Her sturdy bulwarks and waterway timbers, seen here along her starboard deck edge, were another example of the strength and quality of this schooner's construction that kept her working longer than many Bay schooners. (Courtesy of Smithsonian Institution, National Museum of American History, HAMMS Collection, Philip Sawyer)

Like the *Fannie Insley*, the *Smith K. Martin* was built on Maryland's Eastern Shore. Launched in 1899 at Pocomoke City, she originally was intended for the Jersey coast fisheries and was well and heavily built to withstand the battering of the Atlantic. But Bay shipwright E. James Tull built all his boats like that. His vessels were known for the quality of their construction and the 50-ton *Martin* was a good example. By 1936, when this photograph was taken, she had been working the Bay for thirty-seven years, hauling general cargo, stone and building materials, enough to break the back of many a schooner. But the *Martin* showed none of the "hogging" or loss of the graceful curve of her hull from bow to stern that marked so many aging Bay freighters. She was still sound when, in 1940, she was bought by a retired naval officer. He took her to sea and never was heard of again. (Courtesy of Smithsonian Institution, National Museum of American History, HAMMS Collection, No. 5-7-1, Philip Sawyer)

could still get into most river landings. That was important, for the shoal-draft schooners kept working the longest.

Most of the time, in the first years that he owned her, Raymond Evans used the *Fannie* to run seed oysters from tongers on the James River in Virginia to Elliott Island where he'd plant them. He figured he was getting four or five bushels of oysters for every bushel of spat he brought back on the *Fannie*.[3]

Captain Evans took good care of his schooner and always saw to it that she had a fresh coat of paint. He kept her hull painted black, which was common practice with the older schooners. White or light gray was popular with many of the later boats, but black kept a schooner from showing her age. "As they got older, their sides weren't as smooth as they were when they were made," said Calvert Evans, who followed the water as his father had. "The seams got larger and uglier and they tried to hide as much of it as they could. That was when they painted them black."[4]

"My father, he had his colors," said Calvert Evans. "He had a certain shade of buff he used. The deck and the cabin trunk and the tops of the hatches all had to be that color. The *Fannie* had a rounded, push-back forepeak hatch, and it had to be buff too. The tops of everything were buff. The sides of the cabin trunk and the hatches were white. The waterway was green and inside the bulwark was painted white. Her caprail was white, too. She had a brown stripe under her rail inside the bulwark, and there was a bead under the brown that had to be painted orange. The bowsprit was black and the jibboom inboard up to the jib stays was white. The outer end of the jibboom was varnished and so were the masthead and the booms. A lot of the others painted their blocks, but he liked his varnished."[5]

A Dollar a Day

"About 1920, I started going with my father in the *Fannie*," said Calvert Evans. "That would give me seven years. I'd sail with him during summer vacations. I couldn't wait 'til summertime came so I could go on the boat with him. I spent fifteen summers with my father on the *Fannie*.

"I had to work my way up to get a man's pay and when I did, I was getting a dollar a day, which was about as low as it got. I can still remember the day my father said, 'I'm not going to carry a second man this year. You're going to do it.' Gosh I thought I was something and I said, 'You going to pay me the same as you been paying me?'

"'Yessir, a dollar a day,' he says, just like I should be proud to get it. And I was.

"That was about the first time he'd trust me at the wheel, where he turned in solid and went to bed. We'd been planting shells that day down below the mouth of the Patuxent off Cedar Point. When we were done, he said, 'I'm not going into Cambridge tonight. I'm going up in the Patuxent and anchor.'

"'Let's go up tonight,' I says.

"'You think you can take her up?' he asked me and I said 'Yessir.'

"Then I watched him take off his clothes and crawl into that berth.

"'You ain't going to bed, are you?' I asked.

"'Yep,' he says and turns over, leaving me to take her up. We had a crackin' sou'wester that night and we went up that

This view of the after deck shows the wheelbox of the *Smith K. Martin*. She had a pronounced elliptical stern, more shapely and larger than on most Bay schooners. It was topped by a taffrail and turned stanchions as shown here. (Courtesy of Smithsonian Institution, National Museum of American History, HAMMS Collection, Philip Sawyer)

Bay in no time, it seemed like. We were in the Choptank when I called him and he asked where we were.

"'We're almost up there,' I says and, boy, I thought I was something else. That night has always stuck with me. And it was after that he went down to just one other man and me and started paying me a dollar a day.

"In my father's time, they mostly used home crews. My father could always get a man off of Elliott Island. Same way with Hooper Island or here in Cambridge. You could always get local. Got right good experienced help here in Cambridge.

Captain Raymond Evans is seated here behind the main hatch of the *Mildred*, which was captained at the time by his son, Calvert Evans. The lines hanging from the foreboom above his head are "sail stops" used for securing the sail when furled. (Van Name/Perry Collection)

"In Baltimore, during the thirties and forties, you'd go to Pratt Street, to the shipping office where you could find Puerto Ricans and other men to hire on your boat. There was also a clothing store owned by a man named Saperstein. He sold a little bit of everything, and he could get you a crew too. He could send you a man real quick. If you were down the Bay, and a man quit, you could call Saperstein and he'd have a man on the next bus. It was pretty easy getting crews. Of course if you wanted a cook, you'd never know what you'd get, so I'd do the cooking. My father'd always say, I could make a good piece of bread."[6]

It Wrung His Leg Off

"When I started out sailing on the *Fannie* with my father, we hoisted the sails and pulled the anchor up by hand. He was one of the last ones to put a power winch on her. That was 1928. I was fifteen. The first trip he put the donkey engine on her, he got hung up in it and it wrung his leg off.

"He was pulling on the rope and had it all between his legs. I was back aft and when I looked up there, the winch was carrying him over and over and over. Every time it carried him over, he'd try to reach the switch, but he couldn't. By the time I got up there and stopped the engine, there was nothing left of his leg but muscle and veins. He wanted us to cut it off right there, but when we got him to Salisbury, the doctor said if we had, he'd have bled to death. As it was, it was two hours before we got him to the hospital. Had to get a police boat out to take him off. They carried him into Whitehaven, and there we got him in a car and carried him to Salisbury. It was a wonder it didn't kill him, but he was a big strong man. He went back to work with a peg leg that his brother made for him."[7]

Scowing Grain

"A lot of my father's work was from year to year. He'd look forward to seasonal work and most times, he'd get in touch with the farmers or the oyster houses directly to get the work. When he didn't have that, he'd go to the ship broker C. C. Paul in Baltimore. Mr. Paul chartered boats and charged a 5 percent commission at that time. So working through Mr. Paul and with what he got himself, my father could get along pretty good. What time he had off was usually in the late spring and that's when he would paint up, before the wheat started around the first of July.

"Most of his grain work was at the head of the Bay, out of Chesapeake City and Fredericktown and the Bohemia River. It'd be wheat in the summer months.

"When I was little, I'd ask my father, when would I be old enough to know the story on scowing grain," recalled Calvert Evans, who learned soon enough and from then on, asked with dread every time they went out, 'We going to scow any?'

"When we were loading grain in the Elk River, we'd anchor the schooner just below the mouth of the Bohemia and we'd have to lighter it in. That was some work. We'd get just as close as we could get without being ashore. The farmers would drive their wagons loaded with bags of grain out into the water about hub deep. We'd be waiting with a scow we hired from some old man up in Chesapeake City. We'd pull the scow in to the wagon with the yawl boat and fill it with one wagon load, maybe—couldn't have been over fifty bushels. We'd pull it out to the schooner and make the old scow fast, throw the bags up to the deck, and then get on deck and carry the bags over to the hatch. The hatches were small, not over eight foot by eight foot. We'd cut the string on the bag and dump the grain into the hold. There'd be a man aboard to get down in the hold to shovel the grain up under the deck and trim it up while we were going ashore to get another load. That was the hardest work I'd ever done.

"How long it took to take on a load was according to how many farmers came down to the water. We'd move from one farm to another, but they were all fairly close. After a while, we could go up to the docks at Bohemia Bridge and they'd truck the grain up to us, which wasn't too bad. We could load in a day then.

"We loaded them down 'til the water was right up to the deck. That's how we used to load them," said Evans. "About an inch to the scuppers. We swam 'em. We sunk 'em.

"In the off season, when the harvest was over in the fall, we started running down the Bay, lumber mostly out of the Rappahannock, a little out of the Potomac and out of West Point on the York, which we delivered to Baltimore. By 1935, when my father sold the *Fannie*, we were just about seeing the end of the Depression. I remember once, he was running coal into Cambridge from Baltimore where he'd delivered grain. The coal was back freight, and he got seventy-five cents a ton. It just paid the expenses and that's about the cheapest that I remember hearing anybody'd run anything, but at that time, he was glad to get it."[8]

In this 1915 photograph, hands from a farm along the Tred Avon River are shown loading bags of wheat from farm wagon to skiff to be taken to a schooner waiting offshore. There, the bags were hauled on deck and opened, and the grain dumped into the hold to be shoveled back under the wings. "Scowing grain," as it was called, was backbreaking labor. Some schooner captains towed a decked scow or small barge along with them. They secured it to the bank, tied the schooner to the scow, and the farmers used it as a temporary dock to drive their wagons up to the side of the schooner to unload the grain. (Peabody Museum of Salem, No. 27,026, H. Robins Hollyday)

This photograph of the foredeck of an unidentified Bay schooner shows her hoisting machinery: the donkey engine, gears, flywheel, chains, and lines, all exposed as was the one on the *Fannie Insley* that "wrung" Captain Evans's leg off. (Courtesy of Smithsonian Institution, National Museum of American History, HAMMS Collection)

They Just Kept Dying

"When I first went sailing with my father," said Calvert Evans, "the schooners were already on their way out. Them that owned them wouldn't spend any money on them. They couldn't. They just didn't have the work. There were a lot of schooners and rams at that time. But they kept dying out and during the war, they just disappeared. Some of the better ones were sold off the Bay. The dilapidated ones were laid up on the banks to die."[9]

A number of Bay schooners were sold to dredge oysters in Delaware where sail was required until 1945. Some went to Maine as "dude cruisers," or windjammers, and others went south and were put to a variety of uses in Florida, the Gulf of Mexico, and the Caribbean.

Raymond Evans sold the *Fannie* in 1935, and she ended up in the hands of a newspaper woman by the name of D'arcy Grant four years later. Her first winter with the old schooner, Grant got caught by the ice with a load of lumber and was stranded for forty-five days in the lower Bay with most of the rest of the schooner fleet.

"I'd written to borrow money against my freight," she wrote in a story published later in *The Sunday Sun Magazine*, "but the money didn't come before the last of the grub went."[10]

Captain Henry Davis from the *Virginia Carroll*, which was stranded a hundred yards away from the *Fannie*, guessed her plight and went ashore to buy meat for Grant and her first mate to live on until the money came.

Later, inactivity became a greater problem than food. Grant was able to keep herself busy by reading, but the first mate wasn't a reading man. He took to drink and finally jumped ship, leaving her alone with the job of cranking up the engine that ran the pumps morning and night to keep the *Fannie* and her cargo of lumber dry and afloat.

Captain Tom Ruark and his son Edmond came off the schooner *Maggie* to help her out of that predicament, which, as they told her was a "toss-up whether you'd crank that pump or it'd crank you."[11]

The following August, the *Fannie*, in the hands of Captain Wilbur Willey, was running oyster shells from Jones Point in the Rappahannock to Crisfield where the shells were ground up for fertilizer. Lumber and more desirable freight were getting harder and harder to come by, and Grant, who didn't want any part of the "dirty and nasty" cargo of shells, wasn't aboard.

The *Fannie* was eight miles off Windmill Point at the mouth of the Rappahannock. She was fighting a strong wind when her rigging gave way, ripping the chain plates out and sending her foremast over the side. When the foremast fell, it took the mainmast with it, opening up the schooner's seams and nearly breaking her in two.[12]

"There was only time to swing her head into the wind and get the yawl boat over before she went down," Willey reported to *The* [Baltimore] *Evening Sun* the next day. "Not more than forty-five minutes later the [steamboat] *City of Baltimore* came by and picked us up."[13]

As for the *Fannie Insley*, she was gone, lost in fifty feet of water, one of the last of the Chesapeake Bay schooners that once were nearly as plentiful as the vast flotilla of pleasure boats that gets under way on fair weather weekends today. They are all gone now.

And Then, They Were No More

Calvert Evans has a scrapbook, its pages filled with snapshots of the old schooners. Most of them he took with his Number Two Brownie box camera. "We didn't know we'd come to the day when they was no more," said Evans, flipping the pages of his photo album, memories bringing the yellowing images alive again—each one recalled distinctly, like pictures in a family album.[14] He remembers when and where and how he took each one.

Like the day in Tangier Sound when he shinnied out to the end of the bowsprit of the *Fannie*, riding just above the water boiling past the schooner's bow. She was sailing "wing and wing" with the wind blowing steady from behind. The *Fannie* was old then and she'd worked hard, but even so, and even to a young boy, she was a beautiful thing, a powerful symbol of the Bay and the life of the men who worked it. And none of those men knew, until the very last, that there really would come a day when the Chesapeake Bay schooner was no more.

Now, we have come to the very last generation of men who knew and sailed the schooners of the Bay. Soon, there will be none who can remember the sight of the rivers, creeks and harbors of the Chesapeake filled with schooners. Few today know their story.

The *Smith K. Martin* was hauled out at A. Smith & Sons shipyard at Curtis Bay in 1936. The Smith yard, family-owned as were so many on the Bay, figured prominently in the lives of many schooners that survived into the twentieth century. Bay-built vessels like the *Martin* got a good start in life, with oak from the Eastern Shore for keel, frames, knees, and deck beams. By the time she came along, however, southern forests were supplying the pine for planking, deck, and masts. Pine from Georgia went into the *Martin*. No matter how well they were built, to survive, these wooden schooners needed constant, and increasingly expensive, care. (Courtesy of Smithsonian Institution, National Museum of American History, HAMMS Collection, No. 91-14116)

Two

"Oh, How She Scoons!"

There was an old story of the town of Gloucester, Massachusetts, generated by one of the port's early historians as to the origin of the schooner. As it goes, in 1713, a Captain Andrew Robinson built and launched a two-masted vessel curiously rigged with fore-and-aft sails. According to Gloucester historian John Babson, as she slid from the stocks and into the water, a bystander cried out, "Oh, how she scoons!" Rising to the occasion, Captain Robinson immediately replied, "A schooner let her be!"

"From which time, vessels thus masted and rigged have gone by the name of 'schooners,' " wrote Babson in 1860, "before which, vessels of this description were not known in Europe nor America."[1]

Babson's story has often been quoted as the authority for the schooner's origin, but the fact is that the fore-and-aft, two-masted rig of the schooner was in use long before 1713 and was fairly common in Europe.

The term "schooner" itself, however, hasn't turned up in any maritime record before that date. The best guess comes from historian Arthur C. Clark, who in 1904 searched a Dutch-Latin dictionary of 1599 and found the Dutch word "schoon," which means "beautiful," "lovely," or "fair," and concluded that some early Dutch colonist used the word to describe a graceful sailing craft he saw.

At any rate, the term "schooner" has been in use since the early 1700s. The actual rig was a result of the natural progression in the development of the fore-and-aft rig with sails running on a plane with the centerline. This was in contrast to the square rig in which sails were set athwartships or "square" to the centerline. Old records indicate that sailors of northern Europe came back from voyages to Egypt and the Mediterranean with a very basic single-masted fore-and-aft rig as early as 1475. Dutch artists were showing harbor scenes with vessels carrying a schooner-type rig with sails set on two masts before 1620.

Fore-and-Aft

The British eventually adopted the fore-and-aft rig. It proved far handier than the square rig for working in the rivers and channels and along the ragged coasts of England and Northern Europe. They found the same forces, but magnified a hundredfold, in the New World and especially in the Chesapeake Bay. A handy vessel was an absolute must for travel between Maryland and Virginia, between the Chesapeake's eastern and western shores, or simply from one river town or plantation to the next.

On the Bay, where the winds tended to draw up or down its course, or along its hundreds of tributary rivers and creeks, colonial mariners found themselves constantly beating to windward. In that, the square-rigged vessels of the Old World couldn't begin to compete with those rigged fore-and-aft.

The earliest colonists used vessels commonly available back home, such as the shallop, a small vessel of sixteen to forty feet, carrying a fore-and-aft rig on one or two masts. Many were brought in pieces on ships from England and assembled here. For a time, the type was in common use for getting around the Bay. Before long, however, it was replaced by another small vessel, the single-masted fore-and-after called a "sloop"—from the Dutch "sloepe," which was refined by builders in Bermuda and copied on the Bay.

Made in America

Even before the sleek, sharp-built Bermuda sloops began to appear on the Bay in large numbers, there was a two-masted vessel, identified as a "catch" or "ketch." Typically, a ketch carried a square sail on one mast and a gaffsail on the other. It seems to have a strong claim to being the New World ancestor of the schooner, a theory favored by naval architect and historian Howard I. Chapelle. The actual transition from ketch to schooner is impossible to document, but it may have occurred sometime in the 1720s when the term "ketch" disappeared from colonial port records, and "skooner" or "schooner" became a regular entry. The coincidence could suggest that one simply evolved into the other, and people had a catchy new name for the result.

To further hinder any attempt to categorize early vessels was the fact that, until about 1800, they were not identified by their rigs. Their identity was related more to their hull form or to the use to which they were put, not to a particular sail combination. In fact, rig and hull form had little relationship before then. Vessels were known to put into a port under one rig and leave with another, depending on the demands of a particular journey. Changes could be extreme—from one mast to two or from square to fore-and-aft rig. Not until the 1800s did

As early as 1620, Dutch marine artists were painting vessels with schooner-type rigs into their harbor scenes. They were similar to the 1650s schooner shown in this rendering from a painting in an atlas produced by Laurens van der Hem of Amsterdam about 1670. It is a safe assumption that these forerunner schooners were a fairly common sight as handy auxiliary craft by van der Hem's day. (Howard M. Burns)

builders begin to design the hulls of their vessels to carry particular rigs and to identify them by their rig as sloop, schooner, brig, or ship.

Writing about the schooner in particular, naval historian E. P. Morris noted that "in general, the name has been more closely and more exclusively connected with rig, without reference to use or size, than any other type, so closely, that, when other masts were added to the two, the name still went on with the rig."[2]

Perfected on the Chesapeake Bay

In its evolution, the schooner proved to be peculiarly adapted to the winds, waters, and economic endeavors of those who depended on the Chesapeake Bay in one way or another for their livelihood. More than anywhere else in those early days of the colonial experience, the shipwrights of the Chesapeake employed the schooner rig to its greatest advantage, perfecting it as they did so.

Chesapeake shipwrights experimented with the rig, using lessons learned from the swift-sailing Bermuda sloops. They made their schooners faster, larger, and capable of working offshore as well as in the Chesapeake. Eventually, schooners came to outnumber sloops as the prime workhorses of the Bay. Given a schooner and a sloop with hulls of the same size, Bay watermen soon found that it was easier to handle two small sails than a single large one. The two masts of the schooner broke the sail area into more manageable units, providing a lower center of effort for the sail plan and giving better stability on a shoal-draft hull. The rig tended to be more efficient and more economical than that of the sloop when working coastwise and in rivers and bays. A schooner could be handled by fewer men—often only two or three—who could more easily adjust its spread of canvas to the variable wind and weather conditions of the Chesapeake. Also, with lighter masts, spars, and rigging, the cost to build and maintain a schooner was less than that of other vessels of like size.

Small Adaptations to Immediate Needs

Schooners were used on the Bay in the early 1700s, making their first appearance sometime between 1710 and 1718. The name "schooner" was still new. Customs officials seem not to have settled on its spelling in their earliest entries. In June 1717, the "Skooner" *Marlbrogh* of Boston dropped anchor in the lower reaches of the James River. Around the same time, the "Sconer" *Little Bety* brought five negro slaves to the York River from Antigua. The first schooner known to be owned on the Bay was the 20-ton *Ann* built at Salisbury, Massachusetts, in 1728.[4] In

The Spencer Hall Shipyard at Grey's Inn Creek in Kent County, Maryland. This panel was painted circa 1760 and is the earliest known depiction of a Bay shipyard. Of the vessels in this painting, two are schooners. Note that the schooner on the left is more full-built and has two headsails and two gaff-topsails. Both vessels carry lug foresails. The schooner on the left also has a fairly high quarterdeck, a feature that would disappear as Bay shipwrights developed their own distinctive style. The schooner on the right has no headsails or topsails set and the mainsail is both reefed and "scandalized," meaning that the peak halyard has been let go to reduce the span of working sail to that area from the top of the lower mast to the clew on the boom. Maneuvering in crowded harbors and creeks was a fact of sailing life on the Bay and mariners had to be able to reduce sail in a hurry. (Maryland Historical Society)

The schooner was among the first products ever to be identified as "made in America." Colonial shipbuilders may have borrowed heavily from English and European traditions of design and construction, but the end result was their own. Howard I. Chapelle's conclusion is generally accepted that "except for the possible development of the schooner rig for use in seagoing craft, there is as yet no evidence . . . of any distinctive American hull type or rig in the seventeenth and early eighteenth century."[3]

those early days, most of the vessels of any size or distinction were built elsewhere. Unlike New England, where shipbuilding was a major colonial industry and vessels were sold as a product, trade and economic survival on the Bay were not linked to manufacturing or to the building of vessels.

In fact, from the beginning, the economy of the Chesapeake Bay was based upon the growing of tobacco and, to a lesser extent, other agricultural products. Maryland and Virginia depended heavily upon British or northern builders for the ships they required to carry their tobacco and produce to distant markets and to bring in the goods the colonists couldn't get locally.

When a planter or a merchant needed a small vessel to get around on the Bay, it was easy enough to clear a stretch of riverbank handy to timber, hire a ship carpenter—most came with their own tools—and set to building it. "Oaks there are as faire, straight and tall and as good timber as any can be found, a great store, in some places very great," went one colonist's report, which also found among Virginia's natural riches "tall pine trees fit for the tallest masts" as well as iron ore, pitch, tar, rosin, and flax for making rope—indeed, all the raw materials needed for shipbuilding.[5]

And yet, most of the early vessels built in Virginia and in Maryland were small, built strictly for local use. There were no more than a dozen builders on Virginia's Eastern Shore during the 1630s and 1640s, and they were building small boats of fifty tons or so. At the same time, Massachusetts builders were launching three-hundred-ton ships.[6]

By 1720, the economy of the Bay was changing. Tobacco had made many Maryland and Virginia planters wealthy. They were anxious to expand their financial interests and were searching for other sources of income. They found new income in the raising of beef, pork, and grain. On the Eastern Shore of Maryland, Kent, Cecil, and Queen Anne's counties became centers for raising grain. Bay area grain, most of which was shipped through the growing port of Baltimore, was much in demand in European markets because it held up well during the long voyage across the Atlantic.[7]

In colonial days, shipbuilding was carried on in the center of many waterfront communities. In 1718, land was set aside for a "ship carpenter's lot" in Annapolis, which was still a feature of the town's waterfront in the 1850s when this photograph was taken. According to Dr. Edward C. Papenfuse, Maryland State Archivist, Patrick Creagh was the first to take advantage of the space and set up a shipyard in 1735. The yard gave rise to the development of other businesses from a ropewalk and blockmaker's shops to numerous taverns. (Maryland State Archives, MdHR-G-1477-4808)

At the lower end of the Bay, Norfolk became a major transshipment port between Virginia, North Carolina, and the West Indies. Wheat, corn, flour, and items such as beeswax, tar, or finished lumber were profitable cargoes bound for the West Indies, southern Europe, or the northern colonies.[8]

Early Shipbuilding Boom

Suddenly, there was a demand for more vessels and a new class of merchant-planter emerged who found shipbuilding to be an important diversification. Even so, they continued to concentrate on building smaller vessels—sloops and schooners mainly.[9]

The first schooner known to have been built in Maryland was the 35-ton *Sarah*, launched on the Wicomico River in 1731.

Another of 25 tons was built the next year. Three more were launched in 1733 and six in 1734.[10]

Elsewhere in Maryland, in 1733, Dr. Charles Carroll of Annapolis, who was part owner of the newly formed Baltimore Company for the manufacture of iron, contracted with a shipwright, John Casdorp, for the building of a "scooner" to transport supplies to their iron works and carry away the products of their forge.

Casdorp agreed to build in Annapolis

[a] "scooner . . . Thirty eight foot Keel . . . seventeen foot Beam, eight foot or eight foot & a half hold, with Sufficient Rake fore & aft . . . & waist of two foot & half Deep & Cabbin of Sufficient Bigness & fitted in workmanlike manner with hatches, skuttles & all other Requisites. The said Vessel to be square stern, round tuck & of a sailing Body with all her Timbers of Sufficient Substance well hewed & freed from bad or faulty timber, to be skinned with good sound plank full two Inches thick, free from bad worm eaten heart . . . with Wayles of a Sufficient thickness to be well fitted for Burthen, cieled or skinned on ye Inside with good Inch & half Oak plank, the Deck to be good two Inch pine Plank except where Oak Plank is proper to be put in. The said Vessell to be completely fitted finished to a cleat & delivered afloat to sd Charles . . .

The Company agreed to pay Casdorp at the rate of £3 per ton, one half paid in cash, the other half in goods from the company store. As built, she was probably a vessel of 61 tons. Delivery was expected in ten months' time.[11]

Whether the yard was owned by a planter, a merchant, or a shipwright, it was usually a very simple affair. A small lot on the water and a sawpit or pair of trestles to cut the timbers was all that was necessary. There were few sawmills. Most of the timbers and planks were cut and shaped by sawyers employed by the shipyard. Occasionally, the sawpit was "covered with a house to work in all weathers," and there might be a small wharf, but that was about it.[12] Temporary launching ways were built for each vessel.

In towns, such as Annapolis, shipwrights tended to locate their yards in sheltered coves and on little-trafficked creeks outside of the settled area. Some communities, however, such as those along West River below Annapolis or along the Choptank on Maryland's Eastern Shore, grew up because of the shipyard in their midst.

In the mid-1700s, shipyards of Maryland and Virginia often were manned by indentured servants and convicts. Charles Carroll of Annapolis, who owned a yard in the 1750s, followed the common practice and employed indentured servants to work it.[13] While such a labor force was cheap, it was not terribly reliable.

Samuel Galloway, who was another Maryland merchant, contracted for indentured servants to man his yard, but almost immediately a shipwright, a joiner, and a carver ran away.[14] A more profitable venture was to purchase slaves and hire them out as apprentices to a shipwright until they were trained. As a result, much of the skilled labor in colonial shipyards on the Bay was performed by slaves.

Built by Rack of Eye

In the late 1600s, there was a great influx of English shipwrights to the colonies. By 1724, in fact, the exodus had created a severe shortage in England.[15] For the most part, English shipwrights were driven here by a general economic depression at home and the lure of raw materials, land, and greater opportunity in the New World. Many came directly from shipyards in England or on the continent of Europe, bringing a high degree of skill with them.

Frequently, a shipwright used plans taken from any one of a number of seventeenth and eighteenth century English and European shipbuilding books. Usually, however, he drew his own plans or worked from memory, building "from the eye" or by "rack of eye," as they said, to produce a hull.[16] Any colonial shipwright worth his salt wasn't bound by mathematical formulas or textbook methods of building. He knew how to adjust the rules.

Methods had not changed greatly by the mid-nineteenth century, according to Charles H. Cramp who wrote about the building of pungy schooners during that period in a paper he presented to the Society of Naval Architects and Marine Engineers in 1908. "There was no model, no 'laying down' or 'laying off' in the mold loft, nor were molds made there from a 'body plan.'

"Each builder would have a stem and a midship-section mold for all vessels, and as there was little difference in the dimensions of them, these two molds could be adjusted to an increase of a few inches in depth or width to suit contract requirements.

"The little differences in dimensions were easily made by the builder by the adjustment of the stem and midship-section molds. The first thing done was to lay the keel, then the stem mold and a straight board representing the stern post and its rake were tacked on to the keel, and when the amidship section was secured, a grand beginning was made in the form of the vessel.

"Then the stem itself and stern post with transom bolted on would be raised, also a midship-section mold of pine plank would be secured. The next step, which was always considered an important one, was to run the floor ribband which would be just below the floor heads. The adjustment of this floor ribband by means of shores put under it was a second important step in modeling the vessel . . . The relationship of fineness of one end to the other was altogether a matter of judgement or taste, or, as some would have it, 'guess.' But they never departed much from the last boat built. This practice accounted much for the wonderful similarity in all of these vessels built on the Chesapeake and its tributaries, whether they were built earlier or later. In all cases the American instinct was conspicuous."[17]

While this produced many a fine vessel, it gave us little documentary evidence of early ship design and construction. Often the only record of the original plan for a vessel that has survived is a carved wooden half-model. The general practice was to make a half-model and then to make the draft from which

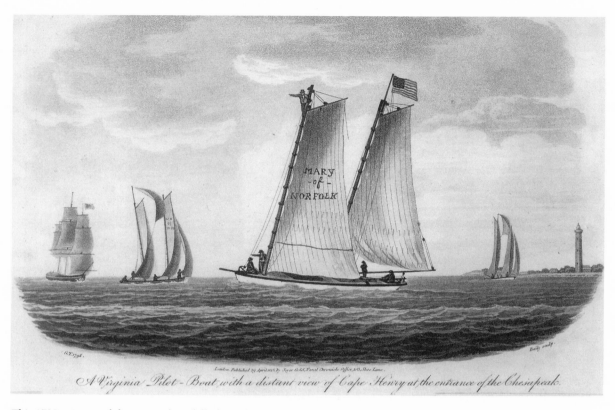

This 1795 painting of the *Mary of Norfolk* shows her on her race to sea to meet and put her pilot aboard the incoming ship. Competition among the various pilot boats was keen and the comfort of pilot and crew was sacrificed to the requirements of speed in these austere schooners. (National Maritime Museum, Greenwich, England, No. B4845)

the actual vessel was built. Half-models circulated from one shipyard to another,[18] and schooners of different sizes were often built using the same half-model.

While colonial shipwrights—and those Bay shipbuilders who came later—started with well-established principles of design, they often altered their original plan to incorporate new ideas, to adapt the vessel to a different use, or, perhaps, to compensate for a lack of suitable materials.

In its evolution, the schooner rig followed a slow process of "small adaptations to immediate needs," as maritime historian E. P. Morris put it. There were "no large motives and no high emotions" influencing the changes.[19] A prime example was the development of the Virginia pilot schooner.

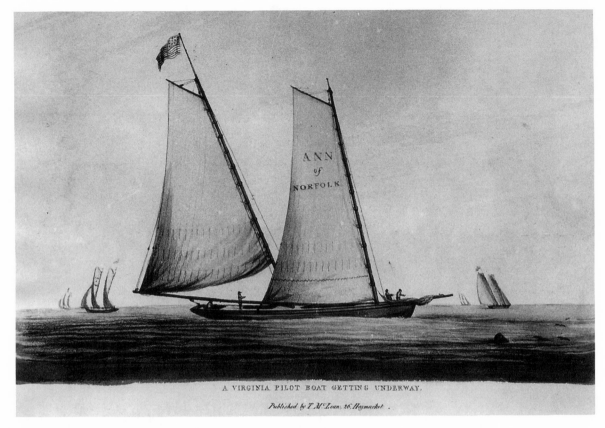

A VIRGINIA PILOT BOAT GETTING UNDERWAY.

Published by T. M°Lean, 26, Haymarket.

Contemporary works of art, such as this 1825 lithograph, are an important source of information about early vessels and how they actually looked. Here, we see the Virginia pilot boat *Ann of Norfolk* getting underway. Since 1791, Virginia law required a boat's name and home port to be painted on her foresail in letters at least nine inches high. Comparisons of late eighteenth century paintings and plans of Virginia and Maryland pilot boats with those of the nineteenth century show us not only that the craft had developed its distinctive characteristics by 1795 but had changed very little over a considerable period of time. Note that the sail area of the lug foresail has been lengthened by the addition of a "bonnet," or strip of sail along the bottom. Bonnets were also found on headsails. As in this rendering, early ship portraits often showed the same or similar vessels on different points of sail. (The Mariners' Museum, No. PK-177, J. Rogers)

Intrepid Seekers: Virginia Pilot Schooners

There was just one way to enter the Chesapeake Bay up until 1829 when the Chesapeake and Delaware Canal opened a northern route, and that was through a twelve-mile gap between Virginia's Cape Henry and Cape Charles. Those mariners who made frequent trips into the Bay knew that if they hit the mid-Atlantic coast at the thirty-seventh parallel and followed it

westward, they would be on a straight course for the sixty-foot-deep channel between the capes. They also knew about the treacherous Middle Ground and Horseshoe Shoals that lay just inside the Bay. Most likely they had a landmark to look for, like the large tree on Willoughby Spit or in the late 1700s Selden's house at Buckroe to keep them out of shoal water.[20]

Entering the Bay was an uncertain course for ships' captains who were new to the route. Very early in the history of the Virginia colony, a system of pilotage was established to guide them through the treacherous Virginia capes and into Hampton Roads, and the James and York rivers. The very first of them were "intrepid, independent loners" in a "chancey occupation," with dangers beyond those of navigation. One of the original Virginia colonists and the earliest known pilot was John Clark, who was captured by Spaniards and carried off to languish in a dungeon for years, after being sent by Virginia's governor to "con" the Spanish ship through the capes.[21]

By law, inbound ships were required to accept the services of the first pilot to reach them and competition among Virginia pilots was keen. Their vessels might sail as far as two hundred miles into the Atlantic, spending days crisscrossing the most traveled courses in hopes of intercepting an inbound ship. In their "mad race to sea" not just any boat would do. Borrowing from the design of the fast-sailing Bermuda sloop, which began trading in the Bay in the early 1700s, Virginia shipbuilders created a sleek, sharp-built schooner that was ideal for the pilots' race to sea "seeking" vessels to guide into the Bay. A clear case of design being driven by need, the Virginia pilot boat was the first identifiable type of schooner on the Chesapeake.[22]

Built for Speed

The pilot boat was a vessel of austere simplicity, unburdened by complicated rigging or anything that would decrease its speed. To keep the vessels light and fast for their "race" offshore, pilot schooners were not encumbered by accommodations for the pilots—sometimes two or three—and the crew who sailed them. There was no room, since most were fifty feet or less. The earliest ones were seldom fully decked. Instead, they had a short, low quarterdeck that gave the pilots some headroom in their cabin aft. In the larger boats, the pilots may have had the meager comfort of a small hearth or scuttle on which to cook. The crew crawled into their bunks forward through the main hatch which was usually where the hearth was found.

The Virginia pilot boat was characterized by its sharp deadrise, narrow body, fine long run, flush deck, low freeboard, fairly shallow draft, and deep drag aft. It was rigged with two raking masts. The mainmast carried a gaffsail on a boom, while the gaffsail on the foremast was loose-footed. The only other sails on the earliest pilot boats were a jib and a main topmast staysail.

Since pilot boats generally were either out "seeking" or tied up at a wharf, they seldom had occasion to anchor. If the need arose, the crew simply threw the anchor on its cable of hemp over the rail. Not until the early 1800s did windlasses and hawseholes for anchor and cable begin to appear on pilot schooners.[23]

Pilot boats were already being identified as such in the 1730s, appearing, for instance, in advertisements in the *Virginia Gazette.* One was reported as stolen or gone adrift from the York River on July 22, 1737. It had a 24-foot keel, a 9-foot beam, and two masts with sails, and it was painted red. Another advertisement described a pilot boat stolen in September 1739 from Newport News. This one was also a two-masted craft, with a 15-foot keel, and, among other things, a tarpaulin upon the forecastle.[24] Obviously, early pilot boats were small, with the rudest of amenities, or more likely, none at all.

The *St. Ann*

The earliest plans known to exist for a schooner built showing the influence of the Virginia pilot boat are those of the *St. Ann.* She apparently was American and, by British standards of the day, "slightly built." Her existence was recorded first in 1736 in Portsmouth, England, when she arrived there under a Por-

tuguese flag. Howard I. Chapelle speculated that the *St. Ann's* "best points of sailing were undoubtedly reaching and running, though she would by no means be deficient in windward work if properly ballasted . . . Her real advantage would be in her ability to reach a relatively high speed in a range of moderate wind velocities."[25] It was for such capabilities that she was undoubtedly bought by the Portuguese for use as a dispatch boat.

The *St. Ann* was 54 feet at the waterline and had a beam of 11 feet 10 inches, which meant that she was very narrow and not at all commodious, with a relatively shoal draft of 5 feet 2 inches. This early example of the pilot boat–type had a long fine run from her bow, which gave only a hint at the sharp-bowed vessels that would develop later. The *St. Ann* carried a mainsail, foresail, a square foresail or "spritsail," two headsails, and probably two square topsails on her foremast. The spritsail and the square topsails were added as "light-weather running sails" sometime early in the eighteenth century, probably in adapting the schooner rig for going farther to sea.[26]

Sharp-built

For all their austerity, the pilot boats caught the eye and imagination of builders throughout the Bay. Even by today's standards, they had the look of a yacht. They served as a prototype vessel and, in a very short time, the "Virginia-built" or "pilot boat" model was used in the design of a wide variety of fast-sailing sloops and schooners. By the mid–eighteenth century, schooners were in the majority and in Maryland by the late 1760s builders were launching three times as many schooners as sloops.[27]

Bay schooners had only the simplest ornamentation or none at all. With the influence of the Bermuda sloop and Virginia pilot boat, the lines of eighteenth century vessels became increasingly fine, with higher masts and lighter, stronger rigging to carry larger sails.

The shipwrights of the Chesapeake continued to improve upon the sharp lines of their schooner hulls, doing everything they could to reduce their weight and thus increase their capacity for speed. They spaced the vessels' hardwood frames as far apart as practical and used the lightest planking they could. They kept the deck structures and freeboard low and eliminated the quarterdeck and quarterdeck rails in favor of a level or flush deck.[28] To further reduce the weight, Bay shipwrights ignored traditional norms, decreasing the diameter of a schooner's masts and keeping her rigging at a minimum.[29]

Stability was a constant consideration with their fast-sailing vessels, sharp-built and top-heavy with sails as they were. Sail power meant speed and as a result there was over-sparring and over-canvassing.[30] Later, inadequately or improperly ballasted clipper schooners occasionally were known to capsize while at anchor, unable to withstand the combined forces of a strong current against their keels and a high wind at work on their top hamper. Under sail, to heel an eighteenth century merchant schooner beyond fifty degrees from the perpendicular was to run the risk of a fatal knockdown.[31]

Such problems did nothing to deter Bay shipbuilders from continuing to produce their long low clippers. While yards in New England and New York built the earliest, and the most, colonial ships, those on the Chesapeake earned an international reputation for speed. By 1755, the Bay was one of two areas on the North American coast that were recognized as centers for the building of fast-sailing vessels. The other was Essex County, Massachusetts, home of the famed Marblehead fishing schooners.

For the most part, New England's schooners tended to be more full-built than those of the Chesapeake Bay. They were known for their large cargo capacity and shallow draft, if not for their speed. Generally, Bay schooners had a heavy rake to both stem and stern. New England's had a relatively straight stem. Lightly rigged, with fewer shrouds than the schooners of the North, the Chesapeake Bay schooner could cause a New Englander to blanch at the sight of her straining under a full press of canvas.

Of course, fast-sailing schooners were being built outside of the Chesapeake—later the pilot boats and fishing schooners of the North became renowned—but the economics and conditions of the colonial period dictated other concerns in northern ports. During the Revolution, builders of New England produced many fast sailers to meet the demands of the war. Afterwards, when it was safe to concentrate on trade again, they returned to building vessels more capable in the area of cargo-carrying capacity than speed.[32]

The same was true of the Bay, as we shall see, although the evolution of the sharp-built schooner from the small but swift Virginia pilot boat to its final and best expression in the Baltimore clipper and the pungy continued. While speed seemed to be a prerequisite for Bay-built schooners, the fact was that other moderate- to full-built schooners were being launched by the hundreds from shipyards up and down the Chesapeake Bay. Designed for their utility, they far outnumbered the fast sharp model and formed a vast fleet, the last of which carried the long tradition of the schooner rig on the Chesapeake Bay into the twentieth century.

Three

In the West Indies Trade

From the earliest days of the American colonies, the Chesapeake Bay figured in the triangular trade between New England and the West Indies. During the French and Indian War, there was great profit to be had in supplying the islands with grain. By 1743, Virginia was exporting 100,000 bushels of corn as well as bread, flour, peas, tallow, candles, and large quantities of barrel staves and shingles. Maryland exports were running apace.

At first, the trade was in vessels built outside the Bay. New Englanders carried codfish, mackerel, rum, furniture, woodenware, and foodstuffs such as cheese, malt, ship biscuit, and peas to the Bay, which they traded for Maryland and Virginia grain for the West Indies. The return leg brought cargoes of West Indian rum, sugar, molasses, salt, ginger, cocoa, cotton, citrus fruits, and wine from Madeira and southern Europe to northern ports. Increasingly, there was a direct exchange between the Bay and the West Indies that depended upon Chesapeake grain, produce, pork, beef, lumber, and naval stores.[1]

This applied the spur to shipbuilders on the Bay to provide the hulls to carry the cargoes so much in demand. Planters and merchants of the Bay preferred to develop their own trade using their own vessels and men rather than leave it to Yankee traders. Fast-sailing schooners and sloops soon were the mainstay of the Bay's growing merchant marine.[2]

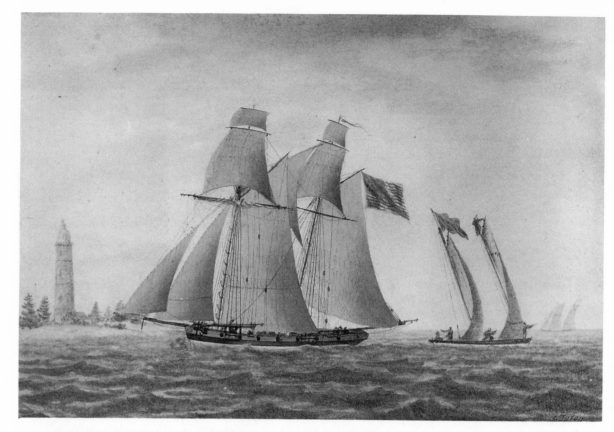

By 1794 when this watercolor was painted, the Baltimore clipper schooner was a dominant type on the Bay, along with its ancestor, the Virginia pilot boat, both of which appear here off Cape Henry. The clipper, a double-topsail schooner, carries square upper and lower topsails on both masts. She is also showing a lug foresail and main-topmast staysail. Her fore course, which is the sail hung on the lower yard of her foremast, has been furled and there is no course on the main. (National Maritime Museum, Greenwich, England, No. 7180, George Tobin)

By the mid–eighteenth century, the Chesapeake Bay was doing a greater volume of shipping than any other region of continental America[3] and in the process had created a sizable fleet of Bay-built vessels—schooners, mainly, and sloops. Basically, the schooners were of two types. The smaller ones were used in the Bay trade and registered twenty to forty tons. Larger schooners of fifty tons or more were West Indies traders, built increasingly on the fast-sailing Virginia pilot boat model.

It was a dangerous age to be about on the seas, and the early West Indies traders had to be fast. They were constantly menaced by Dutch, Spanish, and French privateers and pirates

The identity of this three-masted "tern" schooner is unknown. She is anchored off Cape Henry in this 1825 lithograph. The three-masted rig was not common, and this view shows the earliest known depiction of the type in American waters. She is very similar to the *Flying Fish*, a pilot-boat model schooner whose lines were taken off by the British Admiralty at Portsmouth dockyard in 1806. The clipper schooner is shown at anchor and without sail, a view that shows off the rake of her masts, her stem and sternposts, and the long fine run that characterized Baltimore clipper schooners. The second three-masted clipper, shown under sail, is very likely the artist's attempt to show the vessel in different perspectives, which was a common technique of early marine artists. (National Maritime Museum, Greenwich, England, No. 7186, J. Rogers)

who roamed the Caribbean. Survival for mariners of the Chesapeake Bay in the West Indies trade or in any offshore venture depended upon a vessel that could outsail any other. Out of that need evolved the sharp, fast schooners, described first as Virginia-built. Much later they would be called "clippers," a type known around the world. But in the eighteenth century, before the Revolutionary War, the clipper schooner was strictly a Chesapeake Bay type. The significance of its development is unequaled in the history of naval architecture in the eighteenth century. Its unique characteristics were a product of the perilous, war-torn times in which it was born.

Running the British Gauntlet

At the outset of the Revolutionary War, the Americans had only a handful of warships, a few converted merchant ships, and a small fleet of fishing boats, coasters, pilot boats, and West Indies traders. With this assortment, they meant to oppose the British, who could send ships from one of the most powerful fleets in the world against them. Given the odds, the colonists had to rely upon daring and ingenuity to survive on the seas and even on the sheltered waters of the Chesapeake Bay.

Periodically, the British maintained a blockade of the Bay, the effects of which were quickly felt by nearly every man, woman, and child in Virginia and Maryland. To make matters worse, as early as 1775, Baltimore shippers were suffering significant losses to Tory predators in the lower Bay.[4] Loyalist privateers continued to plague shipping up to and beyond the end of the war.

As a result, any vessel with the temerity to venture from port for the West Indies or Europe ran a gauntlet of Loyalist privateers and British cruisers before even clearing the Bay. And that was only the beginning. They had to elude British warships patrolling the Virginia capes and their men-of-war almost anywhere at sea. The return trip was just the reverse.

For the short term, British and Loyalist vessels preying upon shipping in the Bay caused a disruption of trade, but the British had not reckoned on the enterprising spirit their efforts unleashed in their former colonies. Recoiling from the initial setbacks, Bay merchants ordered new vessels to run the British gauntlet and carry their tobacco, grain, and other commodities to foreign markets.

In May 1776, Maryland's Council of Safety advised merchants of the "impracticability of square rigged vessels escaping the enemy." They offered the opinion "that small sharp rigged vessels would more probably meet with success."[5] Maryland and Virginia merchants already knew that.

Up and down the Bay, shipbuilders began receiving orders for fast and weatherly sharp-built schooners, sloops, and brigs. Surviving records indicate a phenomenal increase in the popularity of schooners in Virginia's merchant fleet. In 1776, only two were built in Virginia, but by 1782 that number had risen to ninety-eight.[6] The navies of both Virginia and Maryland also had a preponderance of schooners, many of which were schooner-rigged pilot boats.

Besides the individual states' fleets of naval vessels, there was a larger fleet of privately owned sloops, schooners, and brigs used to carry supplies for the government and the militia. They continued their freight operations throughout the Revolution, carrying tobacco, grain, flour, and other products of the Bay to the West Indies and returning with guns, gunpowder, flints, bayonets, salt, blankets, clothing, medical supplies, and other war materiel.[7]

Privateers of the Revolution

Knowing they could count on limited support from their state and Continental navies, Virginia and Maryland merchants turned to the business of privateering, a very old institution that originated in Europe during the time of the Crusades. In the fourteenth century, it was every man for himself on the seas. To give their merchants and mariners some means by which to recoup their losses to pirates or the marauding vessels of enemy nations, governments began to issue "letters-of-marque and reprisal" granting their subjects the right to seek redress at sea. Any act against another vessel without such a permit was considered piracy.

The system of licensing privately armed vessels was well established by the time of the British colonization of the New World, and Americans turned to privateering quite early. They had to do so in self-defense, as they were continually caught in the middle and victimized at sea during multiple imperial wars.

Then, too, they went into privateering for the pure profit in it. The Declaration of Independence and the first issuance of "letters-of-marque and reprisal" by the individual states and by the Continental Congress were almost simultaneous.

The commissions issued for privately owned armed vessels were of two types. One was issued to those schooners, brigs, and an occasional sloop, built and operated strictly as vessels of war. "Sea wolves" was the popular term for them. Generally, they had finer lines and little or no cargo-carrying capacity. They were not merchantmen, but privateers, and their mission was to capture or sink whatever enemy shipping they could find. The second type of commission was given to vessels that were armed, but engaged primarily in trade. More burdensome than privateers, but fast nonetheless, these were known as "letter-of-marque" traders or "flyers" and were authorized to seize only those enemy ships that happened to cross their paths in the course of a voyage.[8]

From the outset of the war, which disrupted normal trade, merchants channeled their available capital into new ventures. According to historian Jerome Garitee, "Shrewd merchants intensified their investments in raiders as the small American navy declined and the British navy strangled other profit-making ventures. Little inspiration or education was required as the merchants combined private interests and public duty."[9]

"Private interest and public duty," combined with the rush of circumstances, quickly proved that a unique vessel was needed, and Bay shipbuilders found it in schooners and brigs built on the Virginia model. These increased in number and size as the war progressed.[10]

A rough estimate, taken from various sources, puts the number of different merchant vessels built in Virginia in this period at approximately 430 with more than 300 being schooners.[11] More than 63 Virginians were fitted out as privately owned armed vessels. More than 248 commissions for privateers and letter-of-marque craft were issued in Baltimore, with the number of actual vessels being slightly less.[12] Maryland was second only to Massachusetts which issued some 600 commissions.[13]

About half of Baltimore's fleet of privateers were the small but popular fore-and-aft-rigged schooners, three-quarters of which shipped less than fifty men. There was, however, a trend toward larger vessels and crews as the war went on, and their profits made it possible for merchants to build bigger and better vessels.[14]

By 1777, there were nearly as many men at sea in American privateers as there were on land in Washington's army of nearly 11,000 men. They were a formidable threat to British shipping. Wrote one unhappy British subject from Grenada in 1777, "Everything continues exceedingly dear, and we are happy if we can get anything for money, by reason of the quantity of vessels taken by the Americans . . . A few days ago, from sixty vessels that departed from Ireland not above twenty-five arrived in this and neighboring islands, the others, it is thought, being all taken by American privateers. God knows if this American war continues much longer, we shall all die of hunger."[15]

Chapelle estimates that 50 percent of all American vessels constructed after 1778 were of the Virginia-built type.[16] That year is critical in the history of the American privateers for that is when the French entered the war in support of the American cause against their common enemy, Great Britain. The appearance of the French fleet off the American coast broke the British blockade that had had a stranglehold on mid-Atlantic and southern ports. The result was suddenly to free a large number of privateers trapped in Chesapeake Bay ports and elsewhere.[17] Free to roam the seas, American privateers during the ensuing months of the Revolutionary War captured or destroyed three times as many British ships as did the Continental navy's warships.[18]

Virginia-built

By the end of the Revolutionary War, the predominant choice of vessel for privateering from Bay ports was the double-topsail schooner with square topsails on her main- and foremasts. At this point in the evolution of the type, the so-called Virginia-built schooner still had a raised quarterdeck rather than the flush deck of vessels later to be called clippers. Characteristically, it did not have a raised forecastle deck and had less drag aft than did later schooners. The fast, sharp-built schooners of the Revolution did have fairly low bulwarks and showed the same easy bilge, cutaway bow, raking sternpost, great deadrise, and wide beam of the later Baltimore clippers. A Virginia-built privateer was a vessel with wide decks, towering spars, and lofty sails.[19]

Schooners built as privateers were designed so that the wooden tiller on deck could be unshipped if they expected to do battle. The vessel was then steered with an iron tiller shipped into the rudderhead from the aft cabin below deck. There, the helmsman was protected from fire and was conned from the deck above by the captain calling down the hatch or through the skylight.[20]

The Virginia-built schooner used for privateering had become a distinct type by the time of the Revolution when blockade running created new markets for fast sailers. Bay shipbuilders rose to the challenge of the unsettled times, and out of their efforts evolved the fast, sharp-built schooner known the world over as the Baltimore clipper. Its emergence was one of the most important developments in the history of American shipbuilding.

Baltimore-built

There is no telling where the word "clipper" came from as applied to the fast-sailing schooners developed on the Chesapeake Bay. If you search very old dictionaries, you will find the archaic verb "to clip," which means to fly rapidly, and our eighteenth century forefathers did use it to describe fast horses. So why not the fastest thing on the water? Easier to capture a bird in flight than to catch a Baltimore clipper, they used to say. The word was used to describe the schooners during the War of 1812, according to Jerome Garitee, author of *The Republic's Private Navy*, who found two Baltimore merchants commenting shortly after war was declared that "Six Clippers are fitting out at the Point as Privateers," and added, "Our Baltimore Boats are admirably well adapted to the purposes and there seems to be no want of enterprize here."[21] Ironically, the name Baltimore clipper did not actually come into popular use to identify the fast-sailing schooners of the Chesapeake Bay until the 1830s, by which time the type was dying out.

Up until that time, they were simply referred to as "Baltimore-built," but regardless of what they were called, the impact of the sharp-built Bay vessels on the design and construction of schooners here and abroad was unquestionable. The successes of the swift, Chesapeake Bay–built schooners contributed significantly to the outcome of the War of 1812. The shipbuilders of the Chesapeake Bay earned an international reputation for producing very fast sailers and had few competitors.

While individual schooners differed in some details, the early clipper-type had several unmistakable features. Characteristic were their long, light, and extremely raking masts, which carried very little rigging, and a suit of sails that included a foresail, mainsail, staysail, jib, and, usually, square topsails on one or both masts. They had a low freeboard with a great rake to their stem and sternposts and considerable drag to the keel aft. The degree of deadrise was extreme and their bilges were slack. They were generally flush-decked and wide abeam in proportion to their length, which gave them broad clear decks, suitable for working the sails or handling guns in wartime. Their greatest beam was forward of midships.[22]

The reasons for the speed of the long, black Baltimore-built schooners are found in their design, most particularly their easy lines, the light weight they carried above the load waterline, and their large rig. Howard Chapelle was not alone in his opinion that the lines of the Baltimore model schooners were far in advance of their times and cannot be compared with those of any other vessels of the same date.[23]

The appearance of these schooners never failed to capture the attention of all who saw them. Trelawny, a companion of Lord Byron, describes such a vessel that he came upon at sea:

WEATHER VIEW OF AN AMERICAN SCHOONER UNDER REEF'D SAILS.

The artist captured this clipper schooner sailing with a fair breeze under reefed sails. Reefing and resetting sails was constant work aboard a Baltimore clipper with its tall rig and great expanse of sail. As a result, crews for these schooners tended to be large. (Maryland Historical Society, J. Rogers)

She was a beautiful vessel, long, low in the water, with lofty raking masts which tapered away until they were almost too fine to be distinguished . . . As she filled and hauled on a wind, to cross under our stern, with a fresh breeze to which she gently heeled, I thought there was nothing so beautiful as the arrowy sharpness of her bow, and the gradually receding fineness of her quarters. She looked and moved like an Arab horse in the desert, and was as obedient to command. There was a lightness and a bird-like buoyancy about her, that exclusively belongs to this class of vessels.[24]

This is a rare photograph of a Baltimore clipper. The *Vigilant*, which sailed as a mail packet in the Danish Virgin Islands, is shown here under sail at St. Croix around 1900. Records suggest that she was built in Baltimore in 1809 as the *Nonsuch* before entering Danish registry in 1824. A year later a Danish naval officer with thirty soldiers used the *Vigilant* to capture the much larger privateer *Adolpho*. She then went into service carrying freight among the islands. The *Vigilant* lost her papers in 1876, when she was sunk during a hurricane, and thereafter, because no one could document her origins, became the subject of myth and legend, a fact which gave her value well beyond her freight capacity.

From the 1880s on, the *Vigilant*'s owner did not correct the mistaken belief that his vessel was the *Den Aarvaagne*, a naval schooner involved in a famous battle against British privateers at the close of the eighteenth century. As a result, she was maintained as a historic vessel and thus survived to be feted in 1901, at the celebration of the 100th anniversary of the *Den Aarvaagne*'s action against the British. Danish author Birger Thomsen later proved that the 60-ton *Vigilant* was not the *Den Aarvaagne*, a much larger vessel of 150 tons. But the 119-year old clipper was actually of no less value historically when she was finally lost off Christiansted in 1928, the last of her kind still sailing. (Royal Library of Denmark, Jacob A. Weng)

For all their beauty and speed, the Virginia- or Baltimore-built schooners as a type were ill-suited for peacetime pursuits. Built sharp on the bottom with very little hold space, they were inefficient as freight vessels for all but the most valuable of cargoes. As a result, after the Revolutionary War many were sold to French and Spanish interests.

By 1793, the French Revolution had created a strong market for blockade runners, privateers, naval cruisers, and dispatch carriers. Who better to supply the demand for the sort of fast-sailing craft the French needed than the shipbuilding communities of Norfolk, Baltimore, and the Eastern Shore of the Chesapeake Bay?

Agents of the French revolutionary government came to the Bay with orders for low-cost, fast-sailing craft of moderate size. Most of their purchases were schooners, which proved so effective against the English that the British government protested to the government of the United States.[25] The federal government made an effort to stop the sale of these fast vessels to the French, but Bay merchants and shipbuilders quickly found a way to circumvent their government's strictures and continue the lucrative business of building schooners. The practice was to load a fast sailer with cargo and send it to France, where both cargo and vessel were sold. The schooner was then put into French service. All in all, nearly fifty privateers built in Baltimore sailed under the French flag in the 1790s.[26]

Besides those sold to the French, there were many Chesapeake Bay–built schooners purchased by other Europeans between 1795 and 1815. A fair number also ended up in British hands, obtained mostly by capturing them from the French.

The exploits of schooners sold off the Bay did not fail to receive attention in ports and shipbuilding centers on the Chesapeake. Even when there was not a market for privateers, the drive to design and build the best and fastest schooners possible continued and spurred a strong rivalry between Baltimore builders and those in Dorchester County, in Oxford and St. Michaels, at West River in Anne Arundel County, and in Accomack and Mathews counties in Virginia.[27]

While most of the fast, sharp-built schooners built for use on the Bay during this period came from Maryland's Eastern Shore, the emerging center of shipbuilding on the Bay was Baltimore.[28] In the period following the Revolution, the Patapsco River port became a boomtown. Its merchants were expert in seagoing commerce and their position was strengthened by the devastation that had befallen Norfolk's maritime community during the Revolution.[29]

The growth of Baltimore's waterfront was remarkable, specifically that section of land developed in the 1760s by William Fell on a point east of the new town. Between 1776 and 1783, the shipbuilding center's population nearly doubled, going from a total of 821 to 1,522.[30]

The most dramatic increase was in the area's slave population. The census of 1776 found 65 slaves at Fells Point, while tax records in 1783 showed the total to be 276. The growth in the slave population seems to have been directly related to the growth of shipbuilding there. Most of the growing number of slaves were owned by those engaged in shipbuilding and many became highly skilled craftsmen.[31]

Thirty years later, Fells Point was a bustling shipbuilding center where a yard could build a schooner to order in six weeks. And there was no lack of proven captains and experienced seamen for crews.

The War between the Wars

While Chesapeake Bay builders and merchants profited by the sale of their fast schooners to the French and other foreign interests in the postwar period, there was also a downside to the commerce in vessels to be used as foreign privateers. Even with the achievement of independence and the end of British rule, the seas were not safe for American merchantmen.

The English and French were still at war with each other, and American shipping was in constant peril of attack by warships and privateers of both nations, especially in the Caribbean. The Franco-American alliance lasted just a short time after the

The pilot boat *York of Baltimore*, shown here off Cape Henry, was built in 1848 and served as a Maryland pilot boat until 1854 when she was sold to Virginia pilots. Like many of these swift and handy schooners, the *York* was drafted into the Confederate navy as a privateer. She captured several Union merchant vessels off the Carolina coast before she was run ashore by ships of the Union navy and burned. (Maryland Historical Society, John Wilcox)

Revolutionary War, and it wasn't long before French-owned, Bay-built vessels were preying upon the merchantmen of Maryland and Virginia. By 1800, Baltimore merchants and others trading out of the Bay to the West Indies were suffering from losses not only to French but to British, Spanish, and even Danish and Haitian privateers.[32]

To make matters worse for anyone trading offshore, pirates of various nationalities, often sailing vessels built on the Baltimore model, were having a heyday in the Caribbean throughout the period between the Revolution and the War of 1812.

Privateer- and pirate-infested waters notwithstanding, merchants of the Bay considered the opportunities for trade with both the West Indies and Europe far outweighed the risks and dangers involved. So, as the eighteenth century neared its end, Americans were again in need of fast armed vessels to survive at sea. In 1798, to deal with the problem of France's privateers, Congress once more authorized the commissioning of American privateers. Seventy-four commissions were issued to Baltimoreans and half of those went to schooners.

To further deal with the threat, the U.S. Navy took the 84-foot schooner *Enterprise* into service. Built in 1799 by Henry Spencer at Baltimore, she carried a crew of seventy officers and men and was armed with a dozen six-pounders.[33]

The *Enterprise* spent the year 1800 in the Caribbean where she captured eight privateers and liberated eleven American vessels taken as prizes by the French. Her successes continued as she joined other vessels in the U.S. fleet in action against the Barbary pirates in the Mediterranean.

Soon after her arrival, the *Enterprise* defeated the fourteen-gun Tripolitan corsair *Tripoli*. While she spent most of the next seven years patrolling the Mediterranean, carrying dispatches and convoying merchantmen, the Baltimore clipper took part in countless engagements, alone and in concert with U.S. warships. After her return to this country, she was laid up in New York for almost a year and then was recommissioned in 1811 to operate along the coasts of South Carolina and Georgia.

The *Enterprise* returned to the Bay once more, to the Washington Navy Yard, where she was rerigged as a brig. She fought through the War of 1812 and afterward sailed the Caribbean and Gulf of Mexico chasing pirates, smugglers, and slavers. She was finally lost in July 1823 when she ran aground and broke up on Little Curaçao Island in the West Indies.[34]

In every test to which she was put, the *Enterprise* proved her speed and seaworthiness, not to mention the effectiveness of the design and construction of the Baltimore-built schooners. Their usefulness to the United States and to commercial interests in the Bay did not end completely with the cessation of hostilities after the Revolution.

America's Second War for Independence

Despite U.S. and British naval efforts that drove the French from the American coast and West Indian waters, the shaky U.S./British partnership quickly fell apart. The British replaced the French as the enemy of the American seaman. The terrible demands of the war with France had severely depleted Britain's supply of sailors, which she proceeded to replenish with men impressed from American merchant ships.

Thomas Jefferson, who was entering his second term as president, was determined to avoid another war with Britain and with support in Congress attempted to influence the British with a nonimportation act in 1806. When that didn't work, Congress passed an embargo on American shipping to all foreign ports in order to keep American vessels and seamen at home and out of British hands. The result was that American trade was paralyzed. Men and ships were idle in U.S. ports and as legitimate trade dwindled, illegitimate trade flourished. In 1809, the embargo was withdrawn and trade with all ports but those of Britain and France was reinstituted. Interference from the British and the French continued, however, and American seamen were taken by the British in alarming numbers. Jefferson's attempt to forestall war was a failure. The second war for American independence, which began in 1812, was waged mainly for the protection of the American merchant marine.[35]

Four

Privateer-built

Almost immediately upon the outbreak of hostilities in 1812, British ships appeared to blockade the Atlantic and Gulf coasts of the United States from Long Island Sound to the Mississippi. Baltimore shipbuilders stepped up their production of sharp-built schooners and brigs for use as blockade runners and privateers.

Designed for speed, the Baltimore-built schooner became more and more extreme—light of body with sharply raking stem and sternpost, heavy with rig, and comparable to nothing else on the seas at that time. Generally, they were 80 feet or more on deck.

Privateers usually shipped fifty to one hundred men, a large crew for schooners of less than a hundred feet. Outward bound the crew members were lucky to have space to swing a hammock. They were kept busy and out of trouble working the large number of light sails carried by a double-topsail schooner. When necessary, they were called on to fight, although crews on privateers seldom expected the bloody battles engaged in by naval vessels, a fact, along with the money to be made, that made privateering preferable to naval service.

Whenever possible, a letter-of-marque schooner and even a privateer avoided a battle for fear of damage to its cargo or to the cargo and ship that was its prey. The ultimate purpose for the large crews was to provide a prize master and crew to put aboard a captured vessel to sail it to the nearest friendly port.

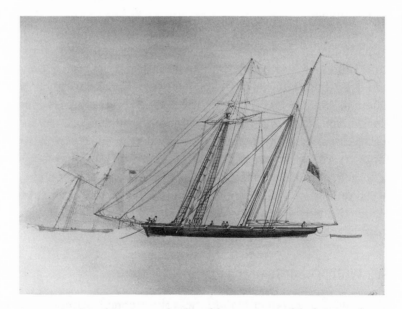

Designed for speed, Baltimore's sharp-built schooners were light of body and heavy with rig. Many, like the topsail clipper shown here, were armed and went to sea as privateers. The clipper under sail in the background displays the long low hull, the sails, and raking masts that gave the Baltimore-built privateer its distinctive profile. (National Maritime Museum, Greenwich, England, No. 7183)

Once in port, the master had to file a suit or "libel," justifying the taking of the vessel, requesting that it be condemned and that it and its cargo be put up for public sale. It was a complex procedure beginning with a trial in admiralty court to prove ownership of the vessel and cargo that justified its seizure. When proved to be under the registry of an unfriendly power, the vessel would be declared a "good and lawful prize" and sold at auction. If ownership by a belligerent was not proven, the ship was restored to its captain and crew or its rightful owners and sent on its way. If put up for public sale, the profits were divided among the privateer's owners, its captain and crew, and the prize captain and crew.

At the outset of the war, many of the schooners were equipped with sails of the new cotton duck, rather than flax. The cotton sails held their shape better than flaxen ones. They were lighter and required less wetting down, which caused the fabric to swell, close the weave, and thereby hold the wind better. They were also whiter than those of flax and, along with the rake of a schooner's masts and the cut of her sails, contributed to the distinctive profile of the Baltimore-built privateer schooner.[1]

In the first decade of the nineteenth century, Baltimore shipbuilders in the yards at Fells Point were turning out sharp-built schooners "finished in privateer fashion"[2] as fast as they could. William Price and other Fells Point shipbuilders, such as Thomas Kemp, who produced the famous privateers *Chasseur*, *Rossie*, and *Rolla* and the letter-of-marque schooner *Grecian*, earned for Baltimore the reputation as a privateers' nest.[3] Baltimore's yards were not the only ones turning out sharp-built schooners, but the greatest number of sharp model schooners, brigs, and ships traced their origins to Baltimore shipyards. Hence the name Baltimore clipper that was later applied to such vessels, wherever they were built.

Sea Wolf: The Privateer *Dolphin*

The privateer schooner *Dolphin* was the second Baltimore vessel commissioned by the federal government at the outset of the war.[4] A "sea wolf," as privateers were popularly called, she began her career in July 1812, and within two weeks, captured the schooner *Fannie*, an easy prey and the first prize of the war to reach Baltimore.[5]

Later, on her second cruise in November, the 161-ton *Dolphin* came up on the 550-ton English merchantman, the *John Hamilton*. After an initial sortie against the much larger

ship to test its strength, the *Dolphin*'s captain, William Stafford, let the clipper drop back, lurking just out of cannon range, dogging the *Hamilton*'s course for a day and a night. At sunrise, Stafford closed on the merchant ship, bringing the *Dolphin* in with cannon blazing.

The *Hamilton* wasn't about to give up without a fight and the action lasted two hours; there were injuries, but no deaths on either vessel. The ship wasn't equal to the hit-and-run tactics of the privateer. Finally, her captain struck his colors and Stafford sent his prize off to Baltimore under command of prize master Anthony Hayman. "Give them a salute of eighteen guns passing Fort McHenry," said Stafford as Hayman set off with the ship and its cargo of mahogany.[6] That one prize was sold for nearly $25,000.[7]

By March 1813, the British blockade had sealed the Chesapeake. The *Dolphin*, along with a number of other privateers, was trapped in Baltimore where she had returned to replenish supplies and crew. Impatient to get back to sea, Stafford set out on March 18 to go down the Bay.

By noon on March 27, the privateer was anchored off Tangier Island riding out a storm. The northeaster brought with it rain and snow—excellent cover to run the blockade. Stafford instructed the pilot he had taken on to get them out of the Bay. As they approached the capes, Stafford and the pilot argued over whether they were in the Cape Charles Channel. The pilot made a wrong call and very nearly ran the *Dolphin* aground.

When the pilot realized his mistake, Stafford wrote in his log, "without further ceremony, he jumped overboard and drowned himself, every exertion of ours to save him proving fruitless."[8]

Sea Wolf and Flyers

Deciding to make no further attempt on the capes, Stafford anchored for the night. Daylight showed him that he was in sight of Cape Charles and a line of English men-of-war as well.

Without a breath of wind to drive the *Dolphin*, he ordered out the sweeps. They rowed the privateer up the Bay until they caught a breeze and the flood tide and clapped on her full suit of sails. She sped north, falling in with three letter-of-marque schooners, the *Arab*, *Racer*, and *Lynx*. The flyers were larger than the *Dolphin*, but unlike the privateer, which was built and manned for a fight, they were less inclined to risk an engagement. The four Americans decided to put into the Rappahannock River.

The 161-ton *Dolphin* carried a crew of 100, which included prize masters and crews, a surgeon, and a fighting force of landsmen. She was armed with two long nine-pounders and ten twelve-pound carronades.[9] The *Arab*, which had been commissioned less than two weeks, was a schooner of 333 tons and mounted two long nine-pounders, a long twelve, and four nine-pound carronades. She had a crew of forty.[10] The 230-ton *Racer* had six twelve-pounders, two long guns, and four carronades and shipped forty men. She was carrying a cargo of cotton, coffee, and sugar.[11] The *Lynx* was a vessel of 225 tons, had a crew of thirty-five and mounted six twelve-pounders. Like the *Racer*, she had a hold filled with cotton, coffee, and sugar.[12]

The 94-foot *Lynx*, which is the most fully documented of the four schooners, was built at Baltimore in 1812 for James and Amos Williams and Levi Hollingsworth. She was commissioned on July 14, 1812. Her spars raked sharply aft and she carried a square topsail forward. Built on the pilot boat model, she must have been very fast. According to Howard Chapelle, "this beautiful vessel is an example of the highest development of the Baltimore Clipper." She was not extreme, he noted, but showed a natural development from the class of Virginia-built vessels being built at the time of the Revolution.[13]

Battle on the Rappahannock

At dawn on the morning of April 3, the four schooners lay anchored in a line across the river at the mouth of Carter Creek. Once the morning mists had cleared, they could see Mosquito Point six miles distant and a schooner being rowed into view. She had the look of a Baltimore-built clipper. Stafford upped

This watercolor painting shows the double topsail privateer *Surprise* capturing the ship *Star* in January 1815. The *Surprise* was built "privateer fashion" by Thomas Kemp in 1813 at St. Michaels. She was 245 tons and measured 79 feet 6 inches by 24 feet 9 inches, with an 11-foot depth of hold. Her captain in 1815 was Samuel Barstow and she carried a crew of 130 men. The *Surprise* ran aground in a storm and was lost at Manasquan, New Jersey, on April 3, 1815. (Peabody Museum of Salem, George Ropes)

anchor and ordered his men to the sweeps to row down to meet her. *Racer* followed.

Stafford's prize master Barriere was at his side at the tiller. As they closed to within a mile of the schooner, they could see the tops of masts over the point—two ships and two brigs they reckoned—and at the same time, Barriere made a chilling dis-

In this view of the *Pride of Baltimore* taken off Sandy Point, Maryland, during Chesapeake Appreciation Days 1984, she looks very much as a privateer might have looked to the crew of a potential prize as she prowled British waters during the War of 1812. The *Pride*, which was lost May 14, 1986, was conceived and built by Melbourne Smith and designed by Thomas Gillmer as an authentic Baltimore clipper, built to nineteenth century standards and using nineteenth century methods. Launched on February 27, 1977, she was immediately successful as a symbol of the city in whose name she sailed. Her success led to the building of the *Spirit of Massachusetts*, the *California* and others, creating a new generation of foundation-owned vessels based on historic types. (M. Staley)

covery. The schooner rounding the point was indeed a Baltimore privateer—the *Highflyer*—and he had once been her captain, but she had been taken by the British early in January. He'd had no word that she'd been retaken by the Americans. Stafford ordered his crew to ship their oars.

By then, the *Highflyer* had cleared the point, and the men on the *Dolphin* could see behind her a flotilla of small craft, barges, cutters, launches, and pinnaces, sixteen or seventeen in all, manned by over a hundred British marines and seamen.

Stafford fired a round from each of his long nines and then turned the *Dolphin* back upriver to where the *Arab* and *Lynx* waited at the mouth of Corrotoman River. The *Racer* was close behind. Together once more, the captains of the four schooners held a council of war and agreed to make a stand, forming a line across the river, keeping their positions with their oars.

Once in position, however, Captain Fitch anchored the *Arab*. The others went to their sweeps—the *Dolphin* holding with three forward oars on each side. On each ship, crews made ready; the seamen putting their cutlasses in their belts; the landsmen loading their muskets and taking positions behind the bulwarks or in the shrouds. Gun crews charged their pieces with grapeshot as their officers went from group to group with words of encouragement. These were not seasoned fighting men.

The British flotilla headed first for the *Arab*, which fired a broadside, but anchored as she was, she was trapped in position. The small boats came on with muskets and cannon blazing. As they closed on the schooner, her crew cut her anchor cable and the *Arab* drifted shoreward. As an English boarding party clambered over the stern rails, the *Arab*'s crew left from the bow, swimming ashore, leaving the privateer to the British.

Aboard the *Racer*, *Lynx* and *Dolphin*, crews were shaken by the desertion of the men of the *Arab*. They turned from their guns with no heart for a fight. Stafford swung into action.

"I'm determined to defend my vessel to the last!" he bellowed. "Will you stand by me? One man has run his vessel ashore. Others may, too. I won't. I mean to defend myself. Those who will fight, give three cheers!"

The cheers of the *Dolphin*'s crew echoed across the Rappahannock as they returned to their posts. Stafford sent for his pistols and ordered his officers to arm themselves also.

In the meantime, the enemy flotilla had engaged the *Lynx* and the *Racer*. British marines raked the decks of the two schooners with their musket fire. The *Dolphin* moved in to help in the defense, firing on the attacking boats with her carronades. Soon, the air was thick with smoke.

The pinnace that was the British flagship moved in on the *Lynx*, coming alongside, but before a boarding party could be sent over the rails, Captain Taylor of the *Lynx* struck her colors. At the same time, a British force had boarded the *Racer*. Her crew fought, defending themselves with handspikes and wielding their muskets like clubs. They were soon overwhelmed and the British had command of the third schooner, immediately turning the *Racer*'s guns on the *Dolphin*. The *Racer*, the *Highflyer*, and several small boats joined in the attack on the privateer.

Stafford met them with broadsides, but under the British onslaught, many of his crew left their posts. Drawing his pistols with a threat to shoot the first man to desert, Stafford got some of his men back to the guns. Several, fearing the British more than their captain, lowered a boat and fled to shore under the fire of Stafford's marines. They escaped unhurt and Stafford rallied his crew—only fifteen remained able to fight—and prepared to make a stand firing into the British boats that were coming alongside.

And then, he was hit, struck in the chest by a twelve-pound cannon shot that had ricocheted off the bulwarks. Beside him, three more men went down, and the attackers quickly beat down the remaining defenders and hauled down the *Dolphin*'s colors.

The captured privateers were rowed downriver to the British squadron that lay waiting just beyond Mosquito Point. The English had lost two men and had eleven wounded; the Americans had six lost and had ten wounded, most of them on the *Dolphin*. Stafford was taken aboard one of the British ships where he was tended by a British surgeon and eventually paroled and returned to Baltimore.[14] The *Dolphin* and *Arab* were taken to Bermuda and sold as prizes, the *Racer* and *Lynx* were taken into British service. The *Lynx* eventually found her way to England where her lines were taken off and the information on her preserved in admiralty records.[15]

No Men for Naval Service

Within a week after the battle on the Rappahannock, word reached Baltimore. It was of particular interest to U.S. Navy Captain Charles Gordon, who was in charge of the naval station at Baltimore between August 1812 and August 1814. Besides following the movement of the British, he had spent much of his time trying to recruit men for naval service or to locate schooners to arm for the defense of the port and upper Bay.

"The enemy are reported to be as high as the Patuxent, and have captured (in the Rappahannock) one privateer and three letters-of-marque schooners belonging to this port," Gordon reported to Secretary of the Navy Jones on April 9, 1813.[16] Later, in May, when Stafford was returned to Baltimore, Gordon recruited him to help locate and command a schooner for naval service. Experienced captains and crews were hard to come by.[17]

Privateering was far more popular than naval service where crews were bound to see battle. There was money to be made on a privateer or an armed merchantman and little on a naval vessel destined for combat. Competition for crews along Baltimore's wharves was keen among privateers, merchantmen, and navy vessels. The privateers usually won.[18]

In February 1813, Charles Gordon's fleet for the defense of the port of Baltimore consisted of a single gunboat, which he could not put into service "entirely for the want of men," he wrote to the secretary of the navy. He could not compete with "the high wages and bounty offer'd to seamen for the Letters of Mark service."[19]

Gordon's Fleet: The Schooners *Comet*, *Patapsco*, *Revenge*, and *Wasp*

Gordon had also been ordered by the secretary of the navy to locate and obtain the loan of four small schooners to complete the naval force that was to protect vessels trading in and out of Baltimore and to patrol the Chesapeake as far south as the Potomac River. Baltimore's builders, however, were concentrating on building privateers and letter-of-marque vessels for going offshore. Gordon wrote to the secretary in March 1813. He'd just returned from inspecting every schooner in port.

"They are very generally too large for your dimensions," he wrote. "I beg leave to observe that none of the Baltimore built vessels of 90 or 100 tons can be got to draw as little as 8 feet of water."[20] Which meant—as far as Gordon's mission was concerned—that they would be no good for eluding the British by taking advantage of the shoal waters of the Bay and its rivers.

A month later he had finally found three schooners that could be armed and outfitted for naval service on the Chesapeake: *Comet, Patapsco,* and *Revenge.* He had also acquired a fourth smaller one, the *Wasp,* to be used as a tender.[21]

Gordon continued to have trouble manning his little fleet. "A great number of the sailors now in Port are still attached to the letters-of-marque," he wrote to the navy secretary, "which deprives us of the use of those fine schooners well fitted and the services of those men."[22]

It was May when he finally got his force under way to patrol the Bay and, in spite of all the trouble he had had, felt well served by the schooners he commanded. He wrote to the secretary of the navy from aboard the *Patapsco* where he was keeping track of a British ship of the line, a frigate, a schooner, and several smaller craft near the mouth of the Potomac. He had requested the assistance of the Potomac Flotilla only to discover that they were "so weakly mann'd and such heavy sailors that they could not be of any service. Indeed, they can be of no use whatever here if that is their state for they will always require such vessels as mine to protect them against the brigs and schooners of the enemy or require some fort to retreat to, and would be driven before the enemy all the way up the river."[23]

The navy suffered for want of adequate vessels throughout the War of 1812, but for private investment, there were plenty to arm and send out to sea. Between 1805 and 1815, 111 privateers and letter-of-marque vessels were built and commissioned at Baltimore. They ranged in size from the 55-ton *Wasp* to the 376-ton *Mammoth.* Ninety-nine were in the one hundred- to two hundred-ton class.[24] Ninety percent of the Baltimore fleet were sharp-built topsail schooners.

At least a dozen private armed vessels sailed out of Virginia ports, but records are scanty. Both Norfolk and Portsmouth were attacked and burned, first by the British and again a half-century later by Union forces raiding Confederate installations there. Most port records went up in flames.

No great fortunes were made from privateering, but during the war, it was just about the only game in town that promised any profit at all, however great the gamble. In terms of the war effort, the private armed vessels were the only successful offensive weapon the Americans had.[25] American privateers preyed upon British shipping, causing $40 million in losses to English merchants. With an economy on the verge of ruin and an angry populace, the British finally sued for peace.[26]

Sailing the Middle Passage

Suddenly, with the end of the war, Baltimore merchants had little or no need for their privateers and there was a serious slump in the business of shipbuilding. Some of the privateers that had survived the war were sold to foreign interests and some fell into the hands of pirates. The remainder wound up sailing the treacherous Middle Passage between the African coast and the West Indies as outlaws in the slave trade.

The importation of slaves was banned in the United States by an act of Congress in 1807, and in 1820 was made an act of piracy, punishable by death. The law applied to the building, owning, fitting out, supplying, or manning of a slaver. It was poorly enforced and some Americans continued to participate in the profitable "Black Ivory" trade. Their role was primarily in providing many of the sharp-built, fast-sailing schooners and brigs that were used in the trade, which was conducted mainly by Cuban and Brazilian slavers and continued through the mid-1850s.[27]

By 1815, with the end of the Napoleonic Wars, England's powerful navy was free to police the seas and enforce treaties with Spain, France, Portugal, and Brazil for the suppression of the slave trade. The treaties allowed British cruisers to stop, search, and seize any vessel of those nations suspected of slaving. Unwilling to trust the British after too recent experience

U.S.B. Washington

La Amistad

Negro Trading

with search and seizure, the United States refused to sign any treaties permitting the British navy to search an American vessel. Cuban and Brazilian slavers lost no time in using that to their advantage to acquire fast-sailing vessels for their trade.[28]

Working through an elaborate system of foreign intermediaries, slave traders bought up the privateers for which the Americans had no further use and, when they needed more, had new ones built on the same model. These were sailed with impunity under an American flag usually with an American captain and crew to England where they were then "chartered" to carry a cargo "particularly suited to the African Coast Trade"— such things as muskets, ammunition, spirits, tobacco, and other trade goods. A cargo of "Coast goods" also included handcuffs, leg irons, oversize cook ranges and kettles, and an unusual number of water barrels.

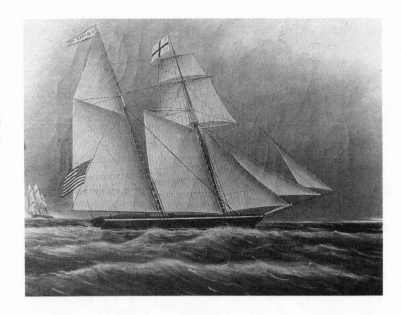

Thus loaded, the vessel continued under the protection of American registry to Havana where it took on passengers and then recrossed the Atlantic to the African coast. On reaching the slave compounds in Africa, the American crew turned the vessel over to the "passengers," who became captain and crew. The American captain, as agent for the vessel's owner, was paid "earnest" money, which was in fact the purchase price of the vessel, and he and his crew returned to Havana or the United States. The vessel got a new name and its registry and flag were changed to Spanish, Portuguese, or Brazilian.[29]

Under its new registry, the slaver was vulnerable to search and seizure, and the key to its success against Britain's cruisers was its speed. At that point in time, there were no faster vessels on the sea than the sharp-built Baltimore-model brigs and schooners that some had begun to call clippers.

Suddenly there was a demand again for sharp-built schooners and brigs built along the lines of the Baltimore clipper schooner. Chesapeake Bay builders, who had fallen on hard times at the end of the war when the need for new sharp-built hulls dropped radically, were in business again.[30]

British government records, though incomplete, show a preponderance of slavers in the late 1830s as having been built on the Chesapeake Bay: in Baltimore and in Dorchester and Talbot counties.[31] This was, as mentioned, in spite of the fact that the laws prohibiting the trade extended to the building, fitting out, supplying, chartering, or manning of a slaver.

During that time, Baltimore clippers—brigs and a few large schooners—new-built as slavers, were altered for the trade, introducing the last real change in their design before these beautiful vessels passed from the scene. The overall result was a vessel of unusually sharp lines, built primarily for speed. As a rule, they were considered expendable and were very lightly built.[32]

A slaver, usually a brig, did have certain characteristics peculiar to it alone. It would usually have large grating hatches on the deck, bulkheads at the ends of its hold, and an unusually large cooking hearth. It also carried an inordinate number of water casks, stored level in the hold and covered with rush mats to form a deck on which the slaves were held.[33]

Up until a slaver arrived on the African coast, it appeared to all but a trained eye as any cargo vessel, albeit not terribly burdensome. Most of the changes necessary below decks to accommodate slaves, such as the installation of the casks, were not made until just before the slaver was prepared to take on its illicit cargo.

During the loading process, a slaver had to be in and out of the African slave compound as fast as possible before a British cruiser came prowling. Working usually at night, they could load the casks, spread the mats over them, and drive some six hundred to eight hundred captured Africans into the hold in as little as seven hours. With their cargo aboard, the slavers made for the open sea and the chief centers of operation in Cuba and Brazil.[34]

Most of the schooners were small, seldom more than seventy feet in length. Often they were used in shallow ports to lighter supplies, crew, or slaves between larger vessels and the shore. Typically, a schooner built for "export" had a very shallow draft—the better to get close to the beaches of slave compounds. Some, according to Chapelle, were "so shallow as to suggest they might have had centerboards," but it is unlikely that these were Bay-built since the centerboard was not in common use on the Chesapeake until the mid–nineteenth century.[35] A slaver was also extreme in her lines to achieve maximum speed. Despite her sinister purpose, she was beautiful.

The *Amistad*

One of the most notable stories involving a Bay-built slaver is that of the schooner *Amistad*, built on the Bay sometime in the 1830s.[36]

In the summer of 1839, a Portuguese slave ship arrived in Havana, Cuba, with a cargo of West Africans. Among them were forty-nine men, one boy, and three girls from Sierra Leone. The Africans were sold to Spanish slave traders who loaded them aboard the *Amistad* and headed for Puerto Rico. The captives sweltered in the schooner's hold where they were confined without food or water. They were beaten and were convinced such barbarisms would end in their deaths. The ship's cook contributed to their fears, using sign language to lead them to believe that they would be boiled and eaten when they reached their destination.

The Africans' Spanish captors paid dearly for misjudging the intelligence and courage of their prisoners. Led by a twenty-five-year-old named Cinque, the Africans escaped from the hold and overpowered the Spanish. They killed the captain and the cook, losing two of their number in the battle, but, in the end, the *Amistad* was in their control.

Cinque ordered the Spanish crew to sail the schooner back to Sierra Leone, using the sun to assure him that they were sailing east for the coast of Africa. At night, however, the Spaniards steered northwest. For two months, the *Amistad* sailed east by day and northwest by night, zigzagging along the North American coast until she was discovered on August 26, 1839, and taken into custody by a U.S. Navy vessel off the coast of Long Island. By then, eight of the Africans had died of disease or starvation.

The captain of the naval vessel claimed the *Amistad* and her cargo of slaves as rights of salvage. Since slavery was still legal in Connecticut, he expected a healthy reward for himself and his crew from the ship and Africans. That was not to happen. The arrival of the vessel and its human cargo was soon an issue of public debate. The question of whether the Africans were indeed slaves and property was raised by antislavery forces and the case eventually went to trial.

The abolitionists were soon at work raising funds to aid the Africans' defense with legal counsel and an interpreter. In 1840, U.S. District Judge Andrew Judson declared the Africans free and ordered that they be returned to Africa. By then, the whole affair had become a controversial political issue at the national level. President Martin Van Buren ordered the U.S. attorney general to appeal Judge Judson's verdict and a year later the case was before the Supreme Court. Arguing in the Africans' defense was former president John Quincy Adams. In March 1841, the Supreme Court upheld Judson's ruling.

By November 1841, when they finally set sail for their return to Sierra Leone, only thirty-five of the original fifty-three Africans survived. With them went a contingent of missionaries, sponsored by the *Amistad* Committee—a precursor to what became in 1846 the American Missionary Association.[37]

The fate of the actual vessel was obscured by events, but it lives on in organizations, music, and literature commemorating the *Amistad* Africans' determination to be free. The outcome of the *Amistad* affair was an inspiration for subsequent abolitionist efforts and for civil rights activists well into the twentieth century.

The Last Days of the Baltimore Clippers

When the slave trade was finally wiped out in the 1850s, it took with it the Baltimore clippers. Because they had become so extreme in their design, they were of no use in general trade. Then, too, because of the terrible work to which they had been put, they were undesirable for any employment. Only a few of the smaller schooners used as tenders in the slave trade survived at all. With the exception of a few scattered revivals, the building of the Baltimore clipper as a type had ceased by the 1840s. Only a few remained by 1860.[38]

A number of schooners built on the Baltimore model in Boston, Portsmouth, and New York were used in the fruit trade where their capabilities in light and moderate weather were an advantage. Extreme versions of the Baltimore clipper schooner were also built in northern ports for smuggling and the opium trade. They remained poor cargo carriers, however, and only in the 1830s and 1840s, when larger ship-rigged Baltimore clippers, such as the *Ann McKim* and the *Architect*, were built in Baltimore, did the type become viable in general trade.[39]

The *Ann McKim* was 143 feet long, drew 17 feet, and was 493 tons. She was a fast sailer, but like her forerunners had too little cargo capacity. Her distinction in the development of the Baltimore clipper is in terms of size rather than design. Her hull was essentially that of an enlarged schooner hull, with considerable deadrise, a rake to her ends, and the sharp lines of earlier clippers. Making her larger did not make her a better cargo vessel, and only proved that there was little to be gained in terms of cargo-carrying capacity by making the Baltimore clippers larger.[40] They could not compete with the slower, more capacious freighters that had begun to dominate the shipping lanes. When more speed was called for, designers went in a different direction, developing the famous American clipper ships of the 1850s. There are two schools of thought as to whether the famed tea clippers evolved from the design of the Baltimore clipper.

The argument against such an evolution is that the clipper ships of the fifties had comparatively little deadrise, were rather wall-sided and flat-floored, and though still not very good carriers could accommodate a large amount of cargo in proportion to their tonnage. The Bay-built "heelers," as Chapelle liked to call the Baltimore clippers, were probably faster than the later clipper ships in light and moderate weather. They were not strong enough or powerful enough, however, to have long survived the heavy weather, such as that encountered rounding Cape Horn, as did the more powerful clipper ships.[41]

Still, some China clippers, like those of New York ship-designer William Webb, did show the long, sharp, hollow bows, long graceful runs, and moderate deadrise that gave them the look of a Baltimore clipper. Thus the difference in opinion persists over the relationship between the Baltimore clippers and the larger and more powerful clippers of the fifties. The weight of the argument seems to come down against there being any direct relationship.

For the rest of the nineteenth century, however, the influence of the Baltimore clipper is seen in nearly every fast-sailing keel schooner built. Elements of its design show up in everything from fruit traders to fishing schooners, to yachts. Pilot schooners, Gloucester fishermen, coastwise schooners, and other commercial traders, all had characteristics of the Baltimore-built "heelers," but the true Baltimore clipper sailed the Chesapeake Bay no more.[42]

The important thing, however, is not how the Baltimore clipper came to its demise, but the part it played in the history of sailing ships and their design. As privateers, most of which were schooners, the Baltimore clippers served their owners and their country well in two wars for independence. They also had much to do with the meteoric growth of Baltimore from a village to a major seaport. But perhaps most of all, the Baltimore-model schooner raised the level of shipbuilding and design to a point that has seldom been equaled in maritime history.

"…[Y]ou Americans are a singular people as it respects seamanship and enterprise," wrote Englishman George Coggeshall in 1856. "In England, we cannot build such vessels as your Baltimore Clippers; we have no such models, and even if we had them, they would be of no service to us, for we never would sail them as you do. We are afraid of their long masts and heavy spars, and soon would cut down and reduce them to our standard. We strengthen them, put up bulwarks, after which they lose their sailing qualities, and are of no further service as cruising vessels."[43]

Howard Chapelle put it best: "Sired by war, mothered by privateering and piracy, and nursed by cruelty, nevertheless, the Baltimore clipper will always remain the type representative of the highest development of small sailing craft, as built by American builders."

Five

A New Era for Bay Schooners

During the War of 1812, shipbuilder Thomas Kemp, whose yard was at the juncture of Washington and Aliceanna streets in Fells Point, was famous for turning out fast privateers. He built the *Chasseur*, captained by Thomas Boyle, one of the more audacious of the Bay's privateersmen. In 1814, while cruising alone in British waters in search of prey, Boyle sent word ashore that the entire English coast was under blockade. After harassing the British on their side of the Atlantic, he crossed to hound their shipping in the Caribbean before returning home with the *Chasseur*, the very first "Pride of Baltimore."

For all their successes during the war, the bold, swift clipper schooners were of little use in a peacetime economy, which by 1819 was in the throes of a general depression. The shipbuilding industry on the Bay suffered along with everything else. Thomas Kemp was among those shipbuilders who experienced a significant loss of business after the war. When the economy began to turn, the market for sharp, fast schooners was gone. Kemp and other Bay builders faced a new era with very different demands.

Except for a few Spanish pirates prowling the Caribbean, the seas were relatively safe for trade and a strong commerce with the West Indies grew up again. Merchants and farmers of the Bay were looking for hulls with plenty of space belowdecks for produce and other goods to send south. Even more than speed, they wanted depth of hold for greater cargo-carrying

By the 1850s, pilot schooners were larger and carried their pilots to sea in somewhat greater comfort than did the earliest pilot boats. The *Commerce of Baltimore* was large enough to "cruise" at sea for several days. While pilot schooners always carried more sail for their size than did most others, later ones, like the *Commerce,* carried an extreme spread of sail. (Maryland Historical Society)

This is an excellent view of the *William A. Graves*, built in Norfolk in 1883 as a pilot schooner for the Virginia Pilots Association. She is not, however, of the "Virginia pilot-boat" type. The *Graves* is a much heavier schooner and her design is not as extreme as that of the original pilot schooners. She carries two headsails and her rigging is also heavier. The association used the *Graves* and two other schooners exclusively until 1891 when they built the steamer *Relief*. (The Mariners' Museum, No. PK-7272)

capacity. Builders like Kemp had to adjust to the new demand. Up to that time, the depth of hold in even the largest of his early vessels never exceeded 10 feet 2 inches.[1]

Records from Kemp's yard show that after the war he was building fewer schooners and a more full-bodied type, which he referred to as an "Eastern Shore Schooner." It showed, no doubt, the influence of St. Michaels shipbuilder Impey Dawson from whom Kemp had learned his trade two decades earlier.[2] Kemp's heart apparently was no longer in the building of boats, however. In 1816, he returned to St. Michaels and his new home at Wades Point Farm on Eastern Bay. Absorbed with orchards and farming, Kemp built no more than two or three more schooners before his death in 1824.[3]

In 1830, another native Eastern Shore builder, who also did a stint in Baltimore building clippers, returned to St. Michaels. Robert Lambdin established his shipyard at Long Wharf and Mulberry streets and, when his four sons were grown, took them on as partners in the building of centerboard schooners, pungy schooners, sloops and, later, bugeyes. Over the next fifty years, the Lambdins found a profitable market for small, fast-sailing cargo vessels and built more than fifty of them for trade on the Bay.[4]

They were not alone. The demand for craft to operate on the Bay and in the West Indies trade supported a large number of small yards on the Eastern Shore, as well as along rivers on the western shores of Maryland and Virginia. The result was that Baltimore, which had never been an exclusive center of shipbuilding on the Bay, suffered for a lack of Marylanders to work its shipyards. Ship's carpenters and other craftsmen preferred to work in their own villages, where they could use the inevitable slack time for fishing, farming, and hunting. Builders like Lambdin found they could take advantage of that preference and profited from their move to the Shore and the new, but sadly brief, age of commercial sail on the Bay.

The Last of the Pilot Schooners

One maritime profession that demanded speed rather than cargo capacity in a vessel was that of pilot. The Norfolk pilots not only developed a suitable boat, but seem to have established the initial standards and practices of their profession as well.

The smaller schooners and sloops—commonly no more than sixty feet on deck—generally were operated by a single pilot. There were larger pilot boats of 100 feet or more that carried several pilots and apprentices. These were fitted out to stay at sea until all the pilots were put aboard inbound vessels. The early pilot schooners carried sturdy dinghies and later yawl boats to take the pilots to and from ships at sea. They were rowed by the apprentices, who then sailed the pilot boats back to port.

During the colonial period, Maryland employed slaves as pilots. In fact, the first mention of a pilot in the laws of Maryland was an act of the legislature allowing a slave to hire himself out as a pilot without recourse to his master.[5]

During the Revolutionary War, some thirty-eight Virginia pilots are known to have served as lookouts and dispatch carriers. Many pilots owned slaves and trained them in the profession, and at least three of the Virginia pilots who served in the Revolution were black: two slaves, Cuffee and Minny, and a Captain Starling, who may have been a freeman. It is known that Cuffee died of wounds he received aboard the pilot boat *William Graves* during an encounter with the British in 1781.[6]

Because of their skill at traversing the shoals at the Virginia capes and at dodging British warships, the Bay pilots provided an invaluable service during the war by conducting merchantmen in and out of the Bay with cargoes of arms, clothing, and other supplies for the American army. On occasion, they even carried gunpowder and other items themselves.

The pilots served similarly during the War of 1812, returning in peacetime to their regular duties of conning ships. They also kept a watch for vessels that might be carrying disease which had to be kept from entering port. In 1856, another distasteful duty was forced on Virginia's pilots. They were required by law to search outbound vessels for runaway slaves or criminals and were fined if a slave got away after they had made their search.[7]

Cruising off the capes for days at a time was no easy life. In late summer and fall came the hurricanes, in winter, gales and ice. In January 1837, it was reported in Baltimore that the "Pilot Boat *Tally Ho* was out to Sea on the 1st. inst. and

At times, the Bay and its harbors were as well-trafficked as are today's highways. Scenes such as this in Annapolis in 1853 were common. A winter freeze is the probable cause of this gridlock at the mouth of the Severn. To a great extent, conditions of the Bay and its weather governed trade that depended upon sailing freighters. An Annapolis girl, Susannah Sands, wrote to a friend in 1857, "Our beautiful river has been frozen over for weeks and no boat of any kind has been down the Chesapeake Bay since last Saturday week." In time, not even a freeze like that of 1857 would keep steam-powered vessels in port and over the next one hundred years, they relentlessly nudged schooners and other commercial sailing craft out of business. (Maryland State Archives, MdHr-G-985-277)

The schooner *Mary and Francis* was built in Baltimore in 1832 by James Haywood and is an example of a typical Baltimore coasting packet schooner of the period. Note the extreme spread of canvas, which was common, and the square sails as well as studding sails on the fore. (Mystic Seaport Museum, No. 62.1153)

encountered a heavy gale from the N.W. and weather very cold. The Boat was so much loaded with ice forward as to bring her down by the head and very much ice on deck, was afraid would have to run into the Gulph stream." Ten days later there was another report. "The Pilot Boats *Star* and *Tally Ho* arrived at Norfolk all safe, having been driven off into the Gulph and been out to sea 8 days."[8]

Aboard a pilot schooner, the pilots lived as well as any master mariner of their day. Their supplies included barrels of salt beef, bushels of onions, potatoes, and cabbages, barrels of beans and flour, and bags of coffee. Accounts show that they had turkeys at Christmas. The pilots had only to command. Their crews—usually three hands and a cook—did the work of "cruizing the boat." A pilot's time came when he climbed over the side of the pilot boat into the yawl to be rowed to an inbound vessel. He had to go, whatever the conditions of sea or weather, or whatever kind of vessel it might be. He could find luxury or filth and disease, but he still had to go, and he had to stay with the vessel until it reached its destination, which could take hours, days or weeks, depending on weather, winds, and tides.[9]

In 1856, there were only five Virginia pilot boats operating: *Reindeer*, *Antelope*, *Plume*, *Hope*, and *York*.[10] It was not a good time for pilots. The coal trade was growing on the Bay, with increasing traffic to Baltimore, Newport News, and Norfolk. Virginia's assembly passed a number of laws revamping the regulations governing pilotage and making many vessels exempt from taking on pilots to encourage the colliers to use the state's coal piers.

Meanwhile, Marylanders were faring even worse. Maryland had far more trade than Virginia, but an act of Congress in 1837 allowed Virginians to pilot vessels to Baltimore and other upper-Bay ports. Then in 1852, the Maryland legislature passed a law allowing any master or vessel owner to pilot his own boat.[11]

The dire situation with which the pilots were faced led them to form the Association of Maryland Pilots.[12] Under the association, the competition that had formerly existed between individual pilots ceased. They took turns going to meet incoming ships, and profits were shared among the association's members. At the time, there were eight pilot boats operating out of Baltimore: *Comet, Selim, Liberty, Henry Clay, Baltimore, Tally Ho, Pocahontas,* and *Constitution.* Each was used by a partnership of six pilots who "cruized" from Cape Henlopen to Cape Hatteras.[13] The system was only beginning to function when war broke out between North and South.

When the Civil War began, some of Maryland's and Virginia's pilots tried blockade running, but their numbers diminished as more and more of them were conscripted into the Union army. Those Virginia pilots who remained were kept from working on the Potomac River or the Bay for fear they'd be taken by Union forces and put to work for the enemy. Virginia's *Plume, Hope, Reindeer,* and *Antelope* were sunk, and the *York* became a Confederate privateer.[14]

Over the course of the war and its aftermath several of Maryland's pilot schooners were lost to the service or simply wore out. They were eventually replaced by the *Eclipse, Dart, Canton, Boston, Coquette, Fashion, Invincible, Maryland, W. H. Silver,* and the last of the sailing pilot boats, the *Calvert,* built in 1873. All were main topmast schooners.[15]

In 1880, the Association of Maryland Pilots built the steamer *Pilot,* the first steam pilot boat used in the United States. She kept something of the look of the schooners, retaining a fore- and mainmast.[16]

The Virginia pilots followed Maryland's lead in forming an association in 1866. The Association of Virginia Pilots owned the schooners *Phantom, William Starkey,* and *William A. Graves,* and the auxiliary schooners *Virginia* and *Hampton Roads.* Virginia's pilots used sailing vessels exclusively until 1891 when they built the steamer *Relief.*[17]

From the very first one built for the race to sea until they were replaced by steamers, the Virginia pilot schooners provided a reliable model for fast seaworthy vessels. The development and refinement of the Virginia pilot boat was an ongoing process that resulted in some significant changes throughout its period of service. The builders of Norfolk pilot boats began to depart from the original model sometime after 1805. The most notable change they made was to sharpen its entrance with a nearly

Up and down the Bay, marine industries, like the shipyard at Solomons Island, Maryland, dominated waterfront scenes in towns where the dock area was often the center of activity. The comings and goings of schooners, such as the one whose bowsprit is just visible on the right, were an important part of daily life. For many tidewater villagers, the nineteenth century freight and packet schooners that served them were their only communication with the rest of the Bay. Note the ever-present flat-bottom skiffs. (Maryland State Archives, MdHR-G-1477-5392)

The *Lula M. Phillips* was rebuilt in 1913 at Bethel, Delaware. She was originally the *Annie M. Leonard*, built at Oxford in 1877 by William Benson who also built the *Arianna Bateman* and the *Clara M. Leonard*. Benson vessels were known for their speed and quality, and the *Annie M. Leonard* served as a packet. It was said that not a piece of wood went into the frames of a Benson-built vessel that was not seasoned at least four years. (The Mariners' Museum, No. PK 3628, Edwin Levick)

upright stempost, a change that was not lost on shipbuilders beyond the Bay.[18]

Ever since the Revolution, builders around the world had been watching and copying the fast Bay-built schooners, and the straight-stemmed Virginia pilot boat model of the early 1800s began showing up on the stocks in yards up and down the Atlantic coast. By 1860, the straight stem was a hallmark of the New York and Boston pilot boats.[19]

Builders in New York and other ports also adopted the Virginia pilot boat's rig with its short bowsprit, large sail area, and raking masts, supported by only one or two shrouds on a side. On the Bay, until about 1845, pilot boats carried a gaff-mainsail with a boom and a large gaff- or lug-foresail having no boom and a clew that came well abaft of the mainmast. They set a single large jib and carried a main-topmast, that set a large staysail, called a fisherman. They rarely carried a gaff-topsail.[20] The rig was designed so that in strong winds, the vessel could work on all points of sailing under the foresail alone. The jib and main were set only when racing to put a pilot aboard a ship, or when the weather was light.[21]

Chapelle offers the pilot schooner *Lafayette* as a good example of the type that began to emerge just before the War of 1812. Designed by Francis Grice and built at Norfolk in 1824, she was considered the fastest pilot schooner working off the Virginia capes in her day. No more commodious than her predecessors, the *Lafayette* was 61 feet 3 inches on deck and, like other pilot schooners, contained much Atlantic white cedar in her construction. She was lightly built with no carvings or decoration, and was flush-decked, with considerable drag, a slightly raking curved stem, a raking sternpost, and a long fine run. The position of her mainmast was far aft of the location usually chosen in schooners. As a result, she carried a very large foresail with which the vessel could be worked in all weathers, but her sail area was well balanced under jib and mainsail as well.[22]

Several schooners were built on the Chesapeake Bay, specifically as New York pilot boats. Chapelle notes a number, including the 69-foot *Virginia*, New York #3, built in 1841, and

New York #5, the 64-foot *David Mitchell*, built in 1846 in Baltimore.[23]

Some Chesapeake-built pilot schooners were used between 1830 and 1857 by New York newspapers to race other newspaper schooners to meet incoming ships for news.[24] One was ordered by the New York *Journal of Commerce*, and bore its name. More commonly, because pilot boats were fast, with excellent seakeeping qualities, they adapted well as yachts, which was how many finished out their lives.

A Well-watered Land: Bay Packets

From the first, shipbuilders throughout the Bay area were well aware of the sailing capabilities of the Virginia pilot boat, and it became the model for the design of other swift-sailing schooners put to a variety of uses on the Chesapeake. Its characteristic features appeared in the design of the more burdensome cargo-carrying schooners of the Bay and in the many packet schooners or passage boats which carried mail, passengers, and cargo between Bay ports.

As opposed to the so-called "tramp" schooners, packets had to keep up a schedule of regular departures and arrivals. The sharp-built schooners were, by far, the most capable at meeting that need. Their cargo capacity was minimal and their accommodations for passengers were often far from comfortable, but they were the "Federal Express" of their day; economy, speed, and efficiency, not comfort, were the keys to their success.

Colonial travelers had to be hardy souls. Doctor Robert Honyman recorded his experience crossing the Bay in the winter of 1775. His trip was not unique in the annals of colonial travel. It was a clear cold afternoon when Doctor Honyman boarded the passage boat in Annapolis for the trip to Rock Hall on his way to Philadelphia. The trip of twenty-five miles would take four or five hours, he was told, and he hoped it was true. Night was coming on and it was getting colder. The wind was picking up too and the schooner was in the hands of "two young lads" who were, at best, "indifferent sailors."

The Eastern Shore and their destination were in sight, but as it began to grow dark, the breeze quickened, driving the schooner off course. They missed the entrance to Rock Hall's harbor, and for several hours thereafter, the boat beat up and down the Bay, grounding several times in the dark. Honyman and his fellow passengers could do nothing but huddle below, out of the wind, but still in bitter cold, on bunks that were too hard and too uncomfortable for sleeping. Few had any stomach for the "sailors salt beef and hardtack" offered for the evening's meal.[25]

As uncomfortable as the good doctor's journey might have been, there was no better way to travel in tidewater Maryland and Virginia than on the Bay or one of its hundreds of tributaries. After all, the Bay area was, as Dr. Charles Carroll of Annapolis pointed out, a "well watered" country where planters could and did "deliver their commodities at their own back doors."[26]

Those deliveries often were made by packet schooners and sloops up until the 1830s when steam-powered boats relentlessly began to take over more and more of their business. Until that happened, though, the packets were a chief means of communication, linking ports from the Elk River to the Virginia capes, stopping at small river towns and private landings in creeks and rivers along the way. They carried passengers, freight, livestock, news, messages, mail, or anything a person wanted sent.

By the 1820s, packet schooners were actually being designed specifically for the service with sleeping quarters for passengers and holds fitted out for light cargo. Larger vessels sometimes had ramps into their holds that would allow them to carry carriages, wagons, and horses or livestock.[27] Captains of Bay packet schooners carried messages between families and friends and at times even acted as agents in business dealings.

Business by Packet

Colonel Henry Maynadier, owner of Belvoir Plantation just a few miles west of Annapolis, and an Annapolis merchant by the name of Joseph Sands, who kept an ordinary on Prince George Street and a shop on Market Space, relied heavily on the packets that ran between Maryland's capital city and the growing port of Baltimore. Between 1808 and the outbreak of the War of 1812, they were partners in the business of butchering, salting, and selling beef, salt pork, and hams to the citizens of Annapolis, to the military contingent at Fort Severn (on land later to be taken over by the Naval Academy), and occasionally in Baltimore.

Henry Maynadier managed their operation from his home at Belvoir. Both he and Joseph Sands had schooners they used for carrying produce and supplies, but when they wanted information, a quick response to a question, or a rush order, they turned to the Annapolis packets. Their correspondence refers to several. Through the good offices of one or another of the packets, they had delivered to Annapolis wooden staves needed to make barrels and the coopers to make them, orders for cattle and hogs, butchers and hands to help slaughter them, and the salt in which to preserve the meat.[28] It was a complicated process in which the successful completion of their business—in this case the slaughter of cattle or hogs—often depended upon the arrival of the next packet.

During one week in October 1808, Henry Maynadier's nephew William, who had a store in Baltimore, sent eight hundred bushels of salt along with a cooper to Joseph Sands aboard an Annapolis packet. Then, less than a week later, he sent along three thousand barrel staves on the deck of a packet belonging to Annapolis Captain George Barber, and the following week, William Maynadier employed yet another packet to carry a letter to Joseph Sands. "Captain Barber informs me that he delivered the staves safe and that you want a grindstone which I send you by the packet," he wrote.[29]

By the end of the month, however, Sands and Henry Maynadier still did not have enough staves and were looking to a vessel from Virginia to bring some up the Bay. "I hope this south wind will produce something favorable to our wishes,"

wrote a discouraged Henry Maynadier to Joseph Sands in Annapolis.[30]

Working diligently at his end, William Maynadier eventually sent staves by two different packets—enough for immediate needs in Annapolis—but at Belvoir his uncle was still concerned. "This northeast wind I hope will send some vessels into the harbor with staves," he wrote in early November. With cold weather upon them, his pastures were nearly exhausted and he feared his cattle were losing weight.[31]

By the year's end, however, everything apparently got sorted out and their butchering of beef and pork was accomplished. All they needed was someone to buy the meat. In January 1809, Henry Maynadier wrote to Joseph Sands, "This hard frost will I hope send some beef and pork eaters into your harbour."[32]

By the following summer, Maynadier and Sands were planning to expand their business and obtained a contract for 200 barrels of salt beef and 150 barrels of salt pork for Fort Severn at Annapolis.[33]

The business continued to be a success, although by November of 1810, they seem to have given up on trying to make their own barrels. Once more the local packets were kept busy, with their attempts to fill their needs—this time for barrels. Joseph Sands began the round with an order by the packet to Joseph Lane, a cooper at Fells Point, for one hundred barrels at $1.50 each to be picked up by Henry Maynadier's vessel. As it turned out, Lane had only four barrels which he sent to Annapolis by the packet. Maynadier was able to get forty-six more from another cooper which were also sent to Joseph Sands via packet, whose captain took payment back to the cooper in Baltimore.[34]

Later, Joseph Sands also operated his own packets, one in partnership with Captain George Barber and another, the 45-foot, 63-ton schooner *Felicity*, with his son Joseph, Jr. The *Felicity* was a sharp-built two-master built in Baltimore by Robert Culley, according to Baltimore customshouse records. When Joseph Sands died in 1832 his son carried on the business, and by then was operating two vessels, the *Felicity* and another schooner by the name of *George Barber*.[35]

He advertised his service in the *Maryland Gazette*, offering the *Felicity* as an Annapolis and Baltimore packet to "freight tobacco and grain from the Severn and South Rivers or any of the several creeks in the neighborhood of Annapolis." The *Felicity* would also carry letters which could be picked up at Joseph Sands's store near the Market House.[36]

Sail or Steam

Joseph Sands, Jr., survived his father by only eight years, during which time he fought a losing battle to keep the family store and the packet service going. By the 1830s, the ability of a steam-powered vessel to keep regular schedules was already changing the attitude of those who depended upon deliveries by water. There was no patience for delays that Sands and his father and others before them had accepted as a normal, if frustrating, course of events in dealing with the sailing packets.

In January 1837, Joseph Sands took a load of hemp aboard the *Felicity*. The hemp was bound for a company in Baltimore, but apparently was held in Annapolis due to the weather. "We can't consent to your remaining at Annapolis with our hemp on board without making some effort to get here," wrote the Baltimore merchant. "We are suffering for the hemp, having already lost the sale of it by your delay in getting here. We hope you will avail of the present open weather to come up, but if this is impracticable and nothing else can be done, we wish you to employ Captain Taylor of the Maryland steam boat to bring you up. He has agreed with us to bring you up for $30 tomorrow and if you cannot get up without, we wish you to let him do so."[37]

There is no record of whether Sands had the *Felicity* towed to Baltimore. The upshot of the whole affair is that experiences

The *R.E. Powell* is shown here at the Otis Lloyd Shipyard below Salisbury. Lloyd had a reputation as a real craftsman and engineer. He built bridges and other structures in addition to schooners and bugeyes. The *Powell* was known as a smart sailer and was used for years as a Wicomico River packet. (The Mariners' Museum, No. PK 1166, Otis Lloyd, Jr.)

like his were becoming increasingly common, in spite of significant improvements in the construction of sailing vessels and many new laborsaving devices.

Eventually there would be patented rigging, deck machinery and fittings, geared capstans and windlasses, iron strapped blocks, geared steering, geared winches, new mast and spar ironwork, improved marine stores, water closets, and donkey engines, all of which made the operation of schooners more efficient and the life of those who maintained and operated them a mite easier.

Viewed from a broader perspective, such improvements kept commercial sailing vessels viable and fed the belief of those who depended on them that they really could continue to compete with the steam-powered boats that were being built in ever-increasing numbers.

The Final Days of the Packet Schooners

As early as 1819, Joseph Sands and other merchants in Annapolis and Baltimore were making use of the newfangled vessels, and in some quarters new steamboats were received with much acclaim. Reports such as one that appeared in the *Niles Register* in June 1832 must have galled the schoonermen of the Bay.

That month, the *Register* reported that besides the "beautiful steam boat *Patrick Henry*," just receiving her machinery at Skinner's yard in Baltimore, there was on the stocks, "a steam boat, which, from present appearances, bids fair to surpass anything of the kind on the waters of the Chesapeake."[38]

That was not good news to those who operated under sail. They were being forced to turn increasingly to bulk cargoes, such as lumber or fertilizer, for which regular, on-time deliveries were not crucial. They did continue for some time to call their schooners "packets," but the age of the sailing packet had just about come to an end on the Bay. Instead, schooners stayed alive in the oyster business in winter and during the rest of the year traveled to the Carolinas for lumber, to the Caribbean for logwood and later for pineapples, and, whenever there was a harvest, shipped grain and other farm produce.

A few Bay-built schooners were employed as coastal packets after 1840 in New England. There was, in fact, a distinct period between 1845 and 1850 in which Maryland-built schooners were introduced into New England's coastal trade, particularly at Cape Cod and at Gloucester.[39]

On the Bay the schooners lingered, their usefulness prolonged by the development of the centerboard that enabled them to serve small river ports and landings that the steamers couldn't reach. Some even survived after the Civil War, but by then most of the packets operating as such had been put out of business by the railroads and steamers. But not all. A few continued to serve the more remote ports not on the steamer schedule.

In 1875, the Oxford Shipyard turned out the first schooner for the Easton Point Packet Line, owned and operated by Captain Edward T. Leonard and Captain Bob Leonard. The schooner was named the *Clara Leonard* and on her maiden voyage took a party of men from Talbot County to the Philadelphia Centennial in 1876. In the same year, the *Anna Leonard* and the *Mary Vickers* were built and added to the Easton Point fleet.[40]

The rivalry between Captains James Gossage, Edward Blann, and Ben Thomas as to the fastest of the three Easton Point packet schooners was keen. It was said that the only time they would resort to the use of an anchor was in the event of a breakdown or if all their spars or sails were carried away.

While schooner captains did race between ports, the actual packet system, which ran a regular schedule on a daily or weekly basis, no longer existed. An individual schooner might occasionally beat the time of a steamer on a particular run, but no amount of economy and efficiency in the operation of a sailing vessel could insure the regularity delivered by vessels powered by steam. Nonetheless, the spirit of the Baltimore clippers was still alive in the hearts of Bay watermen, who continued to build and make a living from their schooners.

Six

Pungoteague or Machipungo? Origins of the Pungy

The story of the Baltimore clipper did not really end with the giant *Ann McKim* or those extreme versions employed by slave traders, pirates, and opium smugglers. At some point very early in the nineteenth century, builders on the Bay used what they saw in the fast-sailing clipper schooners to create an economical vessel for service in the more stable, peacetime environment of day-to-day commerce on the Bay or sailing coastwise to the West Indies. Constructed from native pine and oak with few other tools than the adz, the slick, and the plane, it was called a pungy and is generally considered to have been concurrent with and possibly the final embodiment of the famed Baltimore clipper.[1]

The pungy was a vessel that carried the schooner rig. Its hull was exactly like that of a clipper schooner, just smaller.[2] "The hull was distinguishable by the sharply raking ends, with forepart gracefully curved into the keel, which in turn sloped downwards to meet the stern post at the heel." So marine engineer and historian John Earle described the pungy in a manuscript sent some years ago to his friend and colleague M. V. Brewington. "Sailors call the slope 'drag.' It made for deep draft . . . she never was intended to be a shoal draft vessel. There was, of course, no centerboard. The type operated long before

At one time, pungies such as the *Amanda F. Lewis,* moored here in the Coan River, Virginia, were a common sight. According to Robert H. Burgess, the house in the background is that of Captain Gus Rice whose exploits during the "oyster wars" on the Bay made him a legend in his own time. The *Lewis* was built in 1884 at Madison, Maryland, by Joseph W. Brooks and was affectionately known by watermen as the *Mandy Lewis*. As seen here, her fine lines are accentuated by the traditional paint scheme, bronze green wales and flesh, or so-called "pungy pink," below. As the story goes, when her captain, Gus Rice, couldn't get pure Chinese vermilion to make his colors, he stopped painting her in the traditional style. For a while, he painted her wales gray and her hull white. Note the sailcover on her main; the monkey rail aft. (Peabody Museum of Salem, W. C. Stewart)

This bow detail of the *Amanda F. Lewis* shows her handsomely carved trail boards as well as considerable wear and tear. Her anchor is bent and gnarled after years of dragging through mud and salt water. On the fo'c'sle deck, note the anchor chain running through the chain stop to the windlass and the mooring line running through the chock atop the port knighthead. The trail boards are now displayed at the Radcliffe Maritime Museum of the Maryland Historical Society. (Frank Moorshead, Jr., Mystic Seaport Museum, No. 91-10-132)

the centerboards were developed and competed with shallow draft vessels long after they were introduced.[3]

"Looking at her midship section, the sharp rise of floor, with well-rounded bilge, was characteristic. They were fairly wide vessels with the greatest beam a little forward of amidship, but they were not the apple-bowed and fish-tailed freaks to be visualized from some of the descriptions which have, from time to time, been written of the Baltimore clipper. Their transom sterns were square and wide and high. The quarters were thin and most of the transom was in fact above the deck. The rudder stock pierced the lower edge of the transom, except in some of the older vessels in which it was carried all the way up on the outside of the transom. This variation of the pungy was called a 'Beanie'—why, nobody knows."[4]

Not quite as obscure, the origin of the name "pungy" was nevertheless the subject of considerable debate. Naval architect and historian Eric Steinlein suggested that the word is of seventeenth century Indian origin, derived possibly from Pungoteague or Machipungo, two towns on the lower Eastern Shore of Virginia where a great many of the so-called pungies were built.[5]

Apparently the pungy was common enough to be ordered by name, and carpenters' certificates for vessels built in Accomack County, Virginia, of which the Pungoteague Creek area is a part, include a number of pungies.

Often they were referred to as "pungy boats," which seems to indicate a smaller type of vessel. A similar distinction was made between "schooner" and "schooner boat" in common parlance.

"The pungy's rig was that of a schooner, but characterized by a lightness made possible by a hull with a sharply rising floor and easy turn of bilge which lacked the excessive stiffness of the more full-bodied schooners and which made the latter rather hard on their rigs, necessitating heavy standing rigging," wrote John Earle. "The pungies carried topsails on the mainmast but none on the foremast. The main spreaders, when any were used at all, were of light iron-work, instead of the heavy oak ones commonly used on schooners. Their mastheads were always round, instead of square as on schooners, and finally, their masts were stepped at an angle of rake almost as great as that of the bugeye."[6]

"The two masted rig was generally used," wrote M. V. Brewington, "with a sail plan consisting of one or two head sails, a foresail, mainsail, main gaff topsail and, perhaps, a fisherman staysail. The latter, however, was a development of the 1870s and did not continue long into the 20th century."[7]

Until 1850, the pungy foresail was set loose-footed and overlapped the main, as in the Virginia pilot boats. The mainmast had much more rake than the fore. The single jib was set on the forestay which was supported in part by a decorative longhead.[8]

The loose-footed, or "lug" foresail, "was superceded by the foresail rigged on a boom," wrote John Earle, "but there are a few men living today who have vivid recollections of sheeting lug foresails in a breeze. It was not child's play."[9]

Typical of the type, the *Amanda F. Lewis*, built by Joseph W. Brooks of Madison, near Cambridge, Maryland, in 1884, had a mainmast that was 72 feet long and carried a tremendous spread of sail. Because they carried the simplest form of schooner rig, pungies such as the *Amanda F. Lewis* were very fast. Their "masts were light and fittings small, neat, and yachtlike."[10]

"Instead of having bulwarks around the deck, commonly seen on schooners and other vessels up and down the coast," wrote John Earle, "the pungy had a 'log' some six inches high, fastened to the covering board or waterway; and surmounting the log, there was an open rail made with iron bolts with pipes on them for spacers on top of which was an oak rail cap some three inches thick by perhaps four inches wide. This was not on the privateers for they needed bulwarks when fighting, but it probably was developed at some later date as a means of giving a good measure of safety to the crew on deck in heavy weather and at the same time enabling the vessel to free her deck of water quickly in the event of shipping a sea."[11]

This is a good profile of the Baltimore-built pungy *Banshee*, clearly showing her sheer, her sail plan, and the balance of her rig, the iron crosstrees on the main above which her topsail is loosely stowed, and the water barrel on deck. Pungies had a spike bowsprit as opposed to the bowsprit and jibboom found on many schooners. The *Banshee*'s jib is triced up to get it off the bowsprit—for painting perhaps or to keep it out of a head sea in hard going. This is probably a fairly late photo because she does not show the distinctive pungy paint scheme. (Chesapeake Bay Maritime Museum, No. A-310-4)

A later exception were those deepwater pungies built for New England fisheries, which were given bulwarks. The substantial headrails provided support for the bowsprit as well as "convenience for the necessities of the crew."[12]

Built like a Yacht

Pungies were built for, and often by, working watermen. Whatever their calling, those who built them drew upon a heritage that went back to skills learned from the Indians in the building of log canoes. Many pungies were "chunk-built," which meant that large sections, such as their waterways and transoms, were hewn from a single large log rather than put together in a conventional plank-and-frame style.

Such construction did nothing to detract from the fineness of a pungy's lines or her speed. According to Chapelle, the pungy was a very fast sailer, especially in light and moderate winds, but as low as she was, she was most certainly wet in blowing weather.[13]

Eric Steinlein traveled the Bay and talked to many old-timers who spent the better part of their lives on the decks of pungies and Chesapeake Bay centerboard schooners. Between a pungy and a centerboarder, most would generally agree that the pungy was the handier and the more weatherly of the two. The fact that the pungy was broad of beam, with wide decks that extended well fore and aft, contributed to its stability and sailing power. She still had to be well ballasted. Otherwise, she might not recover when heeled to a point where the lee deck was awash.[14]

According to Charles H. Stevenson, who prepared a report on the oyster industry of Maryland in 1894, pungies were similar to schooners, the chief difference from schooners being that pungies had fuller bows and sharper sterns, "facilitating the rapid tacking desirable in dredging across an oyster reef."[15]

Waiting for a breeze, the *Amanda F. Lewis* is becalmed off Thomas Point Light in the mid-1930s. Gus Rice is at the wheel. The detail in this shot is good, showing her structure and her rigging, the monkey rail aft, the yawl boat, her mainsheet drooping over the top of the port quarter, the preventer rig, and the masthead figure silhouetted against the sky. (Frank Moorshead, Jr., Mystic Seaport Museum, No. 91-10-135)

While the pungy was a handy workboat, built for oyster dredging or for carrying cargo, it had all the appearance of a yacht and never failed to impress those who appreciated fine sailing craft.

"The Pongees, or oyster boats . . . are the most elegant and yacht-like merchant vessels in the world," wrote an English naval captain by the name of MacKinnon in 1852. "It is remarkable that the vessels intended for the lowest and most degraded offices (such as carrying manure, oysters, and wood) are of elegant and symmetrical proportions. An English schooner from Bideford was lying among some of the worst Baltimore coasters. She looked like a hog amid a herd of antelope . . ."[16]

While it was the yachtlike appearance of the pungy that so impressed Captain MacKinnon, there was more to the sleek lines of these vessels than their fine looks. Of greater significance, by Eric Steinlein's calculations, the pungy's light displacement had much to do with the high hull speed for which these schooners were known.

In an article that he wrote for *The Skipper* in April 1965, Steinlein talks of the pungy *Mary and Ellen* built in Baltimore by William Skinner & Son in 1858. Using statistical reckonings such as the "prismatic co-efficient" and "co-efficient of fineness," he judged the *Mary and Ellen* to be very yachtlike indeed. He pointed out that a New England coastal schooner of similar length could have had twice the tonnage of a pungy.[17]

The pungy's yachtlike fineness and her speed were not lost on sporting sailors. The *Hornet*, which was built on the Eastern Shore in 1819, was taken north by a Mr. A. Barker, who entered her, in 1846, in the first regatta held by the New York Yacht Club. She won her race on corrected time. The following year, she was rebuilt by George Steers, designer of the schooner yacht *America* and was still racing when Steers rebuilt her again in 1850 at which time she was also renamed *Sport*.[18]

Said Steinlein of the conversion of the *Hornet* and other pungies to yachts, "Many commercial types of small craft have been converted to yachts, but only a few types lend themselves to practical yacht use without alteration that pretty much ruins

This 1909 profile of the square-rigged bugeye *Alexander Bond*, built by Kirby at St. Michaels in 1893, shows her round stern and monkey rail which along with the square rig contributed to the fact that such vessels were often confused with pungies and schooners. To their builders and owners, however, they were round-stern, square-rigged bugeyes. The *Bond*, which was a handsome vessel, whatever she was called, served most of her working life in the lower Bay. She burned off Old Point Comfort in 1933. (Herman Hollerith Collection, Chesapeake Bay Maritime Museum, No. 137)

The *Amanda F. Lewis* was notable for her beautifully carved stern, which was taken off when she was converted to power. It is now on display at the Radcliffe Museum of the Maryland Historical Society in Baltimore. Important here are the details of the davits, the "lazy-board," or "reef plank" spanning the davits, and the hoisting falls. (Courtesy of Smithsonian Institution, National Museum of American History, HAMMS Collection, No. 663)

their original characteristics. The pungy, like the Friendship sloop, is one of the exceptions."[19]

Pungy Pink

The pungy was known by one other very distinct characteristic which had nothing to do with her conformation. Pungies were almost exclusively painted what old-timers called "flesh" color. Identified today as "pungy pink," it extended from the waterline up to the lower edge of the "bends," or wale strake, which made up the upper 20 to 24 inches of the planking below the edge of the deck. From the bends up to the top of the low log rail was painted a dark bottle green, often called bronze, and the light monkey rail was painted white.[20]

The pungy's distinctive pink color was not arrived at entirely by design. Rather, it came from early attempts to achieve a lighter color at a time when the oxides and pigments needed for producing a pure white were not readily available. Pink was the closest they could come. While pungy pink and bronze were the traditional paint scheme, necessity often dictated otherwise. When Captain Gus Rice could no longer get Chinese vermilion to mix his own "flesh," he painted the *Amanda F. Lewis* white with gray bends.

Pungy or Schooner?

In the records that have come down to us, pungies and schooners were often confused. Because of the rarity of either type in their final days, like the skipjacks of today, they were the subject of countless magazine and newspaper articles. Often, newsmen muddied historical waters by calling any vessel with two masts a schooner—or a bugeye, which was another breed entirely. Or, because the pungy was the dominant vessel in the early days of the oyster business on the Bay, they tended to call anything that pulled up beside Baltimore's Long Dock (later occupied by the Power Plant) carrying oysters a pungy.

To the untrained eye, pungies and schooners were similar. In their deck plans, they were very much alike, according to M. V. Brewington, who wrote of them thus, "in the bows, a windlass; just abaft the foremast, the scuttle leading down to the forecastle; a large hatch came next, then the mainmast at the break of the poop on which was built a small low cabin; then came the wheel and alongside either the port or to starboard, a small lazarette hatch. Over the stern, on davits, was hung a small dory which in later years always contained a single cylinder gasoline engine. The furnishing of the forecastle consisted of nothing more than a couple of bunks, a small table and a cook stove. The cabin itself was not much more elaborate, its chief comfort being a couple of small windows along the sides."[21]

Even in official records, pungies often were classed simply as schooners. John Earle spent years at the National Archives compiling lists of Chesapeake Bay schooners, pungies, and bugeyes. In the process, using the registered dimensions, he developed a system for determining which vessels most likely were pungies if they were not identified as such.

"I consider a vessel to be a pungy if its registered depth was more than one tenth of its registered length," said Earle of his theory, which is as close as any one has been able to come to making a distinction. "If a vessel had a length of fifty feet, I would expect her depth to be at least five feet, to be considered a pungy."[22]

Mainstay of the Oyster Trade

A powerful vessel under sail, with wide decks for working, the pungy was put to use in the 1840s in the flourishing oyster business. Up until the Civil War disrupted the trade, there were easily sixty packinghouses in Baltimore shipping oysters north, where beds off Cape Cod and in Long Island Sound had been exhausted, and west on the brand new Baltimore and Ohio Railroad.

During the 1840s, a number of Chesapeake Bay schooners were in the business of carrying oysters in the shell from the Bay to Cape Cod. Those that were pungies especially caught the

Gus Rice sold the *Amanda F. Lewis* in 1939 and shortly thereafter her new owner converted her to power at the Krentz Shipyard in Harryhogan, Virginia. The graceful curves of her hull are all that was recognizable of the converted *Lewis*, the last pungy to work commercially on the Chesapeake. She was soon sold off the Bay and, according to Robert H. Burgess, was last heard of in 1949, working under Haitian registry. (Courtesy of Smithsonian Institution, National Museum of American History, HAMMS Collection, No. 91-14117)

The 34-ton pungy *Wave* was built in 1863 at Accomack County, Virginia. She sailed out of the Chester River for many years. This photo shows her before she was converted to a yacht in 1937. She was the last pungy to sail on the Bay and was sold ultimately to the Great Lakes where she was abandoned in the late 1950s. (The Mariners' Museum, No. PK 2656, Alexander C. Brown)

eye of the New Englanders who needed fast-sailing vessels for Cape Cod's summer mackerel fisheries, and several were purchased for the fishing fleet. Typically, the pungies were rather shoal bodied and low sided and those conditions turned out to be too wet and uncomfortable for northern winters.[23]

By the 1850s, Bay builders were fitting out pungies with bulwarks specifically for the New England market. At least ten Chesapeake-built pungies were sold to Gloucester and Cape Cod between 1848 and 1854. Among them were the 82-foot *Garland*, built in Baltimore in 1850; the 69-foot *Leading Star*, also built

in Baltimore; the 73-foot *John*, built in 1847, and the 76-foot *Iowa*, built in 1854, both from Dorchester County.

While their speed attracted New England's fishermen to them, the pungies proved to be dangerous in northern ocean waters and by the 1860s, Massachusetts builders began designing fishing schooners more suited to their waters. While the resulting vessels were much larger and deeper, some did appear to have been influenced by the more radical Bay-built boats. One, the packet schooner *Charmer*, was made as an exact copy of the *Iowa*, which was diverted from fishing to packet service and became celebrated around Newburyport, Massachusetts, for her speed. The *Charmer*, however, was built with a New England head and cutwater.[25]

With the end of the Civil War came new prosperity and an oyster boom that spread from Crisfield to Cambridge, Oxford, and Baltimore. By 1869, there were nearly six hundred boats licensed to dredge oysters and the largest number of those were pungies.[26] In an attempt to keep the Chesapeake's oyster beds from being dredged out, the fleet of "drudge" boats as they were called was limited to deep water by the state of Maryland. The shallow waters of the rivers and of the Bay at Tangier Sound and at the mouths of the Chester and Choptank rivers were the domain of the oyster tongers working in small, round-bottomed sailboats of less than 25 feet.[27]

By 1871, the demand for oysters had brought the number of dredge boats to nearly a thousand and since the dredge boats could scrape up many more oysters than the tongers could gather, and could make a much greater profit, they began invading the shallow waters. The result was bloodshed and open warfare between tongers and dredgers. The first phase of the "Oyster Wars" of the Chesapeake lasted into the 1890s, when oyster beds of the Eastern Shore finally began to give out. With their livelihood threatened, Maryland's oystermen moved from the Eastern Shore rivers to Pocomoke Sound below Crisfield and into the Potomac River, both areas where they came into conflict with the oystermen of Virginia. And once more, Bay watermen were fighting each other and dying over the oyster.[28]

As long as there were deepwater beds to be dredged, the pungies dominated the oyster business. But once the deepwater beds were exhausted, shoal-draft centerboard schooners, bugeyes, and, in time, the economical skipjack drove the pungy out of dredging operations in all but the deepest rivers. Later, those rivers began silting up and the working range of the pungies was limited even further. Coupled with the hard times that hit the Bay in the 1890s, watermen turned increasingly to bugeyes and then skipjacks, which were more economical boats to build and maintain than pungies or centerboard schooners.

She-pungy or Square-stern Bugeye?

There were a few attempts to adapt the pungy for use in shallower waters. A small number, known as "she-pungies," were built with centerboards instead of keels and were used in the oyster trade.[29]

"I was fooled several times," recalled John Earle. "I'd see what I was sure was a pungy. It had a pungy stern and didn't have bulwarks like a schooner, but instead had the long gunwale and monkey rail on top of that. Then, I'd walk up on deck and look down in the hold and there was a centerboard."[30]

One known she-pungy was the *Kessie C. Price*, which was converted to a yacht and in her later days was owned by Philadelphia attorney Frank A. Moorshead. Most of Frank Moorshead, Jr.'s extensive collection of photographs were taken from the deck of the *Kessie C. Price*.

To further confuse the issue, what you call a pungy with a centerboard depends upon where you live. "Down around Somerset, they called the type a she-pungy," said Earle, "but around Easton and St. Michaels where they built a lot of them, they called them 'square-stern bugeyes.' It wasn't just the centerboard that distinguished them from other schooners. It was also the square stern that was characteristic of the pungy, which along with the schooner rig set them apart from the bugeyes as well."[31]

A bugeye was a completely different type. A descendant of the log canoe, the bugeye was a two-masted vessel, with the foremast taller than the main. It generally carried triangular sails. Some bugeyes did carry gaff-rigged sails, in which case they were said to be "square-rigged." On the Chesapeake, it was common for the term "square-rigged" to be used when referring to gaff-headed sails, which meant that a vessel's hull had to be given close scrutiny if it was to be accurately classified.

At any rate, the addition of the centerboard only forestalled the coming of the end for the pungy. In the meantime, many that could not continue dredging remained in the oyster trade as buy boats, using their speed to advantage in the race from the oyster beds to the packinghouses in Oxford, Crisfield, Cambridge, or Baltimore. In that service, they were commonly rated by their oyster-carrying capacity. Thus one would be said to carry eight hundred bushels, another fifteen hundred.[32] As nearly as Eric Steinlein could estimate from his talks with Bay watermen, the pungies working the Chesapeake ranged in size from the largest, which was the *Ruth A. Price*, at 69 gross tons and 73 feet registered length, to the *Exchange*, at 22 tons and 42 feet in length.[33]

Some of the larger pungies were used as coastal packets and also in the pineapple trade between Baltimore and the Bahamas. Captain Eugene Herbert of Stevensville on Kent Island shared his memories of the pineapple fleet with Eric Steinlein. The smallest pungy he remembers trading in fruit was the 46-foot *Harp*.[34] One of the so-called "beanie" type of pungy, the *Harp* had her rudder hung outboard to make the most of her length.

"According to Captain Herb," wrote Steinlein in *The Skipper* of April 1965, "as many as forty schooners would sail in a fleet, and, being short on crew, they would heave to at night. In the morning, the fleet would be divided in two, with the pungies to the windward and the centerboarders to leeward. During the day, the pungies would outdistance the centerboarders and would heave to an hour or so before nightfall to wait for the rest of the fleet to catch up."[35]

Ultimately, the pungies were not very successful in the fruit trade. They were wet and tended to be dangerous working offshore. More critical was the fact that their sharp-floored holds prevented the stowage of fruit as other schooners did in open pens designed to keep the pineapples relatively cool and dry so that they would not rot before reaching Baltimore.

Last of the True Clippers

By the 1920s, the fleet of several hundred pungies working the Bay had dwindled to eight, the oldest of which was the *Plan*, built in Accomack County, Virginia, in 1855. There were also two pungies known to be working the Delaware Bay.[36] No new pungies had been added to the fleet since the 1880s.

A decade later, there were only six pungies in active service in the Bay: the 67-foot *Amanda F. Lewis*, built at Madison, Maryland, in 1884; the 63-foot *James H. Lewis*, built at Pocomoke City in 1880 and owned by a Captain Phipps of Annapolis; the *Mildred Addison*, 67 feet long and built in Somerset County in 1870; the *Wave*, 54 feet long, built in Accomack County in 1863 and owned at one time by Captain Robert R. Elderson, an influential farmer of Caroline County, Maryland; the *G. A. Kirwan*, built in 1882 at Madison, Maryland; and the 61-foot *James A. Whiting*, built in Somerset County, Maryland, in 1871.[37]

The career of the *Whiting* was typical of the pungies that survived into the twentieth century. Her winters were taken up with oystering, and she hauled produce during the summer months. The *Whiting*'s final days were hard, wearing her down with loads of rock, gravel, and tar to build the roads for the trucks that were driving her out of business. She was sailed home one last time to Walnut Point, on the Coan River in Virginia, and there run ashore and abandoned.[38]

The *Wave* fared better than most at the end. She was converted to a yacht in 1937. In the 1950s, she was taken to the Great Lakes, where she lived out her days. The *Amanda F. Lewis*, which was the last pungy on the Bay, worked to the very end.

By the 1930s, cargoes were increasingly hard to come by. Pungies and other schooners working the Bay took what they could get. In 1933, Captain Gus Rice made twenty-three trips with the *Amanda F. Lewis*. She carried wheat and lumber from Virginia to Baltimore, coal from Norfolk to Coan, empty cans from can companies in Baltimore to packinghouses in Virginia, canned tomatoes from Virginia to Norfolk and Washington, and fertilizer from Baltimore to Coan.[39]

Even though she kept busy that year, there was little or no profit in trying to compete with power vessels. Finally, the *Amanda F. Lewis* was converted to power in 1939 and taken south. In 1948, she was found leaking badly, with engine trouble off Haiti, and was towed to Port au Prince by another vessel. She was sold to Haitian owners in 1949, which was the last that was known of her.[40]

Wrote Eric Steinlein: "Among the thinning fleet is one schooner—the lone survivor of her type—that has older and better right to the title 'clipper' than have the modern flying boats that have borrowed the term without too much regard for its original meaning." That lone survivor was the *Amanda F. Lewis*—"the last of the true clippers, built for pure sailing without regard to cargo capacity or pay load."[41]

The disappearance of pilot boat, packet, and pungy from the Chesapeake did not close the book on the story of the Bay schooner. A considerable fleet remained to work the tidewaters of the Chesapeake. For more than a century, the Chesapeake Bay centerboard schooner filled harbors from Hampton Roads to Havre de Grace and the uppermost reaches of the Bay. In the early days of this century, harbors looked like a winter forest, they were so filled with masts. The final chapters on the Chesapeake Bay schooner could not yet be written.

Seven

The Centerboard: One More Adaptation to Survive

Bay watermen continually had to adapt to the physical changes taking place in their world. Waterways had been silting up ever since the first settlers arrived and began cutting trees and clearing land to make their homes and farms. Landings became unapproachable as silting and fallen trees and other debris clogged channels. Colonial ship captains regularly dumped stone and brick and other ballast overboard in harbors or rivers. By the time anyone got around to banning such dumping, many harbors had become impassable to all but the most shallow-draft vessels.

Schooner captains changed their routes and when that was not enough, they modified their vessels. Bay shipbuilders delayed the demise of many landings and river towns as viable trading centers by producing increasing numbers of shoal-draft schooners. Then, in the 1840s, they adopted the use of the centerboard, a clever contrivance that allowed a vessel to work in both deep and shallow water.[1]

The 68-foot *Mattie F. Dean* is shown here dredging oysters. Her moderate size of 48 tons enabled the *Mattie Dean* to adapt comfortably to both oystering and freighting. With fine lines and a good overall balance between her rig and hull, she is, in many ways, the embodiment of the Chesapeake Bay schooner, a good example of form following function. She was ideally suited to the conditions dictated by economics and weather conditions on the Bay. Note her long head, light quarters, long bowsprit, and short jibboom. In 1928, according to Robert H. Burgess, she arrived in Baltimore from St. Mary's County, Maryland, with the last cargo of tobacco to be carried under sail. (The Mariners' Museum, No. PK 2702, Frank Moorshead, Jr.)

The *Mattie F. Dean*, built at the Brooks yard in Madison, Maryland, in 1884, is shown here pushed up in a creek near Salisbury, which was one of the advantages of the maneuverable shoal-draft Bay schooner. They adapted very well to the environmental conditions in which they had to work. Note the line of her sheer here and the skiff in the foreground. She was abandoned in Back Creek at Annapolis in 1957, her bones mingled there with those of the *Ella F. Cripps*. (The Mariners' Museum, No. PK 6878, Otis Lloyd, Jr.)

The centerboard wasn't new in the 1840s. A form of centerboard, called a "sliding keel," was in use in England in the eighteenth century.[2] Then, in 1811, a U.S. patent was issued for a pivoted centerboard that was lifted much the same way later versions were in Bay boats.[3] Used first on the Hudson River, the centerboard was known on the Bay in the 1820s, but was not in common use until 1840 or 1845.[4]

The centerboard began showing up first in small boats, but it wasn't long before merchants, farmers, and Bay watermen saw

its advantages over the deep draft, and builders were putting centerboards in the larger commercial schooners. The new contraption not only improved their handling in shallow creeks and rivers where weatherliness and good steering were important, but the new centerboard schooners were also going well on the open Bay.

Emergence of the Chesapeake Bay Schooner

While the centerboard was a significant adaptation, Bay builders were dealing with other problems in the design of their schooners as well. Nineteenth century merchants and farmers on the Bay needed freight vessels to replace the sharp, fast Baltimore clippers that were so sorely limited in their cargo capacity. To meet the need, builders began to construct schooners with full midsections and sharp ends. By so doing, they hoped to gain some of the speed of the clipper and more of the cargo capacity of the slow, but more burdensome, freight vessels. The latter were sometimes called, "clump" schooners,

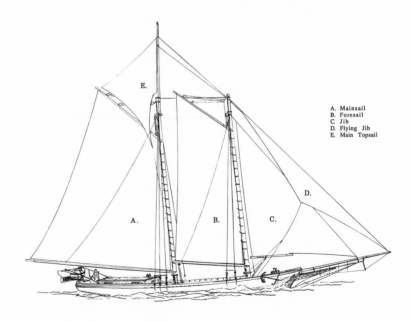

A. Mainsail
B. Foresail
C. Jib
D. Flying Jib
E. Main Topsail

Chesapeake two-masted schooner

The *L. E. Williams* was built in 1875. Notable here is the two-topmast rig, more common on earlier schooners that carried the larger crews needed to handle such things as extra sail. The extra hands were needed for tacking, when the fore-topsail had to be taken down and passed under the spring stay, triatic stays, and topgallant stays on the main and then set again on the other side. The increased competition from steam-powered vessels necessitated economies such as reducing the size of crews. With them went work-intensive features like the foretop, which was eliminated on more and more schooners toward the close of the nineteenth century. (Chesapeake Bay Maritime Museum, No. 662)

This view is looking from the dock aft toward the trunk cabin of the *Minnie T. Phillips*. Her quarterdeck is significantly higher than was usually found on Bay schooners and her bulwarks deeper, indicating that she was designed as a seagoing schooner. (Frank Moorshead, Jr., Mystic Seaport Museum, No. 91-10-106)

another term, like pungy, bugeye, and skipjack, whose origins are obscure.[5] From the 1840s on, the two-masted centerboard freight vessel that emerged was known simply as the Chesapeake Bay schooner.

By 1850, the standard hull for the two-masted Chesapeake Bay schooner, as described by Chapelle, had a straight keel, an upright, flaring stem, a round tuck, and a square stern with an upper and lower transom. She had a flush deck, a short but unusually sharp convex entrance, and a rather long, fine run. Her midsection was characterized by a floor that had a slight rise, a low round bilge and some tumble home in the topsides. The long, exaggerated cutwater was the mark of a Chesapeake Bay schooner.[6]

The *Minnie T. Phillips* was built in Baltimore in 1873 as the *George C. A. Travers.* In 1912, she was renamed the *F. P. Murphy* and finally in 1926 became the *Minnie T. Phillips.* At 100 feet, and 137 tons, she was relatively large for a Bay-built two-master and primarily was engaged in the coasting trade to the Bahamas. (Van Name/Perry)

But clear-cut, surefire identification of a Chesapeake Bay schooner was often impossible. Many boatbuilders traveled from job to job, from the Chesapeake to the Delaware Bay and back again.

"Sometimes they built on that side, sometimes on this side," says naval architect and historian Joe Liener of Pot Pie, on Maryland's Eastern Shore. "If they heard somebody was going to put up a boat down here and they were out of work, they'd come down. If they had new ideas, they incorporated them. That's the way it was all up and down the coast. They had boats up in Jersey built just like ones down here and vice versa.[7]

"They never studied any kind of naval architecture. If it don't look right, it's not right. That was their rule. Those old guys knew what they were talking about when they came down with a set of proportions. You don't have to have formal training in a naval architectural school if you have the practical end of it.

"When they'd set out to build a schooner, they'd make three molds—one for the stern rake, one for the stem rake and one for midships. When a guy wanted a pungy, all they'd need to know was what size boat he wanted. Then, they'd lay out the keel, tack up the bow shape, set the midship and the stern molds up and bend a couple of big long battens around, and then they'd change things from there to arrive at what the owner wanted. They'd take the measurements and develop the rest of the ship from that. The guy who was getting the thing built was going to use it and he knew from experience what he wanted. He could tell from looking at it if it was right."[8]

For the Southern Cause

Bay schooners were still known for their speed and, with the centerboard to enable them to continue running up into shallow rivers and creeks, they were an important means of transportation up to and through the Civil War. For the most part, however, the War between the States brought a slowdown in boatbuilding on the Bay.

Maryland may have remained in the Union, but many of her citizens were Southerners at heart. Because the sympathies of Bay watermen and those who built their boats were known, if not made public, shipbuilding centers were kept under surveillance during the war. In Baltimore, with Union guns on Federal Hill, shipbuilding came to a standstill. A number of Marylanders continued to do business with the South, nonetheless. The schooners of Deal Island were notorious as blockade runners. The Union navy's gunboats were no match for them.[9]

General Benjamin Butler, who seized the U.S. Naval Academy in Annapolis and placed the town under martial law, stationed troops along the Severn River with an outpost of 225 men at Mount Misery near Round Bay to watch for Confederate privateers and blockade runners. The latter were active throughout the war, slipping in and out of coves to pick up contraband from southern sympathizers. Bald Eagle on the Patuxent near Upper Marlboro was a rendezvous for blockade runners carrying medical and other supplies and mail to the South.[10]

Several Bay schooners were claimed by Confederate Navy Captain John Taylor Wood, the famed "Sea Ghost"[11] who made daring raids by night to capture or destroy Union shipping on the Potomac and in the Bay.[12] Generally, however, the Chesapeake was in control of Union forces.

Eastern Shore skipper Samuel T. Hooper was aboard the *Kate McNamara* in April 1865 running coal from Havre de Grace to Washington, D.C. He landed the cargo and was returning to Havre de Grace for another load when the *McNamara* was intercepted by a navy gunboat. She, along with every other vessel on the Potomac, was ordered to heave to and anchor at Piney Point. Later, officers from the gunboat boarded and searched each vessel, then ordered it to get under way and depart at once. Once clear of the Potomac, Hooper learned that Abraham Lincoln had been shot the night before and the navy was searching for his assassin.[13]

This 1933 photo shows the *Australia* with a load of passengers on the Chester River. She was built as the *Ella Alida* at Patchogue, New York, in 1862 under British ownership. Later she was renamed *Alma* and she served as a blockade runner from Bermuda to southern ports during the Civil War. Her Confederate career was cut short in October 1863, when she was captured by the USS *Seneca* and subsequently sold at auction in Washington, D.C. Given the name *Australia*, she went to work as a Bay freighter. In 1879, the 54-foot schooner was lengthened by 10 feet. She continued to haul freight on the Bay until 1941 when the DuPont family bought her for use as a yacht. For years, this schooner was mistakenly thought to be the *Alma* used by Francis Scott Key to sail out to the British fleet before the British bombardment of Ft. McHenry. The legend increased her worth far beyond that of other freight vessels, and she was kept up by her owners when others were being abandoned. That same mystique led to her purchase by the DuPonts. In 1951, Mrs. E. P. DuPont gave her to the Marine Historical Association at Mystic, Connecticut. She has since been hauled out and her hull put under roof as an educational exhibit. Even though her lineage does not go back to 1812, *Australia* is important as a schooner of the Civil War period and the only blockade runner extant. (The Mariners' Museum, Frank Moorshead, Jr.)

The *Minnie T. Phillips* appears to be deep loaded in this view looking forward from amidships across the wide expanse of her deck. (Frank Moorshead, Jr., Mystic Seaport Museum, No. 91-10-105)

But the schooner had not lost its place in Bay commerce yet. Baltimore was one of the country's predominant packing and canning centers. Between 1870 and 1890, schooners carried tons of grain, vegetables, meats, and seafood to the Patapsco River port for processing.

In the 1870s, the A. J. Horsey Co. operated two dozen schooners out of Laurel, Delaware. Most were less than 100 feet and were used mostly for Bay and river trade. Many did go coastwise, however, to Philadelphia, New York, and south to Cuba.[14]

Speed was a factor in the success of a particular vessel and Chesapeake Bay schooners were still known and admired for their swiftness. Even weighted down with loads of oyster shells or tomatoes, they never lost their capacity to excite those who saw them under sail.

Captains and owners never ceased to boast of record-breaking runs their schooners made and someone would always come forth to challenge a claim. Baltimore bankers and merchants as well as shippers and seamen never tired of comparing the feats of schooners working out of that port. Not unlike the football pools of today, men in the taverns and boardinghouses of the city's waterfront bet regularly on the runs of Bay schooners.

Not Yet Replaced

When peace returned, steamboats, which had begun to take business away from the sail-powered freighters before the war, were in an even stronger position. Fewer and fewer new schooner hulls were being built as the nineteenth century neared its end. By 1890, no more than eight hundred schooners worked the Bay, where once they numbered in the thousands.

The Great Schooner Race

Perhaps the greatest contest between Bay schooners took place in 1884 between the *William M. Hines* and the *Judy*.[15] The *Hines* was a two-topmast schooner built in 1883 and at 84 feet was the larger of the two. The *Judy*, built in 1881, was 70 feet and carried a single topsail. The schooners were owned by competing firms, running coastwise with oysters and potatoes in the fall; pineapples from the Bahamas and watermelons from the Carolinas and Virginia in the spring and summer. Whatever the weather and conditions on their routes, the two schooners invariably beat most others into port and with each passing season, their rivalry increased in its intensity. Each schooner had its faction among the sporting crowd of Baltimore's waterfront.

This detail of the mainmast of the *Minnie T. Phillips* shows the Spanish burton, a specific arrangement of block and tackle which in this case raised and lowered her centerboard set alongside of the mast. Note the triple block on the lower throat halyard that provides the threefold purchase on the throat halyard, necessitated by the size of the schooner and her rig. Most two-masters required only a double block. (Frank Moorshead, Jr., Mystic Seaport Museum, No. 91-10-108)

This dockside view of the foredeck and forward house of the *Minnie T. Phillips* clearly shows the bowsprit and jibboom arrangement typical of larger Bay schooners. (Frank Moorshead, Jr., Mystic Seaport Museum, No. 91-10-107)

The *Hines* was owned by Thomas B. Schall, one of the city's largest packers. The *Judy* was the property and namesake of Captain "Judy" Garrett, who sailed for the brokerage firm of R. J. McAllister. Schall and Garrett often got together in Charlie Swearer's restaurant and bar which was next door to the Schall packinghouse on Hollingsworth and Pratt streets.

Tom Schall was quiet and reserved in manner. Judy Garrett was just the opposite, a boisterous man who tended to be a bit of a braggart. As was usually the case when they met, they engaged in a running dispute over the speed of their schooners. One night in May 1884, they decided to settle it once and for all with $500 to the winner of a race from Baltimore to Beaufort, North Carolina, for watermelons.

News of the race spread from one waterfront establishment to another and soon anyone who knew anything about the two vessels had a bet on the outcome of their upcoming contest.

This shot of the steering station on the afterdeck of the *Minnie T. Phillips* shows the wheel, yawl boat, water barrel, and the aft side of the trunk cabin with her bell. (Frank Moorshead, Jr., Mystic Seaport Museum, No. 91-10-104)

Bulack's Saloon at Pratt and South streets, Reilly's at Pratt and Calvert, and several other waterfront bars collected the bets and by the first of June the poolmakers had wagers totaling $60,000—a sum unheard of in those days.

All of a sudden, the race was serious business. To keep everything on the up-and-up, judges were put on each schooner. Captain Walter W. Marsh was the judge on the *Hines* and Captain John Storey was aboard the *Judy.* Captain of the *Judy* was Jacob Holmes and Charlie Terry was at the helm of the *Hines.* The race was set for June 6, starting from the Lazaretto Lighthouse in the Baltimore harbor and ending when the first schooner passed the Morehead City sea buoy just outside Beaufort, North Carolina.

In preparation for the race, the boats were hauled out for inspection and to have their bottoms scraped and painted. Every

halyard, sheet, and sail was checked and repaired. Two days before the race, the two schooners were berthed at Bowley's Wharf (now Pier 1 on Pratt Street) for public view. The talk and excitement they generated along Baltimore's waterfront could only be compared to that surrounding two top contenders for the Preakness today.

Because the *Hines* was larger, she sailed with a crew of eight, among them eighteen-year-old Tom Schall who would act as timekeeper for his father. The *Judy* shipped six men. At dawn on June 6, the harbor was crowded with spectators afloat and ashore as the *Hines* and the *Judy* were towed to the Lazaretto Lighthouse to begin the four-hundred-mile run to North Carolina.

A steady northeast wind gave an early lead to the *Hines*, which passed the Cape Charles Light early on the morning of June 8. The *Judy* was at least five miles behind, but began to

The yawl boat of the *Minnie T. Phillips* is gone in this view that shows the shape of the schooner's transom as well as the chafing boards hung from the rail to be lowered for the yawl boat to ride on when pushing. (Frank Moorshead, Jr., Mystic Seaport Museum, No. 91-10-109)

overtake the *Hines* when the wind hauled to the northwest. By three in the afternoon on June 10, the schooners were neck and neck and as the wind shifted to the south, they tacked close enough to each other for their crews to have jumped from one boat to the other.

Just fifteen miles from the Morehead sea buoy and the finish, the wind died. Captain Terry turned the *Hines* to sea where he found only a dying wind, but Captain Holmes, who had decided to steer the *Judy* shoreward, caught a strong breeze off the land that carried her to the finish line ten minutes ahead of the *Hines*.

The celebrations were necessarily brief because a load of Carolina melons lay awaiting transport north. The *Judy* carried her cargo straight back to Baltimore. The *Hines*'s cargo was destined for New York. Both completed their runs and, when all the furor subsided, went back to work.

The *Hines* was sold off the Bay to Mexico in the 1890s and renamed the *Tres Hermanos*. In April 1898, she became one of the first prizes taken by the U.S. Navy in the Spanish-American War. She was resold after the war and reportedly ran contraband into Mexico for a few years before she disappeared.

The *Judy* eventually came to be owned by Captain Fletcher Russell and in the late 1890s rammed and sank another schooner. Just after the turn of the century, she was run down by a tramp steamer and sank near Sandy Point, Maryland. She was finally raised, rebuilt, and renamed the *Maud Thomas* in 1908. She continued in the Bay trade and continued to be a sharp sailer. The *Maud* was entered in the first of the Chesapeake Bay Championship Workboat Races in 1921 and won the event in her class in the years 1926, 1929, and 1931, which was the last year the races were held. She did not end her career until 1946 when shipping registers list that she was abandoned.

By then, the shipping registers were recording more and more schooners abandoned. Adaptations such as the centerboard only delayed the inevitable, but schooners did not relinquish easily their position as the dominant carriers of freight on the Bay.

This 1890s view of Baltimore's harbor shows not only the large number, but the wide variety, of Bay craft that filled Bay ports in the nineteenth century. Buried in the forest of masts are those of pungies, schooners, sloops, at least one bugeye with a ducktail stern and, in the left foreground, the round-stern, square-rigged bugeye *Edgar M. Schall*, built in Baltimore in 1883 by T. H. McCosker & Co. Patent topsails, which were invented by W. H. Dare in 1877, are seen at the heads of many main topmasts. (National Archives, No. 22CE178)

Eight

The Oyster Boom

The oyster industry goes back in Maryland to the early 1800s, but in those days most of the harvest was shipped north where the bivalve was more in demand. In fact, the demands of the northern markets, which sent fleets of large schooners to dredge the oyster beds of the Bay, were causing concern among Maryland officials. As early as 1820, the state began to regulate the harvesting of oysters. By the 1850s, the oyster beds of Long Island Sound and Cape Cod were exhausted and northern oystermen concentrated even greater efforts in the Bay. In an attempt to further protect its resource, Maryland banned oystering by nonresidents. The result was that a number of New England seafood brokers moved their operations to Baltimore where they opened oyster packing plants.[1] Among the earliest were those of Maltby, Mallory, Hemingway, and Rowe.

By the eve of the Civil War, oystering was a booming business on the Chesapeake, creating a demand for dredge boats and for vessels to carry oysters north. Several fast, sharp-built, centerboard fishing schooners were built in the 1840s and 1850s for New England concerns. The 60-foot centerboard schooner *C. Chase*, built in 1856 in Baltimore by William Skinner & Son, was just one of a number of Bay-built centerboard and pungy schooners purchased to work out of Wellfleet, Massachusetts.[2] In addition to pungies like the *Iowa*, there were centerboarders like the 75-foot *Bloomfield* built in Talbot County in 1850 and the 64-foot *Mary Jones* built in Baltimore in 1851. They were employed in the summer in the Wellfleet mackerel fishery and in winter to transport oysters from the Chesapeake to Cape Cod. Schooners built on the Bay, or modeled after those built on the Bay, were used by the Cape Cod and Long Island Sound oyster fisheries as long as New Englanders continued to use schooners.[3]

During the Civil War, the oyster trade was interrupted, but canning operations continued to develop in Baltimore. Packing-house records noted the arrival in 1865 of the schooner *Alice* with thirty-seven tons of oysters, and there were several larger schooners also at work running oysters into Baltimore.[4] A 70-ton schooner had a capacity of three thousand bushels.[5] In the 1880s, when the peak of the oyster boom was reached, a buy boat made ten to fifteen cents a bushel for shipment to Baltimore. Vessels were clearing $15,000 to $17,000 on a single trip to New England.[6] The largest and most successful of the schooners running oysters after the war was the 77-foot *A. H. Schulz*, built in 1872 and named for the Baltimore oyster packer who owned her.[7]

"When I was a kid, the *Schulz* was talked about more than any other schooner in this area," said Calvert Evans, who later actually owned her. By then she had been renamed the *Sarah C.*

Conway. "She was known because she had that lucrative oyster run up the beach to Long Island."[8]

Generally, the Eastern Shore schooners, which were fewer in number, were owned by their captains. Most of the Baltimore boats were owned by wholesale oyster dealers, packers, canners, or shippers. During the 1879-80 oyster season, there were 800 runners or buy boats—most of which were pungies or schooners—working out of Baltimore. Some 5,600 bugeyes and smaller schooners were dredgers.[9] The boom reached its peak year in 1884, when fifteen million bushels were taken from the Bay.[10]

By 1890, the industry was in decline and the harvest had dropped to ten million bushels due to overfishing and the use of the shells in lime kilns and fertilizer plants instead of leaving them for planting. Records for the 1892-93 oyster season show that there were only 596 bugeyes, schooners, and pungies running oysters.[11] Over two decades, the Chesapeake Bay had supplied 40 percent of the world's oysters, but the age of the "almighty oyster" was nearing its end. By the turn of the century, Bay oystermen were running to Long Island to pick up bluepoint oysters for seeding depleted beds in Maryland's rivers. Captain Sam Brannock of Cambridge and a number of others worked for the state, bringing seed oysters into Maryland, not only from New York, but from the Rappahannock and the York rivers as well.[12]

Starvation Farm to Princess Bay

In the 1870s, a number of oystermen from the north came to the Bay for seed oysters to restock their depleted beds. Among them were Captain Dave Van Name and Captain Benjamin Decker who bought oyster ground in the York and James rivers. There they harvested seed oysters to plant in their beds in Princess Bay in New York. Captain Dave founded a dynasty in Virginia on five hundred acres along the York River near Adams Creek. Most of it was marsh and had little value as farmland. They called it

The *Eddie Cook*, built in 1883 in Cambridge, Maryland, is a handsome little oyster dredging schooner. Although only 43 feet, she has the proportions of a much larger schooner. Of interest is the fact that she has only one shroud per side at each mast. Conservation laws in Maryland counties such as Dorchester and Talbot very likely influenced the size of the *Cook* which was under 10 net tons, the maximum size of vessels permitted by law to dredge the river beds. Larger vessels were made to conform to that tonnage by a method called dunnaging in which temporary bulkheads or structures were built to exempt that space from tonnage measurement. The *Cook* was built as a schooner, whereas many smaller schooner-rigged vessels started out as sloops. One such is the *Rebecca Ruark*, built in 1885. Still working in 1991, she is the oldest commercial vessel under sail on the Chesapeake and was rigged at one time as a schooner. The mast step for her schooner rig was removed during an overhaul in the 1960s. Working with the Bay skipjack fleet in the 1990s, the *Ruark* carries a skipjack's leg-of-mutton rig. (Peabody Museum of Salem, No. 27,018, Richard Goldsborough)

"Starvation Farm." It was valuable property, nonetheless, for just offshore were thriving oyster grounds. There Captain Dave's son, Captain Pete, Sr., his grandson, Captain Pete, Jr., and great-grandson, Arthur, Sr., oversaw the oystering that supplied the family firm in New York.[13]

Captain Dave Van Name's sons, Peter, William H., and Jacob Van Name established the firm of Van Name Brothers. They had a flourishing business selling oysters retail from a scow. It was kept with a number of other retail oyster scows off the Battery in New York City. To keep the retail business going, they employed a number of schooners which they used to run their oysters from the grounds in Virginia to their seafood depot on Staten Island.[14]

Two Van Name schooners that became well known on the Chesapeake Bay were the *David Carll*, which later became the *Blackbird*, and the *William H. Van Name*. The former was built at City Island by her namesake David Carll, a well-known builder of schooner yachts, who also built the *Van Name* in 1872. One hundred and two feet from stemhead to taffrail, the *Van Name* was considered one of the fastest and best of the schooners used in the oyster trade between New York and Virginia.

Doctor Arthur Van Name, Jr., of Urbanna, Virginia, who is the great-great-grandson of Captain Dave, came along after the Van Name brothers had gone out of business and his father, Arthur, Sr., was struggling against forces beyond his control to keep the operation on the York River going. Both Captain Pete, senior and junior, were gone and did not have to live to see the end of the oyster business that had been their life.

"My great-grandfather loved the river," said Urbanna physician and marine artist Arthur Van Name, Jr., who grew up loving the water and the schooners that sailed it. "Although he must have been a good businessman, he was something of a free spirit and I imagine he was happiest on the river. Old Captain Pete had a barge with a cabin on it where he'd retreat and he had a negro who cooked for him there. He also had a small sailboat he loved. One night, there was a storm and the boat began to fill up with water. Captain Pete and the negro got into their hip boots and foul-weather gear and rowed out to try to save the sailboat. Captain Pete fell in and despite the negro's efforts to save him, he drowned. His body washed ashore shortly thereafter. Family legend has it that his body was preserved in rum to be shipped north for burial on Staten Island."[15]

Running out of Hickory Cove

In 1895, the *William H. Van Name* was bought by Captain John Clayton of Cambridge at which time she was hauled out at T. J.

The two-topmast oyster schooner *Alida Hearn* is seen here, bound east off Milford, Connecticut, in 1916 with a load of granite. She was built in 1885 at Pocomoke City, Maryland, and worked on Long Island Sound, carrying sand, bricks, small building stone, and potatoes in the off-season. (Peabody Museum of Salem, Robert Beattie)

Sauerhoff's marine railway in Sharptown. At that time, she had been hauling oysters for nearly thirty-five years, but showed hardly a trace of the work she had been doing. The time book from the yard bears the notation that she "was kept like a yacht."[16]

The *Van Name* continued her career running oysters from the Honga River grounds to Baltimore. "The night before the season opened," wrote eighty-five-year-old William Hooper, one of the few watermen who wrote down his experiences, "Hickory Cove and beyond would be lit up like a city. Boats from Upper Hooper Island, Wingate, Crapo, and Bishops Head would join us here."[17] Hooper spent more than seventy years on Chesapeake Bay schooners.

A large number of the boats that anchored in Hickory Cove were schooners. Several of them claimed the cove as home port. Among them were Captain Sam Brannock's buy boat, the *William Layton*, or the "ol' Bill Layton," as she was usually called; the *Fannie Insley*; the *Flora Kirwan*; the *Laurena Clayton*; and the *William H. Van Name*.

The *Van Name* was one of the larger schooners or "markets," as the buy boats were called, which ferried the oysters to the steam houses in Baltimore for canning.

"Captain Johnny Clayton sailed the *Van Name* in here from Baltimore one day, having gone up there loaded, and, without lowering the sails, reloaded with 3,500 bushels, and sailed out again," wrote Hooper. "The work boats were strung out to the stern of that vessel for a hundred yards, waiting to put their catch aboard."[18]

The *Van Name* worked for another half dozen years under Captain Al Simmons and then near the end of the oyster season in 1902, she was just off the York Spit Light, bound for New York with a load of oysters, when a heavy northwester struck. She put back into Hampton Roads for shelter but struck a sunken, unmarked barge between the Thimble Shoal Light and the ripraps. She was unsalvageable and had to be dynamited the next day.[19]

As for the Van Name family business: "By the time I came along in 1911, the oyster business on the York River apparently was still a going concern," said Arthur Van Name, Jr., "but

The New Jersey–built *Anna and Helen* finished her working life on the Bay with the oyster fleet. She is shown here, powered mainly by her yawl boat, on her way to the oyster grounds. (Maryland State Archives, M. E. Warren, MSA-12664-24)

sometime around 1908, the Chesapeake Corporation, a large papermill, opened up at West Point about ten miles up the river from us. The year after it opened Pop's profits—and he had a nice business—were cut in half. The next year, he ran in the hole. He had training in business and he kept excellent books. The oysters simply went bad there. They died by the score and that was all the way down the York River, but the farther down from West Point you got, the less they were affected. The nearer to

West Point, the greater the loss. I remember taking oysters from that area and punching in the shell with my finger. Because the business went to pieces, I suppose, Pop moved up to West Point in 1916 when I was five and we lived in West Point from then on, until I went out to work for myself as a physician."[20]

Aboard the *Annie Hodges*

Dredging and running oysters was a principal occupation for Bay schooners in the second half of the nineteenth century. Men would live aboard the oyster boats for weeks at a time, and they started young.

William T. Hooper was born in the mid-1880s and lived his life on Hooper Island, a part of Dorchester County lying between

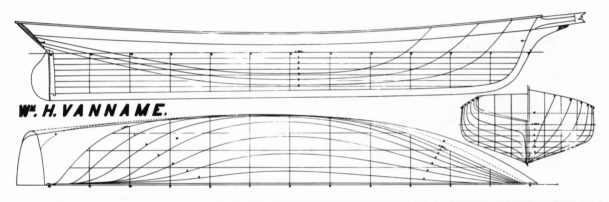

Wᴹ. H. VAN NAME.

The *William H. Van Name* was designed and built by David Carll at City Island, New York, in 1872. She worked twenty years running up and down the Atlantic coast between Norfolk and New York. The *Van Name* went down in winter without ballast and returned loaded almost to the plank-sheer with oysters. According to well-known naval architect W. P. Stephens, "she was long noted as the fastest of the fleet." Her half-model now hangs in Clayton's on the Creek Restaurant in Cambridge, Maryland The schooner was actually built to be 8 feet longer than the half-model indicates. Her lines show her to have been a schooner of good carrying capacity on a moderate draft, with the hull strength required for the heavy rig she carried. Her length, stem to taffrail, was 102 feet, her beam was 25 feet, and her draft 8 feet 5 inches with her center-board up. The *Van Name* was lost in March 1906 when she struck the submerged wreck of the barge *Oak* at Hampton Roads. No photographs of the Van Name have yet come to light. (Mystic Seaport Museum, Ships Plans Dept., W. P. Stephens)

the Bay and the Honga River on Maryland's Eastern Shore. Coming from a family of thirteen children, he quit school at the age of fourteen to go to work on the water with his father, Samuel T. Hooper. William was seventeen when he signed on with Captain Ellie Phillips as cook on the main topsail schooner *Annie Hodges*.[21]

Young Hooper was paid $15 a month in 1902. So were the captain's sons, Amos and Goldsborough. Not bad pay, said Captain Ellie. He'd started out at $10 a month. Hooper's main job was cooking, but he helped on deck, handling sails, steering the boat, or loading and unloading freight.

In the late fall and winter, the *Hodges* was used for oyster dredging. In the spring and early summer, she ran oysters. By late summer and early fall, she was hauling freight: railroad ties, coal, and lumber. Hooper worked three seasons on the *Hodges* running seed oysters from the James River to Maurice River Cove near Port Norris, New Jersey.[22]

To get to Port Norris, Captain Ellie took the *Hodges* through the Chesapeake and Delaware Canal. They entered at Chesapeake City and locked out at Delaware City. Then it was down the Delaware Bay to the Maurice River on the New Jersey side. In those days, Delaware Bay had a narrow channel full of bars and shallows that was best only traversed in daylight, so usually they would stop at sundown in a safe anchorage midway to Maurice River Cove.[23]

Planting oysters was backbreaking work. Once the schooner arrived at Maurice River Cove and dropped anchor, a scow hauled platforms on pontoons out to the *Hodges*. The oysters were shoveled from the deck of the schooner onto the platforms which were then poled out to the planting ground, where the oysters were shoveled overboard. The crew of the *Hodges* was paid an extra $3 each for every load of oysters they helped to shovel off the vessel. Captain Ellie also hired extra help from among the boys who inevitably showed up on the beach.[24]

There was more than shoveling oysters to make the trip to Port Norris memorable. "The tides in that area behave in a most disconcerting fashion, with an ebb and flow of from seven to nine feet," wrote William Hooper in his memoirs. "On one of our runs to Port Norris in the *Hodges*, we anchored offshore in approximately eight feet of water and after the vessel was unloaded, decided to go ashore awhile. While we were on the beach, the tide went and left the vessel high and dry, resting on the bottom. We walked back to the boat and climbed aboard on a ladder.

"The first rush of incoming tide may be several feet, and it comes in strong, sometimes with enough force to sweep a man off his feet. A vessel left resting on the bottom would refloat in about two hours."

Low tides were a boon to local fishermen. They'd haul their traps out into the receding water in wagons and catch hundreds of fish. While the crew of the *Hodges* waited for the tide to get the schooner off the bottom, they had a supper of fish supplied by the fishermen.

"The fish made good eating," wrote Hooper, "and were especially delicious with the hot bread I made. We called it yeast powder bread—made with white flour, salt, baking powder, and plenty of lard to make it tender and flaky. Our saddle-back stove baked it beautifully, with the loaves browned as evenly on the bottom as on the top.

"The saddle-back stove was one especially designed for use aboard a vessel, and was particularly adapted for cooking in rough weather. It was square, with rods built across the top structure to hold cook pots in place. Either wood or coal could be used as fuel . . . We cooked and ate in the forepeak, in the bow of the vessel. The cabin aft in the stern section provided sleeping quarters."[25]

On the return trip, they entered the canal at Delaware City and locked out at Chesapeake City into an area known as Back Creek. Their course took them from there to the Bay.

Hooper recalled one trip home when he and Goldsborough were sailing the *Hodges* while Captain Ellie and Amos were below eating breakfast. They'd been sailing all night, but had lost their breeze with the dawn. Goldsborough just happened to look over the stern and noticed some corks bobbing in the schooner's wake.

The round-stern, square-rigged bugeye *Catherine* built in 1911 at Solomon's Island, Maryland, by M. M. Davis, is shown here in the process of coming about on Tolchester "clump," as oyster grounds were often called. This photograph was taken in September 1941; the *Catherine* dredged oysters until she was abandoned near Annapolis in 1956. (Frank Moorshead, Jr., Mystic Seaport Museum, No. 91-10-151)

"We decided to launch the skiff and have a look," wrote Hooper. "I put the wheel in the becket [a device for holding the wheel in a pre-set position, which usually consists of a length of rope attached to the deck, with the other end of the rope forming an eye which can be slipped over a spoke of the wheel]. The vessel was so becalmed, she was scarcely moving. There was no danger in leaving the wheel unattended for a short time.

"We took the boat hook and rowed around to the stern to investigate. It was part of some poor guy's shad seine. We removed it from the rudder with the boat hook and were pleasantly surprised to find three large roe shad entrapped."

The boys figured that they had hooked the shad seine as they passed the Swan Point fishing ground off Rock Hall. The fishing area was in a busy traffic lane and fishermen were

warned to put their nets deep, so that a boat, light or loaded, could clear them. If they failed to do so, they lost their nets.

"Although we sympathized with the [seine] owner's misfortune, we did enjoy his fish," said Hooper. "We cooked one shad and all the roe for dinner. Captain Ellie salted down the other two for later."[26]

Oystering on the *Arianna Bateman*

Two years later, Will Hooper was sailing with Captain Avalon Simmons on the schooner *Arianna Bateman*. His first voyage was in December, delivering oysters to the Rappahannock River. Oysters were plentiful that year—a glut on the market, in fact. They could be bought for fifteen cents a bushel and Simmons had loaded the *Bateman* "as deep as she would swim."

"We loaded 3,200 bushels of the most beautiful oysters I ever saw," wrote Hooper. "Taken from sandy bottom, they were big as horse shoes and fat as butter."[27]

They left the Honga River in late afternoon and had unloaded their cargo at the planter's oyster ground in the Rappahannock by noon the following day. Up most of the previous night, Hooper went below to sleep as they were rounding Windmill Point to head up the Bay for home.

"I had been asleep about two hours and the vessel was long since past the Windmill Light, when I was awakened by a commotion on deck and horns blowing in the distance," Hooper recalled. "When I opened the cabin door and poked my head out . . . it was as if I had thrust my face in a wad of cotton. We were enveloped in a thick fog—so dense I was unable to discern the others on deck.

"Avalon assured me they were getting along alright and told me to go back to sleep. My response was to the effect that in such a situation, I would rather be on deck."

Hooper took the wheel while Avalon Simmons joined the rest of the crew on lookout. "The Bay was full of noise from horns and whistles. Several steamers were navigating the area, honking continuously. It was altogether a dangerous time to be abroad in the Bay."

And under full sail, no less. "We had all five sails on and all of them drawing, that is, each was filled with wind and furnishing its fair share of propulsion. She was sailing smartly; really cutting the water. We were bound home light and, of course, this increased the vessel's capacity for speed."

Hooper asked Simmons how long he thought it would take for them to reach the Southwest Middles where they would turn east into Hooper Straits headed for the Honga River. The captain checked their location, the time, and the breeze. "An hour and five minutes," he said.

"In exactly sixty-five minutes, he picked up the lead line sounder, threw it over the side and measured exactly two and one-half fathoms. This was the depth he expected . . . I held the vessel in east by northeast for the Straits and . . . we were anchored in Hickory Cove and ashore in Captain Johnny Simmons's store by 9 p.m."

Avalon Simmons sold the 3,200 bushels of oysters he bought on that trip at fifteen cents a bushel to a planter for twenty-eight cents a bushel. Hooper's pay was twenty-five dollars, which was a lot of money in those days. The standard wage for experienced crewmen was still only eighteen dollars a month. But Simmons didn't mind sharing his good fortune, especially since it was just two days before Christmas.[28]

A Shifting Lot

From the point of view of the captains, getting reliable crews was a constant problem. The dawn of the twentieth century was

Many of the schooners that were fast sailers were used as buy boats to carry the oysters to market. In this shot taken in 1915, a hand tonger is selling his catch to a buy boat, possibly the *Kate McNamara*. The flag on one of her forestays lets the tongers know she's buying. Buy boats were generally owned by their captains who bought oysters for their own accounts. Run boats were owned by the oyster packing companies and were operated by hired captains and crews. Note the schooner's spike bowsprit which appears to be hogged down. Rather than being hogged or bent, it is shaped that way as a matter of style. A number of pungies show the same style of bowsprit. Her topsail is stowed in a patent fashion and she shows a band for a fore-topmast, but has none fitted. (Peabody Museum of Salem, No. 27,022, C. L. Johnson)

The two oilskin-clad men shown here are probably the captain and mate of the oyster dredging pungy *John Nelson*. The handle of the hand winder is visible over the shoulder of the man on the left, and the dredge is hanging on the rail behind the man on the right. This Federal Fisheries Commission photo was taken in the winter of 1891. (National Archives)

twilight for working sail. The more experienced men could get easier work and better pay elsewhere. As a result, many of those available for hire along Baltimore's waterfront were the neediest and least experienced—recent immigrants and blacks, especially. They were "a shifting lot," prone to desert. Few had ever worked the water and they weren't prepared for the hardships they found on the Bay.[29] A schooner dredging oysters could stay out two months, and in the worst weather.

Before the start of the oyster season, the dredge and run boats began arriving in Baltimore to get their outfit, crews, and licenses. A fleet of over a thousand bugeyes, schooners, and bateaux gathered at the docks where wagons arrived in a steady stream, delivering supplies from the ship chandlers and grocers. There was always an assortment of men hanging about—some looking for work, others just looking, and still others up to no good.

Captain Charles Barnard, owner of the scow schooner *Ella Barnard* remembered Baltimore's harbor in 1911: "Ruffians along the docks made it unsafe to walk the waterfront after dark and he [Barnard] always carried his little .32 caliber American Bulldog wherever he went," wrote Louis Sayer. "On one occasion just before going on board the *Ella B.*, two 'Jaspers' as he called them, tried to do him in. One carried a piece of pipe and the other a section of an oar. They advanced on him and he fired first over their heads. At this point, they decided on a hasty retreat, leaving their weapons behind and disappearing into the darkness.[30]

"Many evenings, while left alone on board . . . for his own safety he would leave a tin cup over the cabin door. If someone tried to enter, it would dislodge the cup and the invader would be 'given away.' "[31]

Schooner crews going to and from their boats at night walked in the middle of the street and most of them carried "knuckles" in their pockets. Dock lines were often stolen from tied up vessels while the crews slept.[32]

A crew, in the best of times, was made up of the captain, mate, cook, and a deckhand. Ideally, all were experienced. It seldom worked out that way in the waning years of the Chesapeake Bay schooner.

"My father went up to the shipping office in Baltimore to hire men. He could always get a fellow off of Light Street," said Harry Porter, captain of several converted schooners and later the *Maryland Lady* and other yachts kept for governors of the state of Maryland. "Most were black. Occasionally he would get a white man. He'd go on down the Bay and make out best he could. A lot of the men you'd get weren't terribly reliable.[33]

"I remember one time during the wheat season when we were scowing off. My father had two men on. One was called 'Root.' A lot of times in those days you didn't know a person's real name and this one black fellow was just called Root. Now, my father wasn't easy to get along with, hollering and yelling, and that day, he was down in the hold raising hell about

The 43-foot schooner *Frolic* was built by Brusstar Shipbuilding in Baltimore in 1874 for the Maryland "oyster police." Her half-model is in the Smithsonian collection. Two vessels were actually built from the same half-model for the "oyster navy," as it also was called. The other schooner was the *Folly*. Even though they were centerboarders, the two were fairly sharp-built schooners, built more like yachts. The *Frolic* has a relatively long bowsprit and a large rig for the size of her hull, all of which meant speed in terms of carrying out her police function in chasing the "oyster pirates" on the Bay. Note her long trunk cabin amidships to accommodate her crew. The *Frolic* had a long career and was rebuilt several times. (Peabody Museum of Salem, No. 27,020, C. L. Johnson)

something. Next thing we know, this fellow Root has got an ax and was standing over him saying 'I'm gonna kill you!'

"Nobody made a move. Dad didn't either and finally the fellow put the ax down and went on forward and down into the forepeak. Dad came out of the hold and went into the after cabin for his gun. He called him up out of the forepeak and made him go ashore. He had to walk ten or fifteen miles to the ferryboat to go back to Baltimore and when he left he swore he'd get Dad when he got back to Baltimore, but nothing ever came of it.

"Pa would go up to Pratt Street to get a man," said William Seaford Stevens, of Kent Island. "One man we picked up, we brought him aboard one night but the next morning when we got ready to pull out, we set him ashore and went off by ourselves. Another one we got, we carried him down and laid him off in Virginia. We caught him stealing, taking cooked meat from the galley and hiding it under his bunk. The other we just didn't feel right about."[34]

With reliability in question and profits slim, an extra hand was often seen as a luxury a captain was better off without. The feeling among most of the men who followed the water was that the only time you really needed more men was for loading and unloading and you could generally hire local hands at either end of the voyage.

"Usually all you needed was the captain and one man—two head of us that was all," said Woodrow Aaron, who sailed out of Cambridge aboard a number of schooners. "Sometimes you'd go by yourself. If you hit a storm, you'd just drop the sails, throw the anchor overboard and ride it out."[35]

"When the Depression struck, we had to load our own boats," recalled William Stevens. "Usually, when we went down to Virginia to the York River to load lumber, they had men to load, but during the Depression, we had to do it ourselves or go find our own stevedores. We paid them ten cents an hour and we did a lot of the work ourselves."[36]

Paid Off with the Boom

Work on the water is dangerous under any circumstances, but the peak years in the nineteenth century, when there were

The 51-ton *Oystermen* was built by Kirby & Lang at St. Michaels in 1889. She is shown here in the Maurice River, New Jersey, laid up awaiting the oyster season. Note the stowage of her anchor and the bowsprit/jibboom arrangement. The *Sarah C. Conway* is just behind her. (Frank Moorshead, Jr., Mystic Seaport Museum, No. 91-10-102)

hundreds of boats and thousands of men "drudging" oysters, posed unique perils. For decades, oystermen fought each other, tonger against dredger, Marylander against Virginian, all of them against the "oyster navy." During the period known as the "Oyster Wars" that extended from the Civil War to the opening decades of the twentieth century, oystermen regularly died at the hands of other oystermen or the "oyster police." In pursuit of profit, life sometimes came cheap. Not everybody had to be accounted for. Seldom was an itinerant deckhand missed.

There are not many now who could tell of it, but their fathers heard many tales—some true, some not—of the cruelty

This is a view of the deck winders of the *Minnie Mae Kirwan*. By 1936, when this photograph was taken, such machinery was common and perpetuated the use of vessels of this size for oyster dredging. (Courtesy of Smithsonian Institution, National Museum of American History, HAMMS Collection, No. 665)

of the early oyster boat captains; how they shanghaied their crewmen, worked them all season, and then "paid them off with the boom." It was easy enough. Accidents happened. Without a word of warning, a captain came about or jibed, hard and fast, and as the heavy boom swept across the deck, it took the unsuspecting crewman with it. In a good breeze, the cries from the water were out of earshot in minutes. Sometimes, the captain would just put the man ashore. If it happened to be a deserted island or a barren stretch of marsh, so be it. His chances were seldom better than in the water, since most of them knew nothing of the Bay—land or water—and died of starvation or exposure before they found civilization.

Eventually, an increasingly effective oyster police force and a dwindling number of boats put an end to the particularly ruthless years when huge profits drove the oyster industry. Hometown crews became the norm. White and black, the men came from families who had lived and worked together on the water for generations. There were a few black captains dredging, a few who owned schooners and carried freight.

"When my grandfather was running schooners, there'd usually be three people, him, a mate, and a cook," said Earl Brannock. "The cooks were usually black. Later they had all black crews. The blacks were the only ones that would stay on up into the thirties and forties."[37]

Dredging the Potomac

Oyster season began October 15 on the Potomac and several hundred boats put out from Baltimore, dropping down the Patapsco River to the Chesapeake bound for Breton Bay, forty miles up the Potomac. Some five hundred vessels gathered in Breton Bay.

By day, the assembled boats sorted themselves out according to their specific tasks. The dredgers were schooners of sixty feet or less, an occasional two-sail bateau, later to be known as a skipjack, and bugeyes, some of which were schooner-rigged with a gaff-foresail and a triangular main. According to law, the dredging was done only in the open river, and there was usually an oyster police schooner on hand to see that the dredgers adhered to the law.

The dredge boats worked in water ten to thirty feet deep, with the wind in their sails providing the power that dragged the teeth of their iron dredges across the oyster beds. They used either a hand or gasoline windlass to haul the dredge aboard, where the catch was culled for shells and small oysters to be thrown back. The marketable oysters were tossed in a pile. Once they had a fair catch, which could be forty to sixty bushels depending on the size of the boat, they looked for the buy boat or runboat, where the captain would hoist an empty bushel basket on the mainmast if he was ready to take on oysters.[38]

If he was, the dredge boats came alongside, one at a time. Until their turn, they waited off the stern of the buy boat, with their mainsails holding them in place and their jibs left to blow in the wind. The oysters were shoveled into tubs, hoisted aboard the buy boat, or market boat, by a whip crane and lowered into the hold, there to be shoveled back by the crew. The captain of the dredge boat called out the tally and the mate of the buy boat repeated it, recording the figure in his ledger. The buy boat usually left when it was loaded to the sheer plank.[39]

Most of the buy boats were pungies or schooners, measuring sixty or seventy feet on deck. They were also called runboats, because run was just what they did; back and forth between the dredging fleet and Baltimore, as fast as they could load and discharge two thousand to three thousand bushels of shell oysters. A round-trip usually took a week.

Throughout the oyster season, working other oyster grounds in the Potomac, the Bay, and its other tributaries, the routine was essentially the same for the schooners and pungies that served the fleet as runboats. They continued to prove that the speed for which Chesapeake Bay schooners were known had not been worked out of them.

Two schooners and a sloop are tied up discharging their cargoes in front of this Cambridge, Maryland, oyster packing-house. The masts of other schooners can be seen in the background. The power yawl boats indicate that this is a relatively late photograph. (Maryland State Archives, MdHR-G-1477-6640)

Nine

Managing a Schooner

Over the two centuries that commerce in the Chesapeake Bay region was dominated by commercial sail, a definite pattern grew up that lasted in schooners converted to power up into the early 1970s. Even as sail began to give way to power, watermen worked the Bay very much as their fathers, grandfathers, and great-grandfathers had before them. Schooners carried grain, lumber, cordwood, oysters, and farm products to Norfolk, Richmond, Alexandria, Washington, Baltimore, and Annapolis from river landings and small towns from one end of the Bay to the other. The same Bay freighters returned with manufactured goods, coal, fertilizer, and news to be dispensed with the goods at the local general store or ship chandlery.

Some of the larger two-masters, three-masters, and Chesapeake Bay rams, which were unique schooners designed specifically for the narrow passage of the C & D Canal, worked in the coastwise trades from Bay ports south to Cuba and north to Halifax, Nova Scotia. As in the old West Indies trade, they carried northern goods south and returned with lumber, turpentine, and other naval stores.

The schooner *Clara M. Goodman*, built in the 1870s and owned in Laurel, Delaware, carried coal, pig iron, Peruvian

The *Columbia F. C.*, named for a District of Columbia fishing club, was built at Mundy Point, Virginia, in 1874. She is shown here with her topsail set, sailing on a broad reach. Her yawl boat is down—probably for use by the photographer—giving a good view of her stern with the ever-present "scum line" that vessels carried away from their moorings in polluted harbors. The height of the line on her transom suggests that she was heavily laden in her last port of call. (Van Name/Perry Collection)

guano, logs, and lumber. She traded between Richmond, Washington, D.C., Philadelphia, New York, and Hartford, Connecticut. She also made several trips to Cuba.

The *Goodman* was a profitable vessel, averaging three or four charters that earned her investors $300 to $400 a year. One trip to Manzanillo, Cuba, earned a profit of $1,500 after paying for crew, food, chandlery, and other expenses.[1]

In the management of vessels such as the *Goodman*, the captain's share was one-half of each charter. He handled the schooner's finances, obtained the cargoes, figured the tariffs, kept the ship in repair, and managed the crew. The owners received the other half of the amount received from a charter.

The captain took what shares he could afford, but often sold his shares. Shipyards, ship brokers, sailmakers, and chandlers were the usual shareholders other than the captain. Shares in schooners were popular and profitable. A person could buy one-eighth, one-sixteenth, one-thirty-second, or one-sixty-fourth part ownership of a schooner for a return of 5 to 20 percent annually.

Schooners working the Bay or going coastwise sailed twenty-four hours a day in all kinds of weather and often were loaded beyond their designed capacity. Such use meant that they were in constant need of refurbishing and repair. Record books that have survived show numerous entries for marine railway charges, the purchase of new fittings and sails, not to mention cordage, hardware, and paint.

Bills for the *Clara M. Goodman* show the captain and crew purchased needles and thread, firewood and coal, cargo books, cabin furniture, pots and pans, and even spittoons. They also show payments for wharfage, pilotage, towing, hire of a chronometer, customhouse clearance, commission on charters, loading and unloading, charges for "trimming" or stowing the cargo so that it would not shift in heavy seas, fresh water, blacksmith work on block and tackle fittings on booms and gaffs, and hauling out to apply copper bottom paint to prevent the growth of barnacles and other marine life.[2]

Always Pushing

Many of the schooners were owned by store proprietors who depended on them to carry local produce to city markets and return with molasses, kerosene, sugar, clothing, hardware, and other store supplies to stock their shelves. Frequently, the schooners carried passengers and were used by families from the Eastern Shore and the more remote river towns on the western shore for semiannual trips to the city—most often Baltimore—to shop, see the sights, perhaps attend a play, and visit relatives.

In the last century, schoonermen like Captain Charlie Porter, who was a Kent Islander, delivered coal, barrels of molasses, and store supplies by schooner from Baltimore to stores at different places on the island. His son, T. Harry Porter, did the same later in schooners converted to diesel power.

Powered mainly by her yawl boat, the *Columbia F. C.* is under sail in light air. Note her unusually large standing jib, her topsail, and the deep scum line on her hull. The flying jib is furled on the jibboom. (Frank Moorshead, Jr., Mystic Seaport Museum, No. 91-10-124)

This photograph was taken in St. Mary's County, Maryland, around the turn of the century. Schooners went from farm to farm at harvest time, and the wagons were driven out into the shallows for the bags of grain to be loaded into skiffs or scows. Whatever the carrier, the process was generally called "scowing grain." A schooner might stop at three or four farms to get a full load. (Maryland State Archives, MdHR-G-1477-5227)

"My father had a close run from Kent Island to Baltimore," said Captain Harry B. Porter, who was the third generation of Porters to command Bay freight boats. "It would all depend on the wind. On a good trip, he'd get underway in the morning or afternoon and be in Baltimore by nightfall. In later years, he had the yawl boats with their one-lung engines into 'em and he'd push with them if there were adverse conditions."[3]

Power or sail, they were always pushing, literally and figuratively, from port to port, season to season, boat to boat, and generation to generation.

"We worked hard for long hours and loved every minute of it," said William T. Hooper. "We ate simple, wholesome food, with a hunger born of heavy, muscle-straining toil; and slept the sweet deep sleep of exhaustion. We worshipped God and were awed by his handiwork. It was a good life."[4]

Hauling Grain

Early in its history, Baltimore became a center for the import and export of grain and the milling of flour. The Chesapeake Bay provided much of the flour used in New England. Flour from the Bay was favored in European markets and regularly commanded the highest prices. Schooners brought grain from the Carolinas, Virginia, and the Eastern and western shores of Maryland to Baltimore. They anchored by the dozens to await their turn at the grain piers in Canton.

It was seasonal work, but then, much of what the schooners relied on followed the seasons. Late summer into early fall was harvest time, and hauling grain was big business if a skipper didn't want to go out of the Bay. Most of it was wheat for Baltimore. Schooners carried grain—corn and wheat—in bulk in the hold and in bags on deck. They were usually chartered through Baltimore brokers, such as C. C. Paul, one of the largest.

"With the schooners, you went to the individual farmers," said Harry B. Porter. "Each farm had its own landing and all the farmers got together to help each other thresh the wheat. They went from one farm to another. We'd go in and load up and when one farm would finish, we'd get up the anchor and push on down to the next farmer's landing. When they got set up, we'd start the operation. In those days, production wasn't near as great. A thousand or two thousand bushels of grain was a good crop. A schooner would carry a couple of crops at least."[5]

Captain Ira Stevens and his son William freighted wheat and corn from Kent Island to Baltimore. "The farmers would bring the wheat down in farm wagons with their horses and run them overboard," said William Stevens. "We had a scow and we'd go up close and take the wheat off the wagon. It was in bags and we took them up on deck and opened them up and dumped the wheat down in the hold. That was hard work."[6]

"We didn't get home at night," said Harry Porter. "We'd lay around in these coves and we'd go ashore and pick up wood to cut up for the stove in the forepeak. We had a water barrel forward and if we got close to a wharf, we'd fill it. If not, we'd bring it out in buckets. Everybody drank out of the same tin cup. Didn't have any ice.

"When we were loading wheat, we'd sleep on deck. It was too hot below, especially with a load of grain that had a lot of onions and garlic in it. That just created heat. You'd make your bed wherever you could. Maybe you'd throw an old blanket down or roll up in the sail or climb up on top the bags of wheat. You'd roll up and the mosquitoes would turn you around once or twice, there'd be so many of them."[7]

The schooners loaded as much as they could possibly carry. "One time we loaded the *Ruth Decker* 'til the water wasn't quite on her deck," said William Stevens. "By the time we got to Baltimore, the water was two inches on the deck and as soon as Pa got to the dock, he started unloading her.

"Whenever we'd load grain or fertilizer in the hold we'd always seal the hatches. Sometimes on the *Edwin and Maud*, the water'd be coming across and you could have rowed a skiff around on deck if it weren't so rough. Of course we didn't mind 'cause she was a nice boat."[8]

Some of the grain went south aboard schooners headed for North Carolina or Georgia for lumber. "Those boys down there

A below-deck shot of any Bay schooner is rare. This one taken in the hold of the *Amanda F. Lewis* shows a tightly ceiled aft bulkhead between the hold and the cabin. The stanchions lying on the keelson amidships give her extra support for deck loads. The light is coming through the main hatch aft. (Frank Moorshead, Jr., Mystic Seaport Museum, No. 91-10-133)

Here the *Annie C. Johnson* is inbound for Baltimore loaded to her scuppers with watermelons. She was built at Solomons Island in 1891 by M. M. Davis. In the 1920s, she worked dredging oysters on the Delaware Bay, then returned to the Chesapeake. She left again in 1953 for the Delaware where she was abandoned in 1957. (Frank Moorshead, Jr., Mystic Seaport Museum, No. 91-10-128)

in Georgia, they didn't measure their corn the way we did ours," said Cambridge shipwright Jim Richardson of stories he heard during Prohibition. "A barrel of corn up here was fifteen baskets of grain but theirs down there was measured by the gallon. So they'd go down there and get a load of lumber and a little something else. They could make quite a bit of profit on corn liquor."[9]

Lumber kept schooners working, loaded on deck and below, as shown here. This is a view of the hold of the *Sarah C. Conway*. She was built with both "hanging" or vertical knees and horizontal or "lodging" knees for additional strength, a factor that undoubtedly accounted for her longevity. (Chesapeake Bay Maritime Museum, No. 120-1)

Fertilizer Capital of the World

By the 1930s and 1940s, there were as many as thirty fertilizer factories along Bay rivers. A dozen in Baltimore earned it the title "fertilizer capital of the world." The industry had gotten its start in Baltimore in the 1840s, driven by the need of Maryland farmers to increase the production of their land to meet the tremendous demand for wheat and flour.[10]

In 1849, in Baltimore, Philip and William Chappell patented a chemical compound for making fertilizer and a new and thriving industry was born. By the time things returned to normal after the Civil War, Baltimore and Maryland factories were supplying half the fertilizer used in the United States.[11]

It was largely schooners that transported the fertilizer Bay farmers needed for their own fields. A load of fertilizer typically became return freight once a cargo of grain was unloaded in Baltimore. Like the grain, it was carried bulk in the hold. Usually it was phosphate from Florida that the schooners carried to mixing plants in Salisbury, Pocomoke, and Cambridge, Maryland, and Seaford and Milford, Delaware. "It was loose in those days," remembered Calvert Evans, "and if the wind was blowing, you'd get solid covered up with it."[12]

Later, when the fertilizer was regularly warehoused and there were distribution centers, the product was more often carried in bags.

"When we were running fertilizer in the small schooners, we'd carry 150 to 200 tons in bags," said William Stevens. "We got it in Baltimore, and some was loose, some was in bags, and we unloaded in Virginia. We went to seven or eight different piers. We never ran many bags on the *Edwin and Maud*. We carried it loose in her hold."[13]

Load Her 'til She Tilts

More than grain and fertilizer, the standby was lumber. "If you couldn't get a better paying cargo, you could always get a load

The *Edward L. Martin* built in Sussex County, Delaware, in 1882 was 84 tons and 87.2 feet long. A pineapple schooner at one time, she is shown here with a deckload of cordwood. Note that the mainsail is reefed due to the height of the deck load, not the strength of the wind. To get the main boom up over a deck load, it was common to put a reef in the sails. Such a reef was often referred to as a lumber reef. Converted to power, the *Edward L. Martin* was destroyed by fire at Oxford in 1956. (Frank Moorshead, Jr., Mystic Seaport Museum, No. 91-10-118)

of lumber," said Calvert Evans, who owned the schooner *Sarah C. Conway*. "Most of the time, it was out of Carolina or southern Virginia. You figured a load of lumber by the board foot. The *Sarah C. Conway* could load about 80,000 board feet and we'd gross around $200 a load.[14]

Evans used the *Sarah* to haul lumber to Baltimore from mills on the Rappahannock. "When the *Sarah* was loaded with lumber, most times it would be so high you had to stand on the wheelbox and steer with your feet," said Evans. "Lumber would be sticking right out over the side. When it was loaded like that,

Built originally as the *Venus* by Joseph Sauerhoff at Cambridge in 1893, the *Edna Bright Hough* was one of the larger pineapple schooners. She was reputedly a smart sailer and was sold to Portuguese fishermen in 1913. After she returned to the Chesapeake in the 1920s, the *Edna Bright Hough* freighted lumber and other bulk cargo until she was abandoned at Norfolk, Virginia, in 1938. She is shown here in Baltimore at Pier 6, Pratt Street, in 1933, but her home port was Moss Neck, Virginia, at the time. (Robert H. Burgess)

we had to raise the boom, but we didn't fool with what they called a lumber reef. We'd just put a single reef in her."[15]

Lumber was one of the *Arianna Bateman*'s regular cargoes and one of her most frequent ports of call to load lumber was Walkerton on the Mattaponi River. William Hooper remembered especially a very narrow, but deep, twelve-mile stretch of the York River where tall trees grew so close to the river's edge that the *Bateman*'s crew had to pull in the booms to prevent large tree branches from damaging the sails and rigging. The heavy stands of timber also restricted visibility and allowed only the slightest breeze to penetrate, which made it a slow and tedious run. This was before the advent of the powered yawl boat with its gas engine. When the wind died completely, two

The *Mildred* carrying a load of boxboarded timber is being pushed by her yawl boat. Built at Solomons Island in 1911, she was one of the later schooners and economy was the key to her construction. She was skeg-built, which meant her planking was not faired to her sternpost, making her very bargelike. (Van Name/Perry Collection)

for the canning factories, or store supplies for merchants in river towns near the lumbering operations. They would discharge their cargo and head for the timber area to take on lumber or cordwood for Baltimore. Some runs would take them to the head of the Bay on the way to Philadelphia via the C & D Canal.

Those schooners and rams that went below Norfolk for lumber generally passed through the Dismal Swamp Canal and the Chesapeake and Albemarle Canal to Albemarle and Pamlico sounds and then on to Elizabeth City, Belhaven, Morehead City, and New Bern, North Carolina. It was not usually worth the trip for the smaller schooners to go as far as North Carolina. They could expect to come out with no more than 80,000 board feet of lumber, whereas the much larger and more burdensome rams averaged 200,000 feet.

William Stevens and his father made several trips to North Carolina in the three years they sailed the ram *Edwin and Maud*. Generally, they carried soft coal or fertilizer down from Baltimore. They usually ran between North Carolina and Philadelphia, depending on the yawl boat almost all the way. They would burn over seven hundred gallons of gas on the monthlong trip.[17]

At the mill, the lumber was loaded by hand and carefully distributed. If it was dry, a third of it was placed in the hold and two-thirds on deck. A load of green lumber was split half and half and it was often so heavy that, instead of figuring the rate by board feet, the captain charged a flat rate for the load.

"We'd load the *Maud* with dry lumber until she'd tilt," said William Stevens. "When she'd tilt a little bit, we knew we could only put on another 4,000 or 5,000 feet. We'd pile it eight feet on deck and could hardly see over it standing on the quarterdeck. We had to shorten the sails and hoist the booms up high or else we couldn't carry the boom off the saddle.

"We didn't tie the lumber on. Most of it was lumber for houses, one by tens, one by twelves, one by sixes and eights. The way we loaded, the boards tied themselves on. Nothing could move. Never had to tie nothing down. With the light lumber, you couldn't load her high. She'd tilt. We filled up the hold first and then started on deck. When we got green lumber we loaded that to about an inch from water being on the deck.

men, each with a sixteen-foot oar, rowed the schooner, giving her just enough steerageway, or headway, to make her manageable by the helm and keep her from drifting into the trees. If they were lucky, they might catch a flood tide to help them on their way upriver.[16]

On their down-the-Bay passage to Virginia or the Carolinas for lumber, schooners might carry coal, fertilizer, empty cans

When we did that, we'd patch the hatches real good to keep the water from getting in."[18]

Woodrow Aaron of Cambridge remembered carrying lumber aboard the *Columbia F. C.*, whose captain used to load lumber so deep he had water on deck up around the cabin doors. "He used to nail the doors shut and go down through the top. If ever there was a boat loaded, he loaded it."[19]

And when a captain did load the lumber like that, especially high on deck, he would never attempt to go to windward, or the load would surely carry her over. Of course, with a load of lumber in the hold, she wasn't likely to sink.

The *Bohemia*

The 81-foot, main-topmast schooner *Bohemia* had a long life on the Bay and finished it in 1947 hauling lumber. The last two-master to carry lumber on the Bay, she was built in 1884 by Thomas H. Kirby of St. Michaels, Maryland, for J. H. Steele of Chesapeake City. John Chelton, who lived on the Bohemia River, served as her first captain. She started out freighting wheat and bore a carved sheaf of wheat as a stern decoration.[20]

Between 1915 and the mid-1920s, the *Bohemia* did a stint dredging oysters in the Potomac River and the Bay for Captain Edgar Riggin, who owned her then. When the Potomac was closed to dredging, she began freighting lumber to Baltimore from the Rappahannock, Piankatank, York, and James rivers. The *Bohemia* could carry 75,000 feet of dry lumber, for a rate when she began of $1.50 per 1,000 feet. She was capable of a five-day run from Baltimore to Smithfield on the James River and back. During World War II, she was still working under sail and getting as much as $7 per 1,000 feet on a run from the Mattaponi River to Baltimore.[21]

When Captain Riggin decided to retire, he sold the *Bohemia* to a New Englander, Ira Cheney, who had dreams of turning her into a "dude cruiser." He was never able to get together the money to make that dream come true, and she eventually sank at anchor in the Elizabeth River at Norfolk during the winter of 1950. She was raised with plans for her to be converted to power, but those came to nothing and in 1951 the *Bohemia* was abandoned on a mudflat in Sarah Creek off the York River east of Gloucester Point.

Aboard the *Mary Vickers*

Not all the lumber hauled by Bay schooners was for building. A fair amount of the timber went for fuel. Called cordwood in the trade, such rough timber was a regular cargo for schooners like the *Mary Vickers*. She was owned just after the turn of the century by a Baltimore cordwood firm located along the Union Dock which later became Pier 5 on Pratt Street.

The *Mary Vickers* was built in Oxford by William Perry Benson in 1881. By all reports, the *Vickers* was one of the fastest schooners on the Bay. Wrote H. Osborne Michael, who sailed on her in 1905: "She had a fairly sharp bow, a clean run aft and considerable deadrise. Her stern transom drooped slightly at the quarters" in the style of much earlier schooners. She had tall, raking masts and her main boom and bowsprit were exceptionally long. Her standing rigging was of tarred hemp.[23]

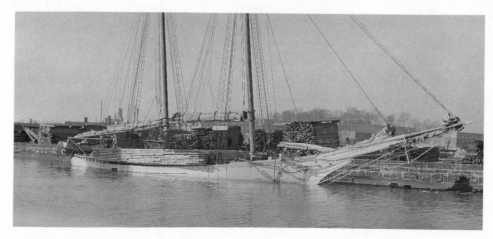

The *Columbia F. C.* is docked at Baltimore discharging a cargo of lumber. She is deeply loaded, with her scuppers at the water's surface at the main chainplates and shrouds, which meant that her decks undoubtedly were awash during the voyage. (Frank Moorshead, Jr., Mystic Seaport Museum, No. 91-10-122)

"She was well balanced and handled beautifully," wrote Michael. "When close hauled, her foresail and mainsail could be trimmed flat aft, 'block to block' and only two spokes of the wheel were necessary to keep her on her course."[24]

The *Vickers* was flush-decked with a low trunk cabin aft, "where the white members of the crew—captain, mate and deckhand—slept and ate. This was lighted by three rectangular, barred windows, while a small square opening alongside the companionway, gave the helmsman a limited view of the compass, lighted at night by a small kerosene lamp.

The *Gracie May* is seen here loading cordwood in the Piankatank River in 1911. Her cargo was bound for Baltimore and the William H. Michael Co. that owned her. She was renamed the *Ruth Conway* in 1923 when she was sold to Captain Harvey Conway of Cambridge. She was converted into a powerboat in 1929. (Peabody Museum of Salem, No. 27,021, H. Osborne Michael)

"The cabin interior was conventional," Michael continued. "There was a small stateroom on each side, the one to port, the mate's, being barely wide enough to turn around in. Each had a berth under the side deck, while under the afterdeck were two additional berths, with a seat locker before them, one almost blocked by the companion ladder. A small table was attached to the forward bulkhead.

"There were two cargo hatches, one between the foremast and the mainmast and the other between the mainmast and the cabin. The bilge pump was amidship just forward of the cabin, and on the forward deck was a 'scuttle' which gave access to the forepeak under the windlass, where any negroes in the crew slept.

"The galley (often called a caboose) was a mere box about five by six feet and six feet high which rested on the forward deck to port, between the fore shrouds and the foremast and was flanked by a water barrel. It had two sliding doors, one forward and one aft, and was fitted with a woodburning Shipmate stove, a shelf for cans of baking powder, salt, etc., and nails for cooking utensils.

"It also had a low bench extending along the side between the doors where the cook sat and worked over whatever was in his skillet. The cook also tended the jib when beating to windward."[25]

H. Osborne Michael sailed on the *Vickers* with Captain Ed Brewington of Salisbury. Captain Ed carried cordwood from the Wicomico River to Baltimore and returned with coal, fertilizer ingredients, tin cans, and store supplies for Wicomico ports. During the summer of 1905, Michael, who was fifteen or sixteen, shipped aboard the *Vickers* with Captain Ed; young Ed, the mate; two other teenage boys; an eight-year-old; and a six-foot black cook.

He remembered one voyage down the Bay in particular. The *Vickers* was three-quarters loaded with hard coal, which was about 110 tons, or three cars of coal. They had gotten a tow out of Baltimore harbor—for a fee of $2—and were turned loose by the tug just off Fort McHenry. The yachtlike schooner *Blackbird* was soon towed out to join them in the dead calm of the river and the two drifted slowly down the river with the tide.

The schooners were soon passed by a score of market boats, bugeyes, skipjacks, and a sloop. "We kids didn't like that at all and began whistling for wind," wrote Michael. "Before the market boats had gotten halfway to Fort Carroll, a distance of four miles, a southwest wind came across the water and filled our sails. The *Blackbird* straightened out on the course down the river and we followed. The wind freshened and caused us to heel a little and both schooners passed the market boats before they reached Fort Carroll."

The *Vickers* routinely outsailed just about everything going her way on the Bay until she was finally sold to a firm in Reedville, Virginia, and finished her days running brick from a brickyard on the Potomac to Washington, D.C. The schooner was eventually abandoned in a Potomac backwater.[26]

Long Boats

The cordwood business led to the development of a type of boat built just for the trade. Simply built and generally known as "wood boats" or "long-boats," these schooners were "of a style peculiar to the Chesapeake bay and the Potomac River," according to Henry Hall in his notes on "Ship Building in the United States," written in 1880 as part of his research for a U.S. government census report on the shipbuilding industry.[27]

As Hall described it, the long-boat was "an undecked centerboard schooner with two fore-and-aft sails and a large jib. They were shallow, flat on the floor, had round sides, straight bodies, and sharp bow with quarter decks and cabins aft, drew only 18 inches of water light and 3 feet loaded and will carry from 60 to 80 cords of wood each."[28]

Hall records one such boat that he saw at an Alexandria wharf as having a green 12-inch band along the waist with a brown stripe above and below it. Above the stripe was a 6-inch white band. Below the brown stripe, Hall said, the vessel was "white or a very light pink" or "flesh color" as it was known locally.

The long-boats were loaded with cordwood, "laid fore and aft on the frames until the hold is full and the gunwales are then

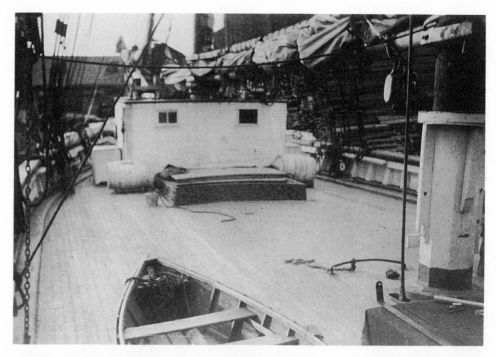

According to Captain Calvert Evans, the two-masted *Kate Darlington* was called affectionately by those who knew her "Katie-My-Darling." Built by H. Brusstar & Bros. at Baltimore in 1889, she was engaged in the pineapple trade early in her career. She was said to "always have had a distinguished air about her," according to Robert H. Burgess. This 1934 photo was taken at Pier 44N in Philadelphia. The *Darlington* was large enough to carry a forward deckhouse which is seen here. Note also the water barrels flanking the forward hatch and the rod for raising and lowering the centerboard just in front of the mainmast. (Philadelphia Maritime Museum, Edward Brownlee)

piled up with sticks laid transversely. The space within is then filled up with sticks, laid athwartships as high as convenient." He noted also that these boats were "fit only for river use, being too clumsy for rough water."[29]

In the Fruit Trade

In the latter half of the nineteenth century, the trade in pineapples between Baltimore and the West Indies flourished, reaching a peak in the 1890s. At that time, Baltimore was the principal center for importing, packing, and distributing pineapples in the United States. Most of the fruit came from Eleuthera, Gregorytown, Tarpon Bay, and Egg Harbor in the Bahamas to

The pungy *Francis J. Ruth*, built in 1871 in Dorchester County, Maryland, is shown here carrying a deckload of railroad ties. She's sailing "wing-and-wing" or "reading both pages." At 60 tons, the *Ruth* was one of the larger pungies and was used in the pineapple trade between the Bahamas and Baltimore. The pungies were fast and more weatherly than centerboard schooners, but they were wet sailers. Also due to the degree of deadrise of their hulls, they had deep holds. As a result, they were less desirable than the flat-floored centerboarders for carrying pineapples because the fruit could not be spread out and was too apt to rot in the hold before it reached Baltimore. (Peabody Museum of Salem, No. 27,019, C. L. Johnson)

Bowley's Wharf on Pratt Street, which is now Pier 1.[30] Among the dozens of fruit packing companies in Baltimore, that of the Thomas B. Schall Co. was the largest.[31]

April marked the beginning of the four-month pineapple season when the fleet of Chesapeake Bay schooners and a few pungies set out on the first of three 1,200-mile trips to the West Indies. Among the two-masted schooners that were used in the pineapple trade were the *William H. Van Name, David Carll, Bill Nye, Kate Darlington, Eva S. Cullison, Flora Kirwan, J. Edwin Kirwan, Kate McNamara, Levi B. Phillips, Emily E. Johnson, Lillie, Rover, Laurena Clayton, Edward L. Martin, Maggie A. Phillips, Richard Cromwell, Clemmie Travers,* and the *William Layton.* The pungies *Ruth A. Price* and the *Francis J. Ruth* were also a part of the fleet, as was the three-masted *Venus,* later renamed the *Edna Bright Hough.* Schooners were preferred for carrying the fruit because they could handle the shallow harbors of the islands far better than steamers and their holds were far cooler for the delicate cargo than were those of steam vessels.[32]

The pineapple schooners ranged from 60 to 200 gross tons and a vessel of 130 tons could earn roughly $1,200 a trip. Records show that in May of 1905, the *Flora Kirwan* arrived in Baltimore with 3,000 dozen pineapples for the Kirwan-Schall Fruit Company. Often, because Bay captains had little experience offshore, they carried a navigator to get them safely from the Virginia capes to the Bahamas.[33] Going down, the schooners carried grain, lumber, wood products, tar, turpentine, naval stores, meat, produce, other foodstuffs, and general merchandise upon which the islands depended heavily.

A round trip took roughly thirty days, with the return taking a greater length of time. As a result, the fruit was picked while it was still green, so that it could ripen on the trip north. If a schooner was delayed, it often meant that the fruit spoiled and the whole cargo had to be dumped.

One of the two-masters that was best known in the pineapple trade was the *Flora Kirwan*, which was built in Baltimore in 1892 for Captain Charles Kirwan of the Kirwan-Schall Fruit Company. It was many years before the Bahamians would accept paper currency or checks and the *Flora*, like others in the trade, had a safe in the captain's quarters where gold was carried to pay for the fruit. The *Flora* was known for her speed, especially with Captain Sam Creighton at the helm.[34]

The dawn of the twentieth century saw the annexation of Hawaii with its growing pineapple industry. That, along with the diminishing productivity of Bahamian soil, caused a radical decline in the pineapple business on the East Coast of the United States. By 1909, it had dropped off considerably. Also, by then, canning factories were beginning to operate in Cuba, Jamaica, and Puerto Rico where harbors could accommodate larger vessels.[35] By 1910, only two schooners were scheduled to sail to the Bahamas, the *J. Edwin Kirwan* and the *Clemmie Travers*. In 1913, the last year, the *Kirwan* was alone in the trade. In 1966, two of the fruit schooners, the *Flora Kirwan* and the *William Layton*, renamed the *Carol Ann*, were still working the Bay hauling freight, but as power-boats, not under sail.[36] The *Carol Ann* sank off Puerto Rico in 1973. The *Flora Kirwan* lasted until 1983 as a clam dredge operating out of Ocean City, Maryland.

Cans and Tomatoes

Baltimore had grown dramatically as a port in the first half of the nineteenth century. Among other things, it was this country's first canning center and processed everything from oysters to fruits and vegetables. The city's first cannery, established in 1826, packed oysters and peaches. Canning eventually became a major Bay industry. Tomatoes began to be processed in 1850 and by 1892, Maryland was the leading tomato canning state in the nation. Most of the factories were located on Maryland's Eastern Shore, but Delaware, the western shore of the Bay, and Virginia also had a number of canneries. At the outset of World War I, there were over four hundred vegetable canneries in Maryland alone, and most of those were in Dorchester County.[37]

During the first quarter of the century, cans continued to be manufactured in Baltimore. Schooners ran empty cans down the Bay to such river ports as Kinsale or Nomini on the Potomac and then returned to Baltimore with a load of canned goods. The

Built as the *A. H. Schulz* in 1872, the *Sarah C. Conway* was a pineapple trader in her early years. She was renamed by Captain Harvey Conway for his wife. He owned a small fleet of Bay freight schooners, but sailed the *Sarah* himself. (C. Calvert Evans Collection, John Frye)

Columbia F. C. and *Thomas B. Schall*, were two of the schooners that made that particular run to the tomato canning houses on the Potomac.[38]

Baltimore merchant Preston Webster had a canning business with a retail wharf on Foster Street. Among the schooners in his fleet were the *William Booth*, *Flora Kirwan*, *Minnie Mae Kirwan*, and the *Silas Webster*.[39]

"I carried tomatoes on the *Sarah C. Conway* to Langnall's Cannery," recalled Calvert Evans, who ran out of Onancock and Cape Charles on Virginia's Eastern Shore for three years after the *Sarah* was converted to power. "The tomato season lasted three weeks to a month, but it paid good. Ten cents a basket at that time and the *Sarah* could carry 5,500 baskets. You couldn't put them in the hold. You had to carry them on deck. One time, they were glutted. I was the only one there and the wharf was full of tomatoes. Said they might as well rot in the hold as at the dock, so they said fill that hold and carry every one you can. So I had the hold full and had the deck loaded 'til they went right up to the windows of the

Woodrow Aaron, who sailed as mate on the *William T. Parker*, a three-master, remembered the state hospital in Cambridge as a frequent stop. It was a heavy user, with railroad tracks and cars to carry coal up from the wharf.[41]

A number of schooners also ran coal to the many canneries and fish factories up and down the Bay, when they weren't running in with empty cans and out with full ones. As back freight on runs from Baltimore, coal paid expenses. Usually.

"I was leaving Baltimore in the *Mildred*," Calvert Evans recalled, "when Bob Walthan, who did a commission business with smaller boats, called me and said he had some coal going to the Cambridge Gas Company. I assumed he was talking about a full load and the *Mildred* could carry 140 tons. So I went to the coal pier and it turned out to be just 75 tons. At a dollar a ton, that didn't even make expenses. After I'd taken the boat's part out, and the captain's part to pay for crew and groceries and what have you, I made $35 on that trip."[42]

A Lively Run on the *Bateman*

Carrying coal was like any other freight in one respect, you were at the mercy of whatever wind and weather the Chesapeake dealt you.

William Hooper made several trips aboard the *Arianna Bateman* with soft coal from Baltimore and Norfolk to a fish factory on Carter Creek and other points on the Rappahannock River.[43] On one trip in particular, the *Bateman* was loaded with 147 tons of coal from Norfolk bound for the Carter Creek factory. Half the load was on deck so that it could be unloaded faster once they got to their destination. The schooner wasn't dangerously overloaded, but the weight had put the scuppers—the openings in the bulwarks to carry water off the deck—close to water level. They had just begun the fifty-mile journey when a thunder squall ran them into Portsmouth. There, they ran down all the sails and let go both anchors.[44]

wheelhouse. Kept salt and pepper shakers right on the shelf in the wheelhouse and all we'd have to do was reach out the window and take one."[40]

Coal Carriers

Havre de Grace, and later piers in Baltimore and Hampton Roads, supplied coal to Bay ports and beyond. It was carried mainly by two-masted coal schooners to towns on Maryland's Eastern Shore and many ports along western shore rivers in Maryland and Virginia.

"It was hard work getting the sails back on the vessel and tugging the anchors aboard, but we were all sturdy men and soon we were on our way again," wrote Hooper, who was mate. "By this time, the wind had struck up to the southward, as it sometimes does after a squall has passed. Avalon said, 'Boys, we'll have a lively run up tonight.' He had us set the topsail over the single reef mainsail and put the flying jib on her. This made the vessel steer smoothly.[45]

"We continued outside Hampton Roads and out into the open Bay. The wind hauled around a bit to the southwest. It was a beautiful night, with the full moon riding high and casting a greenish hue on the wind-churned water. There were no other voyagers in sight.

"The wind kept picking up; a real humdinger of a southwester. It was a rough ride. In fact, it appeared several times that night that the vessel would founder. Waves rolled over the deck that must have removed as much as a ton of that coal at one time. It would be safe to say that at least twenty-five tons of that coal were casualties of the sea. We ploughed on through wind and wave and drove her into Carter Creek just after midnight. The next morning, we noted that her scuppers were well above the water and she was bend free—that is, the rib that rimmed the deck and contained the scuppers was riding above the water."[46]

On the trip home, they cleaned out the hold. The soft coal had gotten wet and created a mess. They kept the pumps going to keep the bilge pumped out while the cleanup crew had the plug out of the centerwell. As a reward, the cook fried up a bucket of fresh trout and bluefish they'd gotten from a fish steamer docked at Carter Creek.[47]

Coal was dirty and was not a popular freight. But, then, there came a time when the captain of a small schooner had to take whatever he could get. Some, at times, even had to stoop so low as to run manure, fish scrap, and tobacco stems, which were about the worst cargoes.

William Stevens remembered that he and his father carried fish scrap in the *Ruth Decker.* "We carried it just once," he said. "That was enough. Another cargo that was an awful load was tobacco stems. We hauled them from a cigarette company in Richmond to a fertilizer factory on the Pocomoke. They were bulky and real light and we loaded them seven or eight feet high on deck and then had to cover them to keep them from getting wet."[48]

As for coal, the trade extended well beyond the Bay, supplying industries in the north. For a time, the two-masters carried the coal for New England's factories, but the demand rapidly increased to the point where larger vessels were needed. The two-masters were supplanted going coastwise by three-, four-, and five-masted colliers, loading out of Newport News, Norfolk, and Baltimore.[49]

Whether it was tomatoes, lumber, or coal, running a freight schooner on the Bay was sometimes dirty, sometimes dangerous, always hard work. But for those fathers and sons who "followed the water" for two hundred years and more, the schooners and the hard work were a way of life.

Ten

Hard Drivers

For men to survive working the Bay in schooners, they had to be good sailors. "Hard drivers" was what they were called in their day. A successful run up or down the Bay depended on three things. One was the condition of the vessel. If a schooner was old and hogged and leaking, a voyage could take a long time, too long to keep her working and paying her way. The weather was the second thing, and last but not the least was the captain and the kind of sailor he was.

Vandalia Perry, who was president of the People's National Bank in Salisbury, owned the schooner *North Carolina* for a number of years in the early 1900s. She traded mostly off the York River where Mr. Perry was a partner in the lumber firm of Perry and Bradley in King and Queen County, Virginia. The *North Carolina* was built in 1856 in Dorchester County. She was 88 feet long, had a beam of 22 feet, and drew 6.8 feet. She could carry 110,000 feet of lumber. While Vandalia Perry owned her, she carried lumber and coal between Virginia and Pennsylvania. For much of the time that Perry owned the *North Carolina*, she was sailed by Captain William C. Johnson, who was known to be a hard driver.[1]

Lynn Perry, who grew up in West Point and eventually retired to Urbanna, Virginia, heard many a story of Captain Johnson and the *North Carolina*. "The way my father'd tell it," said Perry, "my grandfather would be in Baltimore and sometimes, instead of sailing back to West Point on the *North*

These two unidentified schooners are on opposite tacks in the Patapsco River in 1921. (The Peale Museum, Baltimore City Life Museums, No. MC 9048)

Carolina, he would take the steamer from Baltimore. Now it was the height of Captain Johnson's ambition to beat that steamer into West Point and meet my grandfather on the docks and, sure enough, he did it, not once, but several times."[2]

Not every skipper was determined to set records. Lynn Perry recalls a story he heard about one captain of the *Ivy Blades*, a ram built for the Blades Lumber Co., of New Bern, North Carolina. She had a regular run with lumber from New Bern to Elizabeth City, and the ram's owners didn't want any dawdling along the way. They kept the anchors on the *Blades* freshly painted so that they could tell when she got back if she'd been anchored on the trip. Her captain got around that easily enough by running into shallow water and dropping the centerboard which held the schooner as well as the anchors.[3]

Making good time had to do with the captain, the boat and the wind and weather, and sometimes everything would come together just right. William Seaford Stevens worked with his father Captain Ira Stevens aboard several schooners running grain and produce from Kent Island to Baltimore and lumber and other freight between Baltimore and Virginia or the Carolinas. During World War II, they were sailing the *Ruth Decker* for C. C. Paul of Baltimore.

"I remember one time in particular," said Stevens. "We left Baltimore with the *Ruth Decker* to get a load of lumber in Virginia. It took us seven days. Going down, we struck everything just right. We went down at night with a northwest wind going as fast as a Norfolk steamer. Night was always the best time for sailing. We never laid up just because night come on. All we had to worry about was the ships coming up the Bay. We carried a five-cell flashlight to shine on our sails when one of them got too close. At any rate, that time, when we got back to Baltimore and Pa went into the office, C. C. Paul said, 'Captain, when are you going to leave?' "[4]

Conditions were not always as fortuitous. As Captain Harry Porter said, "There were some days when the water would just roll over one end of the boat and out the other for hours at a time and you'd wonder if you were going to make it. Like one old fella said, 'You can run more water out of the seat of your pants than most people will see in a lifetime.' "[5]

The 74-foot schooner *Caradora*, which was built in St. Michaels in 1881 by Kirby and Lang, was captured by Frank Moorshead, Jr., from the deck of the she-pungy *Kessie C. Price.* This view shows her from broad on the port bow. Note the single reef in her main, the full fore and her standing jib. (Frank Moorshead, Jr., Mystic Seaport Museum, No. 91-10-129)

It helped to have a sense of humor. Marshall Pritchard, master of several Bay schooners, was known as a crack sailor. "That man could sail," said Lynn Perry. "One time, he went up the Bay in twenty-four hours and someone asked him how he'd done it.

" 'Well,' he says, 'I didn't have but halfway to go.'

" 'What do you mean halfway? You sailed from York Spit all the way to Baltimore.'

" 'Yea, but she leaked so bad I pumped half of the water out, so I only had half the way to go.' "[6]

Shipwright Jim Richardson likes to tell the story of the skipper of the *Flora Kirwan* when she was sailing out of Cambridge in the pineapple trade. Besides the skipper, there was a "colored man" named George who stayed with the schooner until her last trip to the Bahamas.

"They had left the Bahamas and were up in the Bermuda Triangle," said Richardson. "It was calm and hot and not a

This view was taken from the bowsprit of the *Columbia F. C.* and shows her deck layout. Her jib is furled, but her standing jib is set, as are the fore and main. Note her running light in the foreshrouds and the guards encasing her windlass chains. (Van Name/Perry Collection)

ripple of wind on the water and there she lay until by and by fish and all kinds of things began to break on the water.

"The skipper said to George, 'Get out your oil bag and the sea anchor and rig it up.'

"'Cap'n, it's too hot,' said George.

"'Don't you worry,' said the captain. 'It ain't going to be hot too long. Those fish flying all over means there's a change coming.'

"George got out the storm trysail and set it up between the two masts. The trysail was like a jib and the schooner would balance under it and sail under it too. They got the other sails down and battened down the hatches and got everything squared away.

"They didn't have long to wait and George, he never questioned the Captain again. The first puff that hit, blew the trysail right out of the bolt ropes. George let the oil bag go and the sea anchor and the skipper kept her head into the storm through the whole thing. If he hadn't, he would have gone all the way with it to Spain most likely."[7]

Sometimes, the weather was more than patience could bear and Captain Sam Brannock who owned the *Flora Kirwan* and sailed out of Cambridge was not long on patience. Earl Brannock, Captain Sam's son and founder of the Brannock Maritime Museum in Cambridge, remembers hearing of the time his father and the *Flora* were holed up in the Patuxent with several other schooners. The wind had been blowing a gale for three or four days and the schooners were waiting for it to let up so they could go on down the Bay. "My father had made three or four passes down into the cabin to look at the glass," said Brannock, "and finally he reached over on the bulkhead, grabbed the barometer, threw it overboard and said, 'Let's get this thing underway.' He went on down to North Carolina, came back with a load of lumber and those other schooners were still anchored in the river. The mate he had then left him after that. Scared the hell out of him."[8]

The *Chesterfield*, built in Talbot County, Maryland, in 1878, is shown here sailing into Urbanna Creek. This is a good illustration of the tight quarters in which these vessels had to sail in order to make their way. She is close hauled with her yawl boat aiding in her progress. The *Chesterfield* was sold off the Bay to become a "dude cruiser" and by the mid-1950s was abandoned in New York Harbor behind Staten Island. (Van Name/Perry Collection)

With some of the old schooner captains, you didn't make idle challenges. Samuel T. Hooper, father of William T. Hooper, sailed aboard the *Arianna Bateman* early in her career. She was owned originally by Captain John H. Simmons, and Captain Johnny ran her for one season before going ashore to open a general store at Hoopersville. Henry Meekins took over as captain and Samuel T. Hooper went aboard as mate.[9]

Captain Henry drove the *Bateman* hard in all kinds of weather, Hooper recalled, and one stormy night in particular stood out in his memory. The *Bateman* left Baltimore in company with the Dorchester County–built pungy *Southern Beauty*, which was headed to the Bahamas to load pineapples. The pungy was supposed to be the fastest boat on the Bay, but Captain Henry kept the *Bateman* with her as they tacked from one side of the Bay to the other in a strong head wind. When they reached the mouth of the Patuxent River, the *Southern Beauty* anchored.

"Looks like she found the going too rough," Sam Hooper observed as Captain Henry kept on going.

"Captain Johnny told me not to let any barnacles grow on her anchors," said Henry Meekins, and then added, "He said I couldn't make her leak. We'll see."

The wind was picking up as Meekins drove down the Bay. The boat was continually dipping her leeward waist under. Eventually, Captain Henry ordered the crew to lower the flying jib, but it was too dangerous for any of the crew to climb out to tie it up. The sail lay cradled on the guy ropes (rope hammocks suspended from below the bowsprit to catch the lowered sail—and crewmen if need be) and was carried into the water repeatedly as the schooner rolled and pitched. The only solution Captain Henry could see was to raise the sail again.

"It was a rough and rather frightening ride," said Sam Hooper, "but it was a fast one."

They arrived at Hickory Cove shortly after midnight. The next morning, Hooper discovered eight inches of water in the *Bateman*'s hold. The severe pounding of the night before had forced the water inside. Remembering Captain Henry's comment, he woke him and led the way to the hold. "Damned if we didn't make her sweat a little bit," was the captain's only comment.[10]

There Were Some Smart Skippers

A skipper could be a hard driver, but his success depended equally on his being a good helmsman and navigator. The bridge at West Point on the Mattaponi in Virginia was a special challenge. Lynn Perry was on the shore one day when Captain Robert Banks sailed the *Ruth Decker* through the draw.

"The bridge wasn't exactly true with the channel," said Perry, "and that day, Captain Banks had a northeaster and all her sails on her, but no yawl boat down. He blew for the bridge and the bridge tender got it up just in time. He got her right in that draw and held her until she got through. She was in irons, but he had enough headway on her that he got her through the draw and then he rolled that wheel down and she picked up the wind and went right on. That was one beautiful piece of sailing."[11]

The *Mildred* was built at Solomons Island in 1911. She was slow and not very weatherly, according to Calvert Evans who captained her for a time, but she was a good carrier and had a shallow draft which kept her working. The *Mildred* was converted to power in 1943 and worked the Bay until 1972. (Frank Moorshead, Jr., Mystic Seaport Museum, No. 91-10-149)

The 69-foot *Ella F. Cripps* was built in 1900 at St. Michaels by Kirby & Son. Here she is being towed by her yawl boat. In the late 1940s, the *Cripps* was converted to a powerboat and taken north to Long Island Sound. In the late 1950s, Robert Burgess notes that she was brought back to the Bay to be refitted with sail for use as a dude cruiser, but the loss of the ram *Levin J. Marvel* caused those plans to be canceled. She was eventually abandoned alongside the *Mattie Dean* in Back Creek outside Annapolis, Maryland. (Chesapeake Bay Maritime Museum, No. 475-6)

Old-timers on the Bay will tell you that a good schooner captain was the one who'd been aground on every spit and sandbar in the Bay. He had the feel of every shoal and when schoonermen gathered around a galley stove to talk away a winter's evening, the Pocomoke Muds or the shoal waters of Piscataway Creek or the Elk or Chester rivers were the subject of many a tale they'd tell on each other. There were some smart skippers in those days. They knew their boats and knew the Bay. No question of that. And they went up and down the Bay with only a pocket watch, a compass, and a lead line. No Loran. No radar. No ship-to-shore radio.

George W. Rappleyea wrote in *Motor Boating*, March 1945: "I once met an old darky skipper who for 50 years made from two to three trips a year between the West Indies and Baltimore . . . When he left home, he steered a northerly course hitting the North American continent somewhere between Frying Pan Shoals and Diamond Shoals, following the coastline to Cape Henry and thence up the Bay to Baltimore . . . 'Going home,' he told Rappleyea, 'I go down the Bay to Cape Henry, follow the coastline to Diamond Shoals and then I set a due south course by the compass and keep her on that due south course until the pole star is one handspike above the taffrail [A handspike is 9 inches, the taffrail 3, which equals 24 degrees of latitude at arm's length.]; then I turn west and pretty soon I pick up one of the islands. Boss, when I pick up one of them islands, I knows where I is.'"[12]

Generally on the Bay, if you knew your time and course, then all you would have to do was estimate your speed and you would have a pretty good idea of your location. If you were running at night, you couldn't tell how fast you were going, so you used the lead line. The lead, which weighed between seven and fourteen pounds, was attached to a line marked with strips of leather for two and three fathoms, a white rag for five fathoms, red for seven and two knots for twenty. You would throw it from the schooner's bow and then haul it in as the vessel moved ahead. When the line was taut and vertical, you would take the reading. It was said that all one of those old captains had to do was feel or taste the mud he brought up on his lead line and he knew where he was.[13]

Later sailors had increasingly sophisticated charts and navigational aids, as well as lighthouses and buoys, but for years, watermen depended on what they had learned from each other or from their own experience. "You had to know the landmarks, when you were going into one of these little creeks or narrow channels," said Calvert Evans. "If you were telling someone, you'd say, 'You see that white house up there? You keep it over that big pine tree on this reach . . . ' You kept it all in your head."[14]

Many of the older captains, even those who ran the four-masters and went coastwise, could barely read or write. Most started out in their early teens and had little or no schooling before that. They knew just enough to get by. It was not uncommon on the larger vessels for a captain to dictate entries for his log to his cabin boy, some of whom were not above editorializing. Wrote one cabin boy following the captain's dictated entry, "I don't believe the old son-of-a-bitch knows where he's at."[15]

You Had to Have a Shallow-draft Boat

From the time of their ancestors—and most of the watermen come from families that go back two, three hundred years on the Bay—the harbors and the river channels were getting clogged with silt. Development and deforestation caused the shores of the Bay to erode so fast that whole islands and peninsulas disappeared in a man's lifetime. In some places, shores eroded as much as twelve feet a year. But Bay watermen were used to the changeable character of the Chesapeake. As long as there was enough water anywhere to float a boat on, they went on sailing into shallow creeks and rivers to where cargoes of grain, tomatoes, or melons waited.

"A man that had a flat-bottom schooner, he always had a job," said Calvert Evans. "Had to have a shallow draft to go in

The *Columbia F. C.*'s yawl boat in her davits is clear in this photo, as is the aft side of the cabin trunk. The powered yawl boat played an important part in maintaining the economic viability of the schooner well into the twentieth century. (Frank Moorshead, Jr., Mystic Seaport Museum, No. 91-10-122)

these shallow water creeks. The average schooner of 100- or 150-ton capacity had a light draft of about five or six foot. My father's boat, the *Fannie Insley* was six foot and she was about average."[16]

Before he owned his own boats, Calvert Evans was captain of the *Mildred*. Built in 1911 at Solomons Island, she was 82 feet long with a 22-foot beam and drew 5 feet 6 inches. According to Evans, she was flat-bottomed, straight-sided, and "the meanest boat I think ever was built. She was like a sharp-bowed barge," said Evans. "You couldn't steer the *Mildred* loaded no way in the world. I had to put a skeg on her to keep her stern from

The *Kate H. Tilghman* and *Charles G. Joyce* are shown drying their sails in Hoskins Creek, at Tappahannock, Virginia, about 1940. It was important not to allow cotton canvas sails to remain wet. In a very short time, they could mildew and rot. It was common at the time to see vessels tied up alongside with their sails set to dry, but uncommon to see in photographs. (Van Name/Perry Collection)

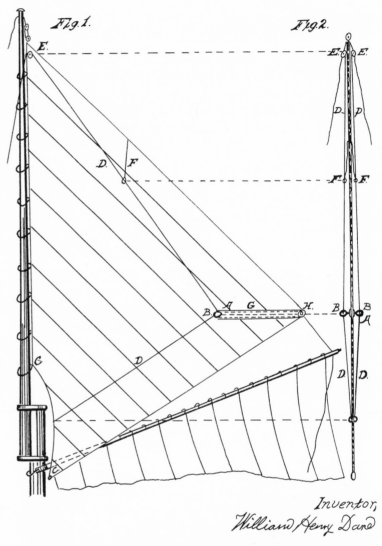

swinging around. She had a barn-door rudder on her and it wouldn't take hold. You'd look back there and it was just like a pot aboiling, but nothing happening. They called that dead water when a rudder wouldn't take hold in it. The *Sarah Conway* had a sharp stern and she'd cut right through the water and you'd turn the rudder just a bit and it would take hold with all that clean water running by, but the shape of the *Mildred*'s stern was so blunt that she'd just pull the water behind her creating all that turbulence and the rudder wouldn't take hold."[17]

The *Mildred* was owned by L. A. Clark who was in the railroad tie business and ran ties from Tappahannock to Portsmouth until the railroads lost out to the trucks. Then Clark had no more use for the *Mildred*. She was sold, converted to diesel, and eventually was abandoned in 1972. "She carried a good load for her dimensions," said Evans. "A lot of bigger boats couldn't get into places she could to get cargoes like lumber and grain. You had to have a shallow-draft boat to get over the Pocomoke Muds and places like that."[18]

In 1877, William Henry Dare invented a "New and useful improvement in the mode of clewing up gaff-topsails." This method of hauling up or furling a gaff-topsail had the advantage not only "as a great saving of labor, but as a means of averting danger to life and property, by a quick and sure method" of handling the sail from the deck. This was done in such a way as to spill the air from the sail, increasing the ease with which the sail was taken in. (Boston Public Library)

Yawl Boats

Up until the advent of the gas engine, long oars or sweeps were used to maneuver a schooner when wind or other conditions prevented the use of sails. Roy Brewington, who started out aboard his father's schooner at the age of seventeen, recalled the days when getting up and down the Bay's rivers depended upon the tides and oars. There would be one deckhand in a boat out front rowing and pulling while other hands wielded twenty-foot oars from the deck. Even then, they counted on a lot of help from the tide.[19]

Later, the sturdily built yawl boat with its gas engine provided a much better means of propulsion. Most yawl boats carried by two-masted schooners were about eighteen feet long. Those for the larger rams, other three-masters, and four-masted schooners were as much as twenty-six feet long. Typically, a gasoline engine provided the power the small boat required to push a schooner along. When not in use, the yawl boat was carried on stern davits. Yawl boats and their engines were limited in size. Too heavy and the boat couldn't be hoisted back up onto the davits when it wasn't being used to push.

That was critical when there was a small crew, as with William Stevens and his father who regularly sailed the ram *Edwin and Maud* by themselves to North Carolina. "We could sail in the Albemarle Sound," Stevens said, "but the rest of the trip to North Carolina we used the yawl boat all the time. It was just me and Pa. When we'd put the yawl boat on deck, he'd be up there at the wheel and I'd go to one side and pull the boat up a bit and then go to the other side and get that end up, and so on until it was up.

"We carried 750 gallons of gas and we hauled it over the stern to the yawl boat, 20 gallons at a time. That was all right when the *Maud* was loaded, because you didn't have to step far, but when she was light we'd have to get a ladder."[20]

The patent topsail of the *Ida May* is visible in this view of the schooner alongside the Annapolis city dock. The chain hanging below the dolphin striker was used by the yawl boat to tow her. She was built in Urbanna, Virginia, in 1898 from the hull of the *Jacob S. Barnes,* which was built in Baltimore in 1870. The *Ida May* left the Bay in 1946 to go north as a dude cruiser and was abandoned in 1955 in Maine. (Frank Moorshead, Jr., Mystic Seaport Museum, No. 91-10-112)

This shot shows the *Columbia F. C.*'s trunk cabin and wheel very well. Note the small "slide" to the starboard of the companionway, behind which is her compass box, protected but handy to the person at the wheel. Also shown is the wheelbox, the turn stanchions, and a bilge pump and portable bench on the housetop. The turnbuckles indicate a later period in her life. (Van Name/Perry Collection)

The yawl boats on rams were usually powered by a Lathrop, which could be started on gas and then pushed over to fuel oil. Most of the smaller boats had Hubbard or three-cylinder Palmer engines.

"The yawl boat on the *Sarah Conway* had a 1937 Master 6 Buick engine in it when I got her," said Calvert Evans. "That thing would really push her. Loaded it wouldn't get over 4, 4½ knots, but she'd push that schooner light, 6 knots."[21]

You Had to Have Good Sails

Harnessing the power of the wind was what schooners were all about and a good set of sails was a matter of great importance. Most of the Chesapeake Bay schooners worked with a mainsail, foresail, one or two headsails, and a main topsail. Very few two-masters carried a fore-topmast. Under most conditions, a fore-topsail was too much extra sail. It also was just too much work because to tack, the sail had to be lowered to get it over the spring stay.

The first sailmaker on the Bay, as far as anyone knows, was brought to Maryland from Ireland as an indentured servant in 1736. By 1776, there were four in Norfolk. The flourishing port and shipbuilding center of Baltimore had 119 in 1850, but that number began to diminish rapidly as the nineteenth century came to an end.[22]

In 1904, sailmaker William L. Godfrey arrived in Baltimore where there were nine sailmaking businesses employing about forty sailmakers. He eventually set up his own loft on Pratt Street. In the beginning, Godfrey had as many as five assistants, but eventually, he was down to himself, his wife, and one other old-timer. In 1952, he closed his loft, the last of its kind in Baltimore.[23]

Typically, a sail loft provided a long, open space in which the largest schooner sail could be spread out. A sail for a schooner was made of heavy canvas, which replaced flax. Twenty-two inches wide, the canvas came on bolts of one hundred yards or more. Until heavy-duty sewing machines came into use, sails were hand-sewn. The sailmaker used thread waxed with beeswax and shoved the needle through the canvas with a lead pad embedded in a rawhide palm. These tools were very much the same, if not the exact tools used by past generations of sailmakers.

The sewing machine was one of the principal advances in the craft coming into general use in the 1850s. In terms of the product, a number of innovations appeared. Among the more notable laborsaving devices that showed up from time to time was a patent topsail that could be furled and unfurled on the topmast. It appeared on very few boats in New England, but was fairly widely used on the Bay, especially on the multimasted schooners.[24]

Boston Street in Baltimore was where a number of sailmakers had their lofts. Calvert Evans and his father could row in from where they anchored the *Fannie Insley* in Canton Hollow and walk from there. "My father tried quite a few around to see who made the best sails at the best price," said Evans. "When I was a kid, I used to like to go up in a sail loft. It had a smell of its own: beeswax, rope, and canvas."

Tagging along with his father, Evans learned some of the things to look for in a sailmaker. "There was one on Boston Street," he recalled. "You always could tell one of his sails because it didn't have enough peak. It wasn't a pretty sail at all. My father wouldn't use him. Don't care how you talked to him, he just wouldn't give that sail no peak. Marshall & Godfrey made most of mine. They were on the same street as Vane Brothers, which was our favorite ship chandlers store in Baltimore."[25]

Boy, She Could Pull

In the early days of sail, when crews were easier to come by, sails were raised by hand and so was the anchor. When steamboats came along offering better pay and more regular work, it got to be harder and harder to find crews for the schooners. The advent of the gasoline-powered deck engine had a lot to do with keeping many a schooner working after the turn of the century when fewer and fewer experienced men would ship aboard a schooner. A good Palmer, Hettinger, or Fairbanks engine could take the place of an extra hand or two.

"When the gas engine came into use, they'd put a six- or seven-horsepower deck engine in the starboard side of the forward house and the galley in the port side," said Lynn Perry. "If there was no forward house, the engine was usually under a protective wooden cover of some kind. They also had a smaller

This shot, taken from the foredeck of the *Columbia F. C.,* shows her donkey engine, hoisting machinery, and anchor windlass, as well as her standing jib club, the forecastle skylight, and the forecastle scuttle just aft of the foremast. The deadeyes and lanyards on her standing rigging indicate that this is an early photograph. Later photos of this vessel show that the deadeyes and lanyards have been replaced by turnbuckles. (Frank Moorshead, Jr., Mystic Seaport Museum, No. 91-10-121)

pump engine just forward of the main cabin. The seven-horsepower engine was used for hauling in the anchor and raising the sails and the smaller one was for running the pumps."[26]

William Stevens, who sailed on several Bay schooners with his father, remembered the Bulldog engine they had on the *Edwin and Maud.* "Boy, she could pull," he said. "She could pull anything on that deck apart. There was a shaft went from the engine through the galley to a big spool you'd wrap your rope around to bring your yawl boat up or your sails, or whatever you wanted to carry up."[27]

He and his father depended heavily on the deck engine for they almost always sailed the three-masted *Maud* alone. "When we'd get ready to get underway," Stevens said, "we'd lay into the anchor and using the engine, we'd both hoist the sails. Then when we got ready to get the anchor up, he'd be back at the wheel waiting to take off. When I got the anchor up, I'd hoist the jib and she'd be off on her own."[28]

Always Busy Underway

You were always busy underway. On the Bay, there was never any great constancy of weather and the sails always needed attention. A schooner's crew was regularly trimming the sheets as wind and weather changed. In between times, while one man steered, the others rested, or did the cooking or other chores. If the wind died, there was the yawl boat to be lowered to push the schooner along.

The gas engine was a great boon to those who worked the Bay under sail. Besides taking over the backbreaking jobs of hauling up anchors and hoisting sails, engines were an absolute necessity for pumping out the bilges. Even the best kept of the boats leaked and every schooner carried a gas engine to run one or two pumps. Soundings were taken daily to determine how much water was in the bilge. The pumps were usually run in the morning and again at night.

According to Captain Clarence Heath, who sailed as a teenager under William C. Johnson aboard the *North Carolina*, the schooner was generally a good sailer, but she leaked badly. Her planking was so thin that it would not hold caulking, which meant the pumps were running morning and night.[29]

As a boy, Lynn Perry of Urbanna, Virginia, learned first-hand about life aboard a Chesapeake Bay schooner. He grew up in West Point where for fifty years, his father, Frank A. Perry, operated the Texas Oil Company's bulk plant and pier at the foot of 7th Street. While Lynn Perry was still in grammar school, his father bought him a thirteen-foot skiff and the boy spent most of his free time in the skiff with his friend Arthur Van Name, Jr., rowing out into the Mattaponi River at West Point to photograph the schooners lying at anchor there. With their box cameras, the two boys documented a significant portion of the fleet of schooners under sail on the Bay in the 1920s. The Van Name and Perry collection of photographs recorded the final days of many Bay schooners although the young men did not know that was what they were doing at the time.[30]

If he knew a schooner captain, Lynn Perry went aboard to visit. One spring day in 1929, he tied up his skiff alongside the 96-foot, 154-ton schooner *Florence A.*, which had anchored at West Point with a load of lumber. He was aboard when her captain, Will Marsh, decided to get underway. The wind was light and Marsh told the boy to stay aboard since the schooner would not have enough way to prevent Perry from getting safely back into his skiff.[31]

"I stood up on the deckload of lumber and was amazed at the work required to get a vessel underway," Perry remembered. "There was a gasoline deck engine of about six or seven horsepower in the bow. It had meshing gears that would transfer the power to the anchor windlass or to the winch head. The anchor chain was heaved up short, so that the anchor was holding and still in the mud.

"When the chain was short, the captain gave the order to stop heaving and the crew—two in addition to the captain—began to hoist the mainsail, then the foresail. This was accomplished by running the throat and peak halyards through a snatchblock to the winch head which was powered by the deck engine.

"Once the sails were set, the captain gave the order to break out the anchor, which was hoisted up and secured to the cathead. The ring of the anchor was made fast in the cathead with the fluke over the rail.

"The captain told me to go aft and steer while they secured the anchor and hoisted the jibs. As the mainsail and foresail filled and I felt the pressure on the rudder in the wheel, I was one happy thirteen-year-old boy. Feeling the power of a schooner under sail was a thrill I'd never forget. I'm sure that I was at the wheel less than fifteen minutes, but I was hooked with a love of sail that would last the rest of my life."[32]

A Trip aboard the *Charles G. Joyce*

That summer, Lynn Perry had his first real experience on a schooner when Captain Bennie Collier of the *Charles G. Joyce* agreed to let him make a trip from J. H. Coulbourn's lumber mill at Water Fence Landing on the Mattaponi River with a cargo destined for Baltimore and the Canton Box Lumber Co.

Once the cargo was loaded, the *Joyce* got underway, using the yawl boat, powered by a twelve-horsepower Palmer gas engine, to shove her through the Mattaponi bridge where she anchored. There, the mate, Gayle Sears, went ashore for ice.

"None of the schooners had electrical power, so there was no refrigeration, except an icebox that was kept cool with block ice," explained Perry, who helped to load it into the yawl boat. "I went aboard with the mate to meet the captain for the first time and to spend my first night on a schooner. The captain's stateroom had double bunks and I slept in the bottom. The captain, the mate, and "Uncle Frank," the black man who was the cook, all slept in the cabin aft."[33]

The *Joyce* got underway the next day along with the 77-foot *W. H. French* under Captain Todd and the 81.3-foot *Bohemia* captained by Edgar B. Riggin. Captain John Insley of the *L. E. Williams*, which was also headed up the Bay with lumber, decided to wait until the next morning. Leaving the Mattaponi, the three schooners were joined by the 126.5-foot ram *Agnes S. Quillin* that had been loading lumber at the Chesapeake Corporation on the Pamunkey River.[34]

The four caught a good ebb tide as they dropped down the York River. They all had sails up, but with very little wind, their yawl boats were providing most of the power. Just above Almonds Wharf, a summer thunderstorm swept down on them. The sails came down in a hurry, but they kept the yawl boats shoving.

It was late afternoon and still pouring rain when Captain Bennie anchored the *Joyce* on the south side of the river opposite Pages Rock Light House. The three other schooners kept going with their yawl boats shoving them down to anchor under Gloucester Point.

"We got underway early the next morning with a good northeast wind," said Perry. "With the mainsail, foresail, and standing jib, the schooner did some beautiful sailing for the short distance from our anchorage to join the others at Gloucester Point. We anchored there to wait for a fair wind and about noon, Captain John Insley sailed the *L. E. Williams* into the anchorage close to us. She was old and hogged with no topmast, but a beautiful sight."[35]

The square-rigged bugeye *Alexander Bond* was built at the Kirby yard in St. Michaels. She is shown here getting underway, as suggested by the two men, one on the foredeck and one in the small boat working to get her away from the dock—not an easy task, but a routine one in the age of sail. (Herman Hollerith Collection, Chesapeake Bay Maritime Museum, No. X 405)

The four schooners and the ram waited there under Gloucester Point for three days with northeasterly winds or none at all. Then late in the afternoon of the third day, the wind came southeasterly and they got underway.

"We sailed all night and were opposite Smith's Point at sunup," said Perry. "We had some wind, so the flying jib and topsail were set. We sailed all day and anchored in Patuxent for the night. The next day, we sailed and shoved to the mouth of the Patapsco, where we anchored until early morning. Then, we shoved into Baltimore to tie up at the Canton Box Company."[36]

They were in Baltimore for about ten days; three or four to unload the lumber and the rest for minor repairs or maintenance to the hull, the sails, and the engines. Some of the crew visited with their families in Baltimore. A number of the schooners, like the *Joyce*, which was owned by the shipbroker C. C. Paul & Co., had crews from Baltimore, although their captains often came from Virginia or the Eastern Shore of Maryland.

The return trip to Virginia began late in the afternoon, with the yawl boat shoving the *Joyce* down the Patapsco. They anchored for the night after only a few miles. Still plagued by light winds, they shoved and sailed to Annapolis and on to the Great Wicomico before anchoring at Fleeton. The next leg of their trip took them to the mouth of the Piankatank River where they anchored under the lee of Gwynn Island.

Those were the days when it was not unusual for a schooner to find herself in company with others when she dropped anchor for a night. At Gwynn Island, the *Joyce* was joined by the three-masted topmast schooner *Josephine Wim-satt* under Captain Will Brinsfield. He sailed the 95-foot Delaware-built three-master until she was sold off the Bay in 1939.

A very different picture was presented by a second schooner that sailed into the anchorage with all sails up, including four jibs. Freshly painted green, the New Jersey–built *Sarah Quinn* was 88 feet long and had a crew of six or more. She was owned out of North Carolina and Lynn Perry learned later that she was lost on the Outer Banks that fall.

Captain Bennie got the *Joyce* underway early the next day with a good wind out of the northeast. "The *Joyce* did some beautiful sailing with three sails and we made it to York Spit in time to catch the first of the flood tide up the York River," said Perry. "It took a long and a short tack but it was a good sailing breeze. We anchored below West Point. The next day, there was no wind but with a flood tide, we shoved the vessel up to Water Fence in time to start loading lumber that day."[37]

He was sorry to have to leave the schooner when his parents drove up to pick him up at Water Fence Landing, but that wasn't the last time that Perry was aboard the *Joyce*.

"Whenever the schooner was in the river, I was always aboard," he said. "I would row my skiff the seven miles up to Water Fence and spend the night aboard. If it was a school night, I did my lessons before going to bed. The next morning, I would sail down the river with them to West Point. Uncle Frank always cooked rice or bread pudding for me."[38]

Eleven

Like Father, like Son

It was common for sons to follow their fathers onto the water as Calvert Evans, Harry Porter, and William Stevens did. Stevens quit school at the age of twelve to go sailing with his father. That was 1926, when Ira Stevens was captain of the *Alice Hodges*. The two of them, father and son, worked until the elder Stevens left the water. A Kent Islander, Ira Stevens was captain of many of the old boats, but never owned one of them. There were few schooners that claimed the island as home port. Ira and his son generally went to Baltimore to get on their boats.

The *Alice Hodges* was an exception. She belonged to a doctor in Trappe and the Stevenses freighted her out of Kent Island.

"Me and my father went down to Trappe to get the *Alice Hodges* in our canoe that we oystered in," said William Stevens. "We freighted her down Patuxent and out of Kent Island, but we only had her two years. She was round and drew a lot of water, so we had to keep her in deep water all the time.[1]

"When we got through with the *Alice*, we got the *Ruth Decker*. We were on her when things started getting rough around 1929, but we stayed on her up into the forties.

"She carried everything on deck. She was built wide and she could stand it. She was a real strong boat. We carried a lot of fertilizer to Seaford in the *Ruth Decker*. She was a good boat. There was nobody to sail her but me and my Pa, and it was easy to get her sails up, easy to pump her out. We had the yawl boat

Deep-laden, the *Annie C. Johnson* is sailing "wung out" or "reading both pages," with the Baltimore light ahead to port. (Frank Moorshead, Jr., Mystic Seaport Museum, No. 91-10-126)

to push her. Even during the rough times, we always kept busy. If we had to do the loading ourselves, that's what we did.

"After that, we went on the ram *Grace G. Bennett*, but we only stayed on her a year. We didn't like her because her bow was so weak. In a big sea, her bow would be moving up and down, but back where you were steering, it'd be quiet."[2]

Life Aboard

The larger schooners, those of a hundred feet or more on deck, which were three- and four-masters mostly, had a roomy cabin aft and usually a deckhouse forward. The forward house was a large room that housed the galley with its wood- or coal-burning stove, a dining area, and an engine room if the schooner was so equipped. Aft were the captain's, mate's, bos'n's, and steward's quarters. Furnishing, though sparse, was often much the same as that in a home ashore. They used kerosene oil lamps for light and in later days, some carried a battery-operated radio to catch weather and news reports. For the most part, however, a captain relied more on his own observations and experience to judge the weather. The most useful news came from other vessels and what they learned when in port.

On most of the larger two-masted and smaller three-masted schooners, the deckhouse arrangement was different. The galley generally occupied half of the forward deckhouse, the deck engine the other half. The captain and mate slept in a cabin aft. On the smallest schooners no deckhouse was carried. Cooking was done in the forecastle, which was a bulkheaded space in the bow extending some twenty feet aft below deck. This was where the crew ate and slept. If the schooner was fitted with a hoisting engine, it generally was left exposed on deck or covered with a tarp when not in use.

It was a rare schooner that had a head or washroom. The crew bathed from a bucket on deck in summer, using first salt water, then fresh water. In the winter, they heated their bucket of water on the galley stove. For toilet facilities, the men used a bucket in bad weather or sat on the headrails up forward. Not until after 1900 did the larger schooners begin to have flush toilets and then only a few.

Bound for Baltimore, a pungy and a schooner lead an oyster fleet of other schooners, bugeyes, sloops, and skipjacks past the Canton Railroad Piers in 1912. (The Peale Museum, Baltimore City Life Museums, No. MC 9039)

William Stevens and his father went on to a second ram, the *Edwin and Maud*. They worked her for three years until 1946, when they could not make any more money running freight under sail. Ira Stevens got off the water then. It was that or go to powerboats and he was a sailing man. His son kept on working the water, but it was hard going if you wanted to stay on a boat.

"I went on the ferry boat *John M. Dennis* as mate, and I was aboard her when the ferry stopped running in '52," he said. "The last trip of the *Dennis*, I carried my wife and car and two children."[3]

His career took an ironic twist when he went to running the boat that carried inspectors and others supervising the building of the Bay Bridge, the very structure that brought the end of the ferry. Stevens retired finally in 1972 to a home on Kent Island where he could see the traffic brought to the Shore by the bridge. If he had a mind to look.

While he was working for the Historic American Merchant Marine Survey in 1936, Phil Sawyer spent time aboard the *Federal Hill*, built in Baltimore in 1856. This drawing is based on his sketches of the accommodations for captains and crews aboard a Bay schooner. The after cabin was often finished with a high standard of joinery and frequently served as home at least part of each year for the captain and his family. (James A. Mitchell, artist)

Never Saw a Cookbook

"You cooked with coal if you had a load of coal aboard, with wood if you were hauling lumber," said Woodrow Aaron. "The stove was up forward in the galley house. If we had a load of lumber, we cut that to keep warm. We had an old bucksaw to cut it up."[4]

Breakfast was served at dawn, dinner at noon, and supper just before sundown. When a schooner was underway, the captain ate first. He and the mate, if there was one, spelled each other at the wheel. Unless the forward deckhouse was large, the cook would prepare the meal and bring it aft in a basket and the crew ate in the main cabin. The water they drank was stored in wooden barrels on deck and everyone shared the tin cup with which they scooped it out.[5]

"You never saw a cookbook on board," said Lynn Perry. "Salt codfish was regular fare because it would keep a long time. The fish was split and spread out flat and salted. To prepare it, they had to soak it overnight. Then, the next morning, they'd scrape it to get the skin and salt off, parboil it, cut up some potatoes and onions, and throw it all in the skillet with some fatback and that's as near perfect eating as you'd ever get in this life. You had it with biscuits and coffee.

"They had no refrigeration, but there was usually an icebox on board that was good for a few days. If they had cold storage, they'd carry eggs and other fresh items. The captain bought the food and didn't spend any more than he had to. Bacon might have been a bit too much. Mornings they would have eggs and biscuits, the usual breakfast. For other meals, they'd pick up fresh seafood from passing watermen—clams, fish, whatever; if

The crew bunked in the cramped forecastle with few furnishings and berths finished with plain boards. They often provided their own mattresses, which were generally straw-filled, hence their nickname, "donkey's breakfast." (James A. Mitchell, artist)

New England needed wood and coal from southern ports. In the late 1890s, the crew of this large schooner, identified only as having been captained by a man named Crowley, seem to be taking a break from loading cordwood for New England at the C & O Pier in Newport News, while the captain's son entertains a visitor. (The Mariners' Museum, No. PH 2610)

the fresh seafood wasn't available and they'd used all their ice, it would get down to canned items—corned beef hash was a real go-getter. They made rice and bread puddings—with a little touch of coconut and some raisins that was some kind of good going."[6]

Everybody Had to Know How to Cook

"On those old schooners, sometimes you'd have a cook, but a lot of times you did it yourself," said Harry Porter. "Everybody had to know how to cook something in those days. They made their own bread and hot biscuits and used a lot of fatback and potatoes. A lot of potato stew. You had to carry things that wouldn't spoil. If a farmer came down and brought you fresh eggs, you had a treat."[7]

Vernon Hopkins went to sea in 1894 at the age of 14. He shipped aboard the brand new *Grace G. Bennett,* built in 1893 for his uncle W. J. Hopkins. The boy pestered his uncle until finally he signed him on as cook. "I was some cook," Vernon Hopkins told Orlando Wooten of Salisbury's *Sunday Times* years later. "I could make apple dumplings as big as your head, and bread tender and smooth. They paid me $8 a month. I had my rear end kicked six times a week and on Sunday for good count. I got out of that ship and out of the cooking business as soon as I could for a place before the mast." The opportunity came in Philadelphia when Hopkins jumped ship and went aboard the ram *Harland W. Huston* in the coastal service.[8]

"They carried a lot of dried fish and fruit and salt fish," said Earl Brannock. "In the summertime, they'd catch mackerel and bluefish and salt them down to use during the winter. They always cooked them in grease two inches thick. Did a lot with hake, a sort of codfish they called "heck" fish. And they made their own bread. A lot of it was stovetop bread, like a shortcake. One-pot meals were a favorite. If you're underway and it's rough, you can handle one big pot better than a lot of small ones bouncing around. A lot was done in cast-iron skillets, or spiders, whatever you want to call them. They ate a lot of chipped beef and gravy, the old navy standby."[9]

"On the *Edwin and Maud*, I did all the cooking, all except for the bread," William Stevens recalled. "Pa made the bread. Every time we baked bread, he'd make enough for two meals. He made it and I cooked it. That was shortbread. We didn't make biscuits. Just rolled it out. We used to call them turn cakes and they were shaped according to the kind of pan you had handy."[10]

"The living quarters weren't that bad aft," said Earl Brannock. "My father had almost what you could call a stateroom on the *Flora Kirwan* and out from that room was the galley and an area where you could sit at a table. There were usually a couple of other bunks up on the side in there too. They weren't too bad, but some of the crew had to sleep up forward."[11]

"On the big schooners, the captains had a nice cabin," said Cambridge marine artist Shirley Brannock, who came along just in time to see the last of the schooners pass from the scene, "but not all of them did. Not on the smaller schooners. But they had more space than the crew, who slept up in the bow in the forepeak. You went down this tiny little scuttlehole and there was no light. It was dark and damp and just barely wide enough to sleep. They didn't really have bunks, just boards that you put a mattress on. On the bugeyes and skipjacks, there would be four stuffed in that forepeak and I'm sure the small schooners were much the same."[12]

And Ma Went Along

Usually, women waited at home, watching the shipping columns of the Baltimore *Sun* or other papers for the comings and goings of their husbands' schooners. Some couldn't take the waiting and sailed with their husbands, making the schooners their homes, at least a part of each year. As in the earliest times, schooners offered the only opportunity that those on the Eastern Shore and in tidewater areas of the western shore had to visit relatives or friends or get to any of the larger towns to shop and tend to other matters.

"My mother, my sister and I would get on the old sailboats in the summertime and go to Baltimore with my father," said

The schooner *D. J. Ward*, built as the *Elijah S. Adkins* in Salisbury in 1910, is shown here in Baltimore in April 1939. Her skiff is lashed alongside just aft of the main shrouds, a technique employed on a number of larger Bay vessels. She shows a flat sheer and evidence of hogging aft. According to Robert H. Burgess, the *Ward* was manned only by Capt. Brinsfield and his wife in the schooner's later life. Many husbands and wives made their homes aboard the larger schooners. (Frank Moorshead, Jr., Mystic Seaport Museum, No. 91-10-119)

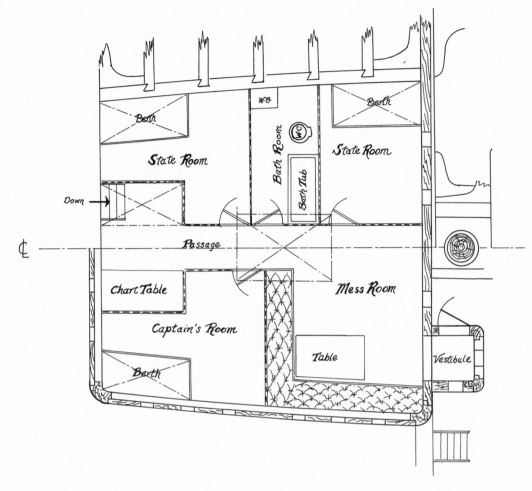

Labels in figure: Berth, W.B., Berth, State Room, Bath Room, WC, State Room, Bath Tub, Down, Passage, Chart Table, Mess Room, Captain's Room, Table, Berth, Vestibule

This plan of the aft cabin of the four-masted *Charles M. Struven* shows that captains, their wives, and/or other officers lived in relative comfort aboard the larger schooners. (Mystic Seaport Museum, Ships Plans Dept.)

Harry Porter. "He'd always take us to the Century or the Hippodrome Theater to see a stage show. Sometimes, we'd just go for a ride on the trolley cars to see the sights."[13]

"I liked the life aboard the smaller schooners," said William Stevens. "From as far back as I can remember, Pa carried Ma and the three of us children with him in the summers. When Ma was along, she did the cooking.

"The *Ruth Decker* had a nice captain's cabin. You could go in and shut the door and be to yourself," Stevens continued. "It had bunks you crawled into. I always took the captain's cabin and Pa slept on a cot, out where the coal stove was. Except when Ma would come aboard, then I would take the cot. We never ate there. We ate in the galley.

"In the forties, Ma went down with us on the *Maud* when my little sister was about three years old. The *Maud* was built high, her sides were waist high to me, so it was safe enough, and we kept an eye on her. But that trip, all the way down to North Carolina, Ma had a toothache. When we got to where we were loading, I jumped in the yawl boat and carried her uptown to a doctor to have her tooth pulled. That was the last trip my mother made."[14]

Captain Howard O'Day wrote of life years before aboard the ram *Jennie D. Bell*.[15] His wife and son Hilliard had spent four or five months out of every year with him.

"Things were always a lot livelier when they were aboard the *Bell*," wrote O'Day, "what with Hilliard chasing Teeny, his little white fox terrier, or shooting up and down the deck on his scooter, zipping round and round the big kegs we carried our drinking water in."[16]

The narrow beam of rams like the *Bell* "made them a bit tipsy at times," he wrote. They were sailing up the Bay and Hilliard, who was "just a tyker then," was sitting in a high chair in their cabin. "My wife was standing close to him and it's a good thing, because the first thing I knew a heavy puff came up, we listed and over went the high chair. My wife caught it—and Hilliard—but he never did forget that. In really rough weather, we'd have to push all our furniture to the side the *Bell* was listing toward so it wouldn't slide all over the cabin.

"Several of us shared the cabin. My stateroom was on the starboard side. The mate's was on the port and the two crewmen had rooms aft. The galley was forward, but although all the cooking was done there, the food was brought back to the cabin to be eaten."[17]

For her last twenty-four years, the *Jennie D. Bell* was owned by Captain Clarence Heath, whose wife lived aboard with him year-round. She gave up a career as a schoolteacher for her life on the water with her husband.[18] A number of wives who stayed with their husbands kept the books and served as business managers.

Captain Edgar J. Quillin, skipper of the *Erminie*, took his bride on a honeymoon aboard the schooner to Bermuda. Once there, Quillin left his new wife, for what they thought would be a brief separation, to help search for a ship in distress just offshore. The time came and went when he was due to return and his wife had an anxious two days thinking she was a widow before he returned safely.[19]

Filling the Grub Bill

Up until World War II, Cambridge was a grain entrepôt and a center for tomato and oyster canning. The harbor of the port was a busy place and much of the waterfront part of town was given over to the homes of men who worked the water and the businesses that served their boats. The scenes there were repeated in other large ports up and down the Bay.

Shirley Brannock remembered many days spent along the Cambridge waterfront as a child. A few schooners would still tie up there. She often heard stories of the days when the big schooners were hauled out at Johnson's yard, their bowsprits extending over the roofs of a row of small houses on Bridge Alley. In her day, Jim Richardson was building boats about where Johnson's used to be, but a couple of the little houses were still

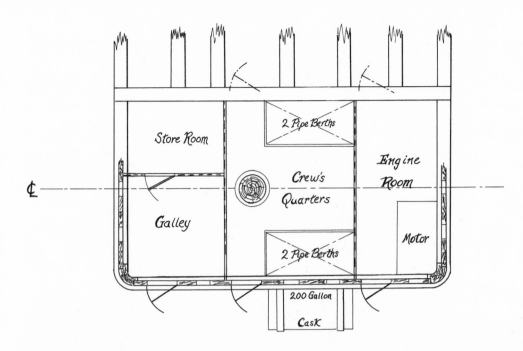

Accommodations for crew aboard even the largest schooners were austere. Four men were housed in the forward deckhouse, a space only slightly larger than that allowed for the captain's cabin on the *Charles M. Struven.* (Mystic Seaport Museum, Ships Plans Dept.)

standing when she was a girl. "There were two rooms up and two rooms down. They were for the oyster 'paddys,' which was what people in town called the itinerant workers," she said.[20]

"The captains and mates generally owned their own homes. You could tell their affluence by the houses they built. The Conways built big homes. All along West End and Willow streets there are rows of almost identical houses, very comfortable and adequate, and their boats were kept at the foot of the street."[21]

Her grandfather, Milton Sullivan, came ashore from sailing and went into the oyster-packing business, and then opened a grocery store and ship chandlery on Cambridge Creek. Next door was Brocato's blacksmith shop where Joseph Brocato made and repaired the dredges of the forty or fifty skipjacks that made up the diminishing oyster fleet of the thirties and forties. Sullivan's chandlery and the blacksmith were but two of a

Captain Clarence Heath, shown here on the foredeck of the *Jennie D. Bell*, was her last owner. When her cargo-carrying days ended, the *Bell* continued to serve as a home for Captain Heath and his wife until 1961 when she was run ashore on the mudflats near Salisbury to prevent her sinking at the dock. In the midseventies, her hulk was broken up as part of a statewide cleanup of the waterways. Note the foredeck details, showing some of her construction, head rigging, and machinery, including the winch head coming from the donkey engine inside the forward house and the windlass with the chain from the donkey engine that operated it. She was in good condition when this was taken in 1948. Her windlass is preserved today in the town square of Bethel, Delaware, as a monument to the men who built and sailed Bethel sailing vessels. (Peabody Museum of Salem, No. 27,024, Otis Lloyd, Jr.)

mast hoops, caulking and rope, deck hardware, foodstuffs, everything.

"I remember, several of the captains could write their names but that was it. They couldn't read or write. One would come in every week and hand my father his entire week's money and Daddy would divide it up in envelopes, one for the boat, one for the captain, and one for each member of the crew. Then he'd take out for the grub bill and hand him back his money to pay out.

"As a kid I filled many a grub bill for the oyster boats. Food was never referred to as anything but 'grub.' The grub bill was a long check sheet printed with the staple items that the boats normally used: the dried beans, peas and fruits, the canned goods, and meats. At the height of the time I remember, in the midthirties, the dredge boats would leave early on Monday morning to go down the river for a week. They'd anchor at night in one of the coves down there and they didn't come home 'til Friday afternoon. They would come in on Friday and pick up their sheets and we'd check off the staples they needed and write in whatever else they wanted. That was spoken of as 'grubbin' up.' We had barrel molasses and kerosene and they'd bring their kerosene cans and molasses jugs for us to fill.

"Saturday nights the store stayed open until midnight. Everybody came to town on Saturday night. They'd go downtown and shop 'til nine o'clock and then they'd come to the store and hang around until midnight and go home. On Saturday night, just before we closed, we'd make up the dredge boat orders. When I was a little kid of seven or eight, Daddy would give me the job of weighing out the dried beans and apricots. When I got big enough to fill the molasses jugs I thought that it was great to turn the crank that ran the pump. Daddy's store was long and narrow, and when we finished, it would be lined up both sides with double rows of boxes ready to be delivered Monday morning. The perishable meats would be cut and put in the refrigerator and Daddy would go down about four o'clock

cluster of waterfront businesses that supported the fleet of skipjacks, schooners, and bugeyes that filled the harbor.

"My father was Howard J. Sullivan, and he went into business with his father," said Shirley Brannock, who helped out in the store when she was not in school. "We carried all the things that the dredgers needed or, if we didn't have something, we ordered it from W. H. Whiting in Baltimore. We supplied

Monday morning, and put the meats and boxes aboard. Occasionally, we would go down Sunday afternoon and put the staple items aboard. The boats used to be stacked six and eight deep all the way down the dock. You always hoped the one you had to drag all those groceries to wasn't the outside boat. I used to think it was great fun to scramble over the boats."[22]

The Ship Chandler's Store

In the heyday of the schooners, every port had its Canton and its waterfront communities of dozens of chandlers, sailmakers, and other businesses who served Bay freight boats and the oystermen. As many as thirty or so were still in business in Baltimore up into the 1960s, but their numbers steadily dwindled as individual firms grew larger and their operations became more streamlined and efficient.[23]

Today, companies like the Vane Brothers of Baltimore exist mainly to serve tugs, barges, pleasure boats, and the giant freighters and ships that use the port. The firm has been outfitting vessels since 1898, however, and was started by two Dorchester County brothers, William and Allen Vane. In the early days, they carried hundreds of items from kerosene oil, paint brushes, and white lead to barrels of beef, pork, flour, black-strap molasses, potatoes, and coffee. Eggs came barreled and packed in salt to preserve them.[24]

In the early part of this century, Vane brothers' chandlery regularly supplied more than 150 sailing vessels. The company also had several sail and powered vessels of its own. The Vanes were owners or part-owners of a number of schooners, including the *Kate Darlington*, the *Brownstone*, the *Maine* and the *Thomas J. Shryock*, a ram. In the early 1930s, they also operated the four-masted *G. A. Kohler* and the *Doris Hamlin*.[25]

The name "chandler" comes from the fact that the earliest function of these harbor merchants was to make and supply candles to their customers. Later, they added other items and eventually carried just about anything a vessel needed from equipment and clothing to foodstuffs. The ship chandler's store was also a meeting place for the captains in port and a place away

Taken at Curtis Bay in 1937, this view from the bowsprit shows the deck of the *Caradora* and the raised quarterdeck aft, which is not typical of Bay schooners. Also uncommon is the jibboom which is set to one side on top of her bowsprit. (Courtesy of the Smithsonian Institution, National Museum of American History, HAMMS Collection, No. 5-9-1, Frederick Farley)

from home where they could pick up mail and other messages. Many large firms had a "Captain's Room."

Writer D'Arcy Grant, who was owner and captain of the *Fannie Insley* for a while, described a Baltimore chandlery in a *Sunday Sun* article she wrote in the 1940s: "From bay freighters

This view of the *Ida May* was taken at Annapolis. She freighted in the Bay for most of the year, but in the summertime was often used by a troop of Sea Scouts from Washington. In the 1930s when the *Ida May* and other freight schooners put in to Annapolis, the dock area was encircled by businesses catering to working watermen and their vessels. (Frank Moorshead, Jr., Mystic Seaport Museum, No. 91-10-111)

all around the harbor sailing men are converging on the chandler's store—the heart of their little world. The clean, sweet smell of new manila hemp pervades the place. In precise coils, it waits to be measured out for sheets, halyards and spring lines . . .

"The odor of coffee in bulk mingles with a flat, rubbery smell of new oilskins that swing from the rafters like thieves on a gibbet. From the rafters also hangs an assortment of 'gum' boots, sou'westers, life preservers, running lights, oil lanterns, flitches of bacon, hams, oil heaters and an assortment of seagoing gear that makes the dark recesses of the store resemble some strange, seaweed-hung undersea cavern.

" . . . Bails of sail twine and marlin . . . battens of cotton caulking and rolls of oakum redolent of tar, wait to fulfill their destiny.

"Midway in the store is the 'social circle.' Its center is a stove, and in winter the circle of chairs surrounding it is never

empty . . . From the farthest reaches of the inland waterway seafaring men bring their news and yarns."[26]

When Howard O'Day ran the *Bell*, her home port was Baltimore. "We usually took aboard all the food we'd need for a voyage," he wrote. "We got it at Vane Brothers, the ship chandlery that was on Pratt Street. If we were going down to the York River, we knew we'd be gone for at least five weeks so we'd take on five weeks' supply of food—salted meats, potatoes, things like that. Of course we could buy fresh vegetables and eggs and chickens from the farmers along the York. And there were always fish."[27]

Sometimes, in some ports, the schooners could come right up to a dock, but usually there were too many, and even in Baltimore, they had to anchor out and drop the skiff for getting ashore. There was a time when nearly every waterfront town on the Bay that could justify being called a port had a "Shanghai," a place that a more sophisticated and worldly age now calls a yacht basin. Once, however, it was where the oyster boats and freight-hauling schooners anchored. The chandler usually owned sleek, fast rowboats and later powerboats to deliver fuel, water, and supplies to them at their mooring.

Blue Paint, Black Suitcases, and Broomhandles

Whenever men would gather in the ship chandler's store or on one or another boat in the anchorage, they'd always have some tale to tell on themselves. Each had his little quirks. Most were just a little bit superstitious.

"There was no one more superstitious than my father," recalled Calvert Evans. "If you had a broom, sweeping the deck or whatever, don't lay it with the bristles pointing forward, lay it with the handle pointing forward. And when you brought the skiff aboard, you had to put it the same way the boat was going, never crossways. Now the standard length of a skiff was 12 feet and that's a lot of room to take up laying lengthwise on the deck. Most people put them crossways and I'd tell him, 'Pa, it'd be so much more convenient if you'd turn that skiff crossways.' 'Don't you turn it!' he'd say and there was no use arguing.

"The worst thing was to bring a black suitcase aboard. We had a fellow name of Elwood Hughes came on with a black suitcase once. Pa didn't say a word, but he didn't like it. We'd been down the Bay to get a load of seed oysters. Going down we had a good fair wind, but when we started back, before we got to the Rappahannock, the fog set in. Daddy pulled up into the Rappahannock and anchored in Butler's Hole. And there we sat. We had a pea soup fog every morning for a week and it was warm weather. You could smell them oysters.

"My father knew it was Elwood with that black suitcase. Now, my father wouldn't cuss. He never did cuss, but he did everything else to let on how he felt about that black suitcase. One day Elwood, who was staying up in the forepeak, found the paint locker up there. He came back to my father and he had that suitcase in his hand. It was the damnedest looking thing you've ever seen. He'd painted it buff, but you could see the black through it.

"'Captain Raymond,' he says, 'when's the fog going to lift? The suitcase ain't black no more.'

"'Yes it is,' was all my father said and he'd never believe otherwise and it was a couple more days before the fog broke and we got on up the Bay with those oysters."[28]

Raymond Evans wasn't the only one who believed a black suitcase was bad luck. At the shipping office in Baltimore, Captain Harry Porter remembered that if a man came down to a boat with a black suitcase, they'd make him take his clothes out and leave the suitcase on the dock. There were enough things could go wrong without taking any chances.[29]

A lot of Bay watermen wouldn't think of setting foot on a boat painted blue—not even the trim. And don't turn the hatch cover upside down or drop it in the hold on their boats either, or use red brick as ballast, or have a leaf, nut, or twig from a walnut tree on board. Some wouldn't allow a woman on board

This view shows the *William H. Michael* tacking into the Annapolis harbor. Built in Queen Anne's County, Maryland, the *Michael* was owned by the commission merchant business of William H. Michael & Sons on McElderry's Wharf in Baltimore. (Courtesy of the Smithsonian Institution, National Museum of American History, HAMMS Collection, Philip Sawyer)

Baltimore's Canton Hollow just outside of the Inner Harbor was filled with sailing vessels in 1918. This was a favorite anchorage for inbound vessels awaiting a berth or for those outbound waiting for a fair breeze. Such views were commonplace in most nineteenth and early twentieth century Bay ports. (Frank Moorshead, Jr., Mystic Seaport Museum, No. 91-10-141)

captain's wives aboard at all times, were some of the last of the freight schooners to work on the Bay.

The business about luck wasn't all about things not to do. "I've set in the Bay with my father just smarting, not a breath of air around, and the sails all hanging limp on deck," recalled Harry Porter, "and he'd reach in his back pocket and throw a penny overboard for a penny's worth of wind."[32]

"Old folks had a lot of belief in lucky and unlucky boats," said Calvert Evans. One of the luckiest ones was the 105-foot, three-masted *William T. Parker.* Built by C. C. Davidson at Milton, Delaware, in 1891, *the Parker* sailed for forty-four years, working mainly hauling lumber coastwise and in the Bay. In 1899, she was grounded off Cape Henlopen, Delaware, and refloated. Then, in 1908, the schooner had another near disaster and was almost lost in a gale off the North Carolina coast. Seven years later, in 1915, she was again off the Carolina coast when a storm hit. This time, the *Parker* was abandoned and given up for lost.

She survived, however, and drifted north as far as the coast of Maine. There, northerly winds turned her around and drove her back down the coast where she was found and taken in tow. She ultimately ended up in the fleet of Baltimore broker C. C. Paul.[33]

Over the years, local newspapers and magazines recorded accounts of the occasional lucky boat and, more often, of the unlucky ones. Most people who lived on or near the Bay and did not make their living from it, knew little more of schooners than such accounts. Few realized when they read those tales of storm-tossed vessels that they were reading the final chapter of the story of the Chesapeake Bay schooner.

or change the name of a boat. And they'd be mighty uneasy if three crows flew across a boat's bow.[30]

But there were always exceptions. The ram *Edward R. Baird, Jr.,* for instance, was painted blue and white. She survived a German U-boat attack during World War II, was set adrift, and retrieved to work another ten years.[31] In fact she, the *Jennie D. Bell,* and the *D. J. Ward,* which finished out their days with the

Twelve

Survival in the freight business meant that a schooner never sailed light if it could be avoided. Not all cargoes could justify a trip, so they were paired with ones that were more profitable. In the smaller schooners, grain and fertilizer or cans and tomatoes were combined to keep holds filled coming and going. For the larger schooners, three- and four-masters, ice and stone provided back freight on colliers. Ice alone, for instance, could not justify a trip to Maine, but as return cargo for a coal schooner, it made economic sense. The same was true of most other cargoes whether a schooner sailed between Baltimore and Eastern Shore river landings or offshore to New England or the West Indies.

Logwood

One of the earliest cargoes carried by Bay schooners that ventured offshore was the dark, gnarled heavy timber called dyewood or, more commonly, logwood. From colonial days, it was used to produce black and dark blue dyes for cloth and also for making certain medicines. Only sugar was a more important or more profitable cargo in the early West Indian trade.[1] Carried first by the larger two-masted schooners, logwood became a return trip payload for three- and four-masters, when in the late 1800s and early 1900s, their owners found that there was as much profit to be had from carrying coal from Newport News to the West Indies as to New England.

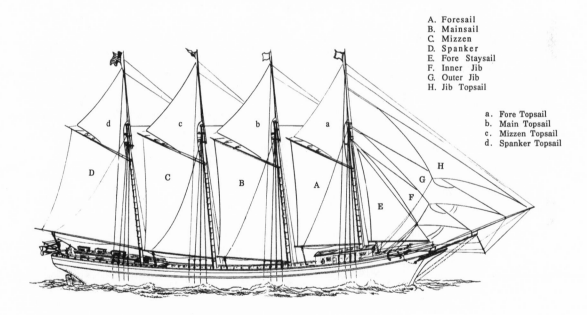

A. Foresail
B. Mainsail
C. Mizzen
D. Spanker
E. Fore Staysail
F. Inner Jib
G. Outer Jib
H. Jib Topsail

a. Fore Topsail
b. Main Topsail
c. Mizzen Topsail
d. Spanker Topsail

Chesapeake-built four-masted schooner.

The *Granville R. Bacon*, the last ram built, is shown here in January 1934 on the beach at Weekapaug, Rhode Island. Her captain, George E. Jones of Norfolk, Virginia, had been using her to run coal from New York to Camden, Maine, and she was running light from Maine to New York when a southeast gale caught up with her. The *Bacon* was under her staysail and spanker only and was making more to leeward than was figured by her navigators. The combination of sail and sea conditions prevented her from tacking out of danger and the southeast breeze pushed her ashore. (Mystic Seaport Museum, No. 59.1401.2, Robert H. Goddard)

After delivering their cargoes of coal to Cap-Haïtien, Port-au-Prince, and other Haitian and Jamaican ports, the large schooners took on logwood.[2] While profitable, logwood often was filled with snakes and spiders from tropical ports and was an unpleasant cargo to handle.

The loading could take anywhere from two to four weeks, because the tremendous amount of logwood a four-master could carry had to be lightered out to the schooner in large rowboats and barges. The hold was filled to capacity to prevent the cargo from shifting once the vessel was underway. Its hatches were then sealed and caulked and more logwood was piled on deck, often as high as six or eight feet. The wood was secured there with heavy chains.[3]

Much of the logwood went on to Philadelphia, but many cargoes were destined for the J. S. Young dye works in Baltimore. Located in Canton, the J. S. Young Co. manufactured tanning extracts and licorice for flavoring tobacco as well as dyes.[4]

The Coal Schooners

While lumber was perhaps the cargo that was responsible for the survival of the Chesapeake Bay schooner into the twentieth century, and logwood was a profitable return cargo for those that went offshore, coal was the principal freight that gave rise to and kept the largest schooners operating. On the Bay, Havre de Grace was the site of one of the earliest and largest coal terminals for the shipment of Pennsylvania coal to southern ports. For Bay two-masters, coal was a reliable, if not popular, cold-weather cargo. Of far greater significance was the fact that the steady stream of coal from Bay ports gave rise to larger multi-masted schooners.

Other terminals followed those at Havre de Grace, with several opening along the Patapsco River. According to Lt. W. J. Lewis Parker of the U.S. Coast Guard, "The first important American soft coal fields had been tapped when the Baltimore & Ohio Railroad reached Cumberland, Maryland on November 5, 1842, providing a tidewater outlet at Baltimore for the rich Georges Creek mines." Growing numbers of schooners loaded coal at the Baltimore & Ohio's piers at Curtis Bay and Locust Point for transport north to keep New England's mills and industrial plants running.[5]

To the south, in the 1850s, Georgetown and Alexandria became terminals for Cumberland coal with the opening of the Chesapeake and Ohio Canal. One of the earliest and largest coal shippers in Alexandria was J. P. Agnew. He also operated a shipyard where shipwrights from Maine built several large coal schooners.[6]

The peak year for Alexandria as a coal terminal was 1871.[7] By 1880, the wharves at Georgetown and Alexandria were suffering severe backups of sail and steam vessels loading coal. Finally, in 1881, the Chesapeake & Ohio Railway was extended from Richmond to Newport News under the ownership of Collis P. Huntington. "Almost overnight, Newport News became one of the great coal ports of the world," wrote Parker. At the same time, the Norfolk & Western Railway had opened West Virginia's coal fields to the Bay, and "by 1885, bituminous coal had become Norfolk's chief export." By 1886, the terminals at Newport News and Norfolk had put Alexandria out of business and were in serious competition with Baltimore.[8]

In the meantime, Maine shipbuilders were building larger and larger three-masted schooners to meet the growing demand for hulls, and then in 1880, came the *William L. White,* first of the four-masters that would become the standard carriers in the coal trade. As Parker writes, "It is worthy of note how closely the advent of the four-master preceded the opening of the Hampton Roads coal ports."[9]

In the 1870s, the traffic of the three-masters split after clearing the Virginia capes, some sailing north to Baltimore, others making the "tedious passage" up the Potomac to Alexandria or Georgetown. By the 1880s, the majority of the coal fleet still went on to Baltimore. Fewer visited Potomac ports and a growing number went into Hampton Roads. By 1910, the trade was divided equally between Newport News and Baltimore, with a few stopping at the terminal at Norfolk.[10]

Loading and unloading coal was a dirty job, which produced smutty black clouds that coated everything. There was no escaping the dust that penetrated cabins and galley. When loading, gangs of black men worked in the holds shoveling the coal away from the hatches. They earned seven or eight cents a ton. When the holds were filled, the crew battened down the hatches and the schooners were nudged by tugs into the channel where they were hosed down before being towed to sea. The whole process of loading could take as long as a week.[11]

If they faced a northeasterly wind, the schooners anchored in Hampton Roads to await a shift. Usually only eight or ten

The largest schooner and the last four-master built on the Chesapeake Bay watershed, the *Anandale* is shown here at the Galveston Coal Co. unloading coal—a dirty process, hence, the sail covers. Her booms are swung out to allow access to the hatches for loading. Note the four workmen, aloft, scraping or "slushing" the topmasts. Slushing was part of regular maintenance and involved coating the masts with grease—usually tallow—to protect the wood and facilitate the movement of the mast hoops up and down. (Peabody Museum of Salem)

would be gathered in the anchorage, but on occasion as many as seventy-five schooners set sail with a fair wind. From then on it was a race to be first to reach the unloading docks in Boston or Portland to avoid as much of the wait at the other end as possible. Once free of the Bay, the voyage north took about a week and unloading, a week. A round trip averaged twenty-two days.[12]

Parker quoted one old captain, "You could go aloft and the fleet would be scattered a little, and there'd be sails all around the horizon, just as far as you could see."[13]

Under sail the men stood four-hour watches, four on, four off, or longer if there was bad weather. They lived in the forecastle in an area roughly seventeen feet by ten feet in the forward house, where the bulkheads were lined with a double tier of bunks. The men signed on for a round-trip voyage.[14]

That voyage was often extended by delays caused by groundings—in the Potomac, in the channel below the coal docks at

KNICKERBOCKER ICE CO.'S RANDOLPH AND CHELSEA PLANTS—CAPACITY 60,000 TONS.

Each year, 60,000 tons of ice from icehouses like this one in Maine were carried to Chesapeake Bay ports by three- and four-masted schooners. (Mystic Seaport Museum, Fowler Collection, No. 89-69-23)

While weather was always a problem for seamen, collision with steam-powered ships was a relatively new one that imposed a growing threat as the sea lanes grew more crowded. The coal schooners were especially at risk because on their voyage from Hampton Roads to New England they cut across the main steamer lanes from Europe and the West Indies to Philadelphia, New York, and Boston, three of the world's busiest ports.[15]

Economics, not collisions or storms, brought on the end of the coal schooners and other sailing freight vessels in general. The year 1907 was a year of general economic depression, but it also saw the arrival of the first of the steam colliers, which would join the railroads and barges and tugs in usurping the schooner's place in the trade.[16]

Added to the forces already at work, the development of other cheaper sources of coal for northern needs and a flood in 1924 that devastated the Chesapeake and Ohio Canal brought on the end of the coal trade on the Potomac. The last schooner belonging to Agnew left Georgetown just before the flood. The entire schooner fleet was dwindling by that time. In carrying coal to northern ports, the schooners couldn't compete with the steamers.[17]

By the thirties and forties, most of the coal carried by schooners from Virginia was going to the West Indies or Bermuda. On a typical voyage from the Chesapeake & Ohio Railway's coal pier in Newport News, a vessel would sail to St. George's, Bermuda. There, the coal was unloaded by laborers using large reed baskets and lightered to shore. A week later, the schooner set sail for Cap-Haïtien to take on a return cargo of logwood. The entire journey took approximately two months.[18]

In July 1948, a British-owned three-master, the *Frederick P. Elkin*, was the last sailing vessel to load coal at Newport News.[19]

Ice

As early as 1665, Governor Berkeley of Virginia had issued a patent to preserve ice and snow, and in 1784 one of George Washington's concerns was the construction of an icehouse. In 1803, Thomas Moore, a farmer in Brookeville, Maryland, wrote

Curtis Bay, and at other spots within the Bay. Offshore, storms could blow a schooner off course and add days and even weeks to the voyage. In winter, channels clogged with ice slowed a schooner's progress and once on the open sea, the going was no easier. The schooners were so deeply loaded that their decks were always awash in heavy weather. When winter added freezing temperatures, every exposed section of a vessel would be covered with ice, its sails stiff as iron.

an essay on the construction of icehouses and discussed a new invention called a "refrigerator."[20]

The ice trade as such actually originated in 1805 when Frederic Tudor of Boston sent a shipload of 130 tons of ice to Kingston, Jamaica, and Havana. By 1830, he had established an ice wharf on Washington's waterfront.[21] At least one New York ice dealer was in the business of selling ice from the Kennebec River in Maine to the Army of the Potomac during the Civil War.[22]

Along with the ice industry, a number of others developed as a direct result of the availability of ice. Among these were businesses dealing in fresh fish, meats, fruits and vegetables; milk, butter, and other dairy products; and in the manufacturing of beer, wine, and ale. The production of ice cream took a big leap forward.[23]

One of the most successful early ice operations in Virginia was that of David King who first sent a schooner to Maine in 1856 and for five years supplied businesses and homes in Richmond with ice. The Civil War put an end to King's enterprise and he finally died in 1873 while trying to re-establish himself in Ohio. David's widow, Jane King, returned to Richmond the following year, brought back by the death of her brother who had gotten an ice business going there after the war.[24]

In the middle of the summer of 1874, the widow King took over the icehouse on East Cary Street. In spite of a national economic depression, and the fact that women in such businesses were practically unheard of, by the next summer, she had the icehouse operating at a profit. It wasn't easy.

The crew of one schooner balked at taking orders from a woman and though they did their job, they poured half a barrel of varnish over the ice, spoiling twenty tons. Jane King was not intimidated. She deducted $50 in damages from the schooner captain's freight charges. He had to deal with his crew.

The scow schooner *Morning Star* was a type usually associated with San Francisco or Gulf Coast ports, but was also found in the Chesapeake, especially around Havre de Grace, Port Deposit, and in the Norfolk area. Stone from the Susquehanna River area was an important cargo for scow schooners on the Bay. The 34-ton *Morning Star* was built in 1892 at Church Creek, Maryland, and is said to have carried stone used to build many buildings in Cambridge. (Herman Hollerith Collection, Chesapeake Bay Maritime Museum, No. X439)

"One rough old schooner captain said he'd be damned if he'd talk business with a woman. He found he'd be damned if he didn't; at least he would be paid. That calmed him. He left the lady ice dealer's office hat in hand, vowing he'd never talked straighter business with any man."[25]

During the time that Mrs. King ran the ice business, eighteen others came and went. She discontinued the handling of northern ice in 1892 when an ice plant opened in Richmond that could produce cheaper ice. She contracted for the plant's entire output. Soon ice plants would be springing up all over the Eastern Seaboard, ending the trade in natural ice and the schooner's part in it.

The scow schooner *Ella Barnard* was built in 1892 by J. W. Brooks in Madison, Maryland. She was named for one of the daughters of Captain Charles Barnard for whom she was built. She hauled produce, granite, and timber from Port Deposit and other upper Bay ports. Her home port was Havre de Grace. Barely visible on her side is her port leeboard, found on only a few scow schooners on the Bay. It could be lowered instead of the centerboard to prevent the leeward movement of these shallow-draft scow schooners. (Chesapeake Bay Maritime Museum, No. 584-11, H. Osborne Michael)

The harvesting of the Kennebec River's ice began in 1870, shortly before Jane King returned to take over her brother's ice business in Richmond. Several villages grew up around the ice operations on the Kennebec, including Cedar Grove, now a part of Dresden, Maine. Besides the icehouses, offices, and ice weighing scales, the Cedar Grove company kept a stable, provided employee housing, and ran a boardinghouse, a general store, a post office, and a grain mill, as well as blacksmith and carpenter shops. In short, they built a company town.[26]

The year 1880 appears prominently in accounts of the ice trade because that was the year that Henry Hall, a special agent with the U.S. Department of the Interior's census division, used for his study of the ice industry in the United States.

According to his study, in 1880 American industries were using ten million tons of ice a year taken from northern rivers, lakes, and ponds. Ice from the rivers in Maine was the most desirable because of the purity of the water. The principal markets for Maine ice were Philadelphia, New York, Baltimore, and Washington, D.C. Between 1850 and 1890, the consumption of ice tripled in Baltimore alone.

Hall's report showed that in 1880, 177 vessels brought nearly 112,000 tons of ice from Maine to Baltimore, where it was sold by seven different companies. Three companies served Washington, where 97 vessels delivered more than 63,000 tons. Thirty-two vessels served Richmond that year. Ten went to Georgetown, two to Norfolk, and one delivered 460 tons to Annapolis. Retail prices for ice in Baltimore began at 20 cents for 100 pounds in April. By August, it had risen to 75 cents for 100 pounds. In Washington, the cost of ice ran between 75 cents and $1 in the winter and $1 to $1.50 for 100 pounds between April and October.[27]

Ice was cut from rivers and lakes and stored between January and early March to await the arrival of three- and four-masted schooners that would carry it to southern ports. The most common carrier was the three-master because any vessel that drew more than eighteen feet was limited in its ability to load in many of the rivers where the ice was produced.[28]

The ice fleet began arriving in April, after the schooners had delivered their cargoes of coal to Boston and Portland. Those that arrived first went up the Kennebec with great care to avoid damage from drift ice set free by the spring thaw.

The peak time of the season was between June and September. Tugs towed the schooners to the icehouses located thirty miles and more up the Kennebec. That trip usually took seven or eight hours.

On the way to the icehouses, the schooners' holds were washed clean of the coal dust and opened up to dry. Usually the schooners had to wait to be loaded with ice and, while at anchor, their captains took the opportunity to put boats over so the crew could paint the hull. In 1880, there were as many as sixty schooners waiting to load ice at Cedar Grove on the Kennebec.[29]

It took two days to load and stow 600 tons of ice in blocks measuring 22 inches by 32 inches by 14 inches and weighing about 250 pounds. The blocks were weighed on their way to the loading dock where they were lowered into the hold by machine. The ice was tightly stacked in blocks and packed with wood shavings or sawdust to insulate it from the heat. Filled to within a foot of the deck beams, the hold was tightly sealed to keep it as air-tight as possible. The schooner's pumps ran regularly. Every four-hour watch got a "suck" on the pumps. The normal loss to melting was between 10 and 20 percent.[30]

Ice took its toll on the schooners that carried it. Rot due to prolonged contact with fresh water was a common problem that shortened the life of many vessels.

Houses at Pittston on the Kennebec River provided ice for the Independent and the Great Falls ice companies in Washington, while ice for the Cochran-Oler Ice Co. in Baltimore came from houses at Cedar Grove.[31] Ice schooners were in and out of Baltimore and Washington with reasonable dispatch because the icehouses in both cities were adjacent to the wharves. Some of the cargo was loaded directly into delivery wagons, the rest went into the houses. During one four-year period from 1892 to 1896, 536 schooners discharged ice at the wharves in Washington. Some 230 came into Alexandria at the same time.[32]

In 1868, the Washington & Georgetown Ice Co. was selling "lake ice" at the 10th Street wharf in Washington and at Godey's Ice House in Georgetown. In 1879, the yellow wagons of the Independent Ice Co. were all over the nation's capital peddling "Northern Ice" from the firm's depot at the 9th Street wharf.[33]

Captain Freeman Reed of the Bath (Maine) three-master *Samuel P. Hitchcock* recorded a typical round-trip for a schooner in the ice and coal fleets. He left Boothbay on March 23, 1882, with 980 tons of ice for Washington. On April 1, Reed picked up a pilot at Piney Point at 4:00 A.M. They passed Mt. Vernon at 5:30 P.M. and were anchored at Alexandria by 7:00 P.M. The *Hitchcock* was towed to Washington on April 3 where Reed had to wait four days before he could pull up to the Great Falls Ice Co. wharf to begin discharging his cargo of ice. The schooner was unloaded by April 11 and was then towed to Winship's coal dock in Georgetown. There, it finished loading 902 tons of coal on April 14 and was towed down the river and sent on its way to Boston, arriving a week later.[34]

Captain Tom Chadwick, of the Thomaston (Maine) three-masted schooner *Jennie F. Willey*, left Cedar Grove on April 25, 1885, with 580 tons of ice and arrived in Baltimore on May 8, making the 725-mile trip in 12 days.[35] That was good time. The average trip was two weeks.

Manufactured ice was in serious contention with natural ice by 1900, and icehouses along the Kennebec began closing one by one. Schooners were still loading ice at Cedar Grove and other Maine icehouses, but their numbers were diminishing. In 1910, a fire that destroyed the American Ice Company's houses at Iceboro, along with two four-masted schooners at the wharf, marked the beginning of the end of the natural ice industry.[36] The four-masted schooner *B.S. Taylor*, built in Wilmington, Delaware, in 1919 brought the last shipment of ice into Alexandria in 1925.[37]

Lime and Stone Schooners

Lumber was not the only building material carried in bulk by schooners that worked the Chesapeake. Lime for mortar, plaster, and huge blocks of granite came to Bay ports aboard three- and four-masted schooners from New England.

Much of the limestone came from kilns in Rockland, Rockport, and Thomaston, Maine. It was carried in wooden

The abundance of white oak and the reputation of the region's shipwrights for building stout vessels led New England owners to seek vessels in the Chesapeake Bay. The 86.8-foot *Amy M. Sacker*, a New Bedford whaling schooner, was built in 1885 at the J. W. Crowell yard in Cambridge, Maryland. She sailed in the 1920s out of Venezuela and lasted into the 1950s. She is one of several whaling vessels built on the Bay. The *Zaine*, a half brig, and the barks *Canton* and *Daniel Webster* were built in Baltimore for the whaling industry. (New Bedford Whaling Museum, No. 7811)

casks which had to be kept from any contact with water because it would cause the lime to ignite. A limer's hold had to be leak free, and the casks were stored on platforms to keep bilge water from reaching them.

If ever the lime began to burn, the only recourse was to seal up the hold with plaster made from some of the lime, in order to smother the flames. Meanwhile, the schooner made for the nearest port, there to anchor well offshore for as long as two or three months to see if the fire would go out. If it didn't, they would have to abandon the vessel in some backwater.[38]

While the smaller schooners were used as limers, much more burdensome hulls were needed for carrying granite. Stone for many of the public buildings in Washington and Baltimore was brought to the Bay from "Down East" quarries by large two-masted schooners built in Maine and by several three- and four-masters built in New London, Connecticut.

A single block of granite could weigh as much as 185 tons and stone droghers were equipped with a special boom to hoist the granite blocks aboard. The blocks could also be loaded through a port cut in the bow. To get maximum support, the blocks were laid along the keel on a platform of sturdy timbers.[39]

Scow Schooners

Not all stone was transported by the big schooners. According to John Earle of Easton, many of the churches and other public buildings in that town, in St. Michaels, and in other towns on the Eastern Shore were built from granite brought in by scow schooners from Port Deposit.[40] A very different type of vessel, the scow schooner developed on the Bay to meet specific needs, such as hauling heavy materials on very shallow waters. The type was used as early as 1743 to carry pig iron from the furnaces at the upper end of the Bay to large ships anchored in deep water.

The hull of this particular schooner was that of a common scow, wall-sided with a uniform width from square-raked bow to an identical stern. Hatches filled most of the deck.

Scow schooners and sloops were built in many areas, and even after the iron supply was exhausted around Havre de Grace, they were being produced at Norfolk, Washington, Chesapeake City, Princess Anne, Virginia, and Charleston, South Carolina. A few sloops were still around in the 1940s.

With their flat bottoms, straight sides, and square ends, they were homely vessels, but served their purpose very well. Built for use in shallow rivers and creeks, they could go where other deeper schooners could not and, if the bottom was solid enough, could be loaded or unloaded from wagons driven out into the water. Like the skipjacks of today, they were simply and inexpensively built, requiring only the most basic of carpentry skills.[41]

The *Ella Barnard*, built in 1892 at the Brooks yard near Madison, on the Little Choptank River in Dorchester County, was one of the few scow schooners that have been identified as such. At one time, she was used by a brickyard on the Rappahannock River to haul bricks. At others, she freighted grain and farm produce from Bay creeks and rivers to Baltimore and returned with farm and cannery supplies.[42]

Whaling Schooners

A little known fact is that at least two schooners were built in Cambridge, Maryland, for the New England whaling fleet. The Brannock Maritime Museum in Cambridge houses records of the schooner *Amy Sacker*, built for the New Bedford Whaling Co. There was also the *Zaine*, which was a half brig, built for the Salem Whaling Co. The main distinction of these vessels was that they were generally larger, more full-bodied, and deeper than the typical Bay freighters.

In the 1890s, the brig *Alexander* was built for the New Bedford Whaling Co. She operated out of San Francisco with the only black captain in the entire West Coast whaling fleet.[43]

Logwood, coal, ice, stone, lime; these last cargoes required a much more burdensome vessel than the doughty two-master. Less than ever was speed the requisite for a profitable schooner. Just before the Civil War, three-masted schooners began showing up in harbors on the Bay. As the nineteenth century progressed, four-, five- and six-masters joined them in one last effort to compete with the steamers and the tugs and barges that were threatening their livelihood and the very existence of commercial sail.

Thirteen

Reviving an Old Concept

By the 1850s, cargo capacity was the prime requisite for the survival of vessels working the Bay. Steam-powered freighters, with their ability to deliver cargoes on schedule, regardless of most wind and weather conditions, had captured all but the bulk cargoes such as fertilizer, grain, coal, ice, and lumber. While two-masted schooners were adequate for the Bay, most could not carry payloads large enough to make coastwise trade practical. To operate a two-masted schooner of more than 100 feet became prohibitive in terms of the manpower required to handle the tremendous sails. Only a few with lengths up to 135 feet were built. The addition of laborsaving devices such as the donkey engine was only a stopgap measure as competition from steamers increased the demand for larger hulls.[1] The only way that schooners could remain viable was by increasing the volume of cargo they could carry with the addition of a minimum number of crew members.

The solution was to add a third mast, increasing the number of sails to gain the amount of canvas needed to power a larger hull. At the same time, this reduced the size of the sails, making them lighter and easier to handle. Three-masters were not new on the Bay. Several three-masted Baltimore clipper schooners were built as fast-sailing dispatch boats. The earliest on record was in 1806. These early three-masters were referred to as tern schooners, with "tern" meaning a set of three or three of a kind.[2] This term continued well into the nineteenth century in the United States and into the early twentieth century in Canadian waters.

Writing in the *American Neptune*, Dorothy R. Brewington reported finding one of the earliest three-masters, the *Ferrata*, built on the Miles River under the direction of Captain Miles King in the early 1800s. In addition to being one of the early three-masters built in the Bay, the *Ferrata* was "apparently one of the first American vessels to be rigged with iron instead of hemp." Brewington quotes a contemporary description in the November 1, 1827, edition of Philadelphia's *American Daily Advertiser*.[3]

> There is now lying at Jackson's Wharf, Baltimore, a vessel which appears to us a novelty in naval architecture. She has three masts, rigged fore and aft fashion as it is called, or similarly to the ordinary schooner. Her standing rigging is all of iron served with rope yarn—the shrouds are continuous bars, and the cross pieces usually termed ratlines are strips of wood. The stays are composed of long links about a yard in length. The tonnage of this nondescript is 336 tons, custom house measure. She is expected to sail very fast and it is said works well . . .[4]

Few three-masted schooners were built outside the Bay until just before the Civil War, and the type was not widely in use until the 1870s. The later three-masters were a very different sort of schooner from their predecessors. The cargo-carrying three-masted schooner of the late nineteenth century was generally a shoal-draft, centerboard model. Most carried topmasts. More than sixty were built on the Bay—in Maryland, Virginia, and Delaware—through the end of World War I. During that time, they more than paid their way in the lumber, coal, and ice trades.

One of the earliest of the second-generation three-masters was the 284-ton *Amelia G. Ireland* built in 1866 in Somerset County, Maryland. The largest Maryland-built three-master was the 714-ton *William A. Marburg*, built in Baltimore in 1883. The same year, William Crawford came to Alexandria from Kennebunkport, Maine, to build the 753-ton *Henry S. Culver* for coal dealer John Agnew. A number of shipwrights and carpenters came to Alexandria from Maine driven by the lack of timber and capital in their home state.[5] After the end of the Civil War, Maine shipbuilders had gotten the white oak they needed to frame their ships from the shores of Maryland and Virginia. In fact, in the winter, some would send a yard foreman and crew to cut out the frames for vessels on order. The prefabricated parts were then shipped north aboard schooners.

As a rule, the Virginia-built three-masters tended to be larger than those built elsewhere on the Bay. Virginia's largest was the *Ellwood Harlow* at 835 tons, also built by William Crawford.

The *Harlow*, which was built in 1882, was the third three-master built by the Alexandria Marine Railway and Shipbuilding Co., established in 1874 by Robert Portner and owned in the 1880s by John Agnew. Her overall length was 179 feet, her beam, 36 feet. Her lower masts were 95, 96, and 97 feet respectively; her topmasts, 50 feet each. The mizzen boom was 65 feet and the others 43 feet. She had a centerboard and a power windlass. Her standing rigging was of wire. The *Harlow* cost $35,000 to build.[6]

The simple rig of the three-masted schooners, plus a donkey engine to help with hoisting sails and anchors, enabled them to operate with as few as seven men: the captain, mate, cook, and four sailors.

This view of the Annapolis harbor shows the three-masted *William Linthicum*, built in 1894 at Church Creek, Maryland. She was built by Benjamin Linthicum who also built the three-masted *Josiah Linthicum* and *Richard Linthicum* and the two-masted *Charles Linthicum*. She was tied up at the Johnson Lumber Co. at the foot of King George Street. The *Linthicum* was sold to Bermuda in 1940, cut down for use as a barge, and was lost shortly thereafter. (Frank Moorshead, Jr., Mystic Seaport Museum, No. 91-10-98)

For a time, the three-masters earned a fair profit for their owners and captains. In 1910, Vernon Hopkins was captain of the 269-ton *Bayard Hopkins*, running from New York to Jacksonville, Florida, with coal and fertilizer on the southbound trip and lumber on the return north. The round-trip took three weeks. Hopkins was paid half of the usual $1,200 charter, out of which he paid for food, the crew's salary, and half of the port charges. He cleared around $400 every three weeks.[7]

Three-masters that worked the upper Bay carried a variety of bulk freight. Chief among those who employed schooners until the very end was the Baltimore ship brokerage firm of C. C. Paul and Co. The company, founded by Charles Cornelius Paul, was located at the intersection of Pratt and Gay streets, popularly known as Gaff Topsail Corner and was in business until 1946. C. C. Paul operated a fleet of fourteen freight schooners. Among them were the three-masters, the *William Linthicum, John L. Martino,* and *William T. Parker*.[8]

The 105-foot *William T. Parker* was not bought by C. C. Paul until 1919. By then, she had had a long and eventful career. Built by C. C. Davidson at Milton, Delaware, in 1891, the *Parker* sailed in the coastal trade. She operated first out of Wilmington, Delaware, and then Philadelphia, surviving severe storms in 1899, 1908, and 1915.[9]

The three-masted schooner *Robert* was built as the *John A. Curtis* in 1874 at Laurel, Delaware, for Captain J. B. Quillin of Bethel. One of her captains reportedly said that the *Curtis* sailed like a fish in water. She was rebuilt and renamed *Robert* in 1908. With her mizzen "wung out" and obscured by her mainsail, she appears to be a two-master in this photo. (Maryland Historical Society)

By 1929, the *Parker's* three topmasts and jibboom had been removed and she was badly hogged, but she continued to work, carrying lumber from North Carolina and Virginia to Baltimore.[10]

Woodrow Aaron of Cambridge was a member of the crew of the *Parker* on the night of February 24, 1935, when she was returning to Baltimore with a load of lumber from North Carolina. The steamer *Commercial Bostonian* was headed down the Bay. It is possible the helmsman saw the schooner too late and was in the process of turning to get out of her way. At any rate, "the *Bostonian* cut the bowsprit off of her," Aaron recalled, "but she didn't sink. We used old mattresses and rags and everything we could think of to stop the hole. I'll never understand how it happened. She was coming down. We were going up."[11]

The steamer suffered hardly a scratch. The *Parker* made it to Annapolis to check the full extent of the damage and then continued under sail to Marley Creek near Baltimore to unload her lumber. That done, she continued on to A. Smith & Sons Shipyard in Curtis Creek where a survey showed that repair would be too expensive. The *William T. Parker* was tied up at Locust Point and used as a home until 1945 when she made her last trip to Curtis Bay where she was abandoned.[12]

Just as two-masted schooners were often called bugeyes and almost any two-master in the oyster fleet was erroneously called a pungy, three-masted schooners without topmasts often were mistakenly called rams, a different breed of boat which will be discussed in the following chapter. The *William Linthicum,* which finished out her career without her topmasts, was often called a ram. She did not have the typical wall-sided construction that characterized the rams, however, and was generally remembered as a handsome schooner. The 73-ton *William J. Stanford,* smallest three-master on the Bay, was another that was mistaken for a ram because of her lack of topmasts. In fact, she began life as the two-masted schooner *John P. Connor.* Built in Barkers Landing, Delaware, in 1868, she was lengthened and rerigged with three masts in 1903. About 1930, she was replanked from the waterline up at A. Smith and Sons yard in Curtis Bay. She was then renamed the *William J. Stanford* and worked the Bay until the early 1940s.[13]

Eastern Shore shipwrights built their share of three-masters. E. James Tull of Pocomoke City built half a dozen, among them the 160-foot *J. W. Somerville* for a Gulfport, Mississippi, shipping company. She was launched in 1919 intended for the transatlantic and coastwise trade.

Two, the *Margret H. Vane* and *Phillips M. Brooks*, were built by J. W. Brooks of Madison. In 1893, in Cambridge, G. T. Johnson built the *Venus*, destined to become one of the most long-lived of the three-masters on the Bay. She was 204 tons and was originally engaged in the pineapple trade. Then, for a time, she served as a fisherman under Portuguese registry. The *Venus* eventually returned to the Bay as the *Edna Bright Hough* and finally was abandoned in Norfolk's harbor in 1938.[14]

If Three's Good, Four's Better

As three-masted schooners proved their worth, builders took the next logical step when even larger hulls were needed to carry coal from southern ports to fuel-hungry industries in the north. They added a fourth, a spanker mast, creating the last incarnation of the Chesapeake Bay–built schooner.

Eight-hundred tons was considered the largest size practical for a three-masted schooner. With four masts, the tonnage could be pushed well above 1,000. The first four-masted schooner, the 189-foot *William L. White*, was built by Goss & Sawyer at Bath, Maine, in 1880, a date which coincides closely with the opening of the Chesapeake & Ohio Railway's coal terminal at Newport News, Virginia.[15] By 1897, the largest of the four-masters, the *Frank A. Palmer*, had been built and measured more than 2,000 tons. By the time the four-masters came along, it was recognized that schooners were only viable in bulk cargo trades and the bigger they were, the more economically they could be operated.

Shown here at Machiasport, Maine, the *Lillian E. Kerr* was built by E. James Tull as a three-master in 1920 at Pocomoke City, Maryland. She was 160 feet long and was the last large sailing vessel launched in the Chesapeake watershed. The *Kerr* was well and heavily built, but was somewhat slow. In 1938, she was sold to Captain James Publicover of Nova Scotia who rerigged her as a four-master. That didn't seem to increase her speed, but it did make her easier to handle. (Mystic Seaport Museum, No. 50.705, Robert H. Goddard)

A typical crew was five men before the mast, two mates, and the captain. The fact that they could run with fewer, less skilled and less experienced men was an economy measure that resulted in the loss of a large number of these schooners and many of their crews in the waning years of commercial sail.

Bay-built

Only eleven four-masted schooners were built on the Bay. The earliest were built in direct response to New England's demand for southern coal. Once schooners went beyond the Bay, it was

This view shows the *Lillian E. Kerr* in 1941 rerigged as a four-master and underway in Long Island Sound with a deckload of lumber. She traveled frequently between Halifax, Nova Scotia, and New Haven, Connecticut, with lumber and returned either light or with coal from New York. She was running north from New York on the morning of Friday, November 13, 1942, when she was run down by the steam vessel *Alcoa Pilot* in convoy in the Gulf of Maine. She and her crew were lost. (Mystic Seaport Museum, No. 48.53, C. A. Owens)

depth of hold from deck to keel, not draft, that was the important measurement. The last were built to meet the need for hulls during World War I. Unlike their predecessors, these schooners weren't built for the Bay trade.

The *William T. Hart* was the Bay's first four-master, built in Alexandria in 1883 in the John Agnew yard. Maine builder William Crawford was foreman on the job. A centerboarder, the *Hart* grossed 934 tons and was 198 feet long with a 38-foot beam. Her owner, Captain Joseph Davis of Somerset, Massachusetts, paid $45,000 for her, but got only two years' use out of the

schooner.[16] She was lost at sea in December 1885, and that story was repeated often as more and more of the larger schooners put out with inadequate crews.

The second four-masted schooner built on the Bay was the 173-foot *The Josephine* built in 1890 by J. S. Beacham of Baltimore. She was owned by J. B. Hopkins and worked out of New York City in the 1890s. *The Josephine* was back on the Bay in 1910, when Captain Reuben Quillin bought a share in her. He was her master in June 1912, when a storm came up out of the northeast. *The Josephine* was on the way from Cape Henry to Mayport, Florida, with a cargo of coal. Quillin used the winds to make that trip in sixty-five hours. On the way, he passed the four-masted ram *Judge Pennewill*, shortly before she went down. Reuben Quillin left *The Josephine* in 1913 and went as mate with his father William John Quillin on the schooner *Laura C. Anderson*. In 1916, he left the schooners for steam as many captains of the larger schooners would do. *The Josephine*, which was owned by C. C. Paul & Co., took three of her crew with her when she was lost south of Kill Devil Hills, North Carolina, in 1915.[17]

The 159-foot *Van Lear Black* was built by J. S. Beacham in 1889 and was registered at various times at Philadelphia; Wilmington, Delaware; Jacksonville; and Tampa, Florida. In October 1929, the *Van Lear Black* burned at Nuevitas, Cuba.

The 174-foot *Sallie C. Marvil* was built by T. J. Sauerhoff at the Sharptown Marine Railway in 1901 and sailed out of Laurel, Delaware, for five years. Her owner and captain at the time was William John Quillen who gave his eighteen-year-old son, Reuben, his first taste of the sea aboard her in 1902.[18]

The *Marvil* was one of the few keel schooners built on the Nanticoke. When loaded, she was reportedly a fast sailer with a good wind and all sails drawing, but her heavy rig with its four topmasts tended to make her top-heavy when sailing light. In 1908, her principal owner was A. H. Bull & Co. of New York. Her captain was Harold G. Foss, who owned an interest in her.[19]

"The masters of vessels such as the *Sallie C. Marvil* were not paid wages," said Foss, quoted in the September-December 1959 issue of *Log Chips.* "They sailed the vessel on what was known as 'square halves' and owned an interest in her. The master received one half of the net freight money and out of that paid the crew's wages and for the food or provisions. The balance was for the master. If the vessel made a quick and profitable voyage, then the master did very well for himself."[20]

A. H. Bull & Co. "received five percent commission on all gross freight money, kept the ship's books, made all charters, paid all bills including one-half net freight to the master, and then divided the balance among the various other owners."[21]

The *Marvil* was eventually lost off Venezuela in July 1915 with a cargo of guano.

Maritime historian Robert H. Burgess noted that the four-masters filled Baltimore's harbor in their heyday, "discharging lumber or logwood, loading fertilizer materials or bricks." They anchored in Canton Hollow off Riverview, or tied up at Jones Falls at Pratt Street or at the Redman-Vane or Woodall ship-yards.[22]

Another four-masted ram was the *Albert W. Robinson,* built by the Sharptown Marine Railway in 1907. She was owned by the Boston Ship Brokerage Co. when she foundered three hundred miles off the Virginia capes in 1926.

The *Anna R. Heidritter* was originally the *Cohassett,* built by Kelley, Spear & Co. of Bath, Maine, in 1903 for the transatlantic trade. She was very nearly destroyed by fire in Baltimore's harbor, but enough of her hull remained for her to be rebuilt. In 1910, she was launched at the Sharptown Marine Railway Co. as the *Heidritter.*[23]

Robert H. I. Goddard, Jr., described her in 1943: "She was a handy little vessel of 694 gross tons, 610 net. Her dimensions were 185 × 37 × 13½ feet. The after cabin contained very comfortable accommodations, being remarkable for its amount of headroom."[24]

In 1918, she was caught in the Atlantic and shelled by a German submarine which left her still afloat but a wreck. A British cruiser found her and towed the hulk to Gibraltar where she was repaired and eventually sent back to the United States.

The *Anandale* is shown here at Hoboken, New Jersey, on the New Jersey side of New York Harbor. By the time she came along, the large coastal carriers had evolved to a fairly standard hull form—full-bodied and designed for bulk cargoes such as coal. She was stranded at Andicora, Venezuela, in 1929. (The Mariners' Museum, No. PK 5472)

This on-deck view of the *Charles M. Struven* was taken just before her launching. Note the caulkers who paused in their work for the picture to be taken. The caulking iron is still sticking out of the deck seam and one of the workmen is holding a large caulking mallet called a "beetle." The caulking was a two-man operation to set the cotton and oakum hard in large seams with the beetle. On her maiden voyage, she carried 930 tons of coal loaded at Newport News, Virginia. The *Struven* also could carry 475,000 board feet of lumber. She ended her days as a barge, the *Maurice R. Shaw*, and foundered in 1942 off Point Jupiter, Florida. (The Mariners' Museum, No. PK 6144, Gilbert)

She was bought by Captain Bennett D. Coleman, who was also her captain for most of his remaining years.[25]

In 1942, returning to Baltimore from Port au Prince with a cargo of logwood, the *Heidritter* was run ashore by a storm at Ocracoke, North Carolina. Coleman and the rest of his crew had lashed themselves to the doomed schooner's lower rigging to keep from being swept overboard by the seas sweeping across her decks. The *Heidritter* came ashore with her bow to the sea. Her masts held until the storm abated and her crew could be rescued. Some of her cargo was salvaged but nine hundred tons had to be abandoned with the hulk. The sea and area residents carried much of it away. Captain Coleman was killed in an automobile accident a little more than a week after surviving the wreck of the *Heidritter*.

Building Boom

Following a gap of several years, the last of the Bay-built four-masters came along during World War I, as a result of the scarcity of steamship tonnage to carry food and other supplies to England and Europe. "For a few weeks, ships were going down at the rate of fifteen million deadweight tons a year," wrote Lewis Gannett in 1920. "Barely twenty million tons were available for Allied war needs. The pressing necessity was to build any kind of ships which could get across the Atlantic."[27]

In the emergency, a call went out from the government for the creation of a "bridge of boats," of wood, not steel. The idea was to provide a variety of wooden hulls for domestic as well as transatlantic use to free up steel-hulled steamships for transporting war materials and supplies.[28] As a result, four new four-masters were built on the Bay: the *Purnell T. White*, built in 1917 by Alonzo Connelly at Sharptown; the *Charles M. Struven*, built in 1917 by E. James Tull of Pocomoke City; the *Alexander H. Erickson*, built in 1918 by the Delaware Steamboat Co. of Seaford; and, in 1919, the *Anandale*, largest of the vessels carrying the schooner rig built on the Chesapeake Bay.

The 184-foot, 751-ton *Purnell T. White* was built for Captain R. B. White of Baltimore. Bad luck seemed to stalk the *White* from her very first voyage, which took her with a load of railroad materials and general cargo from New York to the coast of Africa. On the return trip, her captain died of what was called African fever and was buried at sea. Two days after she got home, the *White*'s cook was found murdered in her galley. Over the next seven years, which she spent mainly in coastwise and West Indies trade, two more captains would die aboard. Finally, early in 1934, the *Purnell T. White* foundered south of Cape Henry, Virginia. Her captain and three of her six crew members were lost. The unfortunate schooner was raised and towed to Baltimore and the Locust Point ship graveyard in 1935. In 1957, the *White* made one last trip, to Hawkins Point outside of Baltimore's harbor where she was abandoned.[29] As late as 1990 some of her bones would be exposed during extremely low tides off the point just inside the Key Bridge.

The *Struven* was one of a number of four-masted schooners built from a design by Henry J. Gielow. A prominent naval architect and senior member of the firm of Gielow & Orr, he began work at the outset of World War I to perfect the design of wooden cargo carriers that could be built quickly, economically, and in large numbers to meet the demand for additional hulls. On her first voyage, the 171-foot schooner carried 930 tons of coal from Newport News to Martinique. She made the trip in twenty days and then returned to Philadelphia with logwood.[30]

The 197-foot *Alexander H. Erickson* was owned and registered in New York City. She was renamed the *Wellington* in the mid-1920s.

The *Anandale* was the last and largest of the four-masted schooners built on the Bay. She was also the only two-decked four-master built here. Had it not been for World War I, the *Anandale* might never have been started. For a time, American shipyards, with government assistance, had as much work as they could handle to meet war demands. The order for the *Anandale*, however, came along at the very end of the wartime shipbuilding boom when government assistance suddenly ceased.

Construction was begun by the Eastern Shore Shipbuilding Co., but with the drop-off of the demand at the end of the war, not to mention the source of funds, the company went into receivership and was eventually bought by the Thirty-Six Corporation, which completed the *Anandale* for Miller & Houghton of New York.

The *Anandale* very likely was designed by Cox & Stevens.[31] Built of yellow pine and oak, the *Anandale* was 1,530 tons, 227 feet long, with a 42-foot beam. She drew nearly 23 feet. The four-master was lost off Venezuela in July 1929.

Designed by Gielow & Orr of New York, the four-masted, 171-foot *Charles M. Struven* was said to have embodied the most progressive methods in ship construction of her day. The *Struven* was built in Pocomoke City in 1917 by E. James Tull, who considered her one of his finest achievements. Tull was also the mayor of Pocomoke City from 1901 to 1924 and was largely responsible for the development of the shipbuilding industry in the area. It was said that Tull "cut his teeth on a ship mould." He is credited with building over two hundred craft, and, in 1893, he won an award at the World's Columbian Exposition for his model and design of the bugeye, *Little Jennie*. (The Mariners' Museum, No. PK 4045)

Albert F. Paul

Built in Milford, Delaware, the 174-foot *Albert F. Paul* did not qualify as a Chesapeake-built four-master, but she was in all other respects a Bay schooner. The pride of the fleet that flew the white pennant with the red and blue P of shipbroker C. C. Paul, she was named for the son of the company's founder who eventually became the firm's president. Charles Paul's daughter, Elizabeth Paul Bacon, christened the schooner at her launching into the Mispillion River at Milford on August 2, 1917.[32]

Remembering the christening of the *Paul,* Elizabeth Bacon said, "I was told this was the largest vessel to have been built in Milford," which she noted was undoubtedly what brought out a larger than usual crowd. It was a gala occasion and the *Paul*'s builder, William G. Abbott, entertained the assembled guests at lunch.

"The schooner was launched without masts," said Mrs. Bacon. "She was towed to Baltimore to be rigged at the shipyard of J. S. Beacham. Two months later, the *Albert F. Paul* was ready for sea duty. On October 28, 1917, after loading 1,129 tons of coal at Norfolk, she set sail for Pernambuco, Brazil. Then began a succession of voyages [99 in all] that took her to several South American ports, Bermuda, the West Indies, and Gulf and East Coast ports.

"Her cargoes were mostly lumber, coal and logwood and for the first ten years, she showed a profit on every voyage . . . The *Albert F. Paul* is probably the best remembered four-masted schooner to have sailed out of Baltimore, which she did until 1941 . . . Much of [her] success could be attributed to her master, Capt. Robert O. Jones, who took command of the *Paul* in 1924 and remained in her until 1941."[33]

In 1936, C. C. Paul was one of only three companies operating sailing ships on the Atlantic seaboard. Its president was Albert F. Paul. He realized the days of commercial sail were limited. His schooners could not compete with tugs and barges and vessels powered by steam or oil. "When people want goods tomorrow, they want them tomorrow," he told author Lee McCardell in 1936.[34]

"A month before Pearl Harbor, my family sold the *Albert F. Paul* to a New York firm," said Elizabeth Bacon, "and on her first voyage for her new owners [February 1942], after delivering a cargo of coal at Bermuda and then taking on a cargo of salt at Turks Island, Bahamas, for Norfolk, she was sunk by a German submarine . . . with the loss of all hands. Her master then was Capt. William M. Martino."[35]

Betwixt the Bark and the Tree

One schooner built during the World War I building boom existed as both a three- and four-master. The 160-foot *Lillian E. Kerr* was built by E. James Tull and was launched in 1920 at Pocomoke City, Maryland, as a three-masted schooner. She was not only large for a three-master, but strongly built. Under three-masted rig, the *Kerr* was a difficult vessel to handle and was generally considered a slow sailer.

"Doubtless her stiffness under sail may be attributed to the strength of her hull which was tried many times during her existence," wrote Robert Goddard in the 1940s.[36]

The *Kerr* was owned in the late 1920s and early 1930s by a New York firm and was engaged in coastwise trade. In 1937, she was sold to Captain James Publicover of Dublin Shores, Nova Scotia, for use in trade to the West Indies. After studying the schooner's hull and rig, Publicover and his son William decided that she would serve them better as a four-master. She received her fourth mast in the spring of 1938 and the change apparently made her easier to handle.[37]

When the Publicovers lost their other four-master, the *Laura Annie Barnes*, they put the *Kerr* on her run carrying baled wood pulp between Nova Scotian ports and New Haven, Connecticut. She continued in her trade in pulpwood, lumber, and coal, all considered essential war materials, after the declaration of war in 1941.[38]

Because the *Kerr* depended upon the wind for her power, she could not keep up with the scheduled convoys. She was running on her own shortly after midnight on November 13, 1942, with a load of coal from New York for Halifax when she was run down by the steamer *Alcoa Pilot*. The steamer was part of a convoy headed west in the Gulf of Maine. The schooner was cut in two and went down in two minutes. The cable ship, *Cyrus Field*, which was also in the convoy, found only one of the seven-member crew. He died aboard the rescue ship.[39]

A Diminishing Fleet

Reporter Lee McCardell noted in 1936 that the *Doris Hamlin*, owned by W. B. Vane, was the only four-master other than the *Albert F. Paul* sailing out of Baltimore.[40] In little more than a decade, all of the others, Bay-built or New England–built, had been lost, never to be replaced.

In 1924, the Maine-built *Dorothea L. Brinkman* ran ashore at Oregon Inlet, North Carolina, and had to be abandoned.[41] The *Anandale* was stranded on July 13, 1929, off Andicora, Venezuela. The *Charles M. Struven* had burned at the pier of a New York lumberyard and became a barge, which foundered off Point Jupiter, Florida, in 1942.

The *G. A. Kohler*, which was employed mainly in freighting coal to the West Indies and logwood from Haiti back to Baltimore, was lost in a storm off North Carolina in 1933. Her captain was George H. Hopkins. His wife, as usual, was aboard. She was a seasoned sailor, prepared for just about anything after her first trip aboard the *Kohler* to Haiti for logwood in the 1920s. The *Kohler* anchored off Bimini when the schooner's cook died suddenly and had to be buried at sea. George Hopkins assumed he had consigned the man's body to the Gulf Stream, but the next morning, his wife was shocked to look over the side into the crystal clear water and see the canvas covered body standing upright, weaving from side to side. At her urging they hoisted the anchor and got under way posthaste.[42]

This view of the Sharptown Marine Railway was taken some time after 1901. The vessel at the left is the 174-foot *Sallie C. Marvil,* one of the handsomer four-masters. She was built in 1901 at Sharptown by master builder Thomas Sauerhoff, who built also at Bethel. His brother, Joseph Sauerhoff, built at Cambridge, Maryland. In the middle is the *John Q. Ferguson,* rebuilt in 1888 from the *James Diverty,* which was built in New Jersey in 1857. She eventually became the three-masted *Virginia.* At the right is the ram *George F. Phillips,* built at Bethel, Delaware, in 1901 by J. M. C. Moore. (The Mariners' Museum, PK 4512, Dr. J. E. Marvil)

Death came closer that August 23rd of 1933 when a hurricane caught the schooner off Cape Hatteras. The *Kohler* was driven ashore and the Hopkinses and the rest of the crew spent the night tossed about by the wind and the sea before the Coast Guard came along and rigged a breeches buoy to take them off. All were saved and when the storm subsided, most of the

The wooden schooner barge *Ruxton* is shown here just before her launching at Baltimore in 1920. The 1,281-ton three-master was built by H. E. Crook. She was owned by the T. J. Hooper Co. of Catonsville, Maryland. This type was designed mainly to be towed with sails added to lessen the drag and increase the efficiency of the tow boats. Many of these barges were former fully rigged sailing vessels, cut down when they became too expensive to operate under sail. The fully rigged clipper ship *Mary Whitridge*, built in Baltimore in 1855, for instance, was cut down and rigged as a schooner barge in the 1880s and lasted into the early twentieth century. (Maryland Historical Society)

Hopkinses' belongings were retrieved as well. Five years later, the hulk was burned in order to salvage her metal fittings.[43] The Hopkinses, in the meantime, had survived the loss of another schooner, the five-masted *Edna Hoyt*, of which we will hear more later.

The 200-foot *Doris Hamlin*, which was built in Harrington, Maine, in 1919, was sold to Baltimore owners in 1930. She was owned by W. B. Vane, and, in 1933, took over the logwood trade following the loss of the *G. A. Kohler*. Her normal complement was a crew of eight: the captain, bos'n, engineer, cook, and four seamen. Typically, the donkey steam engine did most of the heavy lifting, weighing anchor, pumping, hoisting her sails, and shipping her yawl. She carried sixteen sails. Early in 1940, the *Hamlin* loaded coal for the Canary Islands, set sail, and was never heard from again.[45]

The Boston-owned *Herbert L. Rawding* was another four-master that carried logwood to Baltimore. In 1942, the *Rawding* carried the last cargo of logwood to arrive in Baltimore under sail. The *Rawding* survived the war carrying general cargo only to be lost off the coast of Spain in 1947.[46]

More Is Not Necessarily Better

The first of fifty-six five-masted schooners was the *Governor Ames* built in 1888. She was 245 feet long with a 49-foot beam. Her first voyage out, the *Ames* lost her rig and was $20,000 in debt for rerigging before she delivered her first cargo. She worked the West Coast for four years from 1890 to 1894 and then returned to load coal in the Chesapeake Bay until she suffered a fatal stranding in 1909.[47] The *Ames* was followed in 1900 by the Maine-built *George W. Wells*, the first six-master. She was "hailed as a symbol of the rebirth of the American merchant marine," according to Lewis Parker.[48] There would be ten six-masters in all, ranging from 2,800 to 3,700 gross tons, built one a year from 1900 to 1909. The *Wyoming* was the last and largest of the six-masters, and the largest wooden vessel built. Anticipating the success of the six-masters, the steel-hulled, seven-masted *Thomas W. Lawson* was launched in 1902 by the Fore River Ship & Engine Co. of Quincy, Massachusetts. The

Lawson, like many of the six-masters, listed Baltimore and the coal piers at Curtis Bay as a regular port of call. She was 375 feet long, with a 50-foot beam and drew 22 feet.

The giant *Lawson* was eventually converted to an oil tanker and in 1907, was on her first transatlantic voyage, bound for England with nearly two and a half million gallons of lubricating oil. She had a crew of seventeen including officers. The crossing took six weeks, during which she was battered by storms. On her arrival off England's shores, one more storm hit, causing her to break in two between her sixth and seventh masts. All but two of her crew were lost and her cargo of oil spilled into the sea.[49]

The 224-foot *Edna Hoyt*, built in 1920, was the last five-master to be built on the East Coast. She was small for a five-masted schooner, but that was an advantage that kept her working when larger ships were idle. Early in her career, the *Hoyt* carried general cargo outbound for the West Indies and returned with guano or salt. In the late 1930s, she entered the coal trade, running between the Chesapeake and New England under owners Foss and Crabtree of Boston.[50]

In 1937, her captain was George H. Hopkins, and his wife was along when the *Hoyt* became the last wooden five-master to cross the North Atlantic. On the outbound voyage, she carried 1,350,000 feet of lumber from Halifax, Nova Scotia, to Belfast, Ireland. There, in November of that year, she loaded coal briquettes for Venezuela. The schooner was twenty-one days out of Cardiff, Wales, when she ran into a storm in the Bay of Biscay and the 'tween decks collapsed, causing severe leaking. The *Hoyt* barely kept afloat for twelve days, during which time Mrs. Hopkins and the crew were never out of their life preservers. Finally, a steamer came along to tow them six hundred miles to Lisbon where the schooner had to be abandoned.[51]

One of the chief flaws of the five- and six-masted schooners was the length of their hulls, which made them extremely vulnerable to hogging. John Wardwell, who designed the *George W. Wells*, admitted, "Six-masters were not practical. They were too long for wooden construction and when loaded with coal became badly strained by overlapping the beds on which they rest at low tide, while discharging cargoes."[52]

The five-masted schooner barge *Dykes* is shown here at anchor in New York in 1926. The steel-hulled barge was built in Baltimore in 1919 and is an example of the final incarnation of the commercial schooner rig. She was designed by Cox and Stevens of New York to haul aluminum ore for the Aluminum Company of America. (Peabody Museum of Salem, No. 20,503, P. L. Sperr)

In the building of such large schooners, weatherliness was sacrificed to obtain the greater size and cargo capacity. In the process, the largest multimasted schooners lost the advantage of the fore-and-aft rig that had made the schooner the mainstay of America's maritime fleet. They did not come about easily in heavy weather and constantly ran the risk of being blown onto a lee shore. As a result, they did not work as well as was hoped in the coastwise trades and were similarly ineffective on the open seas. It really made little difference, however, for they were doomed regardless of their sailing capabilities. The steam collier and the tug and barge took their cargoes one by one and the large schooners, like most of their smaller cousins, were either abandoned in ship graveyards or were converted to other uses. In the case of the multimasted schooners, that was generally conversion to towing barges.

Fourteen

Shipbuilding on the Nanticoke

The Nanticoke River, birthplace of the Chesapeake Bay ram, originates in central Sussex County, Delaware, and winds its way down to meet Broad Creek. The two flow as one into Tangier Sound in the lower third of the Chesapeake Bay. One of the narrowest of the Bay's tributary rivers, the Nanticoke once flowed through great forests of white oak, pine, and cypress and supported a flourishing shipbuilding industry in the towns of Bethel and Seaford, Delaware, and Sharptown, Maryland.

In the 1870s, David W. Moore was building schooners at Laurel, on the town side of Broad Creek, launching them sideways because the river was so very narrow. He built the *Annie E. Moore* in 1870, the *Amelia Hearne*, with two topmasts, in 1873, the *John McGinnis*, also with two topmasts, in 1874, and, under the supervision of W. R. McIlvaine, the *John A. Curtis*, with three topmasts, in 1874. David Moore wasn't known to be a ship designer, and the likelihood is that the design of the graceful vessels built in Laurel was influenced by his brother, J. M. C. Moore, who was also building schooners in Laurel and later, at Bethel, or Lewisville as it was called then. Construction was probably supervised by Minos Dulaney, a black man, who was noted as a skilled builder of canoes and ships.[1]

Until 1883, when Broad Creek was dredged, most vessels did not go up to Laurel. They stopped at Bethel, which was a major shipping point to Baltimore. Their cargoes were lightered in shallow-draft scows either rowed or poled back and forth to Laurel.

This unidentified schooner is passing through the locks of the C & D Canal in 1892. It clearly illustrates why the canal had the effect that it did on the design and construction of schooners. Any schooner meant to take the inside route to Philadelphia from any Bay port had to pass through these narrow locks which were not eliminated until 1927. (Courtesy of the Staten Island Historical Society, No. A369, E. Alice Austin)

Following the dredging, schooners, with the aid of the tide, could be towed upriver by yawl boats rowed by four or five men.[2]

An Innovator

In 1870, J. M. C. Moore took over as manager of the newly built horse-operated Lewisville Marine Railway. Shortly thereafter, Moore built his first schooner, a three-master, the *Hattie E. Giles*, in 1874. In 1883, when an attempt was made to haul the large coastal schooner, *Clara M. Goodman* (later the *Mary E. Bacon*), which was reckoned to be more than three hundred tons, the horse-driven winch broke and sent J. M. C. Moore in search of a solution. An innovative man, Moore solved the problem with a steam engine from a nearby lumber mill to operate the railway's hauling-out cradle. The *Goodman* had the honor of being the first vessel hauled out at Bethel by steam.[3] Another of Moore's innovations was the use of copper bottom paint, which he began using in 1875. His greatest innovation, however, was the design for the Chesapeake Bay ram, the first of which was laid down in June 1889.[4]

Variously called the Nanticoke or the Chesapeake Bay ram, Moore's new schooner type was built specifically for passing through the locks of the Chesapeake and Delaware Canal.

At the head of the Chesapeake Bay was the thirteen-mile C & D Canal, which joined the Bay and the Delaware River, cutting three hundred miles off the trip from Philadelphia to Baltimore by water. It was completed in 1829. The canal's maximum width in its earliest days was 66 feet, its depth, 10 feet. During World War I, the federal government took over operation of the canal, eventually eliminating the locks. (Today, it is 450 feet wide and 35 feet deep.)[5]

Originally, there were four 24-foot-wide locks; one at Delaware City, Delaware, one at St. Georges, Delaware, and two at Chesapeake City, Maryland. The water level in each lock was maintained by a giant waterwheel, 38 feet in diameter and 10 feet wide, which lifted 1,200,000 gallons of water every hour.[6]

Canal Barges

In the early days, several canal barges built in Hamburg, Pennsylvania, for work on the Raritan Canal were converted to

The *Jennie D. Bell*, built in 1898 in Bethel, Delaware, was the last ram to serve on the Bay, and, in 1956, carrying a cargo of grain from West Point, Virginia, to Baltimore, became the last schooner to freight a cargo on the Bay as well. She is shown here at the dock in Salisbury, Maryland, in 1948. Note her boxy wall-sided hull, which was typical of many of the rams and unlike those such as the *Granville R. Bacon*. (Peabody Museum of Salem, No. 27,016, Otis Lloyd, Jr.)

schooners at the Lewisville Marine Railway for transit through the C & D Canal. The *William J. Donnelly, Lulu M. Quillin, Robin Hood,* and *Three Friends* were all converted in the early 1880s. All had one or two topmasts.[7]

The *Donnelly*, which was typical of these converted barges, had a beam of only 17 feet. She worked well enough when loaded below decks, but great care had to be taken when heeling her

The *Granville R. Bacon*, built in 1911 at the Bethel Marine Railway, was the last ram J. M. C. Moore built. She was considered to be one of the best looking of the outside rams, as those built too wide for the 24-foot locks of the C & D Canal were called. (The Mariners' Museum, No. PK 5263, Waller)

with a load on deck as her main boom trailed in the water up to the sheet blocks. One of her captains, Vernon Hopkins, used to say that "he had to walk on one foot and on one knee when the boat was heeling."[8]

To meet the growing need for vessels to traverse the C & D Canal, several canal barges, such as the *R. J. Camp*, also were built at Bethel.

Note the name change here. In 1880, the name Lewisville was changed to Bethel, a biblical name meaning "sailor's retreat."[9] The choice of name was appropriate, for not only were vessels built and repaired in Lewisville, they often got their crews from the area as well. In the late 1800s, the total population of the town was less than 250 and 25 percent of its men were mariners on the Bay or in the coastwise trades. With the change in the town's name, the Lewisville Marine Railway was renamed the George K. Phillips Company after one of its owners.[10]

A New Type

With the increasing importance of the canal, the need arose for a more versatile vessel than the canal barge. The solution was J. M. C. Moore's ram, the *J. Dallas Marvil*, launched in November 1889. The type acquired the name "ram" sometime around the turn of the century. Local lore has it that someone saw one moving through the locks of the C & D Canal and said, "That ship is pushing through just like a ram."[11]

Another explanation is that the term came from a Civil War–era vessel designed for military use to ram enemy ships. Thereafter, any ungainly, wall-sided, blunt-bowed vessel was known as a ram.

The most successful ship of its size and type, the ram was "a three-masted, baldheaded, narrow, shoal, flat-bottomed, slab-sided, shovel-sterned centerboard schooner with a spike bowsprit."[12] Their block coefficients (gross tonnage divided by the product of length times beam times depth) distinguish them from conventional schooners and indicate their origin from the same or very similar models, built narrower and more shoal than other schooners of like size and rig. Their width was narrow, between 22.5 and 23.9 feet, enabling them to pass through the original 24-foot locks of the Chesapeake and Delaware Canal. Their draft, which seldom exceeded 8 feet, was limited by the canal and by the shallow Hatteras inlets through which lumber from the Pamlico and Albemarle sounds had to pass on its way to northern markets.[13]

The development of the narrow, shoal-draft ram extended the life of commercial sail by making it possible for sizable cargoes of lumber to be carried under sail in the relative safety of the inland waterway all the way from Beaufort, North Carolina, to Philadelphia.

The first and smallest of the rams, the *J. Dallas Marvil* was 112.8 feet long, with a beam of 23.6 feet and a depth of 7.4 feet. In comparison, the last of the rams, the *Granville R. Bacon*, which was built in 1911, was 133.6 feet by 31.6 feet by 11.8 feet. The *Bacon*, with its broad 31-foot beam was what was called an "outside" ram, a development which will be discussed later.

All but two of the rams were three-masters, the exceptions being the four-masted *Judge Pennewill* and the ramlike *Albert W. Robinson.* Only a few had topmasts. As a result, they were referred to as bald-headed. Because they were narrow and of shallow draft, tending to be "tender" or top-heavy to begin with, the rams could not carry a lofty rig. Their sails were cut to have as low a center of effort as possible. Hence the absence of topmasts.[14]

Howard O'Day, captain of the *Jennie D. Bell*, explained the reason for the lack of topmasts on rams: "In the first place, they didn't need the extra sail. Their foresails, mainsails, and spankers provided enough canvas to push them through the water at a reasonably good clip, even when fully loaded. In the second place, the extra weight up there would have made the ships topheavy—and they were topheavy enough as it was, what with their narrowness and their shallow draft. Even with a full cargo, the *Bell* would draw only 9 feet or so . . . In a heavy wind, they'd list a good bit and I never took the *Bell* out into the ocean because of that."[15]

Getting through the C & D Canal still had its problems, even with a vessel designed for the transit. "How fast you got through the canal was according to how you got the tide," recalled Woodrow Aaron, who served on several schooners and rams during his career on the Bay. "You had to push through and only had that fifteen-horsepower yawl boat. A lot of times you were going against the tide and it was stronger. A boat'd get in there and wouldn't move. You either had to wait for the tide to change or a powerboat to come along and pull you through."[16]

Captain Roy Brewington freighted phosphate rock from Baltimore to the Worcester Fertilizer Company in Snow Hill aboard the ram *Edward R. Baird, Jr.* in the forties and early fifties. He thought nothing of taking ten days to make the trip. Often enough he'd have to heave to for days in Tangier Sound, Solomons, or Annapolis to wait for the wind to change.[17]

"Nowadays, you don't find many people willing to wait so long for a change of wind—or for anything else for that matter," Brewington told a newspaper reporter back in the forties. "But in this business, you've got to be a good waiter.

"I have been sailing this bay for 41 years. In that time, I calculate I have actually been on the water for 25 years. I have not yet figured how much of those 25 years I have spent waiting for a breeze or been under way. What difference does it make? All I know is that 25 years is a right long 'sweat' to be afloat. But they have been pretty good years."[18]

The ram was also his home, which was the case with many of the captains of these large schooners. Brewington's wife and son lived with him aboard the *Baird*.

Brewington died in 1953 and the *Baird* had been tied up at the Worcester Fertilizer Company dock in Snow Hill for some time before that. An engineer by the name of George Staples bought her and in September 1955, had her towed from Snow Hill to be hauled out for repairs in Baltimore. After sitting idle for more than two years, her seams had opened above the waterline. In Tangier Sound, a Coast Guard cutter took her in tow and soon the bow waves filled the schooner enough to sink her in thirty feet of water. The *Baird* was finally dynamited so there was no wreckage above twenty-five feet of water and became a fishing reef.[19]

To Build a Ram

At J. M. C. Moore's yard three or four rams could be built in a year. A crew of fifteen men per ship got the construction under way and then as many as fifty or sixty were added to finish her. They'd work ten hours a day, five or six on Saturday. Ship carpenters earned $1.50 a day. J. M. C. Moore paid himself $.30 an hour.[20]

Local timber went into the first rams. It was hauled in from nearby swamps by cart and six- or eight-mule teams. These were the large oak timbers used for keels, keelsons, frames, beams, and stanchions. The timbers were used just as they came from the mill. Oak timbers were easily worked when they were green and as they dried, they got an unbreakable hold on metal fastenings. By the time the rams came along, the building of large wooden ships was on the wane and the last of the rams built on the Nanticoke were planked and decked with pine from North Carolina or Georgia.[21]

Captain John S. Smith of Bethel recalled schooners arriving at Bethel loaded with enough Georgia pine to build a ram. The steamer, *Carrie*, which had a daily run from Sharptown, Maryland, to Laurel brought in the ship chandlery, rope, paint, galley stove, and blocks and whatever else was needed from Baltimore.

The keel was laid first in the order of building a ram. Then came the floor timbers, the ribs, the stem, the knightheads, the transom, the rudderpost, and deadwood. The measurements for the shape of the frames for the bow and stern were taken from patterns or molds used for the prototype *J. Dallas Marvil*, which were laid out in Moore's pasture.

Once the sheer line for the deck beams was established, the 24-foot centerboard well and centerboard were put in, usually on the starboard side of the keel, slightly forward of amidships. This was followed by the deck beams, the keelsons, and the side and floor ceiling. Next the hull was planked with pine, except for that around the bow and stern which had to be bent. The latter was of oak, which could be bent without breaking when put through a steam box. A gnaw hole or section of planking was left out of the port side of the bow so that timbers and other materials could be fed to the inside of the hull. That was closed and the seams caulked with oakum. Then came the bowsprit of Oregon pine (now known as Douglas fir) followed by the two deck hatches, approximately 8 feet square, one located about 16 feet forward of the mainmast and the other 16 feet aft.[22]

Early steering gear, such as that originally on the *Thomas J. Shryock*, was called a "deck-chaser," or a "walking bedstead," because its rolling action between two upright stanchions looked like a bedstead. Later, the rams got a more modern "diamond screw" steering gear.

Typical of ram construction, the *Shryock's* frame was of Maryland oak, her hull and deck of Georgia pine, which continued to ooze its resin in the hot summer sun long after a boat was built. The deck seams were caulked with oakum and then filled with hot pitch. Finishing steps were the addition of the log rail, the cabin, and forward deckhouse. Chain boxes were built on the forward deck. They had to be large enough to hold 400 feet of one-inch chain. The *Shryock* carried a wooden barrel windlass. The chain passed several turns around the "barrel" then was coiled or "flaked" on deck and in the chain boxes.

Most rams were also painted below the waterline with copper bottom paint. After the schooner was completed, salt, which is an effective preservative, was poured between the frames, filling the space between ceiling and planking to within two feet of the deck. Finally, the decks were oiled. The masts were almost always stepped after the ram was launched.[23]

The Launching

Launching was a holiday in Laurel and Bethel. The schools were let out and everyone in town gathered at the water's edge to watch. Any who desired could go aboard the schooner to ride it down the ways or skids. Between launchings, the skids were moored in the water next to the wharf. When needed, they were hauled out, cleaned, greased well with tallow, and put under the bottom of the boat. Wielding "pin malls," men from the yard drove wedges to lift the boat off the keel blocks so that it rested only on the launching skids. They then stood ready with axes to cut through the stern props at the moment of launching, which was timed just when the flood tide had begun to ebb.

If the schooner did not begin to move on its own, the visitors on its decks, usually 150 or 200, were asked to move to the bow and then run to the stern and "stop all at once." That was a sure-fire method of getting the vessel moving. The schooner hit the water with a great splash which sent large waves up and down the river. Its momentum carried the vessel several hundred yards upstream, but the ebb tide soon carried it back to where workmen from the shipyard could get lines on it to bring it back to the dock.[24]

The *J. Dallas Marvil* was launched with more fanfare than most. Delaware Governor Joshua H. Marvil, father of J. Dallas, stood at the *Marvil*'s bow, the wind billowing his long black cape, as the first ram ever slid into the Nanticoke River. At her helm when she began her career on the Bay and along the Atlantic coast was a Bethel man, Will Eskridge. She shipped lumber, coal, fertilizer, and cement and worked until June 1910, when she collided with the steamship *Everett* and sank off Sandy Point, Maryland.[25]

A very different sort of spectacle was provided for the crowd at the launching of the *Mabel and Ruth* in 1896. A Miss Amelia Gordy, who was watching the proceedings from the decks of the schooner *Robin Hood*, earned a place in maritime history when she fell overboard. As was the custom of ladies of that day, she was wearing several petticoats beneath her dress. Not only did her attire save her from a thorough drenching, but Miss Gordy landed upright and remained that way to the astonishment of onlookers. Buoyed by her skirts, she seemed to be standing in the water and floated that way until she was rescued by Captain W. J. Quillin, who dove in after her.[26]

Stepping the Masts

Once the ram was launched, she was towed or pushed to J. M. C. Moore's wharf, which lay along an open stretch of shore. There Dan, his driving horse, powered a derrick that hoisted the ram's three masts, all three of which could usually be stepped

Launch day for a ram usually brought out the whole town. Schoolchildren were given a holiday for the event. Here, the *Reedville*, built in 1910 by E. James Tull, is being launched in Pocomoke City, Maryland, in 1911. She had a somewhat finer hull than most of the more full-bodied Bethel rams. Her block coefficient was in the area of .78 whereas most of the others were up over .80. The *Reedville* was lost in February 1927. (The Mariners' Museum, No. PK 4518, Waller)

in a single day. A ram's masts stood 70 feet or more above the deck. Equidistant between the fore and mizzen masts, the main was slightly forward of center. The foremast was in the center of the forward deckhouse.[27]

The 100-foot mast timbers were usually of Oregon pine transported to Philadelphia by ship and there put in the water. A raft of six logs was made and then towed to Bethel by the first

The *Judge Pennewill*, built in 1906 at Bethel, Delaware, was the largest, and one of only two, four-masted rams. She was built with two centerboards, which probably gave her a fairly versatile helm when sailing. Having two centerboards was unusual, but not unique. She is brand-new here and freshly painted with no scum line or staining from her scuppers. The workman on the scaffolding under her cathead is just beginning to paint the name on the vessel. The *Pennewill* was lost off the South Carolina coast carrying cement to Florida in 1912. (The Mariners' Museum, No. PK 3012, Waller)

tug headed that way. On a few occasions, the mighty mast timbers were shipped by rail from Oregon, requiring two railroad cars to transport them. They arrived square or octagonally cut and were rounded by broadax and drawing knife.[28]

"They'd finish up to around ninety feet," says Joe Liener of Pot Pie on Maryland's Eastern Shore. "They would chop for a long time and did a beautiful job. The finished mast looked like it'd been turned on a lathe. Of course, one side was straight. You're making a flagpole if you put the taper on all sides. The side your sail's on is straight."[29]

The masts of the *Thomas J. Shryock* were 85 feet with a 20-inch diameter and cost $600 each when she was built in 1891. Her booms were of Maine fir. With the masts set, the spars were put in place and the rigging completed. The rams were rigged by Arnold Elzey and William Bennett of Sharptown, Maryland. Their rig consisted of a flying jib, a standing jib, a staysail, a foresail, a mainsail, and a spanker or mizzen. The foresail was

the largest sail of the three on a ram. On a conventional schooner, the foresail was the smaller of the two it carried. The sails were made by Ben Gravenor, also of Sharptown, or were bought from John McGinnis of Philadelphia or from Baltimore sailmakers. At the last, the anchors, chains, other hardware, and accessories were put on for delivery to the new owner. A ram generally carried two 900-pound anchors and a 200-pound kedge.[30]

Economical and Efficient

Put up against any other three- or four-master of comparable size, a ram couldn't be beat for economy and efficiency. With its topmasts, an ordinary freight schooner of comparable size would normally need a crew of eight to get under way and set its sails. The bald-headed ram required four fewer crew members. Later with the addition of a donkey engine to raise sails, one man, if necessary, could do the job. The standard crew for a ram, however, was the captain, a mate, a cook, and two sailors.[31] Because the rams were much larger than the two-masted schooners working the Bay, they could carry larger cargoes, travel longer distances, and make a greater profit for their shareholders.

A Smart Sailer

The ram was said to be a "smart sailer and good sea boat" by those who knew her, although she did not work well to windward. Ten knots was not unusual, however, with the wind aft or on the quarter. According to Captain Orlando Moore, one of the better known skippers, a ram would head into the wind within five points of the compass versus four points for a conventional schooner.[32]

In a storm, Captain Moore advised that all sail be "stripped" and the anchor "let go." Some fifty to sixty fathoms of chain might be let out when anchoring in a storm. Hauling the anchor back in again, storm or no storm, kept four men at the hand windlass for as much as a half hour. Once the anchor was up, the mizzen, main, foresail, and headsails were raised. When the one-cylinder donkey engine came into use, temperamental as it was, it made hoisting the larger sails a much easier task.[33]

The light winds and narrow, winding rivers of the Bay frequently made sailing an impossibility. Rams relied heavily on their yawl boats, even more than conventional Bay schooners did. Their yawl boats were powered by fifteen- or thirty-horse-power engines. Lathrop engines were among the most popular.

Inside and Outside

There were two types of rams, designated "inside" or "outside" depending on their size and general use. The early, inside rams were smaller, with a beam under 24 feet, conforming to the width of the locks of the C & D Canal.[34] They worked best in the protected waters of the Bay or its tributaries. Later, with a growing demand in the Bay for lumber from the Carolinas and other southern states, larger, beamier rams were built. These were too wide for the original locks of the C & D Canal, but they were more seaworthy and capable of going coastwise. Their greater capacity for carrying bulk cargoes such as lumber, which did not have to be delivered according to a tight schedule, kept some of them working until the mid-1950s.

The ten larger, outside rams had beams up to 34.5 feet and were used in coastwise and even oceangoing trades. The *Alverda S. Elzey*, which was 135.9 feet long, had a beam of 28.5 feet, and drew 8.2 feet, was one of the outside type. Although her hull was built wall-sided like a ram, she was rigged like a schooner with three topmasts, a jibboom, and trailboards. The *Elzey* also had five headsails. She was said to have been one of the best looking rams, which were built for work, not looks. She was lost off Mexico in 1910.

Largest of the three-masted outside rams was the *Joseph P. Cooper* at 150 feet, with a 28.2-foot beam and a 10.2-foot draft. She was built at Sharptown, Maryland, in 1905. This ram was one of those that maritime historian and author Robert H. Burgess refers to as an "improved model," having a foretop, a jibboom, a more graceful sheer, and a handsomer bow and stern.[35] Her home port was Crisfield, Maryland, but she spent her first years as a New York to Miami packet. During World

These unidentified rams are inbound for Baltimore, both deep-laden with lumber. The Chesapeake Bay rams were economical and efficient freighters and were a common sight on the Bay up until the 1940s. (Chesapeake Bay Maritime Museum, No. X598)

This view, taken near Annapolis in 1936, shows the ram *B. P. Gravenor*, deep-laden with lumber, being pushed by her yawl boat. According to Robert H. Burgess, the *Gravenor*, renamed the *May Fair*, was lost off Cape Hatteras in 1942, making her the last large commercial sailing vessel lost on the Outer Banks. (Courtesy of the Smithsonian Institution, National Museum of American History, HAMMS Collection, Philip Sawyer)

War I, her captain, John Beauchamp of Baltimore, took a charter from New Orleans to Spain with a cargo of barrel staves for wine casks. The return cargo was salt. Many of the owners were nervous about the voyage and sold their shares to Beauchamp, who collected $50,000 on his gamble—some $30,000 more than the *Cooper* cost to build. He sold the schooner, which was subsequently lost in the Atlantic in November 1918.[36]

The *Judge Pennewill* was the only bald-headed four-masted ram. She was 155 feet long, 34.5 feet abeam, and drew 12.2 feet. Built by J. M. C. Moore at Bethel in 1906, she had two centerboards, one forward and one aft. The *Pennewill* was

abandoned by her crew and lost in a storm off the South Carolina coast in June 1912.

In 1909, J. M. C. Moore's yard, which was by then known as the Bethel Marine Railway, was sold to Samuel J. Furniss and James M. Eskridge. Moore remained to build the *Granville R. Bacon*, which was the last ram built on the Bay and was said to have been the best looking of all.[37] One of the outside type, the *Bacon* was owned by Captain George Jones of Norfolk. In her final years, she carried coal from Norfolk and New York to Camden, Maine. Running light out of Camden in December 1933, she hit a strong southeaster. Under forestaysail and spanker, the captain drove her south through the blizzard, not realizing that she was drifting dangerously close to shore. By the time he sighted lights on land, it was too late to keep the *Bacon* from beaching herself at Weekapaug, Rhode Island. Her crew of six and valuable fittings and gear were brought off and she was burned when the Coast Guard could not pull her off the rugged shore.[38]

The Bethel yard was bought in 1916 by Smith and Terry, Inc. The company built two oceangoing barges, No. 1 in 1917 and No. 2 in 1918, but by the end of World War I, the yard was idle and remained so until it was dismantled in the 1940s.[39]

Jennie D. Bell

While others among the twenty-six rams built at Bethel, Delaware, and at Sharptown and Pocomoke City, Maryland, may have had more distinguishing features or longer, more eventful lives, the *Jennie D. Bell* is one of the best examples of this unique Chesapeake Bay craft.

She was built at Bethel in 1898 for Captain William S. Bell and was named for his wife. Captain Bell's ownership was brief because he died three years after she was built. The *Bell* was 125 feet long, 23.5 feet abeam, and she drew 7.5 feet. At various times the *Jennie D. Bell* was owned by as many as twenty-one shareholders from Laurel, Bethel, Seaford, and Baltimore.[40]

Lumber was one of her main payloads, but she also hauled coal, canned goods, vegetables, and grain. Although she was never inspected by the American Bureau of Shipping for voyaging offshore, she did so and weathered the experience well.[41]

Howard O'Day of Bethel bought into the *Bell* in 1918 and was her captain for three years. She was owned then by C. C. Paul. O'Day's wife and small son sailed with him four or five months out of the year.[42]

The *Bell*'s last owner was Clarence Heath. He became her captain and part owner in 1927. Born on the Nanticoke at Jesterville, Maryland, Heath started on the water with his father when he was fifteen. At age seventeen, he went aboard the schooner *North Carolina*, under Captain William C. Johnson, sailing from the James River to Philadelphia and New York with lumber.[43]

Heath went from the *North Carolina* to become captain of the two-master *Brooklyn*, at the age of nineteen. He was captain of a succession of schooners, including the *Blackbird*, known on the Bay as a real sailer; the *Murray Vandiver*; and the three-master *Abel W. Parker*. He gave up the *Parker* when he bought one-eighth share of the *Jennie D. Bell*. He sailed her for C. C. Paul and then shared ownership with the Worcester Fertilizer Company, hauling fertilizer materials between Baltimore, Snow Hill, Salisbury, and Pocomoke City.[44]

Real trouble struck the *Bell* only once. As Captain Raymond Evans had discovered on the *Fannie Insley*, deck engines were handy but treacherous. The hoisting engine on the *Bell* managed to entangle one of the deckhands in the jib halyard, which wrapped several times around his neck and left arm before Captain Heath was able to reach him and stop the engine. His left arm was almost completely severed at the shoulder when Heath lowered him to the gas-driven yawl boat for the three-and-one-half-hour trip to Salisbury. The man lived, but lost his arm.[45]

In 1955, Clarence Heath bought out the Worcester Fertilizer Company's shares to become sole owner of the *Bell*. Calvert Evans recalled that the *Jennie D. Bell* was home to Captain Heath and his wife, who lived aboard for twenty-four years. They almost always had dogs, thirteen at one time. "When they weren't tied up at a wharf, it took him the first hour when he got up in the morning to clean the deck," recalled Calvert Evans. "Those dogs would be yapping so much sometimes, you couldn't talk."[46]

The *Bell* was one of the best-kept schooners on the Bay in spite of the dogs. Calvert Evans remembered that she held her shape to the very end.

By the time Captain Heath acquired full ownership of the schooner, she served him as little more than a home. He had a difficult time keeping the *Bell* busy. She brought the last schooner-load of lumber under sail from North Carolina to the Bay in the early 1950s.[47] In 1957, the ram's donkey engine gave out after raising the mizzen three-quarters of the way. There was no replacing the engine and no raising the other sails with only Captain Heath and one other elderly man to hoist them by hand. The *Bell* worked through the winter with headsails and partially hoisted mizzen and then made her last trip up the Wicomico to Salisbury, Maryland.[48] Captain Heath and his wife lived aboard until 1961, a year before his death. The *Jennie D. Bell* was pushed onto the flats just off Riverside Drive in 1961 and there slowly rotted away.[49]

A latecomer in the history of commercial sail on the Chesapeake, the ram was the largest of the distinctly Bay craft. Although not as comely or as fast as the other freighters carrying the schooner rig, the Nanticoke ram fulfilled its purpose admirably. The economy of its operation, its sturdiness, and its size forestalled the coming of the end of commercial sail on the Bay. The *Jennie D. Bell* was the last sailing freighter on the Chesapeake.

One other ram, the *Edwin and Maud*, survived, but not on the Bay and not hauling freight. She was converted to a dude cruiser at the end of World War II and operated on the Bay until 1954 when she went north to become a successful Maine "windjammer." The dude cruisers, fitted out to carry passengers not freight, were the last stage in the decline and disappearance of commercial schooners working under sail on the Chesapeake Bay.

Fifteen

Sail Was Fading Out

Even though steam had been coming on strong since before the Civil War, Bay schooners held their own. For bulk cargo, they still could offer the cheapest rates. But if you looked around, you could see they were being used up, wrecked, or just plain worn out. There was no money in building new ones. By the turn of the twentieth century, a new-built two-masted schooner was a rarity on the Bay. Powerboats were inching ahead in the race into the future and over the next half century, they would leave the aging schooner fleet dead in the water. Quite literally.

In the last half of the nineteenth century, the schooner *Sallie and Ellen* was cut in half by a steamer in the Delaware Bay. Her captain, Thomas Hopkins, and his brother Calvin survived, each on one half of the schooner, as the two sections floated down the Bay. They were rescued before the bisected boat sank beneath them.[1]

Before engine-driven vessels came along to share the waterways, sailing vessels were numerous and often ran into each other. More and more, and larger and larger, steam- and diesel-powered boats gained yet another advantage. In a collision, they usually sent the schooner to the bottom.

Captain W. J. Quillin of Seaford, Delaware, was captain of the four-masted *Herbert D. Maxwell*, built in Maine in 1905. She was off Sandy Point, Maryland, when she collided with the Merchant and Miners Line steamship *Dorchester*. The insurance investigation later showed that the schooner changed course just before the collision. Captain Quillin and Elvey Quillin were in the stern when the steamer carried away the forward quarter of the *Maxwell*, drowning her steward and two sailors who were in the bow. What was left of the schooner floated long enough for the Quillins to be rescued.[2]

More of the schooner fleet were lost during World War I, especially the larger three- and four-masters that went offshore. One that survived a German submarine attack was the *Edward R. Baird, Jr.*, which was said to have been one of the best looking of the rams, with her quarterdeck and forecastle. She was just above the Chesapeake Lightship bound for New York with lumber when a German submarine surfaced. The U-boat captain ordered Captain Robert Coulbourn and the *Baird*'s crew into the ram's yawl boat and then took them prisoner. Before submerging, the submarine fired a shell into the ram's port bow.

During the three days the *Baird*'s crew was aboard the submarine, its captain boasted of attending a show in Norfolk. When finally the Americans were put ashore between Cape Henlopen and Fenwick Island, they passed the information on to the navy, whose investigators used it to help them locate

German saboteurs operating out of a cottage near Virginia Beach.

The *Baird*, in the meantime, was kept afloat by her cargo of lumber until a U.S. Coast Guard cutter found her and towed her into Norfolk. J. M. C. Moore traveled down from Bethel, Delaware, to retrieve the ram, which had the dubious distinction of being the first merchant sailing vessel of the United States attacked by Germans in American waters during World War I.[3]

Another schooner attacked by a German submarine was not as lucky. The *Laura C. Anderson* was off the coast of France in August 1917 when she was fired on. She was lost, but her crew escaped and were eventually rescued.[4]

Others often disappeared mysteriously without clear evidence to tell whether they were victims of enemy action or an act of nature. Generally, however, the end of most of the Bay's schooners was less dramatic.

They Ran Those Schooners 'til They Were Worn Out

Unless a schooner was poorly built to begin with, she had a clean, slightly convex sweep or sheer to her deckline. Over time, however, many developed a definite sag at bow and stern and were said to be "hogged"—a sure sign of age, if not impending demise.

"There used to be some hogged-up boats on this Bay," said Woodrow Aaron of Cambridge. The *William T. Parker* was one with which he had more than a passing acquaintance. "We had a pump on each end of her and had to build her up inside on each end to make it level, so she'd be flat in the hold for cargo.

"They ran those schooners 'til they were worn out," said Aaron. "I asked Marshall Pritchard once about the old *Mary Lee.* 'Isn't she leaking pretty bad?' I asked. 'Oh no,' he said. 'I sleep with one foot out of the berth and when I feel the water come

The *William J. Stanford* was built as the *John P. Connor* in Barkers Landing, Delaware, in 1868. In 1887, she was lengthened and rerigged as a three-master and for a time carried the name *Priscilla.* At 89 feet, she was fairly small for a three-master. There were a number of such bald-headed, spike bowspritted schooners like the *Stanford*, which looked like rams, but were not. In the final days of sail, when schooners could not compete with powered vessels in terms of speed, topsails and extra headsails along with the larger crews to handle them were eliminated to save money. Also, the vessels were getting old and tired and couldn't stand the extra press of sail from topsails and extra headsails. In 1930, the *Stanford* was rebuilt at A. Smith & Sons Shipyard, which eventually owned and operated her. She was sold in 1937 and this view was taken sometime after that. In this photograph she is showing her age; hogging is quite apparent in her sheer. The *Stanford* was abandoned near Rock Hall, Maryland, in the late 1940s. (C. Calvert Evans)

The *A. Victor Neal* was rebuilt from the *John C. Kelso* in 1924. Here she is shown at the Oxford Shipyard in 1938 having some replanking done amidships. (Frank Moorshead, Jr., Mystic Seaport Museum, No. 91-10-137)

lined a dip net with a burlap bag to hold the sawdust and then worked it up and down under the schooner's hull. When sucked into the seams, the shavings or sawdust would swell to make a good seal. A more permanent solution was to drive shingles into the seams where the oakum was working out and then cut them off. They'd swell up, making a tight boat.[7]

Not only time and the normal processes of aging worked on a hull. Notes made by a captain of the schooner *Maggie* tell of how he was finding her "sluggish and down by the head" under sail. He went forward to check and could hear water gushing in somewhere in the bow. On closer investigation, he discovered that rats had gnawed a hole that was only underwater when she was under press of sail.[8]

An Old Enemy

A more pervasive and invasive problem than rats was the *Teredo navalis* or shipworm. It flourished in salt water from June through mid-July, honeycombing unprotected planking in the hulls of wooden vessels. In colonial days a solution was to careen a vessel, or haul it out at the end of the "worm season" so that the worms could be burned off. Another was to coat the bottom of the boat with pitch, tar, lime, or tallow. As it turned out, the best and simplest solution was to make frequent runs up into rivers and creeks where the water was more fresh than salt and thus kill the dastardly worms.[9]

The Last Step

The practice of sheathing a schooner's hull with sheet metal was common on the Bay only when schooners began to show wear. If a schooner was in relatively good shape, metal was used only in a strip below the bends, from the bow to two-thirds of her length aft, to protect her from ice.

When a man covered the hull of his boat with "metal"—usually heavy-gauge galvanized steel—it was one step short of running her into some back creek to die.

up on my foot, I know it's time to get up and pump her out.' I asked him how high was her floor above her ceiling? 'Oh I imagine about three foot,' he said."[5]

"You beat those old schooners up and down the Bay and they leaked aplenty," said Captain Harry Porter. "Down in the country, captains would go ashore to a farmer's yard to get bags of horse manure and carry them on deck. Then, when they stopped overnight, they'd take long-handled dip nets and fill them full of this stuff and shove the nets down under the boat, shaking the manure loose. The boat was sure to be leaking and it would suck it right into the seams."[6]

They would also run the bow of a leaking schooner up onto a mudbank to achieve the same end. Some said the Wicomico River mud was especially good for filling the seams. Probably better than manure or mud was sawdust or wood shavings. They

"We called that putting a boat 'in a coffin,'" said Calvert Evans. "All the old boats went that way. You did that to hold them together. When a boat gets to working in a big sea and the planks are working on the frame, she'll tend to spit the oakum out of her seams. That will send her to the graveyard quicker than anything in the world if you can't keep the caulking in the seams.

"You usually put the metal on from the waterway to below the waterline, but some went halfway to the keel. Before you did that, you'd clean the hull and replace any rotten planks. Then one man would spread the pine tar on with a broom, another would come right behind to put the sheets of felt on right away and finally would come the men putting on the metal. They did it all at once so the pine tar wouldn't dry out before it could soak into the felt. They used narrow sheets of steel and the width of it varied with the curve of the hull, but mostly it was two feet wide. It would lay up against the hull without a wrinkle in it and most of it was a decent looking job. My father used gas tar to paint the hull once he got the metal on the *Fannie* and when that got dry it was hard as enamel. There was very little rust.

"After he put the metal on, that stiffened her up. You could see the difference once she'd been put in a coffin. Before, when she was at sea, she'd start shaking and trembling, but then you'd put the metal on her and that would tighten her up. You got a long time out of her after that."[10]

Old Sails

Besides a tight hull, a man working the Bay in a schooner wanted a good set of sails, but, toward the end, when lean years were coming one right after the other, he'd keep a sail as long as it was possible to patch it. Generally, the life of a sail was six, maybe seven years, but a lot went longer than that.

"It got to the point when an old schooner couldn't go any longer and she'd made her last trip, if she had one halfway decent sail, you'd put it on another schooner," said Calvert Evans. "Some of them didn't fit too good either. Maybe the sail was 50 foot on the mast on the boat it was made for, but on another, it'd be 30 foot. We used to reef them, like we did in heavy

In 1988, the *Lula M. Phillips*, which long since had been converted to power, sank at her berth in the Port Norris, New Jersey, area and in 1990 was purchased by Mark Swiderer from New England, who got her raised and taken to Yanks Boatworks in Tuckahoe, New Jersey. She was hauled out there in the spring of 1991 when this photo was taken. The yard was in the process of sheathing her hull with plywood and sheet aluminum. Note some of the old metal remains. Old-timers called this encasing of a vessel's hull putting it "in a coffin." It was a last resort in order to keep a boat afloat a bit longer. Shortly after this picture was taken, the *Phillips* was towed to Haverhill, Massachusetts, to be rebuilt for the dude schooner trade. (M. Staley)

weather, and when it got to be too much trouble to reef them, we'd have them cut off.

"Years ago, when C. C. Paul was in business, he had five or six four-masters," Evans continued. "They'd put new sails on those that were going outside and sometimes he'd give the old ones to those that had Bay schooners. Some of them would cut them down. Some, you didn't have to do anything with, just put them on and use them. With cheaper freight rates and higher cost of equipment, they'd use anything they could get by with."[11]

You Could Always Get Shell

As schooners gave way to steamers and then to tugs with barges that could carry far greater loads than a typical two- or three-master, any cargo would do. "If you couldn't get anything else, you could always get a load of oyster shells," said Calvert Evans. "But mostly they were seasonal, in the wintertime when they were shucking oysters. Oyster shells and lumber were considered cheap freights but you could always get a load.

"I had steady work running oyster shells and glad to get it back during the Depression—picking them up from the shucking house at Broomes Island and running them to the Potomac Poultry Food Company's plants in Crisfield and Baltimore where they were ground up for lime and chicken grit. There was some dust in those places. You couldn't see over ten feet in front of you. They counted shells by the bushel and we'd get about four cents a bushel. The *Sarah* carried about five thousand bushels, which was $200 a trip before taking out for the boat and expenses."[12]

William Stevens and his father carried shell from Norfolk to Baltimore in the *Ruth Decker*. "We'd always keep our doors tight shut when we were hauling shell," he said. "There'd always be a lot of rats in the shell. When they were grinding them, you'd hear the rats squealing."[13]

A Brief Reprieve

In the late 1930s, a general business revival brought a brief reprieve for the aging fleet of freight schooners, the oldest of which was the *Federal Hill*, built in Baltimore in 1856.[14] The available power vessels couldn't meet the demand for lumber, fertilizer, and other bulk cargoes. Putting the schooners back to work also was good for the business of chandlers, sailmakers, and others supplying their needs. In fact, business hadn't been that good since World War I—at least as far as Baltimore was concerned.

Captain J. Harry Porter of Kent Island sailed for Baltimore broker Preston Webster, who owned a fleet of freight schooners and bugeyes. His story is much like those of many others who captained schooners in the final days of commercial sail. In the winter during the 1920s and 1930s, Captain Porter ran oysters in the pungy *G. A. Kirwan*. In the spring and summer, his cargoes were grain and fertilizer, carried for a time in the bald-headed schooner *Ella F. Cripps*. She was a fast sailer and one of the memorable ones. He sailed a number of vessels for Webster, including the *Corsica* and the *Augusta*, and the bugeyes *Sarah Wingate* and *Vaughn*. The *Vaughn* was the only boat that Preston Webster kept after the Depression took its toll on his business.[15]

"Sail was fading out then and power was coming in," said Harry B. Porter, J. Harry Porter's son. He went to work with his father after World War II. "My father was running corn, soybeans, wheat, and oats from the Eastern Shore, North Carolina, and Virginia to Baltimore, Norfolk, and to Seaford, Delaware, and was buying and selling oysters on what we called powerboats. They were really the old schooners, converted to power—the *Carol Ann*, the *Sarah C. Conway*, and the *Betty I. Conway*, they were all schooners once."[16]

Captain Harvey's Fleet

The *Sarah C. Conway*, *Carol Ann*, and *Betty I. Conway* that Harry Porter skippered as powerboats were the last of a fleet of schooners that once belonged to Captain Harvey H. Conway of

Cambridge, Maryland. Conway was engaged at one time or another in hauling oysters, fish, grain, lumber, slag, fertilizer, and other bulk cargo, as well as produce and canned goods—all the trades that employed schooners on the Bay between the 1880s and 1940s.[17]

Captain Harvey owned a large fleet of schooners, working out of Cambridge under sail and power. With five sons and five daughters, he established a small dynasty in Cambridge. His sons lived with their families in houses their father owned on Choptank Avenue. At one time, Captain Harvey owned most of Choptank Avenue and a large number of houses throughout the rest of Cambridge as well. All of his sons ran schooners for their father and so did two of his nephews.[18]

"I'd say Captain Harvey's most lucrative work was buying and selling oyster shells," said Calvert Evans. "Anytime you're buying and selling, you're either going ahead or backwards fast. Most were going backwards, but not old man Harvey. He'd go around and estimate shell piles. He'd say, 'Well, there are a couple hundred thousand bushels on that and I'll give you x-number of dollars, and most of the time he'd close the deal right there. That was what kept his boats going. They couldn't handle all the shell and he'd use outside boats. My father used to run a lot of shell for him when the work was slack. A lot of others did too. They'd call Captain Harvey and get a load of shells. A lot of people made money buying and selling oysters. He made it with their shells."[19]

Most of the Conway schooners were given family names. The first, the *William Sommers*, Captain Harvey named after himself, *H. H. Conway*, but soon sold her off the Bay.[20] By all accounts, the Conway schooners were the best kept on the Bay. "That Captain Harvey, he was a hard goer," was the way folks on the Shore described him. He was one of a kind, no doubt about it, but the fate of his fleet, taken schooner by schooner, was all too typical.

Most of Harvey Conway's fleet were acquired in the early 1920s and 1930s. None were new. In 1930, Captain Harvey bought the *Richard Cromwell*, which was built by Joseph W. Brooks of Madison, Maryland, in 1888 and in her early career worked in the pineapple trade. He renamed the *Cromwell*, *Harvey*

The *Fannie Insley* is shown here with a load of oyster shell. Beside her is an unidentified bugeye, also with a load of shell. They are waiting to pass through the locks of the C & D Canal at Chesapeake City, Maryland. The *Fannie* was lost on August 20, 1940, when she was bound up the Bay with a cargo of oyster shell. She was dismasted and sank off the mouth of the Rapphannock River, Virginia. Her crew escaped in the yawl boat. (The Mariners' Museum, No. PK 2647, George Barrie)

Here, the *Minnie Mae Kirwan* is entering the Annapolis harbor. She was built in 1882 at Whitehaven, Maryland, as the *G. W. Robertson*. Typical of many Bay schooners, the *Robertson* worked under several names in her lifetime. She was renamed *Minnie Mae Kirwan* in 1907 and then went on to be renamed twice more after she was converted to power in the early 1940s at A. Smith & Sons yard in Curtis Bay. She then became the *W. C. Witt* and in the midfifties, the *L. R. Parker*. Later, she was sold to Florida where she was abandoned in the seventies. (Frank Moorshead, Jr., Mystic Seaport Museum, No. 91-10-148)

H. Conway. She was eventually sold, converted to power, renamed the *Jeff*, and was finally lost off Florida in 1954.[21]

The 105-foot, New York–built schooner *George S. Allison* was added to the Conway fleet in 1921. She was renamed the *Betty I. Conway* after Harvey, Jr.'s daughter and was converted to power in the late 1920s.[22] Later, she was sold to Captain Arthur R. Eubank of Lewisetta, Virginia, and renamed the *Eugenia* after his daughter. She sank in 1972 following a collision with a menhaden fishing boat near the mouth of the Rappahannock.[23]

In the late 1920s, the *James R. Teal* joined the Conway fleet with the name *Eva Conway*. John Conway converted her to power and eventually sold her to Bermuda in the 1930s.[24]

One of the most beautiful schooners on the Bay was the 79-ton *Laurena Clayton*, built in Cambridge in 1892 for the pineapple trade. The *Laurena Clayton* was the only one of nearly a dozen Conway schooners that did not get the family name. She also was the only one that was not rebuilt when Conway acquired her.[25]

Conway was a firm believer in a well-built, or rebuilt, boat and he rebuilt all of his schooners except the *Laurena Clayton*. The first cost of the boat ought to be the biggest, was his dictum. Built or rebuilt with care and the best materials, a boat would serve many years with no more outlay than that required for normal maintenance.

The *Laurena Clayton* carried lumber—rough board pine from Virginia mostly. She was sold in the 1930s, converted to power, renamed the *Effie M. Lewis* and put to work running oyster shells from the Delaware Bay to Baltimore. She was headed up the Delaware Bay in 1941 with a load of shells when she ran up on a tugboat—literally ended up on top of it—and subsequently sank. As the story goes, when her captain reported the loss, the insurance company didn't want to pay off. They said he had only fire insurance. Undaunted, the captain said he knew that. He had a fire in the engine room and when he went down to fight the fire, that's when she ran into the tug. The company paid.[26]

Collisions and sinkings were a common occurrence and a fair portion of the schooner fleet that survived into the twentieth century had spent some time on the bottom of the Bay or its tributary rivers and creeks. The schooner *Gracie May*, which was built in 1909, became the *Ruth Conway* in the mid-1920s and in 1929, was converted to power under the ownership of Harvey Conway's son Jim. She was later owned by Captain L. R. Parker of Cambridge, and sank in a collision with a tugboat in the C & D Canal in 1947. She was raised and used to haul grain until she began to leak so badly that she sank with seven thousand bushels of corn northwest of the Thimble Shoal Light in the Hampton Roads in 1965.[27]

The 79-foot *William Layton*, built in 1873 below Vienna on the Nanticoke River was renamed the *Ida B. Conway*, after Harvey Conway's daughter-in-law. She was sold in the 1930s to a man in Reedville, Virginia, who sold her to Captain Sammy Todd of Salisbury. Captain Todd sold her to Hodges Crouch who converted the *Ida B.* to power in 1948 and renamed her *John J. Crouch* after his father. Calvert Evans bought her in the midfifties and named her the *Carol Ann* for his daughter. The *Carol Ann* was one of two former Conway schooners owned by Calvert Evans. The other was the *Sarah C. Conway*.[28]

"She Raised Me and My Ten Children"

The 77-foot *Sarah C. Conway* was the last survivor of the Conway fleet and Harvey Conway's favorite. She was built in 1872 for the pineapple trade as the *A.H. Schulz* in Baltimore. Harvey Conway renamed her after his wife Sarah Catherine when he rebuilt her in 1924.

Captain Harvey demanded a lot of a boat. "You never make money laying in harbor," he told one of his captains. "Drive her. When the wind blows, you don't have to stop."[29]

Which was how it was, sailing for Harvey Conway. "Head wind or fair wind," said Leonard H. Turner, who sailed in the *Sarah* for several years, "we never stopped." One time, Turner was in another schooner bound for the York River with sails reefed down because the wind was blowing a gale out of the northwest. They were overtaken by another schooner running with three sails set and paying no mind to the wind. It was Harvey Conway and Turner knew he wouldn't take those sails in until he'd reached his destination. Conway was a hard driver, but men liked to work for him. "They did better on his boats than at home and worked right through the Depression," said Turner.[30]

The *Ida B. Conway* was built in 1873 on the Nanticoke as the *William Layton* and worked originally in the pineapple trade. She became the *Ida B. Conway* in 1924 when she was acquired by Captain Harvey Conway of Cambridge, Maryland. In 1948 she was converted to power at the E. L. Deagle & Son shipyard at Deltaville, Virginia, and became the *John J. Crouch*. When she was owned by Captain Calvert Evans she was renamed the *Carol Ann* after his daughter. She was sold to the West Indies and was lost in 1973 off Puerto Rico. (Peabody Museum of Salem, No. 27,017, Otis Lloyd, Jr.)

The *Sarah C. Conway* was sold off the Bay in the early 1930s and in 1934, Captain Calvert Evans found her with her bow into a marsh near Port Norris, New Jersey, where this photo was taken. He soon was forced to convert her to power, after which the *Sarah* worked on the Bay until 1971, when Captain Evans sold her to Captain Rick Savage for use as a clam dredge out of Ocean City, Maryland. (Frank Moorshead, Jr., Mystic Seaport Museum, No. 91-10-101)

Three or four years before he died in 1937, Conway sold the *Sarah* to a Dr. Charles Sharp in Port Norris, New Jersey, where schooners were still finding work dredging oysters.[31] Not even those who drove themselves and their boats the hardest could beat the forces that were taking work away from commercial sail. Captain Harvey and his sons were finding work increasingly scarce.

The *Sarah* was the schooner Conway sailed himself and he couldn't stand to see her lying idle in the shipyard at Cambridge when he retired from sailing. Leonard Turner remembered the day Conway sold her. When he finally struck the deal, Captain Harvey didn't want to see the schooner go and sent word to the captain to take her away before daylight. "She raised me and my ten children," he told Turner. "I rebuilt her twice. She made me $55,000. I do not want to see her go in daylight."[32]

The *Sarah C. Conway* worked the Delaware Bay until the oyster business there began to fall off. All along the Maurice River from Dorchester to Port Norris and Bivalve, New Jersey, schooners were scattered along the shore, run aground and left to die.

Dump Trash Here

About the time that Harvey Conway sold the *Sarah*, Calvert Evans was working in Easton. His wife was tired of his following the water and Evans came ashore and opened an auto body and fender business. After a few years, he had had enough. "We were doing all right, but I got tired of hammering on fenders," Evans said. "Everyday, I wanted to be on the water."[33]

When he heard there were some schooners laid up in Port Norris, Evans made the trip to New Jersey. What he found was a virtual marine graveyard. Four or five schooners were already beginning to rot along the shore. Their masts were piled up in a nearby field.

"That's where the *Sarah* was," he recalled. "I found her up on the shore. She was put up to die. The first day I went to look at the *Sarah*, she was bow into the marsh right by a sign that read 'Dump Trash Here.' They'd taken all her sails off and all her running rigging. Her masts were still in her and her booms and gaffs were still on her. They'd dried her sails and put them away in good shape in a loft. When I bought her, her sails were ready to put on and everything was in good working shape. Even the yawl boat engine was usable. I forget what Dr. Sharp was asking for her, but I said I've only got $1,450. He said, 'I'll take it.'

"She was a crack sailer. It was a pleasure to work her. She was quick and she'd answer her rudder just the minute you'd roll the wheel down on her. Reminded me of a yacht. Her jib would flop a time or two and then she'd take right off the other way. Most of them you have to hold the jib to windward, so it would blow them around, but not her. She'd come around just fine. I was very fortunate. My daddy had a good sailer with the *Fanny Insley* and I had one too."[34]

It Was Convert or Quit

More than a few captains ran their boats and themselves long past their prime, unwilling to relinquish their way of life without a fight. They went under sail as long as they could, and then those that couldn't give up the water or their boats converted them to power to eke out a living a little bit longer. For a long time, the schooners survived because they got the work the powerboats didn't want—anything that didn't have to be picked up or delivered according to a tight schedule.

"They'd pick up a load of fertilizer or lumber in Carolina and if it took a month to get it to Baltimore, that's what it took," said Harry Porter. "In addition to that, a tugboat and barge could carry up to fifty thousand bushels of grain and could charge maybe a cent or two less than schooners that could carry only five thousand or eight thousand bushels at a time."[35]

"With a powerboat, you could load in Baltimore today and unless there was a hurricane, you'd be down somewhere's on the shore unloading the next morning," said Calvert Evans. "But with a schooner, depending on the wind, you could load in Baltimore on Monday and not get to Cambridge or wherever until Friday. So finally, it got so that if you didn't have a power vessel you couldn't make the time and they started dieselizing the schooners—the ones that were good enough. It was either get out or dieselize and that's what I did to the *Sarah Conway*. I sailed her one year and saw the trend. You just couldn't make it under sail. I owned the *Sarah Conway* and the *Carol Ann*. I was forced to dieselize the *Sarah*. Didn't want to. Had to. It was convert or quit.

"We took the *Sarah* down to Deagle's yard at Deltaville, Virginia, and stripped her down," said Evans. "They converted her from end to end and put on a pilothouse and gave her a diesel engine. They drilled a hole in her stern for a three-inch shaft. We started out with a MR-8 Superior Diesel, straight 8. I think that was the first high-speed diesel that came out. She had a three-to-one reduction gear. Every year you had to pull her down and free her rings up or put new ones in her. She'd stick 'em up every year. I tried every kind of lube oil ever made. They didn't last too long. After we got going a little bit, I put a Caterpiller diesel engine in her. I knew I had an engine then. That was a nice engine."[36]

Still Pushing

Power only delayed the end of the small freighters. First the railroads, and then new highways and trucks, took away the freight business that kept the converted schooners working. Ironically, many of them carried the materials that were used to build the highways for the trucks that were taking their cargoes. Competition was keen among Bay freight boats for what work remained. The converted schooners were still carrying much the same cargoes they had carried under sail and they were still pushing.

"We were out there competing with thirty or forty other boats," recalled Harry B. Porter. "Everybody was in a different location loading grain. It wasn't a thing where you had a schedule saying you load today and you have to be up to Baltimore tomorrow to unload. You loaded and got there as fast as you could to get your name on the list to be unloaded. You let somebody beat you out and get two or three boats ahead of you, that could mean a day or two before you would get unloaded and go after another load. The season just lasted so long and then it was all over, so you were always fighting the other fellow. And you were fighting the weather and always pushing. If you didn't, you didn't make any money."[37]

The *Sarah* Goes Down

By the mid-1950s, Calvert Evans was running phosphate rock on the *Sarah C. Conway* from Baltimore to Seaford, Delaware, and grain on the return down the Nanticoke. The trip took him right past his home in Vienna and if he happened to make it before midnight, he would tie up at his dock and spend the night at home. If it was after midnight, he'd sleep on the boat so as not to wake his wife.

"It was just a little before midnight when I tied up there at Vienna with a load of corn," said Calvert Evans, of what seemed like any other night that May of 1957, "and I figured my wife was liable to be sitting up still, so I walked up to the house."[38]

He left Pete the cook and his dog Sport asleep in the pilothouse. Later, in the early morning hours, the captain of a tugboat pushing a barge upriver went to sleep and ran the barge over the *Sarah*'s stern and up into the pilothouse. The cook was trapped and drowned when the *Sarah* went down. They never did find Sport.

"I didn't intend to raise the *Sarah*," said Evans. "When she was sunk, I was making three trips a week bringing down phosphate rock from Baltimore to Seaford. If I didn't want to lose that work, I had to get another boat. So I bought the *John J. Crouch*. She was very similar to the *Sarah* and she was already dieselized. I named her after my daughter, Carol Ann. Captain Harry Porter ran her for me."[39]

The *Sarah* was too good a boat to stay on the bottom though, and Calvert Evans arranged to have her raised in May 1958 by A. Smith & Sons of Curtis Bay. Buck Smith came down with their crane and hoisted the *Sarah* out of the Nanticoke mud. When they finally could go aboard, they made a chilling discovery. The *Sarah*'s eight-inch exhaust pipe had been bent across Calvert Evans's berth by the bow of the barge. "It would have pinned me in there," he said. "And I almost didn't go up to the house that night."[40]

As soon as the *Sarah* had cleared the water, they took the Caterpillar engine out. "That was something in this world to clean up," said Evans. "We took that engine all to pieces and soaked every piece in Varsol and put it back together. Any part that showed any wear, we replaced it. The real damage was to the hull. I favored Deagle's down in Deltaville and that's where she was rebuilt. I rebuilt the *Sarah* two more times before I sold her in 1970."[41]

Evans sold her to Captain Rick Savage who used her for clamming off Ocean City, Maryland. Calvert Evans went out clamming with Rick Savage several times. "That's a hard life," said Evans. But then, it never was easy for anyone who made a living on Chesapeake Bay schooners, power or sail.

One Last Trip

Lynn Perry recalled his last trip on a schooner. It was a short trip, one Sunday in the fall of 1940. Captain Marshall Pritchard, who had been on the schooner *Maine* for about a year, had anchored her in the Mattaponi River off West Point. He was going up the river to load lumber at Newington Landing, just above the courthouse in King and Queen County, and invited Perry to go along. Lynn Perry didn't know that would be the last time he would sail on a Chesapeake Bay schooner.

Captain Gus Rice was something of a legend among his fellow watermen. An audacious skipper and shrewd gambler, he was never without a deck of cards, even in this photo taken late in his life. Gus Rice was quoted by Phil Sawyer, artist for the Historic American Merchant Marine Survey, as saying, "Beauty is the lead of trade. Ain't no man ever seen me in none but a pretty boat." He was proud of the *Amanda F. Lewis*, but here, we can see that both he and the schooner are looking pretty tired. (Frank Moorshead, Jr., Mystic Seaport Museum, No. 91-10-146)

"It was a beautiful afternoon and we had the first of the flood tide," he recalled. "We started shoving with the yawl boat and after going through the bridge, we put the foresail on her—I think that was for me—but it helped and added to our progress. Marshall let me have the wheel from the anchorage through the bridge and all the way up the river. The *Maine* was hogged and showing her age, but still a joy to be aboard and underway, even with only one sail. The river was beautiful that Sunday afternoon with some color in the trees. And I can still taste the clam fritters we had for supper just before we arrived at the landing. It wasn't long after that trip up the Mattaponi that I joined the navy. When I got back after the war, almost all the schooners were gone. The next time I saw Marshall Pritchard, he was the captain of a tug."[42]

Sixteen

No Frills

Schooners on the Chesapeake Bay were always no-nonsense working craft, but, like the family car of today, they also provided recreation. Well into the 1930s and 1940s, they were still the only means of transportation to Annapolis, Baltimore, or other Bay cities for many a waterman's family. Between runs, freight schooners often were hired for a pleasure cruise or perhaps to carry a fishing or gunning party.

The *Columbia F. C.*, which was built at Mundy Point, Virginia, in 1874 for the Columbia Fishing Club of Washington, D.C., served the sporting group and hauled general freight and lumber as well. She was the last schooner to carry a load of "box-boarded" timber into Washington in August 1946. Shortly after that, she was sold to Captain Tom Henry Ruark of Deltaville, Virginia, who subsequently sold her to Cuba in 1948.[1]

By the late 1930s, working sail was in an irreversible decline on the Bay. The 73-foot *Henry Disston*, a two-master built in Portsmouth, Virginia, in 1881, was typical of those that hung on to the very end—those that were not converted to power. In her early days, the *Disston* worked out of Norfolk in the oyster trade dividing her time between Virginia and New Jersey. Up until the 1920s, she frequently kept busy during the summer months taking sailing parties out of Atlantic City, New Jersey. By 1920, however, she was working primarily on the Bay hauling lumber and other general cargo.[2]

On the eve of World War II, the *Disston* made a brief sortie into the cruise business under the ownership of Captain D'Arcy Grant, who had become tired of freighting but couldn't get schooners out of her system.

The *Disston*'s hold aft was fitted out with a galley, dining saloon, and a cabin for two passengers. Forward of the mainmast, the hold was divided into two compartments with three bunks each. Grant left the original master's cabin aft untouched. The schooner left the steamboat dock at Gloucester Point in July 1941 on her first cruise on the Bay. Too small to offer much in the way of comfort, the *Disston* was not a good choice for cruise work and by 1945, had been abandoned.[3] A second attempt at the cruise business was made with the two-masted *Edward L. Martin* whose windjammer career was also short-lived. The *Martin* was bought by Captain John Conway, converted to power, and renamed the *Honey B.* in 1943.[4]

Dude Cruisers

Windjammers were doing considerably better in Maine, and several Bay schooners were sold north at the end of World War

II. Looked on with disdain by many Bay watermen, they were disparagingly called "skin boats" or "head boats." A kinder term was "dude cruiser."

The so-called dude cruiser was a commercial sailing vessel, like the *Disston*, fitted out for carrying passengers on vacation cruises. They were a product of the post-Depression movement toward the more rustic, homespun, and economical vacation. While dude ranches had been around since 1910, they grew in popularity in the thirties, spurred by the economy and movie westerns. The later, waterborne, East Coast version of the dude ranch was the windjammer or dude cruiser that flourished in Maine and Florida and had a limited success on the Chesapeake Bay.

When Calvert Evans's father Raymond Evans sold the *Fannie Insley*, he went into several old schooners, one of which was the *Ida May*. "Keen on both ends," she wasn't large but by all accounts was a "real fine looking boat."[5] The *Ida May* operated as a cruise boat out of Oxford, Maryland, during World War II. In 1946, she was one of the first of the Bay schooners to be sold north as a dude cruiser. The schooners *Maggie* and *Chesterfield* also went north for the same purpose. By the midfifties, the last two had been abandoned, the *Maggie* in Rockland, Maine, and the *Chesterfield* behind Staten Island.[6]

The 125-foot ram *Mabel and Ruth*, built in 1896, was sold south. Renamed the *City of St. Petersburg*, she was used for her namesake city's tourist trade for only a year before she was junked in 1948.[7]

The 135-foot *Grace G. Bennett*, built in 1893, ended her career as a dude cruiser. She worked the upper Bay and took cruises to Annapolis, Cambridge, Oxford, and up the Potomac to Georgetown between 1945 and 1953.[8]

Chesapeake Vacation Cruises

The most successful dude cruiser operation on the Bay began when a retired B & O Railroad man, Herman Knust, discovered an old schooner laid up in Curtis Bay. She turned out to be the 125-foot ram, *Levin J. Marvel*.

Built in just ninety days, the *Marvel* was launched in 1891. She was built for Captain Henry W. Bell, who died aboard her in a blizzard in 1899. Until his death, Bell freighted North Carolina

The *Henry Disston* was built in Portsmouth, Virginia, in 1881. The 73-foot schooner worked primarily out of Norfolk in the oyster trade. She ran oysters "up the beach" to New Jersey ports and New York and during the summer months often took sailing parties out of Atlantic City. In the 1930s, her topmasts and jibboom were removed to lessen the strain on her rig and reduce her manning requirements. In 1941, D'Arcy Grant, who had owned the *Fannie Insley*, bought the *Disston* and fitted her out for the passenger trade. This was the first attempt at dude cruising on the Chesapeake Bay. By 1945, the *Disston* had been abandoned. She is shown here with passengers rather than cargo. (Frank Moorshead, Jr., Mystic Seaport Museum, No. 91-10-143)

lumber to Baltimore and Philadelphia. The *Marvel* worked between other ports as well, carrying coal and fertilizer mainly.[9]

Knust once owned a Gloucester schooner and long harbored the idea of offering windjammer cruises on the Bay. He bought the *Marvel* in 1944 and over the winter had her converted

Between freight runs, schooner captains often hired their vessels out for pleasure cruises or to carry fishing and gunning parties. This party is on a summer cruise on an unidentified schooner rented sometime in the 1930s by George Turner of Prince Frederick, Maryland. (Maryland State Archives, MdHR-G-1477-5964)

to a cruise ship, completely gutting her in the process. Portholes were cut in her hull to give light and air to sixteen cabins, each with double-deck bunks and a washbasin and running water. Also below deck were separate men's and women's heads with electric flush toilets. The dining room was below, while a library and lounge were in the after deckhouse. The galley, which was in the forward deckhouse, was modernized with a gas stove to

replace the *Marvel*'s old woodburner and food was sent by dumbwaiter to the dining room. In addition to a freight schooner's usual complement of engines for hoisting sails, lowering the yawl boat, and pumping out the bilges, there was one to generate electricity for the lights, radio, and toilets.[10]

Knust's investment in the schooner and her conversion to a dude cruiser was $18,000. After three years, business warranted the purchase of another ram, the *Edwin and Maud*. Launched in April 1900, the *Edwin and Maud* was named for the children of her first captain, Robert Riggin of Bethel. With a bit of a curve to her bilge, the *Edwin and Maud* had less of the look of the old wall-sided rams and more that of a typical three-masted schooner. She was last owned by the C. C. Paul Company of Baltimore and operated in the Bay and coastal freight service until Knust bought her in 1946.[11]

The two rams were running at 90 percent capacity throughout the cruise season, which extended from the first of June to the first week of October. Known as Chesapeake Vacation Cruises, they were home ported in Annapolis. A normal run for a five-day cruise, according to Annapolitan Lester Trott, who handled public relations for the cruise company, would take in St. Michaels, Oxford, Cambridge, and Solomons. A two-week cruise added stops in southern St. Mary's County, Crisfield, Tangier Island, Yorktown, Deep Creek (off the James River in Virginia), and Gwynn Island, Virginia.[12]

If they picked up a favorable wind late in the day, the rams often sailed through the night. They sailed as much as possible, but to make the various ports more or less on schedule, the yawl boats were put to work.

Much of the success of Knust's operation was due to the fact that he maintained his schooners and put them in the hands of capable, experienced skippers, such as Marshall Pritchard, a veteran of thirty years as a Bay schooner captain. Usually the mate and seaman were also watermen who knew the Bay and its boats. The rest of the crew consisted of a cook, steward, and hostess.

Passengers amused themselves sunning, playing shuffleboard on deck, or reading and playing cards or other games in the lounge. Whenever the ram anchored, they swam. The hostess took care of the passengers' needs and perhaps, in the evenings, got a moonlight singalong going on deck. The food, prepared Maryland style, was plentiful.[13]

Down the Intracoastal Waterway

Most winters, the *Marvel* and the *Maud* were laid up at Salisbury on the Wicomico River, but in November 1945, Knust took the *Marvel* from Baltimore to Miami, down the connected bays, canals, and rivers that make up the Intracoastal Waterway. The 125-foot ram was the largest sailing vessel ever to make the 1,271-mile trip, and the event was covered by *Life* Magazine. The *Marvel* stopped at Belhaven, Morehead City, and Southport, North Carolina; Georgetown and Charleston, South Carolina; Brunswick, Georgia; and St. Augustine, Daytona Beach, Sunny Isles, and Miami, Florida.[14]

Thirteen passengers were aboard for the memorable cruise, along with a crew of four which included skipper Marshall Pritchard and owner Herman Knust. The *Marvel* used her yawl boat almost the entire way, but had her sails up a good part of the time. The ram drew six feet, but at many places the waterway was little more than that. She got herself off twenty-two sandbars and out of the mud four times during the thirty-three-day trip. There were also 142 bridges to add excitement.[15]

The bridge tender at Sunny Isles, Florida, probably had one of the most unforgettable hours of his career the day he looked up at the sound of a horn to see the 125-foot, three-masted schooner under full sail headed for the bridge. Aboard the *Marvel* there were also a few heart-stopping moments as it became obvious the draw was not going to open in time. Captain Pritchard leapt into the yawl boat, cut the engine, scrambled back aboard the ram, ran to the bow and dropped the forward anchor. The hook held fast, but the schooner's stern was immediately caught in a cross-tide which swung her around. The *Marvel* ended up backwards in the now fully open draw. The bridge keeper kept the draw open as Pritchard used the yawl boat to pull the schooner back out of the opening and turn her around. He then sailed her through under mainsail and foresail.[16]

Although the trip took a week longer than expected and the South experienced one of the year's worst cold waves, most of those aboard the *Marvel* felt the adventure was well worth it.

The rams *Edwin and Maud* and *Levin J. Marvel* are shown here during their days as dude cruisers. The *Maud* was built in 1900 by G. K. Phillips of Bethel, Delaware, and was a somewhat more graceful, better-looking vessel than some of the earlier rams. She has a slight degree of tumble home and a more pronounced sheer. Nine years older, the *Marvel*, on the left, is showing her age. The difference in the condition of the two vessels is evident in the degree of fairness in their sheer lines, even though the *Marvel* always had a somewhat flatter sheer. (Chesapeake Bay Maritime Museum, Trott Collection, No. 484-7, M. E. Warren)

Herman E. Knust, a retired railroad executive who went into the dude schooner business with the purchase of the *Levin J. Marvel* and the *Edwin and Maud*, successfully operated the two rams as Chesapeake Vacation Cruises out of Annapolis, Maryland, from 1946 to 1954. Annapolitan Lester Trott served as business manager for the firm. Knust is shown here aboard the *Maud*. (Chesapeake Bay Maritime Museum, Trott Collection, No. 533-4)

Knust did not, however, proceed with his plan to develop a winter cruise business with the rams in Florida.

As it turned out, the summer business on the Bay provided a good living for the rams' owner. Knust eventually bought an estate in Culpeper, Virginia. With the cruise business demanding more of his time than he cared to spend, Knust decided to cut back. The *Marvel* was badly hogged and otherwise showing

her age by then. Knust took her out of service and retired her to Salisbury.[17]

North to Maine

In 1954, Knust sold the *Edwin and Maud* to a cruise business in Maine. Her captain was Frederick Guild, a true schoonerman who went to sea at the age of fourteen and was second mate aboard the *Edna Hoyt*, the last five-masted schooner to sail the Atlantic coast. Guild had been taking vacationers on windjammer cruises out of Castine, Maine, since 1932. Knust knew the *Maud* would be in good and capable hands.[18]

The ram was renamed *Victory Chimes* and was completely reconditioned and her hull painted green. Captain Guild became her sole owner in 1959. She was maintained in yachtlike condition. Along with her small boats, she was given a complete overhaul every year. The crew in Maine consisted of a mate, bos'n, three sailors, a cook, and three stewards. The *Victory Chimes*'s Filipino cook, Sixto Arasate, served up large portions of hearty New England fare, spiced with an occasional oriental dish. Janet Guild also went along with her husband, taking her turn at the helm and serving as bookkeeper, publicist, and cruise director.[19]

For thirty-two years, the *Victory Chimes* sailed the coast of Maine under Captain Fred Guild and then in 1986, he sold her to a pair of entrepreneurs who took her to Lake Superior, hoping to make a sail training ship of her. Before heading for the Great Lakes, the *Victory Chimes* was taken to Florida with a stop on the Chesapeake Bay in the fall of 1985.

The 85-year old ram showed the stuff of which she was made when she weathered a fierce gale off the Florida Keys in November 1985. In 1986, she went on to participate in the parade of tall ships in New York Harbor for the Fourth of July observance in honor of the one hundredth anniversary of the

Statue of Liberty. The rest of that summer was spent traveling through the St. Lawrence Seaway to her new home port in Duluth, Minnesota.[20]

Financial difficulties befell her owners and the *Victory Chimes* was towed back to the Chesapeake Bay with her masts and rigging stowed on deck. Over the winter of 1987-88, the ram was bought by Domino's Pizza and then was towed to Maine for a major overhaul. She returned to the Bay a year later, this time painted white with blue trim and named the *Domino Effect*.[21]

Ahoy, Matey!

No one knew it at the time, but when the *Edwin and Maud* sailed out of the Chesapeake in 1954, the end was at hand for the commercial schooner working the Bay under sail.

A Pennsylvania man by the name of John Meckling tried to keep the vacation cruise business going with the *Levin J. Marvel*; the *Grace G. Bennett* was to be added the next season Both were in bad shape, but Meckling did not have the experience with boats or the finances to put them in proper condition, assuming that was possible. He bought the *Bennett* at a sheriff's sale for $310. He never really got her going, and she sank at the bridge at Crumpton during hurricane Hazel in October 1955.[22]

By then, disaster had struck Meckling's enterprise. He had very nearly lost the *Marvel* shortly after he bought her in June 1954. Meckling was still in the Wicomico River, on the way to Annapolis, when the wake of a passing boat drove the *Marvel*'s yawl boat into her transom and she soon began to fill with water. The Salisbury fireboat arrived in time to pump her out and get her safely on her way to Baltimore where minimal repairs were made at the Booz Shipyard.[23]

The rest of the summer was uneventful, as was the first part of the season in 1955. Meckling had brochures printed up:

"Ahoy, Matey! There's loads of fun awaiting you on the good ship *Levin J. Marvel* as she starts her tenth season . . . fun and adventure on the Chesapeake Bay . . . You will feel secure and safe . . . the skipper . . . is a veteran of the Chesapeake, the crew is experienced . . ."[24]

Here, passengers are playing shuffleboard on the deck of the *Edwin and Maud*. She was built with full bulwarks as opposed to some of the other rams which had only built-up log rails. The *Maud* operated as a Bay and coast freighter until 1945 when she was bought by Captain Herman Knust for vacation, or so-called dude, cruises. She was sold off the Bay to Rockland, Maine. Her owner and captain was Fred B. Guild who changed her name to *Victory Chimes*. In keeping with the spirit of the times, this was an inexpensive, but unique, vacation experience. The business began in New England in 1935 and thrived during the Depression and war years when money and fuel were scarce. (Chesapeake Bay Maritime Museum, Trott Collection, No. 534-11)

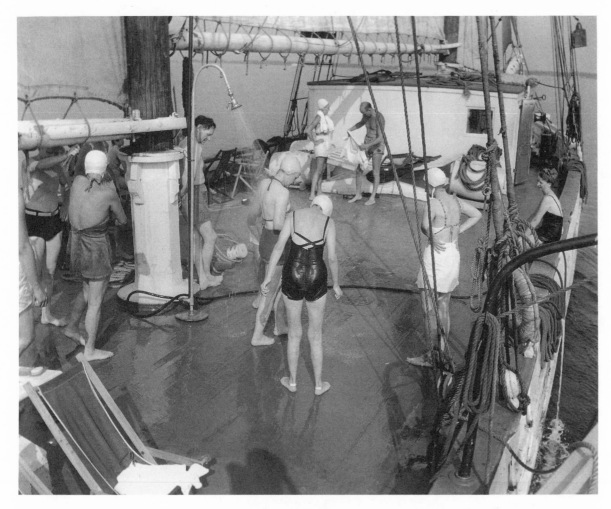

The *Levin J. Marvel* was built in 1891 by J. M. C. Moore. She was the first of Knust's dude cruisers. This view of the passengers showering on deck also shows the *Marvel*'s built-up log rails. Accommodations on the dude cruisers were fairly primitive, which was a part of their appeal. The *Marvel*, however, was destined to bring an end to such cruises on the Bay. Knust sold her in 1954 to John Meckling who operated the aging ram until August 12, 1955, when poor judgment and lack of proper maintenance combined to bring about her loss in Herring Bay during hurricane Connie. Fourteen people were drowned and the tragedy effectively ended dude cruising on the Bay for nearly twenty years. (Maryland State Archives, M. E. Warren, No. MSA 26699-B)

The Last Cruise of the *Marvel*

On Monday, August 8, prospects looked good for a week of that "fun and adventure" when the *Marvel* left the dock at Annapolis with twenty-three passengers, Meckling, a cook, a messboy, and Steve Morton, the seventeen-year-old first mate.[25]

No one gave a thought to weather reports that five hundred miles away, in the Atlantic east of Palm Beach, Florida, hurricane Connie was headed on a northeasterly course.

By noon on Tuesday, the *Marvel* was in Oxford. Meckling received reports of the hurricane alert and warnings that the storm was due in the Bay within twenty-four to forty-eight hours. The passengers were anxious to continue the cruise and persuaded the captain to push on to Cambridge where they spent Wednesday night.

"The hurricane warning had been lifted when we left Cambridge Thursday morning," said Captain John Meckling. "It was a beautiful day. The sun was shining and there was a light, balmy breeze."[26]

Meckling had never taken a course in seamanship or navigation, nor did he hold a master's license or any sort of certification. He carried no barometer, nor did he have experience in judging weather. As the *Marvel* sailed out of Cambridge, he did not know that the flags flying over the Cambridge Yacht Club were storm warnings.[27]

The storm warnings were also being broadcast over the radio, but Meckling yielded to the wishes of his passengers. They felt secure basking in the sun on the decks of the large schooner, which appeared every bit as safe as the buses and airplanes they had taken to get to their vacation afloat on the Chesapeake Bay.

On the way down the Choptank, the *Marvel* anchored so that the passengers could swim. By sundown Thursday, they were in the Bay.

"We proceeded on a northerly course, coming up the Bay toward Annapolis," said Meckling. "The velocity of the wind continued to increase. It grew steadily all night long. We kept under sail with the intention of going into Annapolis or the first port we could make—probably West River or South River."[28]

The skies that night were clear and the passengers stayed on deck enjoying the evening. They finally turned in around 1:00 A.M., and Meckling continued to sail up the Bay. He did not turn on the radio because he didn't want to disturb the sleeping passengers.[29]

"About daylight Friday morning, it started blowing gales. I could see then that on that particular tack we were being blown off our course," said Meckling. "So we changed our tack and tried to run into the lee behind Poplar Island for anchorage off the Eastern Shore."[30]

The winds were recorded later as having been between twenty-five and forty miles per hour with gusts to forty-five miles per hour.[31] Meckling noted that the building clouds promised rain, but he still did not know that Connie had changed course and was due to head straight up the Bay.

The *Marvel* was two and a half miles off Bloody Point light when a terrific gust of wind ripped her foresail. Meckling called below, where the passengers were just beginning to stir, to ask some of the male passengers to come on deck to help the mate, Steve Morton, get the torn sail and the staysail and spanker down. That done, Morton launched the yawl boat and tried to start it with the hope of pushing the *Marvel* toward Poplar Island. He discovered that water in the boat had fouled its engine. The yawl boat was useless. The *Marvel* had no other power beyond her sails.[32]

The Race for Herring Bay

"The staysail forward was raised," Meckling told *The* [Baltimore] *Sun* newspaper, "and we ran before the wind so we would not take the batter of the seas against our sides." By this time, the visibility was about three hundred yards. The wind and rain had whipped a mist off the Bay and "it was like looking into a white wall."[33]

With the winds at her stern increasing steadily, Meckling had little control over the ram's course. He steered now, as best he could, for Herring Bay on the western shore. He assumed that because the hurricane was coming up the Bay, the worst winds would come from the same southerly direction and the gentle curve of Herring Bay would protect them.

"Because the ship rode so well, none of the passengers got frantic or even disturbed," said Meckling. "Everyone was in a very good mood. The chef had prepared hot cakes and scrambled eggs and we had fruit juice and dry cereal for breakfast that morning and everyone chowed down."[34] For fourteen of the people aboard the *Marvel*, that would be their last meal.

After breakfast, the passengers put on raincoats and went on deck, the better to enjoy the ride. None of them realized that they were racing toward the shallows in a bay that would hold them in the path of seventy-mile-an-hour winds roaring out of the northeast. Meckling had not figured on the counterclockwise swirl of hurricane winds.

The *Marvel*'s captain was not in an enviable position. As he stood at the wheel of the 125-foot schooner, careening down the Bay through a blinding rain, his assessment of the situation must have been grim. He had not slept in twenty-four hours. The most experienced person aboard other than himself was a seventeen-year-old who had sailed nothing over twenty feet. He had bowed to the wishes of his passengers who knew nothing of the sea's unforgiving nature and he had completely misjudged the storm that, as yet, was only playing with them.

Around 9:00 A.M., the *Marvel* made Herring Bay, where the crew took her staysail off and dropped the anchor about one and a half miles east of Fairhaven. With the seas running as much as ten feet high, the anchor took some time to hold and bring the ram's bow into the wind.

"Of course, all the time we were lying there, the seas were increasing. The wind was getting more violent, the sea was just turning into . . . a boiling cauldron and the rains were belting down," said Meckling, who drew no comfort from radio reports that hurricane Connie was definitely going to strike the Chesapeake Bay area. At some point, the yawl boat broke away from the stern and was never seen again.[35]

"Now about 11:00, we began taking seas clear up over the bow . . . and the winds were coming down still northeasterly and we were just waiting for it to change to southwest or southerly," said Meckling.[36] Even though the radio was broad-

The *Edwin and Maud* returned to the Bay as the *Victory Chimes* in 1985. Her appearance off Sandy Point, Maryland, during Chesapeake Appreciation Days was the first time in at least twenty-five years that a ram had displaced water in the Bay. After thirty-two years sailing under Captain Fred Guild out of Rockland, Maine, the *Chimes* was sold out of New England. In 1985, she was on her way to the Great Lakes, via the Chesapeake Bay and Florida. The Great Lakes venture proved unsuccessful and, in 1988, the ram was bought by Domino's Pizza for use as a corporate cruise and goodwill vessel. For the next two years she sailed as the *Domino Effect* and then was sold back to Rockland, where she went back to carrying passengers on windjammer cruises in 1991, sailing once more as the *Victory Chimes*. (M. Staley)

casting northeast storm warnings, he still did not understand that the hurricane's winds would not change to a southwesterly direction until the eye had passed over them.

Meckling asked the passengers to stay below because the wind and the seas washing over the bow made it nearly impossible to stand upright on deck. Assuring them that they were in no danger, he asked them to get into life preservers.[37]

The passengers laughed and joked as they put on their life jackets. They did not know that there was no lifeboat and the yawl boat had been swept away. They did not know that hurricane Connie had already claimed another former schooner, the two-masted *LaForrest L. Simmons*, then a powerboat. Her two-man crew had a lifeboat that took them safely to shore not far from where the *Marvel* pulled at her anchor in Herring Bay.[38]

At one point, the *Marvel* pulled her anchor free and swung broadside to the waves, which rolled her over on her side, sweeping away her forward deckhouse and leaving a yawning hole through which the seas poured into the hold. The forward bilge pump would not start, and the passengers took turns at the hand pump. A gas-driven bilge pump was taken down to the dining room, but the tremendous amount of water was more than it could handle. Below, the passengers tried vainly to close the portholes, but few could be secured and they resorted to stuffing blankets in the openings. That was ineffectual and the water climbed higher and higher in the forepart of the vessel.[39]

SOS

At around 1:30, Meckling began sending radio distress signals, but his Mayday signal was never heard. By 2:00 the *Marvel* was losing buoyancy from the water pouring in over her bow.[40] Her foredeck was awash and Meckling gathered the passengers on the afterdeck to explain the method of abandoning ship. They began to fasten themselves to a lifeline to prevent them from drifting apart once they were in the water. "There was no hysteria, no panic and everyone aboard cooperated to the fullest extent," said Meckling. It was shortly after 2:30 on the afternoon of August 12, 1955.[41]

Once more the anchor lifted and the ship swung broadside to the waves, rolling first to port and then to starboard and capsized.[42]

Deborah Killip, a copywriter for a New York advertising firm, was in the cabin below. "I was thrown against the wall. I could feel people clawing around me . . . The water was all around, rushing in . . . I saw the skylight above me. Someone was holding my legs . . . then I was floating." Once free of the boat, she made no effort to swim. It was enough to let her lifejacket hold her up as she struggled to catch her breath after each swell washed over her. At 4:15, Killip was the first to wash close enough to the beach for someone to see her and swim out to help her ashore. Her rescue brought the first word of the wreck.[43]

Meckling had been on the afterdeck and was caught beneath a sail. "The seas grabbed me and I was washed clear of the ship," he said. "When I got out from under, the water around me was full of people."[44]

They fought the seas that were sweeping them shoreward where they could see the surf crashing on the rock jetties that lined the shore. Meckling and four others managed to stay together and paddle away from the rocks. After several hours, they were washed into a duck blind where a sixth person had already found shelter.[45]

Two men ashore at North Beach finally saw a yellow hat waved by the people huddled in the duck blind. At great risk to themselves, they made three trips in a fourteen-foot outboard to save the occupants of the blind. It was about 8:00 by the time the last of the six were brought ashore.[46]

The husband of one of the women rescued from the blind had made it safely to shore only to be drowned trying to rescue others.[47] Seven people, in addition to the six in the duckblind, survived the wreck of the *Levin J. Marvel*. Fourteen died, including two couples and two children with their parents.[48] The last of the bodies, that of a thirteen-year old boy, was found on August 16.[49]

The tragedy was the worst in the history of the Chesapeake rams and was never forgotten by Bay watermen, who believed the *Marvel* should have been retired long before and run aground on some quiet riverbank. The Coast Guard inquiry found that the "casualty was directly caused by the unseaworthy condition of the *Levin J. Marvel* . . . due to the poor physical condition of essential hull structures and fittings, which had been neglected by the managing owner" and that a "contributing cause was the poor judgement used by Mr. Meckling." The inquiry also found that "the vessel was inadequately manned."[50]

The loss of the *Levin J. Marvel* brought an abrupt end to passenger service on the Bay, a hiatus that would last for twenty years. Of greater importance was passage by Congress of the Bonner Act requiring strict regulation of the construction, maintenance, and operation of small passenger cruise vessels by the U.S. Coast Guard.

Epilogue

They Are All Gone Now

By the 1950s, the shores of creeks and rivers from one end of the Bay to another were littered with old, worked-out schooners, run aground and left to die. For a time, men still knew their names and could tell a thing or two about this one or that. They were old friends gone to rest and the watermen who knew them viewed the rotting hulks with an abiding fondness and respect. Every one of the old schooners had worked hard providing a living for the men who sailed them.

As in the earliest days, there were still small fishing villages, farm landings, and ports along the coast of Maine and in the Chesapeake and Delaware bays that were not served by major highway systems. The relatively protected waterways in these areas kept schooners viable after they ceased to be competitive in the freight business.

Once the Chesapeake was bridged and cargoes could be carried more cheaply and efficiently by giant freighters, high-capacity barges, or trucks, the aging and rapidly diminishing schooner fleet was driven from the shipping lanes once and for all. Records indicate that none were built after the *William F. Dunn* was launched in Norfolk in 1924.[1] At that time, there were more than one hundred still working the Chesapeake, but the next two decades would see almost all of them lost, abandoned, converted to power, or sold off the Bay.

The most complete record of the final days of the Chesapeake Bay schooner is found in the photographs and writing of

The *Rose M. Gaskill*, which was built as the *C. W. Hand* in 1915 at Solomons Island, Maryland, worked out of Philadelphia in the Delaware Bay oyster fleet. She was cut down for power in the late 1940s and has been abandoned in Bivalve, New Jersey, since 1989. This photo was taken in 1991. (M. Staley)

historian and author Robert H. Burgess. He captured many of the last of the schooners still working under sail and power before they disappeared entirely. For some, he wrote the final chapter, offering a sad catalogue of rotting hulks, abandoned from one end of the Bay to the other.

Although no one knew it at the time, Bay schooners were beginning to record a series of "lasts," the last load of coal, of lumber, of grain. The last pungy under sail on the Bay was the *Wave*, built in Accomack County, Virginia, in 1863. She worked out of the Chester River until 1939 when she was converted to a yacht and altered so that she was barely recognizable. Eventually, she was taken to the Great Lakes.[2] The last two-masted schooner employed on the Bay was the *Anna and Helen*, which worked with the Crisfield oyster dredging fleet until she sank in Crisfield's harbor in 1957. She was abandoned two years later.[3]

A few schooners were sold off the Bay in the 1930s and 1940s, but their stories are woefully similar. Typical was that of the three-masted, 156-ton, 112-foot *William Linthicum*, launched at Church Creek in Dorchester County, Maryland, in 1894. Early in World War II, she was sold by C. C. Paul and Co. of Baltimore to Bermuda and converted to a lighter for use by the British forces. Chesapeake Bay Captain William Martino sailed her the eight hundred miles to Bermuda, where she served briefly before being abandoned in 1940.[4]

A number of Bay schooners went to Florida and were soon lost or abandoned. Others, like the three-master *Josephine Wimsatt*, were sold to work in the Gulf of Mexico. The *Wimsatt*, renamed *Ruby W.*, was wrecked off Brownsville, Texas, in 1945.[5] Honduras provided a market for several schooners, including the *Levi B. Phillips*, which had been converted to power. The *Columbia F.C.* was sold to Cuba in 1942. The thirty-eight-year-old *Bill Nye* was lost in 1933 bound for the West Indies, not with cargo but with missionaries on their way to combat voodooism among the island's inhabitants.[6]

During World War II German U-boats prowling the Caribbean created a demand for wooden-hulled freight vessels small enough to escape the predators' notice. Sold south for the West Indies trade were the two-masters, *Charles G. Joyce, Minnie T.*

The steel-hulled *Mystic Clipper* was built in 1983 and spent six seasons on the Bay as a dude cruiser. She was designed along the lines of a late Baltimore clipper–style schooner by naval architect Charles Wittholtz. The *Clipper* followed the *Mystic Whaler*, which returned dude cruising to the Bay nearly twenty years after the *Levin J. Marvel* tragedy. The accommodations and safety features of today's passenger schooner or windjammer are very different from those of the former freight schooners that were pressed into the trade in their final days. (M. Staley)

The 72-foot pungy *Lady Maryland* was built in 1986 at Baltimore's Inner Harbor. Designed by Thomas Gillmer, she was built by G. Peter Boudreau and is owned by The Living Classroom Foundation (formerly the Lady Maryland Foundation). The pungy sails as a living classroom for thousands of Bay area students. (M. Staley)

Phillips, and *Thomas B. Schall.* The *Harriet C. Whitehead,* one of the largest two-masted schooners serving on the Bay, was converted to power at Cambridge, Maryland, before she went south. She was eventually lost at sea carrying sugar between the West Indies and the United States.

Though most of the old schooners went south to Florida, the Gulf, and the Caribbean, a few were sold to northern interests. The three-master *Lydia Middleton* ended her career in New Jersey as an Atlantic City tourist attraction, got up as a "pirate ship," and renamed *Vulture.* She was finally abandoned in 1936.[7] The *Australia* was sold to the DuPont family in the 1940s for use as a yacht. They later presented the decaying schooner to Mystic Seaport. There what remains of the *Australia* is maintained as an educational exhibit that offers a unique opportunity to walk through the hull to see its construction.

A number of the strongest schooners and pungies were sold to the Delaware Bay as oyster dredgers in the New Jersey fleet that operates out of Bivalve, Mauricetown, and Dorchester. A few of those were eventually converted to power and were still working in the 1980s.

The 75-foot *Dale Riggin,* built in Accomack, Virginia, in 1873, was one of the Bay schooners that went to New Jersey. She left the Chesapeake in 1924 and was converted to power in 1945. The *Dale Riggin* worked out of Atlantic City clamming and dredging oysters out of Port Norris.

As we've seen, some of the larger schooners and rams, such as the *Edwin and Maud, Ida May, Maggie,* and *Chesterfield* went to Maine in the passenger trade. The final chapter has yet to be written on the *Maud,* which spent thirty years as the *Victory Chimes* and, when last seen on the Bay, was called the *Domino Effect.* She closed out the decade of the 1980s operated by the Domino's Pizza empire. The *Domino Effect* went north, was sold again, and sailed into the 1990s as the *Victory Chimes* once more. She returned to the run she had when she left Maine, tying up at the same dock.

For all intents and purposes, however, the Chesapeake rams, schooners, and pungies have gone the way of the multi-masted schooners, clippers, and pilot boats that supported so much of the trade conducted in the Bay and mid-Atlantic regions for two hundred years. With them went any real awareness of the part the schooner played in the life of the Bay. Few today realize the extent to which this vessel embodied the culture, spirit, and identity of this maritime area.

"In these times, when there is no urgent demand for either personal courage, sound nerves, or stark beauty, we find ourselves by accident," wrote H.G. Wells. "You can go through contemporary life fudging and evading, indulging and slacking, never really hungry nor frightened nor passionately stirred . . . your first real contact with primal and elemental necessities the sweat of your own deathbed."[8]

That is something that can never be said of those who sailed upon schooners and lived within the rules of the demanding, unforgiving environment of the great "inland sea" we call the Chesapeake Bay.

Pride of Baltimore

America's bicentennial generated a new interest in the maritime heritage of the Bay and its sailing craft, an interest which began to take tangible form at daybreak one Sunday in May 1976. That day, work began in a makeshift shipyard in Baltimore's Inner Harbor on the first Baltimore clipper to be built on the Bay in nearly 150 years. Launched ten months later and christened the *Pride of Baltimore*, the clipper was built as a bicentennial project for the city of Baltimore.

The most dramatic representation and embodiment of the spirit of the past was in the construction of the *Pride of Baltimore*—not a museum ship like the *Constellation* or a static display like the Jamestown fleet or the *Dove* of St. Mary's City, the *Pride* was a "real" clipper schooner, built as Thomas Kemp might have built her in the early 1800s, not a copy, but distant kin to Kemp's *Chasseur*, the original "pride of Baltimore."

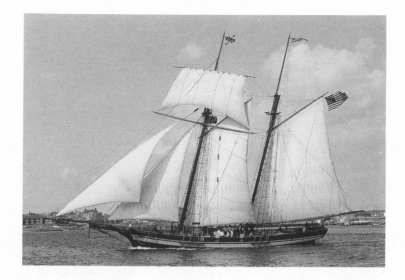

The *Pride of Baltimore II* was designed by Thomas Gillmer and built by G. Peter Boudreau. She sails as a goodwill vessel for the state of Maryland and the city of Baltimore. Larger than *Pride* I, with twentieth century safety features, she was launched April 30, 1988, and is shown here in May 1989. (M. Staley)

Long before Op Sail '76, marine artist Melbourne Smith dreamt of sailing a Baltimore clipper. "I wanted to know the thrill of sailing a ship unknown on the Bay for nearly two hundred years and unknown to any living sailor," said Smith, prime mover and project director for construction of the *Pride*. Until he began putting together plans for how a ship such as the *Pride* could be built, most people would have said his was an utterly impossible dream. By 1975, however, the people of Baltimore and their government shared Smith's dream and at 8:00 A.M. on Sunday, May 23, 1976, work began on the *Pride of Baltimore*.

"She was designed and built in the tradition of the Baltimore clippers of old," said Melbourne Smith, shortly before her launching in 1977. "She is the last of her line," he added, hardly imagining the import his words would have less than a decade later.[9]

Displacing 121 tons, the 90-foot clipper schooner was not a replica, a reconstruction, or a copy of any single vessel in our history's past, according to naval architect Thomas Gillmer who designed her. She was a vessel like no other seen by anyone alive, he noted, and upon her launching, the *Pride* gave modern sailors their first opportunity ever to learn how a Baltimore clipper sailed. "She is a Baltimore clipper schooner, I think the last one

Now known as the *New Way*, this schooner was built in 1939 as the *Western Union*. She was built in Key West, Florida, but was modeled after the schooner *G.W. Garrison*, built in Baltimore in 1885. The *Garrison* was laying cable between Florida and Cuba for Western Union when she was wrecked in a storm in 1937. Her captain at the time defied the company and insisted that another schooner be built. Since he had the charts and knew where the cables were laid, the captain won and instead of a modern motor vessel, he got his schooner, which was christened the *Western Union* and worked repairing cable until the 1970s when she was sold north to become a dude cruiser. In the 1980s, she was bought by Vision Quest of Philadelphia and renamed the *New Way*. At the time of this writing, she was employed by Vision Quest in the organization's program to rehabilitate youthful offenders by placing them in a challenging environment to learn cooperation, self-reliance, and discipline. In that capacity, she is a frequent visitor to Bay ports and winters at the Chesapeake Bay Maritime Museum. (M. Staley)

ever," he said in an article for *Wooden Boat* magazine shortly before the *Pride*'s launching. "She had all the characteristics, the style and details of construction of the fast schooners and brigs," known originally as clippers around the turn of the nineteenth century.[10]

Gillmer gives primary credit to the British for the authenticity of his design. The Americans, who built the famed clippers, kept no drawings or records of their designs; however, when the British captured the fast, sharp-built Bay schooners from the French and from Americans, they sent them posthaste to Portsmouth and other Royal Naval shipyards and took off their lines for preservation in the British Admiralty archives. A second reliable prime source for information on how to build a Baltimore clipper came from French naval engineer, M. Marestier, who also took off the lines of several clipper schooners during a visit to the United States after the War of 1812. As a result, the design was as close to that of the clippers built in the nineteenth century as was possible.[11]

The same is true of the methods and materials used. Only two concessions were made to modern times and those were the Dacron used in the standing rigging, the shrouds, and lower stays, and the installation of an auxiliary engine.[12]

The Loss of the *Pride*

On May 7, 1986, Armin Elsaesser wrote in the log of the *Pride* as the clipper lay at anchor off St. Thomas, soon to set sail for the final 1,500-mile journey back to Baltimore following a tour of fifteen European countries: "What lies ahead is unknown—a source of mystery and apprehension—perhaps the allure of the sailing life—always moving, always changing, always wondering what the next passage will be like . . . this time our destination is home—the Chesapeake Bay and Baltimore. It is always a relief for the captain, and I suspect, the ship, to have our lines ashore and fast where *Pride* is safest—the Finger Piers at the Inner Harbor."[13]

Shortly before noon on May 14, 1986, the *Pride* was in the Atlantic north of Puerto Rico, when it was "hit by a wall of wind and water with wind speed of 70 knots and more," according to first mate John "Sugar" Flanagan. "In what appeared to be slow motion, the boat started laying over to port and in less than 60 seconds the boat was over on its side."[14]

The twelve members of the crew scrambled along the outer bulwarks toward the life rafts located aft and as the *Pride* slipped beneath the surface of the stormy sea, eight of them gathered around one of the deflated rubber rafts. The squall lasted no more than ten minutes before it was over. The eight briefly saw the bodies of two of their fellow crew members. They never saw Armin Elsaesser and the twelfth member of the crew again.

After six hours in the water, they managed to inflate the raft and get aboard. "We entered the six-man life raft with eight exhausted people," said Flanagan. "We spent four days, seven hours in the life raft. The days were barely tolerable, the nights were hell."[15] The eight were rescued from the life raft at 2:30 A.M. on May 19 and the news of the loss of the *Pride* was sent home ahead of them to Baltimore.

Lady Maryland

At the time the *Pride* was lost, another schooner, a pungy, was due to be launched from the very yard in Baltimore's Inner Harbor where the clipper had been built nine years before. Designed by Thomas Gillmer and built by Peter Boudreau, one of those who had built the *Pride*, the 72-foot *Lady Maryland* was unlike the *Pride*, which was built to nineteenth century specifications. The *Lady Maryland* was meant to be a replica of a pungy and had to meet strict Coast Guard regulations in order to fulfill her twentieth century mission, which was to serve as a floating classroom to teach Maryland's young people about seamanship, environmental science, and the Bay's maritime history.

Unlike a pungy of the nineteenth century, she was constructed with three watertight bulkheads, a head, a galley, two engines with feathering props, and external lead ballast to enhance her self-righting capabilities. *Lady Maryland* is true to her origins in many respects, from the Maryland white oak and pine from which she was built to the "pungy pink" of her hull.[16] She was launched in June 1986, a month after the *Pride* went down. Every year since then, the *Lady Maryland* has taken thousands of students on educational cruises of the Bay.

This shot of the *Pride of Baltimore II* (right) and the *Clipper City* was taken at the Preakness Regatta, which has become an annual event in Baltimore Harbor during Preakness Week. The *Clipper City* was built in 1985 in Green Cove Springs, Florida. She is a steel representation of a Great Lakes topsail schooner of 1884 and is not typical of Chesapeake Bay schooners. (M. Staley)

Pride II

In response to the demand from the people of Baltimore and Maryland, as well as the surviving members of the *Pride's* last crew, in October 1987, the keel was laid for *Pride II* in the Inner Harbor yard where the *Pride* and *Lady Maryland* had been built. Designed by Thomas Gillmer and built by Peter Boudreau, she was launched April 30, 1988. This time, Gillmer designed a clipper for the twentieth century, larger and heavier, with a much lower center of gravity, double the ballast, and watertight bulkheads. The new *Pride* also is certified to carry thirty passengers in addition to her crew of twelve. Owned by the state of Maryland, *Pride II* serves as a symbol of the state's maritime heritage and as an ambassador for Maryland business and tourism.

During the spring and fall, four other schooners make appearances on the Bay. Owned by Vision Quest, and sailing out of Philadelphia, the former *Western Union*, now the *New Way*, is a rough copy of the Chesapeake Bay centerboarder *George T. Garrison*. Built in Baltimore in the 1880s, the *Garrison* worked for Western Union, repairing cable between Florida and Cuba until a hurricane damaged her beyond repair in 1937. Her captain demanded another schooner and the *Western Union* was built as a larger and inexact copy of the *Garrison*. It is believed that the *New Way* still carries the compass, binnacle, bell, wheel, brass portlights, and some other fittings of the old *Garrison*.[17]

Also owned and operated by Vision Quest is the *Bill of Rights*, launched in 1971 at the Harvey Gamage Shipyard in South Bristol, Maine. She was followed in 1973 by the windjammer *Harvey Gamage*, which offers cruises on the Chesapeake Bay. Finally there is the *Spirit of Massachusetts*, which operates as a goodwill and educational vessel for Massachusetts much as *Pride II* does for Maryland.

One last member of the fleet of schooners that claim home ports on the Bay is the *Clipper City,* a schooner-rigged cruise vessel designed to give passengers a sense of nineteenth century travel but with twentieth century comforts.

Loss of the *Sarah Conway*

In 1986, as news of the loss of the *Pride of Baltimore* spread around the world, just a few people noted the passing of the *Sarah C. Conway* which slipped quietly away to a watery grave in the Atlantic. Calvert Evans heard of it. So did Lynn Perry and a few others who knew her whereabouts. Purely by chance, the U.S. Coast Guard vessel *Hornbeam* was nearby when the master of the *Sarah* sent his first distress call.[18]

When the *Hornbeam* arrived, the converted schooner was flooding rapidly. All of her pumps were disabled and she was riding dangerously low in the water. A rescue and assist team from the Coast Guard cutter went aboard with pumps, but could not get them working before the *Sarah* began listing to starboard. It was obvious she was going to capsize. As she rolled, her crew of four and the two crewmen from the *Hornbeam* crawled onto her hull and leapt into the water. The master was the last to abandon the *Sarah,* sliding along the bottom and over the keel before dropping into the 36-degree water. The men watching from the *Hornbeam* noticed that the *Sarah*'s propeller was still turning as she went down. In thirty seconds, the *Sarah C. Conway* was gone.[19]

"Sailing's long gone," wrote Captain Vernon Hopkins in his memoirs. "We never had enough men, with only four sailors, a cook, and the master, to handle a vessel. We'd be wet and cold, soaked through for days on end in bad weather; knocked about, sore; just beat from the long hours on deck. But then, when the sun did come out and we got a long run with favoring winds, that was all forgot. This was living. Sails set, an easy wheel, there has never been anything like it. It was a pretty thing."[20]

Writing for the Baltimore *Sun* in 1946, Robert H. Burgess put it thus. "The Chesapeake Bay has been called 'a yachtsman's paradise.' After the last commercial sailing craft on these waters has lowered its sails for good, there will be the sails of pleasure craft to carry on the tradition of canvas.

"But it will not be the same. With the passing of the winged boats that spread their canvas for dollars and not for amateurs' fun, there will pass the men who sailed them, a stout and shipwise breed. No Sunday sailor will ever know the Bay as they have known it, and few will learn most of the tricks it took to wrest a livelihood from it these last few decades, the twilight of sail."

Appendix I – Vessel Lists

The vessel lists that follow have been compiled from the following sources: John Earle's Maryland Vessel Files at the Maryland Historical Society, Baltimore, Maryland; vessel lists in various issues of *Log Chips,* edited by John Lyman; the various works of Robert H. Burgess; *Chesapeake Bay Log Canoes and Bugeyes* by Marion V. Brewington; Francis E. "Biff" Bowker's Vessel Files at the Mystic Seaport Museum; *Merchant Vessels of the United States,* published by the Treasury Department, Bureau of Navigation, Washington, D.C., various volumes published between 1868 and 1989; *The Record* of American and foreign shipping, various volumes; *American Lloyd's Register of American and Foreign Shipping,* 1857-1869; *Lloyd's Register of American and Foreign Shipping,* various volumes; and the Baltimore Customs House Records.

Where there have been discrepancies, apparent errors, or conflicting information among various sources in a vessel's name, its dimensions, or place it was built, for consistency's sake, we have used the names and statistics found in the *Merchant Vessels of the United States.*

Occasionally, there appears to be a conflict between a vessel's builder mentioned in the text and the builder named in the vessel list. This difference is due to the fact that sources, such as master carpenter certificates, customshouse records, *Lloyd's Register,* the American Bureau of Shipping *Record,* or other resources sometimes recorded the name of the building company, rather than the actual master carpenter. For example,

J. M. C. Moore was the master carpenter for several vessels built by the George K. Phillips Company, which appears as builder on the vessel list. Also, Thomas Kirby was the master carpenter for Kirby and Lang.

As for the names of places, we have used the original name. Whites Landing, where the *R. E. Powell* was built, for instance, is now Whitehaven, Maryland.

Discrepancies in lengths may appear from one source to another due to differences in the basis for measurement. For example, lengths over the rail will be greater than the registered dimensions taken from the interior volume of the vessel for customshouse purposes.

Tonnage measurements may also vary as a result of remeasuring after a vessel has been rebuilt, or at the request of an owner.

1. Chesapeake-built two-masted schooners   *page 180*
   The list of two-masted schooners contains only a fraction of the thousands built on the Chesapeake Bay watershed. They outnumbered all other types of commercial sailing vessels. We have included only those that appear in the text, or those not mentioned but long-lived or well-known in their day. We are grateful to Robert H. Burgess and Francis E. Bowker for their assistance and patience in verifying information recorded here.

2. Chesapeake-built vessels carrying
three-masted schooner rig   *page 184*

The list of three-masted schooners is more complete than the lists of two-masters and pungies. They were fewer in number and therefore were more readily identifiable in contemporary records. They generally appeared later as a type. In customs-house records, for instance, they are specified as either three-masted or "tern" schooners. Francis E. Bowker of the Mystic Seaport Museum has made a lifelong study of American-built three-masted schooners and made his files available for our study.

3. Chesapeake-built four-masted schooners   *page 188*

Because of the late appearance of the four-masted schooner and the limited number built, of all schooner types, they were the most easily traced through merchant vessel lists and customshouse records. As a result, this list of four-masters is complete.

4. Rams or ramlike vessels   *page 189*

The list of vessels considered to be rams or ramlike is also comprehensive due to the fact that rams appeared late as a type and were relatively few in number. They were identified as such either by their specific hull form and construction or by using a block coefficient criterion (*see* Glossary).

5. Known pungies   *page 190*

Many more pungies were built than are listed here. This is due to the difficulty, both then and now, in distinguishing a pungy from a schooner. The distinction was seldom made in contemporary records and vessel lists. Those included here are known to have been pungies, identified as a result of first-hand experience of one of our sources, or by the use of John Earle's technique of identifying a pungy by its ten-to-one, length-to-depth, ratio.

6. "Square-rigged" bugeyes   *page 194*

"Square-rigged" bugeyes were particularly difficult to separate from schooners and pungies in government records. The identities of those included here were verified through vessel lists made by M. V. Brewington and John Earle, or through photographs and sail plan books at several institutions.

7. Scow schooners   *page 195*

This is not a complete list of all the vessels built and rigged as scow schooners. They were somewhat easier to identify in customshouse records, which usually specified either "flat-built," or "square-ended."

8. Vessels mentioned built
outside the Chesapeake   *page 196*

Vessels were often renamed many times. In the case of those built outside the Bay, we have chosen to list them under the names by which they were best known while working the Chesapeake. This list includes only those schooners mentioned in the text. Countless others from all over the world called at Bay ports.

9. Schooner barges built on the
Chesapeake   *page 197*

Schooner barges represent the last incarnation of the schooner type. This list, which refers only to those vessels built as schooner barges and not those cut down from fully rigged sailing vessels, is fairly comprehensive because the schooner barges appeared late and are relatively easy to trace. The work of Paul C. Morris was invaluable in this list.

Abbreviations Used in Vessel Lists

abnd	abandoned
m	masted (2m, 3m, etc.)
mi	miles
M.R.	Marine Railway
p.b.	powerboat
rblt	rebuilt
rn	renamed
S.B.	Shipbuilding
schr	schooner
st. bt.	steamboat

NAME	OFF. NO.	TONNAGE:		DIMENSIONS:			BUILT:			COMMENTS
		GROSS	NET	LENGTH	BREADTH	DEPTH	YEAR	WHERE	BY	
A. VICTOR NEAL	224253	81.00	62.00	74.8	24.8	7.2	1924	Oxford, Md.	Kirkwood	Rblt from JOHN C. KELSO
ADMIRAL	106846	41.34	39.27	62.8	20.6	6.6	1885	Baltimore, Md.		rn DAVID ROBBINS SR, Del Bay dredge boat
ALIDA HEARN	106379	28.00	26.00	56.4	18.7	5.2	1885	Pocomoke City, Md.		Foundered 7/18/1928 off Newport, R.I.
ALICE	105578	29.94	28.44	54.0	20.5	5.6	1875	Mathews Co., Va.		
AMELIA HEARNE	105313	113.56	107.88	94.2	23.9	9.1	1873	Laurel, Del.	D.W. Moore	Total cost $9,488.02
AMERICAN EAGLE	1674	18.13	17.22	43.0	14.4	4.3	1869	Solomons Is., Md.		
AMY M. SACKER	106408	119.87	113.88	86.8	22.6	9.6	1885	Cambridge, Md.	J.W. Crowell	Active Venezuela until mid-1950s
ANNA A. CROSWELL	105062	40.00	38.00	61.8	20.5	6.1	1871	Somerset Co., Md.		rn (a) JOHN SCHALL, (b) VICKI PAT,
										p.b., scuttled 1989
ANNIE C. JOHNSON	106831	32.00	21.00	59.0	20.6	5.4	1891	Solomons Is., Md.	M.M. Davis	Abnd 1957
ANNIE E. MOORE	1980	126.21	119.90	96.0	24.0	8.0	1870	Laurel, Del.	D.W. Moore	
ANNIE HODGES	105177	47.00	45.00	61.5	21.8	6.1	1872	Baltimore, Md.		
ANNIE M. LEONARD	105679	68.27	64.80	77.5	21.8	5.6	1877	Oxford, Md.	Wm. Benson	Rblt 1913 as LULA M. PHILLIPS
ARIANNA BATEMAN	105045	63.00	60.00	77.0	23.4	6.2	1871	Oxford, Md.	Wm. Benson	Lost by collision 10/20/1933, Md. Pt.
BALTIMORE	2022	22.39	21.27	57.5	17.3	5.7	1857	Somerset Co., Md.		
BESSIE JONES	217567	46.00	33.00	65.8	20.6	5.4	1893	Madison, Md.	Brooks	Md. oyster police
BOHEMIA	3291	71.00	67.00	81.3	23.8	6.0	1884	St. Michaels, Md.	Kirby	Abnd 1951, Sarah Cr, Va.
BREEZE				63.5	19.3	5.5	1855	Baltimore, Md.		
C. CHASE				60.6	19.1	5.5	1856	Baltimore, Md.	Skinner & Son	
C. W. HAND	213158	35.00	13.00	60.7	19.8	5.0	1915	Solomons Is., Md.	Parsons	rn ROSE M. GASKILL, p.b., abnd 1989,
										Bivalve, N.J.
CALVERT	125199	70.53	67.00	78.0	22.0	7.9	1873	Baltimore, Md.	Skinner & Son	Last pilot schooner of Md. Pilots Assoc.
CANTON							1874	Baltimore, Md.	Skinner & Son	
CARADORA	125936	56.00	53.00	74.1	22.6	5.7	1881	St. Michaels, Md.	Kirby & Lang	Abnd 1952
CHARLES H. RICHARDSON	125605	53.00	51.00	66.8	22.8	5.7	1877	St. Michaels, Md.	Kirby & Lang	
CHARLES G. JOYCE	126078	122.67	116.54	97.9	26.9	7.6	1882	Baltimore, Md.	Wm. Woodall	Foundered 5/13/1944 at Miami
CHARLOTTE MOORE	125641	18.23	17.32	42.5	16.6	4.2	1877	Lewisville, Del.	J.M.C. Moore	
CHESTERFIELD	125699	66.00	63.00	79.6	22.4	5.3	1878	Talbot Co., Md.	Kirby & Lang	Abnd 1955, Staten Is., N.Y.
CLARA M. GOODMAN	125545	191.33	181.36	106.5	29.8	9.2	1874	Lewisville, Del.		rn MARY E. BACON, abnd 1889 at Gibraltar
CLARA M. LEONARD	125434	56.00	53.00	73.8	22.0	5.9	1875	Oxford, Md.	Wm. Benson	Easton packet, stranded 12/1921, Pt. Lookout
CLEMMIE TRAVERS	126314	85.00	81.00	85.9	23.8	7.0	1885	Mathews Co., Va.	F.R. Hayes	Stranded 9/18/1936, Norfolk
COLUMBIA F. C.	125285	49.00	46.00	79.0	22.8	6.3	1874	Mundy Pt., Va.		Sold Cuba, 1942
D. J. WARD	208190	82.00	66.00	88.7	23.7	6.4	1910	Salisbury, Md.		ex ELIJAH S. ADKINS
DORCHESTER	157059	56.00	40.00	80.0	24.0	5.6	1882	Madison, Md.	J.W. Brooks	Rblt as W.J. MATTHEWS, abnd 1969 as p.b.

NAME	OFF. NO.	TONNAGE:		DIMENSIONS:			BUILT:			COMMENTS
		GROSS	NET	LENGTH	BREADTH	DEPTH	YEAR	WHERE	BY	
E. S. JOHNSON	135617	90.00	71.00	88.5	24.0	7.3	1882	Baltimore, Md.	McCosker	Foundered 6/9/1928, Rock Pt., Md.
ECLIPSE	135064	23.00	22.00	47.0	16.6	5.2	1874	Lancaster Co., Va.		
EDDIE COOK	76453	10.50	9.97	43.1	14.5	3.3	1883	Cambridge, Md.	Sawyer & Spicer	
EDITH R. SEWARD	135467	244.71	232.47	116.2	30.5	9.8	1880	Dorchester Co., Md.	W.J. Lambdin	Possible 3m
EDWARD L. MARTIN	135629	84.00	80.00	87.2	23.6	6.8	1882	Sussex Co., Del.		Lost by fire near Oxford, 1956
										as HONEY B (p.b.)
EFFIE A. CHASE	135524	22.00	21.00	53.5	18.2	4.8	1881	Pocomoke City, Md.	Whittington	Converted from sloop, abnd 1939
EFFIE ESTELLE	135236	32.00	31.00	58.0	19.6	4.9	1876	Talbot Co., Md.	Lambdin	
ELLA F. CRIPPS	136851	47.00	47.00	69.2	21.9	5.8	1900	St. Michaels, Md.	Kirby & Son	Abnd 1956, Back Cr., Annapolis, Md. (p.b.)
EMILY E. JOHNSON	135712	121.61	115.53	95.4	26.7	7.9	1883	Piankatank R., Va.		
EMILY E. BURTON	8765	88.41	83.99	95.0	23.5	6.8	1871	Lewisville, Del.		
EUGENIA	8365	43.00	40.85	66.9	23.7	5.2	1864	Baltimore, Md.		
EVA	136840	7.00	7.00	39.1	12.9	3.1	1890	Cambridge, Md.	J. Sauerhoff	Schooner-rigged bateau
EVA S. CULLISON	136016	47.00	45.00	70.5	21.0	6.2	1888	Baltimore, Md.		Abnd 1962, Rockport, Ma.
FANNIE INSLEY	120565	59.00	56.00	78.0	23.2	6.0	1883	Church Cr., Md.	J.W. Brooks	Foundered 8/20/1940 off Windmill Pt.
FEDERAL HILL	9769	72.00	68.00	84.1	23.4	6.5	1856	Baltimore, Md.		Abnd 1941, Colonial Beach, Va.
FLORA KIRWAN	120918	67.00	51.00	80.0	23.8	6.6	1892	Baltimore, Md.	McCosker	Lost 1983 as clam dredge
FLORENCE	21836	45.00	43.00	71.0	21.6	5.1	1867	Somerset Co., Md.		ex REMEDY
FRANCIS E. WATERS	120512	145.63	141.20	99.4	28.1	7.4	1882	Taylors Is., Md		
FRANK M. HOWES	120493	178.90	169.95	119.8	24.7	8.3	1882	Baltimore, Md.		
FRANKLIN	9031	294.81	280.17	112.4	30.0	8.0	1867	Baltimore, Md.		
GEN'L E.L.F. HARDCASTLE	85858	66.00	62.00	79.6	23.4	6.3	1883	Baltimore, Md.	Beacham	Foundered 8/16/1899, salvaged, rn LOUISE
GEORGIA		132.70	89.50		24.0	7.0	1853	Dorchester Co., Md.		
GRACIE MAY	206853	104.00	104.00	99.8	25.5	6.6	1909	Seaford, Del.	Smith	rn RUTH CONWAY (p.b.), sank 10/8/1965
H. M. ROWE	95719	39.00	37.00	66.0	21.4	5.6	1882	Dorchester Co., Md.		Abnd 1949, Belhaven, N.C.
HENRY DISSTON	95644	41.00	26.00	73.0	19.8	5.2	1881	Portsmouth, Va.		Abnd 1941
HESTER A. SEWARD	95859	158.00	150.10	108.8	28.8	7.6	1885	Taylors Is., Md.	Lambdin	Lost 1885
IDA B. CONWAY	80340	73.00	69.00	70.8	24.0	6.3	1873	Nanticoke, Md.	Zac Layton	ex WM. LAYTON, rn p.b. (a) JOHN J. CROUCH,
										(b) CAROL ANN
IDA MAY	100657	70.00	54.00	72.0	21.4	7.4	1898	Urbanna, Va.		Rblt from JACOB S. BARNES
J. EDWIN KIRWAN	111429	138.00	110.00	105.0	28.9	8.7	1902	Gloucester, Va.		ex BESSIE AND RUBY, abnd 1941
JOHN Q. FERGUSON	76764	129.00	122.00	105.2	21.0	7.6	1888	Sharptown, Md.		ex JAMES DIVERTY (2m), rn VIRGINIA (3m)
JOHN R. P. MOORE	75917	99.00	94.00	86.7	27.0	6.5	1877	Snow Hill, Md.		Foundered 10/31/1938, Norfolk
JOSEPHINE	76230	19.00	18.00	54.8	16.0	4.4	1881	St. Michaels, Md.	R. Lambdin	

NAME	OFF. NO.	TONNAGE:		DIMENSIONS:			BUILT:			COMMENTS
		GROSS	NET	LENGTH	BREADTH	DEPTH	YEAR	WHERE	BY	
JUDY	76261	51.82	49.23	70.6	21.8	6.2	1881	Baltimore, Md.		Rblt as MAUD THOMAS
KATE DARLINGTON	14487	135.00	128.00	97.8	28.0	7.1	1889	Baltimore, Md.	Brusstar	Broken up 1939, Locust Pt.
KATE McNAMARA	14291	65.00	49.00	79.0	23.6	6.2	1873	Madison, Md.	J.W. Brooks	Rblt by Kirby 1897
KATE R. WATERS	14299	38.96	37.01	65.1	21.1	4.9	1873	Accomack Co., Va	E. Waters	rn (a) MARGRET E.E. ARMIGER, (b) AMALIE,
										(c) DALE RIGGIN (p.b.) still active 1992
KATHRYN E. RIGGIN	206718	22.00	17.00	52.0	18.4	4.6	1909	Whitehaven, Md.		
L. E. WILLIAMS	140130	100.77	95.73	95.5	23.1	7.5	1875	Wicomico Co., Md.		Foundered 10/5/1930, Travers Pt., Md.
LAURENA CLAYTON	141223	79.00	75.00	95.0	24.0	7.0	1892	Cambridge, Md.	Barclay	rn (p.b.) EFFIE M. LEWIS, foundered
										11/11/1941, Delaware Bay
LEVI B. PHILLIPS	141194	87.00	66.00	86.7	23.8	7.0	1892	Cambridge, Md.	G.T. Johnson	Pineapple trader, sold Honduras, 1946
LULA M. PHILLIPS	210862	61.00	53.00	77.5	22.0	5.6	1913	Bethel, Del.		Rblt from ANNIE M. LEONARD
MAGGIE	90276	72.00	69.00	87.0	23.9	5.9	1871	Dorchester Co., Md.	J.J. Skinner	Abnd 1962, Rockland, Me., burned 1965
MAGGIE A. PHILLIPS	92541	95.00	91.00	98.0	26.0	7.6	1893	Baltimore, Md.	Brusstar	Lost at sea 5/31/1906, in pineapple trade
MAGNOLIA	85066	111.76	106.17	92.0	27.0	6.4	1869	Talbot Co., Md.	Kirby & Lang	ex GEORGE E. SMOOT
MARY A. BACON	125545	191.33	181.76	106.5	29.8	9.2	1876	Laurel, Del.		ex CLARA M. GOODMAN
MARY LEE	75430	130.00	104.00	98.8	23.8	8.2	1872	Laurel, Del.		ex JOHN McGINNES, abnd 1940
MARY VICKERS	91356	68.00	64.00	79.7	23.2	6.2	1881	Oxford, Md.	Wm. Benson	Eastern Shore grain packet
MATTIE F. DEAN	91695	48.00	32.00	68.0	25.0	5.8	1884	Madison, Md.	J.W. Brooks	Abnd 1956, Back Cr., Annapolis, Md.
MATTIE MAY	91589	169.73	161.24	108.3	27.3	7.6	1883	Baltimore, Md.	Skinner	
MAUD SEWARD	90803	143.11	135.95	98.2	26.6	7.8	1875	Little Choptank, Md.	W.J. Lambdin	Lost 1/1/1910, stranded Martha's
										Vineyard, Ma.
MAUD THOMAS	205460	44.00	38.00	72.0	21.3	6.0	1908	Whitehaven, Md.		Rblt from JUDY
MILDRED	208729	81.00	67.00	82.0	22.0	5.5	1911	Solomons Is., Md.		Abnd 1972, as p.b.
MINNIE & EMMA	91550	77.00	57.00	93.0	24.0	5.9	1883	Pocomoke City, Md.		Abnd 1941
MINNIE H. SMITHERS	91754	137.02	130.17	104.6	21.2	7.8	1885	Bethel, Del.		
MINNIE MAE KIRWAN	85752	56.00	53.00	75.7	23.7	6.7	1882	Whitehaven, Md.		ex G.W. ROBERTSON rn p.b. (a) W.C. WITT,
										(b) L.R. PARKER
MINNIE T. PHILLIPS	85255	137.00	123.00	100.4	27.0	6.9	1873	Baltimore, Md.	Skinner	ex (a) GEO. C. A. TRAVERS, (b) F.P. MURPHY
MURRY VANDIVER	90798	112.93	107.28	87.5	26.0	7.0	1875	Havre de Grace, Md.		
NELLIE	18782	142.02	134.92	108.0	26.0	7.1	1873	Dorchester Co., Md.		
NORTH CAROLINA	18006	96.00	78.00	88.0	22.0	6.8	1856	Dorchester Co., Md.		Abnd mid-1933, Fleeton, Va.
OYSTERMEN	155171	51.00	49.00	71.2	20.6	6.1	1889	St. Michaels, Md.	Kirby & Lang	Abnd Port Norris, N.J.
R.E. POWELL	110551	68.00	49.00	83.8	22.9	6.3	1882	Whites Landing, Md.		Wicomico River packet, abnd 1931
ROBERT H. MITCHELL	110264	163.66	155.48	104.0	28.6	7.1	1875	Dorchester Co., Md.	T.L. Vickers	

NAME	OFF. NO.	TONNAGE:		DIMENSIONS:			BUILT:			COMMENTS
		GROSS	NET	LENGTH	BREADTH	DEPTH	YEAR	WHERE	BY	
ROVER	110600	126.12	119.81	85.0	26.7	8.0	1883	Cambridge, Md.		Foundered 7/19/16, off Cape Hatteras, N.C.
S. F. KIRWAN	23872	83.66	79.48	84.8	23.9	6.3	1876	Dorchester Co., Md.	J.H. Davis	
SARAH C. CONWAY	105403	77.00	61.00	77.4	23.5	7.4	1872	Baltimore, Md.	W. Woodall	ex A. H. SCHULZ, lost 3/6/1986 off
										Atlantic City, N. J.
SMITH K. MARTIN	116915	50.00	33.00	73.7	22.7	5.8	1899	Pocomoke City, Md.	E. J. Tull	Lost 1940
STEPHEN CHASE	115485	51.00	48.00	66.6	23.9	6.7	1876	Dorchester Co., Md.		Abnd 1940, Curtis Bay, Md.
SUNNY SOUTH				71.0	22.0	5.4	1855	Baltimore, Md.	Skinner & Sons	
THOMAS B. SCHALL	145302	55.00	52.00	75.3	22.9	6.5	1882	Baltimore, Md.	McCosker	Sold foreign, 1942
THOMAS H. KIRBY	24881	36.00	34.00	63.0	20.2	5.6	1871	Talbot Co., Md.	Kirby & Lang	Stranded 11/24/13, Occohannock Bar, Va.
VAQUERO		370.36		126.7	28.1	11.5	1853	Baltimore, Md.		San Francisco packet
VERNETTA ANN	25935	48.71	46.28	75.0	22.1	5.4	1876	Baltimore, Md.		Oyster dredge, Delaware Bay
VIRGINIA CARROLL	95835	97.00	93.00	91.6	22.6	6.6	1884	Pocomoke City, Md.		ex HESPER A. WATERS, "Out of
										documentation" 1946
W. H. FRENCH	81523	92.00	88.00	77.0	23.4	6.5	1895	Berkley, Va.		Abnd 1936
W. P. WARD	145311	84.77	80.53	85.0	23.9	6.3	1882	Cambridge, Md.	P. Spenser	ex THOMAS RICHARD, sold Honduras as
										p.b. 1947
WILLIAM A. GRAVES	80952	74.00	70.00	81.0	20.9	7.0	1883	Norfolk, Va.		Pilot schooner, Va. Pilots Assoc.
WILLIAM F. DUNN	224197	70.00	42.00	84.0	23.6	6.5	1924	W. Norfolk, Va.		Foundered 2/12/1932, Tangier Sound
WILLIAM H. MICHAEL	80716	48.00	36.00	65.8	21.4	5.7	1879	Queen Anne's Co., Md.	Bonshell	Abnd 1947, Chrisman Cr., Va.
WILLIAM M. HINES	80956	75.59	71.81	84.4	23.8	7.0	1883	Baltimore, Md.		Sold Mexico 1890s, rn TRES HERMANOS
WILLIAM LAYTON	80340	73.00	59.00	79.8	24.0	6.3	1873	Nanticoke River, Md.		rn IDA B. CONWAY (see above)
WILLIAM LIESHEUR	80338	25.00	17.00	53.0	18.0	4.0	1872	Accomack Co., Va.		
WILLIAM M. POWELL	80992	59.00	37.00	78.5	23.2	6.2	1883	Finney, Va.		Abnd 1937
ZINGARA	28005	9.00	9.00	43.8	16.3	4.0	1852	Anne Arundel Co., Md.		Abnd Bellevue, Md.
ZORA AND ANNA	208096	86.00	73.00	83.8	23.8	6.3	1910	Sharptown, Md.	Conley	Rblt from OCEAN BIRD, abnd 1941

CHESAPEAKE-BUILT VESSELS CARRYING THREE- MASTED SCHOONER RIG

NAME	SIGNAL	OFFICIAL	TONNAGE:		DIMENSIONS:			BUILT:			COMMENTS:
	LETTERS	NO.	GROSS	NET	LENGTH	BREADTH	DEPTH	DATE	WHERE	BY	
A. DENIKE	HBSQ	731	427.8	406.4	131.5	30.1	10.0	1866	Greensboro, Md.		Geo. Jones owner
ABBIE P. CRAMMER	HBCG	53	304.8	289.6	119.8	30.6	6.6	1867	Baltimore, Md.		Home port 1873, N.Y., N.Y., lost 9/26/1888
AGNES S. QUILLIN*	KSOD	107174	197.0	187.0	126.5	23.9	7.8	1894	Bethel, Del.	Geo. K. Phillips	Stranded 11/1938, Potomac R., Smith Pt., Va.
ALICE CARLISLE		106148	55.4	52.6	83.0	18.0	5.5	1883	Portsmouth, Va.		Scrapped 1905
ALICE P. TURNER	KTSP	201918	192.0	166.0	127.0	30.7	9.8	1905	Sharptown, Md.	T. Sauerhoff	Reblt from HARRY LANDELL, sold foreign 1914
ALVERDA S. ELZEY *	KPBH	107450	283.0	249.0	135.9	28.5	8.2	1899	Bethel, Del.	Geo. K. Phillips	Topmasts and jibboom, lost 1/1910
											off Mexico
AMELIA G. IRELAND	HBST	733	284.5	270.3	124.0	30.1	12.4	1866	Somerset Co., Md.		Home port 1893, N.Y., N.Y.
ANNA M. HUDSON *	KTJP	201396	338.0	299.0	135.5	31.8	10.0	1904	Bethel, Del.	Geo. K. Phillips	Abandoned 1933
ATLANTIC			91.2		68.0	20.0	7.8	1825	Sussex Co., Del.		"Neptune figure head, square stern"***
BESSIE BROWN	KCRP	123298	260.0	220.0	123.8	32.3	9.5	1884	Bethel, Del.	Wm. R. McIlvane	Wrecked by stranding 5/15/15, Cobb Is., Va.
BRAZOS	KRPM	3928	226.0	190.0	131.5	26.5	8.6	1902	Baltimore, Md.	Beacham & Bro.	Wrecked 11/13/1917, stranded Fla. Tortugas
CHARLES A. WITLER	KHSW	201506	219.0	181.0	124.0	29.4	8.3	1904	Baltimore, Md.	Woodall	Lost 1905 by collision
CHARLES B. LEET	KLNG	126931	305.2	289.9	137.8	32.7	9.3	1892	Suffolk, Va.	Wm. P. Crammer	Lost at sea, 1/1900
CHARLES T. STRANN *	KJMB	126732	215.0	186.0	125.2	23.8	8.9	1891	Sharptown, Md.	J.M.C. Moore	rn (a) CHARLES L. ROHDE (b) KINKORA
											(c) CIUDAD TRUJILLO, Dominican Republic
CLARENCE A. HOLLAND*	KLSB	126984	200.0	179.0	126.5	23.9	8.2	1893	Bethel, Del.	J.M.C. Moore	Abandoned 1949, Elizabeth City, N.C.
CURTIS AKERLY	JRCK	125412	378.3	359.6	122.4	30.7	10.9	1875	Claremont, Va.		Lost 1881
EDNA AND EMMA *	KHVC	136165	182.8	173.6	119.7	22.5	8.2	1890	Baltimore, Md.	Mc Cosker	Lost 1899
EDWARD A. SANCHEZ	JQCB	135050	492.9	468.3	135.6	33.0	15.7	1874	Baltimore, Md.	Skinner	Rerigged as barkentine
EDWARD R. BAIRD, JR.*	KSHN	137061	279.0	238.0	132.0	28.3	9.8	1903	Bethel, Del.	Geo. K. Phillips	Sank 9/19/1955, Tangier Sound
EDWIN AND MAUD *	KPRT	136784	208.0	178.0	126.0	23.8	8.6	1900	Bethel, Del.	Geo. K. Phillips	rn (a) VICTORY CHIMES, (b) DOMINO EFFECT
											(c) VICTORY CHIMES, sails out of Rockland, Me.
ELIZABETH			78.0					1812	Baltimore, Md.		Possible 2m
ELLWOOD HARLOW	JWHK	135597	835.8	794.0	179.2	36.0	18.6	1882	Alexandria, Va.	Wm. Crawford	Lost 1895
EMMA D. ENDICOTT	HGJF	7874	335.6	318.8	120.0	30.0	11.7	1864	Baltimore, Md.		Home port 1893, N.Y., N.Y., lost 1/1902,
											Chatham, Ma.
EMMA P. DOUGLAS		8408	85.0					1868	Somerset Co., Md.		J.E. Ellis of Crisfield, Md., owner
ENGINEER			270.0		96.9	30.4	9.0	1832	Baltimore, Md.	James Beacham	Sold foreign, possibly slaver
EUGENIA			310.0					1832	Baltimore, Md.	James Beacham	Sold foreign, probably slaver
FANNIE H. STEWART		120529	351.0	333.0	136.0	33.0	11.0	1882	Yorktown, Va.	N.V. Lane	Foundered, 5/8/1915 off Cape May, N.J.
FANNIE REICHE	KLGB	120896	463.0	440.0	143.1	34.0	10.1	1892	Baltimore, Md.	Beacham & Bro.	Lost 1905 by collision
FANNIE R. WILLIAMS	JNPC	120109	365.6	347.4	129.0	32.2	14.6	1873	Laurel, Del.		Home port 1885, Wilmington, Del.
FERRATA			336.0					1827	Miles River, Md.		First use of iron rigging (M.V. Brewington)
FRANK M. HOWES	JWHN	120493	178.9	170.0	119.8	24.7	8.3	1882	Baltimore, Md.	Beacham & Bro.	Lost 1893

CHESAPEAKE-BUILT VESSELS CARRYING THREE- MASTED SCHOONER RIG

NAME	SIGNAL	OFFICIAL	TONNAGE:		DIMENSIONS:			BUILT:			COMMENTS:
	LETTERS	NO.	GROSS	NET	LENGTH	BREADTH	DEPTH	DATE	WHERE	BY	
GEORGE AERY	JRWB	85465	323.4	307.2	138.6	34.0	12.2	1876	Jamestown, Va.	J. Mathis	Lost 1889
GEORGE F. PHILLIPS *	KQWS	86572	270.0	237.0	130.2	28.3	8.4	1901	Bethel, Del.	J.M.C. Moore	Abandoned 2/5/1910, 33°25'N; 73°40'W
GEORGE N. REED	LBVF	208508	493.0	429.0	156.5	35.1	13.4	1911	Seaford, Del.	Seaford M. R.	Stranded 6/20/1915, N.C.
GEORGE PEABODY	JLBS	85163	493.0	429.0		30.4	18.5	1871	Baltimore, Md.	Beacham	Rerigged as barkentine, sold foreign 1883
GEORGE W. CHURCHMAN	JQNW	85371	281.0	242.0	120.6	31.1	9.7	1874	Greensboro, Md.	W.C. Satterfield	"W" dropped from name 1886, foundered
											4/5/1921, Port Furna, Cape Verde Is.
GRACE G. BENNETT *	KLPN	86242	210.0	199.0	135.5	23.9	7.8	1893	Bethel, Del.		Abnd 1956, Crumpton, Md.
GRANVILLE R. BACON *	LCFB	209184	385.0	339.0	133.6	31.6	11.8	1911	Bethel, Del.	Bethel M. R.	Last ram built, stranded 1933, Weekapaug, R.I.
H. S. LANFAIR	KCHV	95792	402.0	346.0	138.0	32.7	10.0	1884	Baltimore, Md.	J.S. Beachham	Lost 5/1/1917, St. Johns Is., Me.
HARLAND W. HUSTON *	KJPN	96116	180.0	171.0	125.0	23.6	7.4	1891	Bethel, Del.	J.M.C. Moore	Foundered as barge HERO
HARRISON T. BEACHAM	KVDS	202715	299.0	266.0	143.0	29.0	9.0	1905	Baltimore, Md.	Beacham & Bro.	Missing 1928
HARRY K. FOOKS *	KRLP	96597	276.0	249.0	131.0	28.2	9.2	1902	Bethel, Del.		Foundered 10/19/1910, Gulf of Mexico
HATTIE E. GILES	JPWS	95312	135.0	128.0	110.5	23.7	7.5	1874	Lewisville, Del.	J.M.C. Moore	rn IDA O. ROBINSON, abnd 1929
HENRY S. CULVER	KBVJ	95782	753.7	716.0	178.4	35.0	19.2	1883	Alexandria, Va.	Agnew	Lost 1889
IDA BIRDSALL	HKGD	12018	358.1		140.0	32.0	13.0	1866	Baltimore, Md.		
IDA E. COMLY *		100594	208.0	197.7	133.8	23.8	7.6	1894	Bethel, Del.		Lost 1/1902
ISABELLA GILL	KJGQ	100483	585.0	525.0	153.1	35.5	14.6	1891	Baltimore, Md.	Skinner	Missing 8/1906
IVY BLADES *	KLWR	100584	234.0	222.0	134.8	23.9	8.8	1894	Bethel, Del.	J.M.C. Moore	rn CORAPEAKE, burned 6/1936, N. River Bar
J. B. VAN DEUSEN	JCKB	13788	222.5	211.3	115.2	29.4	10.5	1867	Havre de Grace, Md.		Home port 1871, Philadelphia
J. DALLAS MARVIL*		76852	160.0	152.0	112.8	23.6	7.4	1889	Bethel, Del.	J.M.C. Moore	Sunk 6/15/1910 by collision, Sandy Pt., Md.
J. W. SOMERVILLE	LTGM	219507	547.0	470.0	160.2	35.2	12.7	1919	Pocomoke City, Md.	E. J. Tull	Foundered 10/27/1921 off Tampa
JAMES B. OGDEN	JTVW	76154	678.7	644.8	160.0	36.0	17.6	1880	Alexandria, Va.	Alex.M.R.&S.B.Co	Lost 1896
JAMES BOYCE JR.	JWSQ	76375	729.9	693.4	156.3	35.5	19.5	1882	Alexandria, Va.	Potomac Manuf.	rn ISLEBORO, lost 8/1902
JAMES H. HARGRAVES*	KLSF	77106	184.0	138.0	128.0	23.6	9.8	1893	Sharptown, Md.	J.M.C. Moore	rn (a) B.P. GRAVENOR, (b) MAYFAIR,
											Lost 1942 off Cape Hatteras, N.C.
JAMES H. YOUNG	JFTH	13989	128.0					1867	Newtown, Md.		ABS Record states "canal"
JASON			173.0		76.0	22.9	9.5	1807	Baltimore, Md.	J. Hutton	"one deck, round tuck, flush deck,
											three masts" **
JENNIE D. BELL*	KNPD	77312	194.0	171.0	125.0	23.5	7.5	1898	Bethel, Del.	J.M.C. Moore	Abnd 1961, Salisbury, Md.
JENNIE E. MARSHALL	KCDP	76483	197.8	187.9	123.5	23.8	9.0	1884	Bethel, Del.	Wm. R. McIlvane	Converted to barge 1890
JENNIE M. CARTER			300.0					1874	Newtown, Md.		Home port 1888, Providence, R.I.
JOHN A. CURTIS	JNVS	75589	155.0	147.0	111.2	23.6	8.5	1874	Laurel, Del.	D.W. Moore	Rblt 1908, rn ROBERT, abnd 1933
JOHN E. HURST	JMVB	75528	126.0					1873	Newtown, Md.		ABS states "flat model," lost 1880
JOHN H. CANNON	KJMS	76947	232.0	220.5	120.0	30.8	8.6	1891	Baltimore, Md.	Brusstar & Bro.	Lost 12/1897
JOHN N. PARKER	JQRW	75734	165.1	156.8	118.3	24.0	7.6	1874	Laurel, Del.		Home port 1885, Seaford, Del.

CHESAPEAKE-BUILT VESSELS CARRYING THREE-MASTED SCHOONER RIG

NAME	SIGNAL LETTERS	OFFICIAL NO.	TONNAGE: GROSS	NET	DIMENSIONS: LENGTH	BREADTH	DEPTH	BUILT: DATE	WHERE	BY	COMMENTS:
JOHN Q. FERGUSON*		76764	129.0	122.0	105.2	21.0	7.6	1888	Sharptown, Md.		rn VIRGINIA, rerigged from 2m, abnd 1939
JOHN S. BEACHAM	JQPB	75706	234.0	199.0	107.4	28.6	8.4	1874	Baltimore, Md.		Foundered 4/3/1917, Cape Sable, N.S.
JONATHAN MAY	HLPS	13403	342.0		125.0	31.0	10.0	1857	Berlin, Md.		Original owner Henry May of Philadelphia
JOSEPH P. COOPER*	KVDL	202680	315.0	288.0	150.4	28.2	10.2	1905	Sharptown, Md.	Sharptown M.R.	Lost at sea 11/1918, 36°21'N; 71°41'W
JOSIAH LINTHICUM	KNBF	77255	165.0	146.0	110.0	27.3	9.3	1897	Church Cr., Md.		Lost at sea 1899
LENA M. COTTINGHAM	JQVD	140089	210.0	200.3	113.8	31.0	8.5	1875	Seaford, Del.	M. Griffith	Lost 1888
LEVIN J. MARVEL*	KJWQ	141175	183.0	174.0	125.5	23.5	7.5	1891	Bethel, Del.	Geo. K. Phillips	Foundered 8/12/1955 off N. Beach, Md.
LEWIS EHRMAN	JLSB	15841	406.3	386.0	129.0	31.4	14.0	1872	Baltimore, Md.		Lost 1892
LILLIAN E. KERR	MBQS	220698	548.0	475.0	160.2	35.5	12.7	1920	Pocomoke City, Md.	E.J. Tull	Rerigged as 4m, sunk 11/1942 by collision
LIZZIE A. WILLIIAMS*	KLJS	141221	188.0	179.4	125.0	23.7	7.5	1892	Bethel, Del.	Geo. K. Phillips	Sunk 7/13/1917 by collision, Gulf of Mexico
LIZZIE YOUNG	JNPD	15942	380.5	361.4	128.2	32.8	14.6	1873	Seaford, Del.		Home port 1888, Boston, Mass.
LUCY WRIGHT		15819	198.6		110.0	30.0	9.6	1872	Laurel, Del.		
LULU M. QUILLIN		21739	129.0	122.0	106.0	19.1	8.6	1882	Lewisville, Del.	Lewisville M. R.	Rblt from READING R.R. #34, lost 1917, N.C.
LUNA			126.4		67.0	22.2	8.1	1805	Baltimore, Md.	Wm. Flannigan	"One deck, 3 masts, square tuck"***
LYDIA H. ROPER	JQTN	140084	321.0	305.0	146.0	34.0	10.5	1875	Norfolk, Va.	Sawyer & Taylor	Foundered 3/16/25, Pilot Town, Miss.
MABEL AND RUTH*	KMPQ	92691	190.0	166.0	125.3	23.8	7.6	1896	Bethel, Del.	J.M.C. Moore	rn CITY OF ST PETERSBURG, abnd 1948, Fla.
MAGGIE E. GREY	HMPD	16077	405.5	385.2	127.8	30.0	15.8	1867	Baltimore, Md.	Booz & Co.	Wrecked 1891
MARGRET H. VANE*	KRJC	93222	246.0	204.0	126.4	28.3	8.9	1901	Madison, Md.	J.W. Brooks	Lost 3/23/1908 by stranding, Cobbs Is., Va.
MARTIN L. SMITH	JRNL	90855	384.0	365.2	128.0	32.4	15.2	1875	Jamestown, Va.	Geo. H. Wheaton	Lost 1893
MARY E. ESKERIDGE		209412	378.0	334.0	148.0	30.4	10.0	1911	Seaford, Del.	Seaford M. R.	Stranded 12/31/1911, Big Kennekeet, N.C.
MARY LEE PATTON	KMCT	92618	549.0	522.0	156.2	34.0	15.3	1894	Baltimore, Md.	Beacham & Bro.	Lost 1/1905, W. Indies
MATTIE MAY	KBPD	91589	166.7	161.2	108.3	27.3	7.6	1883	Baltimore, Md.	Skinner	Lost 1903
MATTIE NEWMAN	KCBT	91645	354.9	337.1	140.6	34.0	9.8	1883	Yorktown, Va.	N. L. Lane	Home port 1883, N.Y., N.Y., sold London, 1917
MINNEHAHA		90577	98.0		93.9	23.9	5.8	1864	Seaford, Del.		Home port 1888, Philadelphia, Pa.
MINNIE G. LOUD	JMTC	90503	412.6		132.6	31.5	12.1	1873	Baltimore, Md.	Willener & Buck	Loud, Claridge and Co, owners, lost 1881
MINNIE REPPLIER	HNQW	17154	345.0		119.0	30.0	10.0	1864	Baltimore, Md.		
NEW LIGHT			316.0		135.60	30.1	8.6	1855	Md.		
NORFOLK			183.0					1818	Va.		
ORESTES			136.0		62.7	23.0	8.0	1805	Baltimore, Md.	Wm. Flannigan	Charles Ghequires, A. Kunckel, owners
PANOPE			156.9		72.0	23.0	9.0	1806	Baltimore, Md.	J. Hutton	B. Salenare, owner, cost $7,000
PERCY W. SCHALL	KLVB	150490	239.7	227.7	123.7	28.3	8.4	1891	Baltimore, Md.	Mc Cosker	Burned at sea, 2/1896
PHILLIPS M. BROOKS*	KSPT	200196	243.0	243.0	132.5	28.2	10.1	1903	Madison, Md.	J.W. Brooks	Sold Dominican Republic, 1922
POCAHONTAS			380.0		122.0	29.0		1827	Mathews Co., Va.		Possible 1st use of iron shrouds, see FERRATA
REBECCA R. TOWNSEND	HQKM	21507	352.0					1864	Baltimore, Md.		
REEDVILLE*	LCDM	209062	235.0	212.0	130.0	26.3	8.8	1910	Pocomoke City, Md.	E.J. Tull	Sold foreign, 1920, foundered 2/27/1927

CHESAPEAKE-BUILT VESSELS CARRYING THREE- MASTED SCHOONER RIG

NAME	SIGNAL LETTERS	OFFICIAL NO.	TONNAGE: GROSS	NET	DIMENSIONS: LENGTH	BREADTH	DEPTH	BUILT: DATE	WHERE	BY	COMMENTS:
REVENGE			106.0		59.5	21.2	8.0	1805	Baltimore, Md.	Wm Flannigan	"One deck, three masts, square stern"**
RICHARD LINTHICUM	KSTC	200474	191.0	191.0	121.5	24.8	9.0	1903	Church Cr., Md.	B. Linthicum	Sold Venezuela, rn ALSACIA
RICHMOND*	LBCF	206175	288.0	265.0	135.3	26.5	9.0	1908	Sharptown, Md.	Sharptown M.R.	Lost 9/1926 off Fla.
ROBERT PORTNER	JSDM	110299	631.0		130.0	30.0	17.0	1876	Alexandria, Va.	Alexandria, M. R.	Lost 1878
ROGER QUARLES		110644	25.0	24.0	74.0	15.6	4.5	1884	Norfolk, Va.		Scrapped 1909
SAMUEL T. BEACHAM*	KNQB	116845	185.0	155.0	121.0	23.7	8.2	1898	Baltimore, Md.	Beacham & Bro.	Lost by collision 1913, Fla. Straits
SANANDREAS	KQGF	116989	226.0	180.0	122.0	28.0	9.6	1900	Pocomoke City, Md.	E. J. Tull	Lost 12/10/1900, Bahamas
SARAH AND LUCY	JQFN	115303	252.4	239.8	114.0	33.2	9.0	1874	Holy Fork, Va.		Home port 1885, N.Y., N.Y., lost 8/2/1918
SARAH J. FORT	HQVP	22530	208.2		105.0	20.0	10.0	1865	Greensboro, Md.		A.J. Pharo, owner
SARAH S. HARDING	JMFK	115165	384.6		133.0	32.6	14.6	1873	Seaford, Del.		H.L. Gregg and others, owner, of Philadelphia
SILVER WING	JSHN	115536	142.3					1877	Baltimore, Md.	Beacham & Bro.	Sold Mexico, rn IBERIA, lost 1883
SPOTLESS	JRNC	115429	418.1	397.2	145.0	32.0	13.0	1875	Baltimore, Md.		S.B. Watts owner, Baltimore
STEVEN J. FOOKS	JQTG	115363	430.5	408.9	135.4	35.0	11.6	1874	Solomons Is., Md.	Solomon & Davis	Home port 1883, Baltimore
SUGAR STICK								1855	Baltimore, Md.		Possible 3m
T. MORRIS PEROT	JRFV	145072	308.0	294.8	137.5	33.8	11.6	1875	Jamestown, Va.	J. Mathis	Lost by collision 9/1913 off Fenwick Is., Md.
THOMAS J. LANCASTER	JQGD	145019	653.2		156.0	34.6	18.4	1874	Seaford, Del.	Wm. Lamb	Lost, 10/5/1881, New Inlet, N.C.
THOMAS BOOZ	JFLN	24670	310.4	294.9	116.9	29.8	8.7	1867	Baltimore, Md.		J.C. Cottingham, owner, 1888 home port Phila.
THOMAS J. SHRYOCK*	KJCN	145571	173.0	164.0	117.4	23.7	7.7	1891	Bethel, Del.	Geo. K. Phillips	Abandoned 1945, Elizabeth City, N.C.
VENUS	KLRT	161715	204.0	194.0	108.0	29.4	9.1	1893	Cambridge, Md.	G.T. Johnson	rn (a) SANTA LUIZA (Portuguese flag),
											(b) EDNA BRIGHT HOUGH (U.S.), abnd 1938
VICTOR C. RECORDS*	KSCV	161928	293.0	263.0	136.5	28.3	9.7	1902	Sharptown, Md.	Thos. Sauerhoff	Wrecked 2/16/1920 off Cape Lookout, N.C.
VIRGINIA F. HAWLEY		25844	107.1	101.8	98.5	22.3	6.6	1871	Havre de Grace, Md.		Home port 1905, Baltimore
W. H. DIX	KRDF	81778	212.0	168.0	112.9	28.5	9.2	1901	Pocomoke City, Md.	E.J. Tull	Lost 7/9/1912, New Providence Is.
WALTER W. RASIN	KHTP	81306	679.0	648.3	160.0	35.8	16.2	1890	Baltimore, Md.	Brusstar	Lost 1897
WILLIAM L. FRANKLIN		80223	123.4	117.2	96.5	26.7	7.1	1871	Baltimore, Md.		Home port 1888, Baltimore, Md.
WILLIAM LINTHICUM	KMDB	81494	156.0	148.0	112.0	27.6	8.0	1894	Church Cr., Md.	B. Linthicum	Sold to Bermuda, converted to barge 1940
WILLIAM A. MARBURG	KBPV	80986	714.0	678.0	163.4	33.7	19.7	1883	Baltimore, Md.	Woodall	Lost 1892
WILLIAM H. KNIGHT	JQVS	80510	187.0		116.4	29.3	8.2	1875	Taylors Is., Md.	Lambdin	Lost 1883
WILLIAM H. SKINNER	KLSW	81454	262.0	220.0	129.2	30.2	9.0	1893	Baltimore, Md.	Skinner	Abnd 2/1908, 45 mi. ENE of Frying Pan Shoal
WILLIAM THOMAS MOORE*	KRTC	81825	291.0	261.0	134.3	28.8	10.1	1902	Bethel, Del.	Geo. K. Phillips	Foundered 11/16/1916, 40°05'N; 37°56'W
WILSON AND HUNTING	KBMH	80976	418.0	344.0	152.0	35.0	11.6	1883	Alexandria, Va.	Potomac Manuf.	Lost 1905
* Ram											
** Customs House Carpenter Certificate											

CHESAPEAKE-BUILT FOUR-MASTED SCHOONERS

NAME	SIGNAL LETTERS	OFF. NO.	TONNAGE: GROSS	NET	DIMENSIONS: LENGTH	BREADTH	DEPTH	BUILT: DATE	WHERE	BY	COMMENTS:
ALBERT W. ROBINSON*	KWBQ	204036	498	423	163	34.7	12	1907	Sharptown, Md.	Sharptown M. R.	Foundered 9/5/1926, 300 mi off
											Va. capes, ram with topmasts and jibboom
ALEXANDER H. ERICKSON	LPGQ	217389	970	880	197	39.3	15.4	1918	Seaford, Del.	Del. Steamboat Co.	rn WELLINGTON, foundered 9/10/1928
											off Cape Hatteras, N.C.
ANANDALE	LTWF	219318	1630	1530	227	42.3	22.8	1919	Sharptown, Md.	Eastern Shore Shpbldg.	Largest schr built on the Chesapeake
										Thirty-Six Corp.	Stranded 7/13/1929, Andicora, Vz.
ANNA R. HEIDRITTER	LBKG	207312	694	610	185	37.1	13.5	1910	Sharptown, Md.	Sharptown M. R.	Rebuilt from COHASSETT, dragged
											ashore 3/2/1942, Ocracoke, N.C.
CHARLES M. STRUVEN	LHDM	215086	632	562	171	37	13.2	1917	Pocomoke City, Md.	E. James Tull	Foundered as barge MAURICE R. SHAW JR.,
											11/4/1942, 4 mi off Pt. Jupiter, Fla.
JUDGE PENNEWILL*	KVFG	202826	439	358	155	34.5	12.2	1906	Bethel, Del.	J. M. C. Moore	2 centerboards, abandoned 6/9/1912,
											between Charleston and Savannah
PURNELL T. WHITE	LJCH	215687	751	688	184	37.4	14	1917	Sharptown, Md.	Alonzo Connelly	Abandoned 2/9/1934 off Cape Henry, Va.
											hulked 1935 at Baltimore
SALLIE C. MARVIL	KICF	117067	568	546	174	37.2	16	1901	Sharptown, Md.	Sharptown M. R.	Lost 7/20/1915 off coast of Venezuela
										Thomas Sauerhoff	
THE JOSEPHINE	KJCP	145572	639	563	173	36	15	1890	Baltimore, Md.	J. S. Beacham & Bro.	Stranded 4/3/1915 off Kill Devil Hills,
											N.C., 3 men lost.
VAN LEAR BLACK	KGRN	161615	634	546	159	35.8	12.9	1889	Baltimore, Md.	J. S. Beacham & Bro.	Burned 10/18/1929 at Nuevitas, Cuba
WILLIAM T. HART	KBMG	80927	934	896	198	38	19.6	1883	Alexandria, Va.	John Agnew Co.	Lost at sea 12/11/1885.

* 4 masted ram

NAME	SIGNAL LETTERS	OFFICIAL NO.	TONNAGE: GROSS	NET	DIMENSIONS: LENGTH	BREADTH	DEPTH	BUILT: DATE	WHERE	BY	COMMENTS:
AGNES S. QUILLIN	KSOD	107174	197.00	187.00	126.5	23.9	7.8	1894	Bethel, Del.	Geo. K. Phillips	Stranded 11/1938, Potomac R.,
											Smith Pt., Va.
ALBERT W. ROBINSON	KWBQ	204036	498.00	423.00	163.0	34.7	12.0	1907	Sharptown, Md.	Sharptown M. R.	4m, topmasts and jibboom, lost 9/5/1926
ALVERDA S. ELZEY	KPBH	107450	283.00	249.00	135.9	28.5	8.2	1899	Bethel, Del.	Geo. K. Phillips	Lost off Mexico 1/1910
ANNA M. HUDSON	KTJP	201396	338.00	299.00	135.5	31.8	10.0	1904	Bethel, Del.	Geo. K. Phillips	Abnd 1933
CHARLES T. STRANN	KJMB	126732	215.00	186.00	125.2	23.8	8.9	1891	Sharptown, Md.	J.M.C. Moore	rn (a) CHARLES L. ROHDE (b) KINKORA
											(c) CIUDAD TRUJILLO, Dominican Republic
CLARENCE A. HOLLAND	KLSB	126984	200.00	179.00	126.5	23.9	8.2	1893	Bethel, Del.	J.M.C. Moore	Abnd 1949, Elizabeth City, N.C.
EDNA AND EMMA	KHVC	136165	182.78	173.64	119.7	22.5	8.2	1890	Baltimore, Md.	McCosker	Lost 1899
EDWARD R. BAIRD JR.	KSHN	137061	279.00	238.00	132.0	28.3	9.8	1903	Bethel, Del.	Geo. K. Phillips	Sank 9/19/1955, Tangier Sound
EDWIN AND MAUD	KPRT	136784	208.00	178.00	126.0	23.8	8.6	1900	Bethel, Del.	Geo. K. Phillips	rn (a) VICTORY CHIMES (b) DOMINO EFFECT
											(c) VICTORY CHIMES, sails out of
											Rockland, Me.
GEORGE F. PHILLIPS	KQWS	86572	270.00	237.00	130.2	28.3	8.4	1901	Bethel, Del.	Geo. K. Phillips	Lost 2/5/1910
GRACE G. BENNETT	KLPN	86242	210.00	199.00	135.5	23.9	7.8	1893	Bethel, Del.	Bethel M.R.	Abnd 1956, Crumpton, Md.
GRANVILLE R. BACON	LCFB	209184	385.00	339.00	133.6	31.6	11.8	1911	Bethel, Del.	Bethel M.R.	Last ram built, stranded 12/1933,
											Weekapaug, R.I.
HARLAND W. HUSTON	KJPN	96116	180.00	171.00	125.0	23.6	7.4	1891	Bethel, Del.	J.M.C. Moore	Foundered as barge HERO
HARRY K. FOOKS	KRLP	96597	276.00	249.00	131.0	28.2	9.2	1902	Bethel, Del.	Geo. K. Phillips	Foundered 10/19/1910, Gulf of Mexico
IDA E. COMLY		100594	208.00	197.67	133.8	23.8	7.6	1894	Bethel, Del.	J.M.C. Moore	Lost 1/1902
IVY BLADES	KLWR	100584	234.00	222.00	134.8	23.9	8.8	1894	Bethel, Del.	J.M.C. Moore	rn CORAPEAKE, burned 6/1936,
											No. River Bar
J. DALLAS MARVIL		76852	160.00	152.00	112.8	23.6	7.4	1889	Bethel, Del.	J.M.C. Moore	Sunk by collision 6/15/1910,
											Sandy Pt., Md.
JAMES H. HARGRAVES	KLSF	77106	184.00	138.00	128.0	23.6	9.8	1893	Sharptown, Md.	J.M.C. Moore	rn (a) B.P. GRAVENOR, (b) MAYFAIR,
											lost 1942
JENNIE D. BELL	KNPD	77312	194.00	171.00	125.0	23.5	7.5	1898	Bethel, Del.	J.M.C. Moore	Abnd 1961, Salisbury, Md.
JOSEPH P. COOPER	KVDL	202680	315.00	288.00	150.4	28.2	10.2	1905	Sharptown, Md.	Sharptown M.R.	Lost at sea 11/1918
JUDGE PENNEWILL	KVFG	202826	439.00	358.00	155.0	34.5	12.2	1906	Bethel, Del.	J.M.C. Moore	4m, 2cb, abnd 6/9/1912 off S.C.
LEVIN J. MARVEL	KJWQ	141175	183.00	174.00	125.5	23.5	7.5	1891	Bethel, Del.	Geo. K. Phillips	Foundered 8/12/1955 off No. Beach, Md.
LIZZIE A. WILLIAMS	KLJS	141221	188.00	179.38	125.0	23.7	7.5	1892	Bethel, Del.	Geo. K. Phillips	Sunk by collision 7/13/1917, Gulf
											of Mexico
MABEL AND RUTH	KMPQ	92691	190.00	166.00	125.3	23.8	7.6	1896	Bethel, Del.	J.M.C. Moore	rn CITY OF ST PETERSBURG, abnd 1948, Fla.
MARGRET H. VANE	KRJC	93222	246.00	204.00	126.4	28.3	8.9	1901	Madison, Md.	J.W. Brooks	Wrecked 1908, Va.
PHILLIPS M. BROOKS	KSPT	200196	243.00	243.00	132.5	28.2	10.1	1903	Madison, Md.	J.W. Brooks	Home port 1905, Crisfield, Md.
REEDVILLE	LCDM	209062	235.00	212.00	130.0	26.3	8.8	1910	Pocomoke City, Md.	E.J. Tull	Sold foreign, 1920, foundered 2/27/1927
RICHMOND	LBCF	206175	288.00	265.00	135.3	26.5	9.0	1908	Sharptown, Md.	Sharptown M.R.	Lost 9/1926 off Fla.
SAMUEL T. BEACHAM	KNQB	116845	185.00	155.00	121.0	23.7	8.2	1898	Baltimore, Md.	Beacham & Bro.	Lost by collision 1913, Fla. Straits
THOMAS J. SHRYOCK	KJCN	145571	173.00	164.00	117.4	23.7	7.7	1891	Bethel, Del.	Geo. K. Phillips	Abnd 1945, Elizabeth City, N.C.
VICTOR C. RECORDS	KSCV	161928	293.00	263.00	136.5	28.3	9.7	1902	Sharptown, Md.	Thos. Sauerhoff	Wrecked 2/16/1920 off Cape Lookout, N.C.
WILLIAM THOMAS MOORE	KRTC	81825	291.00	261.00	134.3	28.8	10.1	1902	Bethel, Del.	Geo. K. Phillips	Lost 11/16/1916

NAME	OFF. NO.	TONNAGE:		DIMENSIONS:			BUILT:		
		GROSS	NET	LENGTH	BREADTH	DEPTH	YEAR	WHERE	BY
A. WEISKITTLE	106136	43.34	41.17	66.5	21.6	6.3	1882	Madison, Md.	J. Brooks
AEOLUS	105061	44.90	42.66	69.6	21.9	5.1	1871	Accomack Co., Va.	
ALABAMA	1605	22.90	20.90	51.0	17.5	5.0	1853	Talbot Co., Md.	
ALBATROSS	409	16.61	15.78	46.6	14.0	4.8	1848	Somerset Co., Md.	
ALICE AND MARY	105545	8.30							Casltetonny
AMANDA F. LEWIS	106304	47.00	33.00	67.0	22.3	6.5	1884	Madison, Md.	J.W. Brooks
AMELIA M. PRICE	1848	58.47	55.55	71.3	23.6	6.8	1869	Somerset Co., Md.	
AMERICAN PATRIOT	1634	26.48	25.16	50.3	17.6	5.5	1856	Dorchester Co., Md.	
ANGIE McNAMARA	1862	46.77	44.44	64.6	21.2	6.8	1862	Madison, Md.	J.W. Brooks
ARIANNA	1656	19.71	18.73	46.5	12.2	5.0	1853	Somerset Co., Md.	
B. A. WAGNER	2995	53.40	50.73	68.4	22.5	7.3	1875	Dorchester Co., Md.	
BANSHEE	2991	33.71	32.02	59.0	19.8	5.6	1875	Baltimore, Md.	
CADET	4400	38.80	28.00	59.6	18.4	6.0	1864	Somerset Co., Md.	
CAPITOL	4404	27.45	26.08	50.3	16.6	5.8	1854	Somerset Co., Md.	
CHARLES A. PRYOR	5597	10.50	9.69	39.0	14.5	4.0	1867	Crisfield, Md.	
CHARLES SAMUEL	5617	24.88	23.60	49.6	17.2	5.2	1864	Dorchester Co., Md.	
CHRISTOPHER C. FALLIN	5773	53.89	51.20	66.5	22.0	7.5	1869	Madison, Md.	J.W. Brooks
COQUETTE	4020	43.32	41.15	68.9	18.8	7.4	1855	Baltimore, Md.	
DANIEL AND AUGUSTUS	6563	27.59	26.21	55.2	18.4	5.8	1867	James Is., Md.	
DANIEL J. BALLARD	6504	16.17	15.37	46.0	17.0	5.8	1867	St. Georges Is., Md.	
DEFY	6000	7.37		34.0	10.7	4.2			
DISPATCH	6591	18.97	18.02	47.0	15.0	5.0			
DOVE	6387	16.52	15.69	44.6	15.0	4.2	1856	Hunting Cr., Va.	
ELLEN AND ALICE	135268	38.00	36.00	63.0	20.0	5.8	1877	Gloucester Co., Va.	
ELLEN MATILDA	8379	39.73	37.74	60.9	20.0	6.6	1865	Accomack Co., Va.	
ELLEN TRAVERSE	8411	16.74							
EMILY JANE	7052	17.00	11.00	39.1	16.5	4.9	1842	Somerset Co., Md.	
EMMA BERRY	135330	9.22	8.76	34.9	11.4	3.5	1876	St. Georges Is., Md.	
EXCHANGE	8381	22.02	20.92	42.3	17.7	5.0	1849	Onancock, Va.	
FAIR AMERICAN	9721	13.80	13.11	43.0	13.0	4.0		Somerset Co., Md.	
FLIRT OF THE WAVE	9800	35.53	33.85	55.4	19.0	6.0	1864	Somerset Co., Md.	
FLORA	120599	13.70	13.02	40.0	15.7	5.2	1884	St. Georges Is., Md.	
FLORA TEMPLE	9801	35.00	23.00	63.5	21.0	6.6	1866	Somerset Co., Md.	

NAME	OFF. NO.	TONNAGE:		DIMENSIONS:			BUILT:		
		GROSS	NET	LENGTH	BREADTH	DEPTH	YEAR	WHERE	BY
FOUR FRIENDS	9897	41.93	39.85	59.3	20.3	6.5	1869	Somerset Co., Md.	
FOX	9215	18.82	17.88	44.0	14.0	4.6	ca 1845	St. Georges Is., Md.	
FRANCIS J. RUTH	120011	60.90	57.84	73.0	23.2	6.7	1871	Dorchester Co., Md.	J.W. Brooks
G. A. KIRWAN	85735	44.00	42.00	66.3	21.8	6.4	1882	Madison, Md.	J.W. Brooks
GENESTA*	85910	10.00	9.00	47.4	15.8	2.8	1885	Cambridge, Md.	
GOLDEN RULE	10950	16.56	15.73	50.4	17.0	5.9	1867	Accomack Co., Va.	
GRAY HOUND	10248	18.13	17.22	48.6	17.0	5.1	1851	Somerset Co., Md.	
GUSSIE C.*	200387	21.00	21.00	55.0	20.6	5.3	1903	Fairmount, Md.	
H. P. BARNES	95095	39.00	29.00	57.8	20.5	5.9	1870	Baltimore, Md.	
HALCYON	11036	17.90	17.02	47.8	15.6	5.5	1835	Somerset Co., Md.	
HARP	11900	17.41	16.54	46.0	14.6	4.5	1869		
HATTIE AND FRANCIS	95626	28.06	26.66	53.3	17.4	5.5	1881	Madison, Md.	J.W. Brooks
HOPE	11022	30.42	28.90	56.2	19.2	5.6	1866	Baltimore, Md.	
HOPE	95763	32.07	30.47	56.5	19.5	5.6	1883	Lankford Bay, Md.	
HUMMINGBIRD	11921	12.25	11.64	41.4	15.4	4.8	ca 1867	St. Georges Is., Md.	R. Ball
IDA	100166	42.80	40.66	65.0	20.8	5.6	1875		
ISAAC SOLOMON	100077	27.32	25.95	57.0	18.5	5.8	1872	Solomons Is., Md.	I. Solomon
IOWA		100.40		76.7	23.0	6.6	1854	Dorchester Co., Md.	L.I. Applegarth
J. S. SMITH	75415	30.00	17.00	55.0	19.0	5.6	1872	Somerset Co., Md.	
J. W. BROOKS	75057	47.74	45.35	64.5	21.1	6.1	1868	Dorchester Co., Md.	J.W. Brooks
JAMES A. WHITING	75326	35.00	23.00	61.0	20.6	6.3	1871	Somerset Co., Md.	
JAMES E. RILEY	13980	28.00	20.00	56.0	16.0	5.8	1853	Accomack Co., Va.	
JAMES E. STANSBURY	75325	51.78	49.19	66.2	21.7	6.8	1871	Dorchester Co., Md.	
JAMES H. LEWIS	76146	37.00	35.00	63.6	22.7	5.6	1880	Pocomoke City, Md.	
JENNIE BAKER	12857	15.33	14.56	42.9	16.1	4.6			
JESSIE J. PARKS	13917	29.62	28.14	55.3	18.8	5.2	1866	Somerset Co., Md.	
JOHN E.A. CUNNINGHAM	75905	24.33	23.11	52.8	19.7	5.8	1876	Somerset Co., Md.	
JOHN H. ADAMS	13974	35.62	33.81	58.7	20.5	6.4	1858	Somerset Co., Md.	
JOHN HENRY	13997	12.88	12.24	42.0	13.0	4.1	1867	Crisfield, Md.	
JOHN NELSON	12525	44.99	42.74	60.2	19.3	6.8	1856	Somerset Co., Md.	
JOHN ROWLETT	13993	51.73					1877	Dorchester Co., Md.	Spicer
JOHN W. WILLING	13977	23.00	22.00	50.0	16.0	5.2	1848	Somerset Co., Md.	
JULIA AND ANNIE	75164	42.16	40.05	64.5	21.5	6.4	1869	Talbot Co., Md.	

NAME	OFF. NO.	TONNAGE:		DIMENSIONS:			BUILT:		
		GROSS	NET	LENGTH	BREADTH	DEPTH	YEAR	WHERE	BY
KATE JOHNSON	14270	21.62	20.54	49.4	16.9	5.4	1872	Somerset Co., Md.	
KESSIE C. PRICE*	14477	25.00	17.00	55.6	18.6	5.0	1888	Rock Cr., Md.	
L. McMURRY	15438	34.00	26.00	54.0	18.8	5.9	1862	Somerset Co., Md.	
L. B. PLATT	15944	39.00	27.00	61.6	22.2	6.3	1873	Dorchester Co., Md.	
L. C. SPENCER	15703	44.00	42.00	64.0	20.8	6.4	1870	Dorchester Co., Md.	
LADIES FANCY	15481	20.52	14.47						
LADY EVANS	15465	32.00	30.00	58.5	20.8	6.0	1864	Somerset Co., Md.	
LADY MARYLAND	903524	60.00	54.00	72.1	22.1	7.6	1986	Baltimore, Md.	G.P. Boudreau
LADY OF THE LAKE	14514	21.00	13.00	50.1	17.7	6.0	1846	Somerset Co., Md.	
LaFAYETTE	14522	26.00	19.00	54.4	17.5	6.3	1838	Somerset Co., Md.	
LAURA A. MUIR	15615	28.00	27.00	54.5	18.7	5.7	1869	Somerset Co., Md.	
LIVELY DOVE	15494	9.70	9.22	45.0	13.0	4.0	1867	Somerset Co., Md.	
LUCY J. STEWART	15467	27.14	25.79	51.6	19.1	5.8	1869	Somerset Co., Md.	
M. J. DAUGHERTY	93268	17.00	17.00	49.0	17.2	5.2	1902	Crisfield, Md.	
MAID OF THE MIST	9004	49.02	46.57	65.2	21.2	6.3	1870	St. Michaels, Md.	Kirby & Lang
MARTHA A. AVERY	17877	32.35	30.73	57.5	18.0	6.6	1864	Somerset Co., Md.	
MARY AND ELLEN	91357	36.53	34.70	64.4	20.8	6.3	1881	Baltimore, Md.	Skinner & Sons
MARY ANNA	16034	25.34	24.07	51.7	18.0	5.6	1854	Somerset Co., Md.	
MARY ELIZABETH	16090	17.32	16.45	46.2	15.7	4.2	1834	Dorchester Co., Md.	
MARY ELLEN	16067	53.24	50.58	67.1	21.7	5.5	1859	Baltimore, Md.	
MARY J. BOND	90662	35.06	23.99	61.6	20.7	6.1	1874	Crisfield, Md.	
MARY L. BIRD	17133	22.89	14.89	51.8	17.7	6.0	1850	Somerset Co., Md.	
MARY L. COLBOURNE	17894	23.83	13.64	49.2	17.5	5.5	1851	Somerset Co., Md.	
MARYTENA	17882	34.61	32.88	59.6	20.4	6.1	1867	Somerset Co., Md.	
MILDRED ADDISON	24858	35.00	33.00	67.6	21.5	5.1	1870	Somerset Co., Md.	
MINNEHAHA	90128	37.00	27.00	58.5	20.3	5.8			
MODEL	16018	26.29	24.98	50.4	16.4	6.0	1865	Somerset Co., Md.	
MOORE AND BRADY	91284	34.55	32.82	63.4	20.8	5.9	1880	Dorchester Co., Md.	J.W. Brooks
NEPTUNE	18692	44.90	42.66	69.6	21.9	5.1	1871	Accomack Co., Va.	
NOBLE GRAND	18450	28.25	26.84	53.1	17.9	5.8	1854	Somerset Co., Md.	
OCEAN BIRD	19246	22.43	21.31	49.0	17.6	5.0	1869	Somerset Co., Md.	
OCEAN QUEEN	19235	22.97	21.82	48.0	16.0	5.0	1855	Somerset Co., Md.	
PENSACOLA	19693	24.00	23.00	52.0	18.6	5.4	1862	Somerset Co., Md.	

KNOWN PUNGIES

| NAME | OFF. NO. | TONNAGE: | | DIMENSIONS: | | | BUILT: | | |
		GROSS	NET	LENGTH	BREADTH	DEPTH	YEAR	WHERE	BY
PLAN	19522	25.00	24.00	53.6	17.8	5.5	1855	Accomack Co., Va.	
RUTH A. PRICE	110082	69.00	66.00	73.3	23.8	7.9	1873	Somerset Co., Md.	
SAMUEL R. WAITE	23892	46.15	43.85	63.8	20.0	6.3	1870	Somerset Co., Md.	
SEABELLE	22092	19.00	18.00	50.0	15.0	5.0	1855	Somerset Co., Md.	
SEABIRD	23676	31.32	29.75	58.5	18.7	6.2	1854	Somerset Co., Md.	
SEAMENS BRIDE	22036	28.00	17.00	54.0	16.3	5.8	1856	Somerset Co., Md.	
SERENA C. SOMERS	22048	27.00	25.65	53.4	18.1	5.9	1864	Baltimore, Md.	
SEVERN T. CROSWELL	23677	20.82	19.78	46.5	14.8	5.5	1854	Somerset Co., Md.	
SHAKESPEARE	23647	13.60							
SHINING LIGHT	22410	19.75	18.76	53.0	18.0	6.9	1856		
SPARKLING SEA	22013	27.78	26.39	52.4	17.6	6.0	1856	Somerset Co., Md.	
SPLENDID	23614	15.60	14.83	44.6	15.4	5.0	1867		
STARLIGHT	23628	23.03	21.88	48.6	16.0	5.6	1854	Somerset Co., Md.	
TEMPLAR	24736	6.40		23.0	9.0	2.0			
THE CHICORA	5609	35.43	33.66	58.0	18.5	5.4	1865	Somerset Co., Md.	
THREE BROTHERS	24016	24.52	23.29	50.7	17.5	5.7		Prize Vessel	
TROPIC	24535	18.09	17.19	47.8	16.2	5.3	1866	Somerset Co., Md.	
TWILIGHT	145391	46.00	32.00	66.4	22.3	6.5	1884	Madison, Md.	J.W. Brooks
WAR EAGLE	26958	22.00	21.00	49.1	17.1	5.6	1855	Somerset Co., Md.	
WAVE	26694	34.00	25.00	54.8	16.1	6.2	1863	Accomack Co., Va.	
WELDON	80153	36.84	35.00	62.8	21.0	5.6	1870	Somerset Co., Md.	
WILLIAM J. McKEWEN	80108	54.00		68.0	20.7	7.0	1865		
WILLIAM H. VICKERY	26972	25.00	23.00	49.6	16.4	5.2	1856	Somerset Co., Md.	
WILLIAM H. WHITING	81055	25.16	23.91	59.0	20.0	5.0	1884	Pocomoke City, Md.	
ZEPHYR	28073	30.20	28.69	52.7	18.6	5.8	1871	Calvert Co., Md.	
* SHE-PUNGY									

NAME	OFF. NO.	TONNAGE:			DIMENSIONS:			BUILT:			COMMENTS
		GROSS	NET	LENGTH	BREADTH	DEPTH		YEAR	WHERE	BY	
A. J. LAWSON	106217	24.1	22.9	57	17.6	5.2		1883	Pocomoke City, Md.		
ALEXANDER BOND	107046	32.0	30.0	65.5	19	5.4		1893	St. Michaels, Md.	Kirby & Son	Round stern
AMBITION	106205	17.0	8.0	53.2	15.1	4.3		1883	St. Michaels, Md.	T.L. Dawson	Round stern
ANN MATILDA	106219	10.0	9.0	46.5	12.9	3.7		1883	St. Michaels, Md.		
AVALON	106861	22.0	17.0	59	18.1	4.8		1891	Pocomoke City, Md.		
CATHERINE	209260	51.0	51.0	65.2	22.1	6.1		1911	Solomons Is., Md.	M.M. Davis	Round stern
CENTENNIAL	125692	9.0		51.1				1878	Crisfield, Md.		
CLYTIE	12785	40.0	36.0	81	21	6.5		1901	Solomons Is., Md.		
CURLEW	126170	38.0	29.0	65	19.4	6		1883	Pocomoke City, Md.	W.J.S. Clarke	Patent stern
EDGAR M. SCHALL	135752	30.0	21.0	62.3	17.8	5.3		1883	Baltimore, Md.	McCosker	Round stern
EVA BRAMBLE	135529	23.9	22.7	61.5	16.3	4.8		1881	Brannock Nk, Dor. Co.	G. Bramble	Round stern
G. W. GLENN	85872	16.0	13.0	59.3	16.5	3.3		1884	Accomack Co., Va.		Round stern, log built
GEORGE T. PHILLIPS	85747	32.0	31.0	65.5	18.1	5.5		1882	Solomons Is., Md.	J.T. Marsh	Patent stern
GRACIE	86107	26.0	25.0	58	17.7	5		1890	St. Michaels, Md.	Kirby & Son	
HAZELLEAN	95892	10.0	9.0	51.4	14.2	2.8		1886	Somerset Co, Md.		
IVY L. LEONARD	100343	31.0	21.0	64.2	18.1	4.8		1883	Madison, Md.		
J. HAMMITT LAKE	211624	49.0	49.0	68.5	22.2	5.3		1913	Solomons Is., Md.	M.M. Davis	ex LEROY WOODBURN
J. F. LANGHAMMER	76444	31.0	23.0	60	19	5.8		1883	Pocomoke City, Md.		Patent stern
J. W. LEWIS	76758	19.0	18.0	45	14.6	4.6		1888	Greenpoint, Va.		Round stern
JOSEPHINE	76230	19.0	18.0	54.8	16	4.4		1881	St. Michaels, Md.	R. Lambdin	
LIZZIE LEE	206696	45.0	36.0	68.8	22.7	5.5		1909	Inverness, Md.	J. Branford	Scuttled late 1980s, L.I.
LIZZIE MAY	140786	9.0	9.0	49.3	13.3	3.2		1885	Tilghman Is., Md.	J.T. Harrison	Square stern
LOLA TAYLOR	15958	10.3	9.8	56	16.6	2.3		1886	Westmoreland Co., Va.		
M. J. COVINGTON	91711	9.0	5.0	50.4	13.6	2.8		1884	Tilghman Is., Md.	W.S. Covington	Square stern
M. W. WILLING	91620	13.0	8.0	49.6	157	3.8		1883	Somerset Co, Md.		
MINNIE AND HELEN	91508	27.2	25.8	64.7	17.2	4.6		1882	Easton, Md.		
NORMA R.	130478	27.0	26.0	65	18	5.3		1890	Solomons Is., Md.	W. Parsons	Patent stern
R. B. HAYNIE	111134	31.0	22.0	64.6	19.1	5		1896	Solomons Is., Md.	M.M. Davis	Patent stern
RESCUE	110877	27.0	19.0	60.7	18.2	5		1890	Pocomoke City, Md.		Round stern
RHODA VIRGINIA	111460	18.0	18.0	56.3	17.8	3.6		1903	Madison, Md.	J.W. Brooks	Round stern
RICHARD J. VETRA	110790	10.0	9.0	50	15.5	3.2		1888	Deal Is., Md.		
SAMUEL S. SMYTH	116297	10.0	9.0	53	13.9	3.4		1889	Monie, Md.		
SAMUEL T. WHITE	115976	20.0	19.0	50.5	17.6	4.4		1883	Pocomoke City, Md.		
THOMAS BLADES	145488	27.0	26.0	62	17.6	5.1		1888	St. Michaels, Md.	Kirby & Lang	Round stern
THOMAS H. KIRBY	145316	28.0	26.0	61.1	17.6	5.1		1882	St. Michaels, Md.	Kirby & Lang	Round stern
WINNIE H. WINDSOR	81060	26.0	25.0	63.1	17.2	5.2		1884	Solomons Is., Md.		
WOOLFORD	80958	29.1	27.7	63.2	18.7	4.7		1883	Madison, Md.	J.W. Brooks	Round stern

NAME	OFF. NO.	TONNAGE:		DIMENSIONS:			BUILT:	
		GROSS	NET	LENGTH	BREADTH	DEPTH	YEAR	WHERE
BERTHA MAY	3586	9.29	8.83	35.4	9.8	2.5	1893	Occoquan, Va.
DANIEL	157608	60.00	48.00	64.0	21.5	4.5	1901	Alexandria, Va.
DANIEL BOONE	6944			39.0	14.0	3.0	1879	York Co., Va.
ELLA BARNARD	136266	34.00	32.00	63.8	16.8	4.1	1892	Madison, Md.
EVER AND VINNIE	135896	18.00	17.30	44.0	14.0	4.0	1886	Princess Ann, Va.
GEORGE	215645	14.00	11.00	50.9	13.0	2.4	1917	Alexandria, Va.
HARVEY B. MOORE	95716	35.38	33.61	66.5	17.2	3.9	1882	Havre de Grace, Md.
JOHN E. Du BOIS	77024	32.00	30.00	59.3	17.0	4.8	1892	Havre de Grace, Md.
JOHN FISHER	211516	30.00	30.00	75.0	19.4	2.7	1891	Alexandria, Va.
JOHN S. WILSON	76669	46.00	44.00	69.1	19.1	4.6	1887	Havre de Grace, Md.
JOHN TAYLOR	208888	57.00		75.0			1911	Alexandria, Va.
KLONDIKE	211515	18.00	18.00	60.6	17.0	3.0	1901	Alexandria, Va.
L.B. HATTIE	95896	10.35	9.58				1886	Princess Ann, Va.
LAURA	141193	15.00		44.4			1892	Washington, D.C.
LILLY	141168	39.00		69.4			1891	Alexandria, Va.
M.F. PARKER	91245	13.04	12.39	41.0	15.0	3.0	1880	Norfolk, Va.
MAGGIE MAY	92418	41.00		67.7			1891	Washington, D.C.
MORNING STAR	92477	34.00	32.00	65.3	18.4	4.3	1892	Church Cr., Md.
SUSSEX		49.66		80.5	21.9	3.4	1852	Sussex Co., Del.
THREE SISTERS	59435	36.00		61.0			1887	
VIRGINIA	161548	7.53	7.15	36.3	14.3	3.1	1885	Talbot Co., Md.
W.R. SAVAGE	81163	23.30	22.13	55.0	15.0	4.5	1887	Princess Ann, Va.
WALTER W. MURPHY	80990	50.93	48.35	79.0	15.0	5.5	1883	Havre de Grace, Md.
WILLIE HILLIS	80303	34.52		61.5	17.3	4.5	1870	Havre de Grace, Md.

NAME	RIG	OFF. NO.	TONNAGE:		DIMENSIONS:			BUILT:		COMMENT
			GROSS	NET	LENGTH	BREADTH	DEPTH	YEAR	WHERE	
ABEL W. PARKER	3M	105318	202	148	116.1	32.2	7.9	1873	Boothbay, Me.	
ADA J. CAMPBELL	2M	106655	139	132	91.3	26.5	8.1	1889	Westerly, R.I.	
ALBERT F. PAUL	4M	215632	735	661	174.5	37.0	14.4	1917	Milford, Del.	Sunk 3/15/1942 by U-332
ANNA AND HELEN	2M	209254	32	22	57.0	19.3	5.5	1911	Dorchester, N.J.	Sank 1957 at Crisfield, Md.
AUSTRALIA	2M	25	35	29	67.0	18.9	5.1	1862	Patchogue, N.Y.	Currently at Mystic Seaport
B. S. TAYLOR	4M	217768	1488	1389	212.2	40.0	21.2	1919	Wilmington, Del.	ex W.H. WOODIN, abnd 11/1934
BAYARD HOPKINS	3M	3662	269	212	118.0	30.1	9.1	1895	Bath, Me.	Lost, unreported after 1/4/1919
BETTY I. CONWAY	2M	10420	123	84	90.0	27.5	6.3	1866	Stony Pt., N.Y.	ex GEORGE S. ALLISON
BLACKBIRD	2M	6920	124	96	103.0	27.0	8.5	1876	City Is., N.Y.	ex DAVID CARLL
BROWNSTONE	2M	9860	176	167	105.6	27.9	8.5	1869	Hartford, Ct.	ex (a) FANNIE G. WARNER, (b) GILL AND BAIRD
										(c) MANCHESTER AND HUDSON
DOROTHEA L. BRINKMAN	4M	217914	698	621	184.4	38.2	15.0	1919	Rockland, Me.	Stranded 3/2/1924, Oregon Inlet, N.C.
DORIS HAMLIN	4M	218955	1063	960	200.5	38.8	18.5	1919	Harrington, Me.	Lost, unreported after 2/12/1940
EDNA HOYT	5M	220938	1512	1384	224.0	41.1	20.8	1920	Thomaston, Me.	Last 5m schr built, condemned 2/1938
FLORENCE A.	2M	120804	154	126	96.5	27.4	7.2	1890	Cherryfield, Me.	
FRANK A. PALMER	4M	121037	2014	1831	274.5	43.0	21.0	1897	Bath, Me.	Sunk 12/17/1902 by collision
FREDRICK P. ELKINS (U.K.)	3M	141517	470	152	152.0	34.5	12.7	1919	Cape d'Orr, N.S.	ex SEAMAN O.A.
G. A. KOHLER	4M	219185	1462	1365	212.2	40.0	21.2	1919	Wilmington, Del.	ex CHARLES S. GAWTHROP, lost 8/23/1933
GEORGE W. TRUITT	4M	86679	690	577	183.7	37.2	13.0	1903	Bath, Me.	rn GEORGE W. ELZEY, lost 2/27/1932
GEORGE W. WELLS	6M	86573	2970	2743	319.3	48.5	23.0	1900	Camden, Me.	First 6m schr, stranded 9/3/1913
GOVERNOR AMES	5M	86022	1778	1597	245.0	49.0	21.2	1888	Waldoboro, Me.	First 5m schr, lost 12/13/1909
HERBERT D. MAXWELL	4M	202593	772	640	185.9	38.4	14.0	1905	Bath, Me.	Sunk 5/16/1911 by collision
HERBERT L. RAWDING	4M	218885	1219	1109	201.7	38.5	21.9	1919	Stockton Springs, Me.	Foundered 6/10/1947
JENNIE F. WILLEY	3M	75232	383.9	364.8	128.2	29.8	10.4	1870	Thomaston, Me.	
JOHN L. MARTINO	3M	81300	257	213	126.7	30.4	8.2	1890	Phillipsburg, Me.	ex WINNEGANCE
LaFORREST L. SIMMONS	2M	206347	132	104	88.9	27.8	7.5	1909	Milford, Del.	Lost 8/12/1955
LAURA ANNIE BARNES	4M	216001	629	530	179.5	37.0	13.0	1918	Camden, Me.	Stranded 1/17/1939
LAURA C. ANDERSON	4M	141106	960	766	183.2	38.5	17.6	1891	Bath, Me.	
MAINE	2M	91861	190	181	105.4	28.0	8.5	1886	Bath, Me.	Abandoned 1945, at Baltimore
RUTH DECKER	2M	75839	122	85	98.6	27.0	6.6	1876	Port Jefferson, N.Y.	ex JOSIE CROWLEY
SAMUEL P. HITCHCOCK	3M	115693	604		162.3	35.6	13.9	1880	Bath, Me.	Lost 1903
THOMAS W. LAWSON	7M	145943	5218	4914	375.6	50.0	22.9	1902	Quincy, Mass.	Only 7m schr built, lost 12/14/1907
WILLIAM H. VAN NAME	2M	80311	97.1	92.2	93.5	26.0	7.8	1872	City Is., N.Y.	Lost 3/31/1906
WILLIAM DONNELLY	2M	26590	98.38	93.46	97.8	17.6	7.1	1860	Hamburg, Pa.	Canal boat converted to schr
WILLIAM J. STANFORD	3M	75187	73	70	89.0	23.0	5.5	1868	Barkers Landing, Del.	ex (a) JOHN P. CONNOR, (b) PRISCILLA
WILLIAM L. WHITE	4M	80770	996		189.9	39.9	17.4	1880	Bath, Me.	First vessel built as 4m schr
WILLIAM T. PARKER	3M	81338	178	169	105.0	28.0	7.0	1891	Milton, Del.	Retired from service 1935
WYOMING	6M	207010	3730	3036	329.5	50.1	30.4	1909	Bath, Me.	Largest wooden sailing vessel built

SCHOONER BARGES BUILT ON THE CHESAPEAKE

NAME	RIG	OFF. NO.	TONNAGE:		DIMENSIONS:			BUILT:		
			GROSS	NET	LENGTH	BREADTH	DEPTH	YEAR	WHERE	BY
AGRAM	2M	167796	2129	2049	267.3	46.0	23.6	1919	Westpoint, Va.	York River Shipbuilding Co.
ARMISTEAD	2M	167795	2100	2049	267.3	46.0	23.6	1919	Baltimore, Md.	Maryland Shipbuilding Co.
BALTIMORE	2M	214479	1307	1242	229.7	40.1	16.1	1916	Baltimore, Md.	P. Doughty Co.
BANGO	2M	167793	2129	2049	267.3	46.0	23.6	1919	Quantico, Va.	MI Valley Bridge & Iron
BELMONT	3M	214936	969	896	198.0	34.6	18.0	1917	Baltimore, Md.	Coastwise Shipbuilding Co.
CARROLL	3M	214936	1281	1210	228.0	38.0	19.1	1920	Baltimore, Md.	Coastwise Shipbuilding Co.
CATONSVILLE	3M	219152	1281	1210	228.0	38.0	19.1	1919	Locust Pt., Md.	Coastwise Shipbuilding Co.
CHARLES E. HEARN	3M	206861	657	580	177.0	34.5	13.3	1907	Bethel, Del.	J.M.C. Moore
COHANSEY	2M	216477	807	734	179.2	34.7	15.6	1918	Baltimore, Md.	Coastwise Shipbuilding Co.
DENDRON	3M	201136	592	559	198.0	30.1	11.8	1904	Elkton, Md.	Diebert & Bro.
DRUID HILL	3M	219412	1281	1210	228.0	38.0	19.1	1919	Baltimore, Md.	H.E. Crook
DUNMORE	2M	202381	581	538	167.8	30.2	13.0	1905	Solomons Is., Md.	Dawson Shipbuilding Co.
DYKES	5M	218864	2072	1631	306.8	50.2	20.3	1919	Baltimore, Md.	
E. R. HAGGET	2M	207405	696	655	199.3	32.1	11.7	1910	Elkton, Md.	Diebert & Bro.
EUGENIA HOOPER	2M	209241	730	688	198.6	32.1	12.7	1911	Chesapeake City, Md.	
FLORENCE ELLIOT		215673	455	440	201.9	23.6	10.7	1917	Seaford, Del.	
GEORGIA	3M	212943	1318	1247	230.5	40.0	16.0	1915	Baltimore, Md.	Wm E. Woodall
GLENSIDE	3M	215220	974	900	196.3	34.6	18.8	1917	Baltimore, Md.	Coastwise Shipbuilding Co.
HALLOWELL	3M	219172	1327	1182	231.0	38.5	18.7	1919	Richmond, Va.	Crosby Navigation Co.
HARRY F. HOOPER	2M	207891	836	762	203.0	35.5	13.5	1910	Chesapeake City, Md.	Diebert Barge Bldg Co.
HERMITAGE	5M	218433	2111	1652	306.2	50.2	20.3	1919	Baltimore, Md.	
HOWARD E.	2M	216857	436	421	184.6	23.9	11.2	1918	Pocomoke City, Md.	E.J. Tull
I. D. FLETCHER		206652	1034	1034	215.6	35.0	15.7	1909	Sparrows Pt., Md.	
JOHN H. WINSTEAD II	3M	221970	1160	1120	214.5	36.1	16.2	1922	Baltimore, Md.	Charles L. Rhodes
JOSEPH J. HOCK	2M	217930	1032	982	209.4	36.2	16.3	1919	Baltimore, Md.	
MANOKIN	3M	219409	1289	1213	228.0	37.7	19.1	1919	Whitehaven, Md.	
MERRIMAC		203197	640	595	182.6	35.0	12.0	1906	Pocomoke City, Md.	E.J. Tull
MILDRED	2M	216264	436	421	184.6	23.9	11.2	1918	Pocomoke City, Md.	
MONOCACY	2M	208289	973	904	202.2	40.1	14.4	1911	Elkton, Md.	Diebert Barge Bldg Co.
NANTICOKE	2M	205800	771	735	203.6	35.4	13.0	1908	Sharptown, Md.	Sharptown Marine Railway
NO. 21 (Con. Coastwise Co.)	3M	130910	905	773	196.0	34.3	17.5	1901	Baltimore, Md.	H.G. Skinner
NORFOLK	3M	200785	589	558	197.9	30.0	11.8	1904	Elkton, Md.	Diebert & Bro.
NORTHERN #12	2M	216318	970	901	205.0	35.0	14.7	1918	Elkton, Md.	Diebert Barge Bldg Co.
NORTHERN #14	3M	215821	971	913	204.0	35.0	14.6	1917	Elkton, Md.	Diebert Barge Bldg Co.
NORTHERN #17	3M	216992	961	899	204.6	35.0	14.7	1918	Elkton, Md.	Diebert Barge Bldg Co.
NORTHERN #18	3M	217705	1047	983	226.2	35.1	14.9	1919	Elkton, Md.	Diebert Barge Bldg Co.
NORTHERN #31	3M	218703	1083	1021	231.0	35.0	14.9	1919	Elkton, Md.	Diebert Barge Bldg Co.

SCHOONER BARGES BUILT ON THE CHESAPEAKE

NAME	RIG	OFF. NO.	TONNAGE:		DIMENSIONS:			BUILT:		
			GROSS	NET	LENGTH	BREADTH	DEPTH	YEAR	WHERE	BY
NORTHERN #32	3M	219756	1476	1405	241.3	40.3	16.8	1920	Havre de Grace, Md.	Diebert Construction Co.
NORTHERN #34	3M	218663	1946	1840	246.7	43.5	23.3	1919	Havre de Grace, Md.	Diebert Construction Co.
NORTHERN #35		219829	2051	1907	246.2	43.0	24.4	1920	Havre de Grace, Md.	Diebert Construction Co.
NORTHERN #36	3M	220821	1488	1439	241.3	40.3	16.8	1920	Havre de Grace, Md.	Diebert Construction Co.
NORTHERN #38	3M		1488					1920	Havre de Grace, Md.	Diebert Construction Co.
NORTHERN #43	3M	211179	2215	2128	267.3	46.3	23.6	1921	Sollers Pt., Md.	Maryland Dry Dock Co.
OHIO		216378	1677	1560	224.4	38.7	21.9	1918	Fairfield, Md.	
OLIVE	2M	217180	436	422	184.6	23.9	11.2	1918	Pocomoke City, Md.	E.J. Tull
PENNINGTON	3M	215480	967	894	196.3	34.6	18.3	1917	Baltimore, Md.	Coastwise Shipbuilding Co.
PITTSTON	2M	203157	466	440	180.0	30.0	14.0	1906	Sharptown, Md.	Sharptown Marine Railway
PORTLAND	3M	167794	2129	2049	267.3	46.0	23.6	1919	Quantico, Va.	MI Valley Bridge & Iron
PORTSMOUTH	3M		2215					1921	Sollers Pt., Md.	Maryland Dry Dock Co.
POTOMAC	2M	205675	823	772	203.4	35.0	13.6	1908	Elkton, Md.	Diebert & Bro.
POTTSTOWN	3M	215678	974	901	194.5	34.6	18.3	1917	Baltimore, Md.	Coastwise Shipbuilding Co.
OCTORARO	2M	217556	807	734	179.2	34.7	15.6	1919	Baltimore, Md.	Coastwise Shipbuilding Co.
R. J. CAMP		111323	703	703	179.0	35.0	12.3	1900	Bethel, Del.	J.M.C. Moore
R. W. McDONALD	2M	203687	630	590	199.0	32.1	11.7	1906	Elkton, Md.	Diebert Barge Bldg. Co.
ROSE	2M	215706	443	421	184.6	23.9	11.2	1917	Pocomoke City, Md.	E.J. Tull
RUXTON	3M	219749	1281	1210	228.0	38.0	19.1	1920	Baltimore, Md.	H.E. Crook
SALEM	2M	216211	801	731	177.6	35.0	15.6	1900	Bethel, Del.	J.M.C. Moore
SEVERN	2M	204802	780	762	206.0	35.3	13.4	1907	Sharptown, Md.	Sharptown Marine Railway
SHAMOKIN	2M	201006	829	829	193.0	35.2	13.7	1904	Elkton, Md.	Diebert Barge Bldg. Co.
SHERWOOD	3M	218751	1281	1210	228.0	38.0	19.1	1919	Baltimore, Md.	Coastwise Shipbuilding Co.
SMITH &TERRY #1	3M	215546	1156	1097	203.6	41.2	16.7	1917	Bethel, Del.	J.M.C. Moore
SMITH &TERRY #2	3M	216876	1251	1198	221.1	41.0	16.5	1918	Bethel, Del.	J.M.C. Moore
SWEETSER LINTHICUM	2M	208230	695	652	199.3	32.1	11.7	1910	Elkton, Md.	Diebert Barge Bldg. Co.
T. J. HOOPER	2M	205443	722	697	204.0	35.2	13.5	1908	Sharptown, Md.	
TIOGA	3M	216038	1012	938	197.0	35.0	18.4	1918	Baltimore, Md.	Coastwise Shipbuilding Co.
TRENTON	3M	215835	1013	939	197.0	35.0	18.4	1917	Baltimore, Md.	Coastwise Shipbuilding Co.
TUCKAHOE	2M	216898	792	726	179.0	34.6	15.5	1918	Baltimore, Md.	Coastwise Shipbuilding Co.
WAYNE	2M	215945	436	421	184.6	23.9	11.2	1918	Pocomoke City, Md.	E.J. Tull
WESTLAND	3M	217208	989	933	196.8	35.7	15.6	1918	Baltimore, Md.	Coastwise Shipbuilding Co.
WILLIAMSBURG		81665	319	319	159.6	31.8	9.4	1899	Williamsburg, Va.	
WHITEHAVEN	3M	219399	1293	1217	228.0	37.7	19.1	1919	Whitehaven, Md.	Whitehaven Shipbuilding Co.
WORCESTER	3M	201604	625	594	200.0	30.1	12.6	1904	Elkton, Md.	Diebert & Bro.

Appendix II – Drawings and Plans

This collection of vessel plans, which has been gathered from several different sources, represents examples of the various types of schooners developed on the Chesapeake Bay, particularly emphasizing those that are the focus of this text. Readers interested in Baltimore clippers and earlier vessels will find them well covered in the works of Howard I. Chapelle and more recently, Thomas Gillmer.

The best source for documentation of Bay watercraft is the Historical American Merchant Marine Survey (HAMMS), maintained by the Smithsonian Institution's National Museum of American History. This collection was conceived and managed by Eric J. Steinlein with the support of Frank Taylor, curator of engineering at the Smithsonian Museum of American History. The survey, which was funded by the Works Progress Administration, was an effort to document and record the nation's rapidly disappearing maritime resources. Lasting only from March 1936 to October 1937, the project lost its funding long before reaching fruition. Fortunately the Chesapeake region is the best represented and most complete.

Of the plans included here, the HAMMS plans and several others were taken from the measurement of actual vessels. In these cases, the hull lines and details were drawn to the outside of the planking. Other plans were taken from builders' half-models and represent only the body of the vessel, with lines drawn to the inside of the planking. External construction details, which were built to the standard practices of the builder, are not shown.

Caradora   *Drawings begin on page 203*

The drawings of *Caradora* were taken from the existing vessel by a HAMM Survey party in the spring of 1936 (Survey no. 5-9). The survey took place at the A. Smith & Sons Shipyard at Curtis Bay south of Baltimore shortly after the vessel was rebuilt at that yard.

Built in 1881 by Kirby & Lang at St. Michaels, Maryland, the *Caradora* was originally owned by Joseph Steele (three-quarter owner) and Z. T. Cooling (one-quarter owner), both of Cecil County, Maryland. Her home port was Baltimore. *Caradora* was used principally to haul wheat, corn, and general cargo between Eastern Shore ports and Baltimore.

Materials used in construction: stem, sternpost, keel, planking, frames, clamp beams, and combings were all white oak. Her deck was yellow pine; her knees, hackmatack.

Length overall	78' 6"
Extreme beam	22' 4"
Light draft	2' 3" fwd
	5' 0" aft

Sail plan information was obtained by the HAMM Survey from an unnamed Baltimore sailmaker. The project supervisor was Carl L. Ludloff; H. W. Rust was the delineator. Overall, the documentation of the vessel was very complete.

Smith K. Martin *Drawings begin on page 209*

Smith K. Martin was built in 1899 at Pocomoke City, Maryland, by E. James Tull for Captain Levin Kelly. She was originally intended for the New Jersey fishing or oyster trade, but never entered that service. She served most of her life freighting on the Chesapeake Bay. At the time of this survey, she was owned by Captain Edward Kelly of Eastport in Annapolis. He employed her to carry rock and general cargo.

These plans were drawn from measurement of this vessel taken at the A. Smith & Sons Shipyard in the spring of 1936. The survey party leader was Phillip Sawyer; Leon Hand, delineator. The plans were later redrawn by Charles Bissell.

This is a remarkably complete documentation of this vessel. Included in the survey, but not reproduced here, were many detail sketches by artist/surveyor Phillip Sawyer.

Materials used in construction: keel, shelf, waterways, stem, sternpost, frames, knees, deck beams, and ceiling were all white oak. Her planking and deck were Georgia longleaf yellow pine. She was iron fastened.

Length overall	73' 7"
Extreme beam	22' 7"
Light draft	4' 7" fwd
	5' 5" aft

Minnie Mae Kirwan *Drawings begin on page 214*

The *Kirwan* was built in 1882 at Whitehaven, Maryland, by Stephen Murrell. Her original name was *G. W. Robertson*. Her owner and captain was A. H. Williams. She was homeported in Crisfield, Maryland, and was used in general freight and oystering.

At the time she was surveyed at Baltimore by a HAMMS party in 1937, she was engaged in oystering and her home port was Tappahannock, Virginia. Frederick Farley was the survey leader.

The *Kirwan* was heavily built of oak and pine and was fastened with iron spikes and drifts.

Kate Darlington *Drawings begin on page 217*

The *Kate Darlington* was built at Baltimore in 1889 by Mc-Cosker & Company for T. Hopkins & Brothers. The *Darlington* was a fairly large two-master. In her prime, she sailed in the Bahama pineapple trade. In 1939, her hull was broken up for firewood at Locust Point, Baltimore.

These plans were drawn by Edward G. Brownlee in November 1936. He had measured the vessel at Philadelphia for his own interest in 1934. The drawings are now in the collection of the Chesapeake Bay Maritime Museum at St. Michaels, Maryland.

The *Darlington* was built of mixed hard and soft woods and was fastened with galvanized iron.

George C. A. Travers *Drawing on page 219*

The *George C. A. Travers* was built at Baltimore by Skinner & Son in 1879 for S. H. Travers & Sons. According to Robert H. Burgess, in 1912, she was sold and renamed *F. P. Murphy* after Baltimore's oldest sailmaker. In 1925, she was renamed *Minnie T. Phillips*. At 142 gross tons, she was large for a Bay two-masted schooner. For most of her life, she was engaged in the coastal trade, calling at Philadelphia, Miami, and the Bahamas. She carried sail to the end, which came in 1943 when she was abandoned at Nassau, Bahamas.

These lines were taken from the original builder's half-model now in the Radcliffe Maritime Museum of the Maryland Historical Society in Baltimore. Though no detail is given, her shape, showing her to be a full-bodied vessel, is evident.

The *Travers* was built of oak and yellow pine with iron fastenings.

Wave *Drawings begin on page 220*

The pungy *Wave* was built in 1863 in Accomack County, Virginia. She had been converted to a yacht by 1940 and was the last pungy to carry sail on the Chesapeake.

These drawings were made from data taken off the vessel by C. Loundes Johnson of Oxford, Maryland, in 1940. R. H. Gibson was the delineator. The plans were originally published by the Historical Society of Talbot County, then given to the Chesapeake Bay Maritime Museum. They were retraced for publication here by R. H. Hambidge. The sail plan was based on a Hudgins and Dies sail plan book from 1893.

Amanda F. Lewis *Drawing on page 222*

The well-known pungy *Amanda F. Lewis* was built by Joseph W. Brooks at Madison, Maryland, in 1884. She was built for Captain M. O. Lewis and was named for his wife, whose likeness appeared in her carved stern decoration.

These drawings were made from measurement of the actual vessel by a HAMM Survey party in 1936 (Survey no. 5-7). The plan and its details were drawn by Howard I. Chapelle and are now in the collection of the National Museum of American History of the Smithsonian Institution.

Lizzie Lee *Drawings begin on page 223*

The *Lizzie Lee* was built by John Branford at Inverness, Maryland, in 1909. At 45 gross tons and 68.8 feet registered length, she is the largest square-rigged bugeye we have found.

In 1923, she was renamed *Ishmael,* fitted with a seventy-five-horsepower engine, and registered out of Wilmington, Delaware. In 1943, she was renamed *Norman L. Jeffries,* and in 1945 became the *Twin Harbors* registered in New York. There, she served the Frank Flowers Oyster Farms at Oyster Bay until the late 1980s when she finally wore out. She was stripped of her gear and scuttled as an artificial reef in Long Island Sound.

These lines are from her original builder's half-model, now in the Radcliffe Maritime Museum of the Maryland Historical Society. No construction detail is shown. Scale of the original model is one-half inch to a foot. Her sail plan was copied by Marion Brewington from sail plan books of John R. Mitchell, a Baltimore sailmaker. This plan is now in the Ships Plans Collection at Mystic Seaport Museum and was redrawn by R. H. Hambidge.

Victory Chimes *Drawings begin on page 225*

The ram *Victory Chimes* was built in 1900 as the *Edwin and Maud* by J. M. C. Moore, master carpenter for the George K. Phillips Company at Bethel, Delaware, for Captain Robert Riggin. She was named for his children.

This lines plan for the *Victory Chimes* was drawn by naval architect Roger Long of Portland, Maine. These lines are the only known drawings of an identified ram. Lines from an unidentified ram half-model are a part of the Smithsonian's HAMMS material. The lines were taken off the *Victory Chimes* in 1989 when she was eighty-nine years old. While she showed a fair degree of hog in her keel and some sagging in her chines, she was in remarkably good shape for a vessel of her age, a testament to her builder and a credit to the dedication of her owners in maintaining her.

The sail plan shown was drawn in 1934 by Edward G. Brownlee who recorded the vessel and many of her details when she called at Philadelphia as the freight ram *Edwin and Maud.*

Charles M. Struven *Drawings begin on page 227*

The four-masted schooner *Charles M. Struven* was built by E. James Tull at Pocomoke City, Maryland, in 1917. She was designed by naval architect Henry J. Gielow of the New York firm of Gielow and Orr to fulfill the wartime demand for tonnage that could be quickly and efficiently built.

According to an article in *The Rudder* magazine of June 1918, the *Struven's* "construction throughout embodies the most progressive methods used in modern shipbuilding today." E. James Tull was quoted as saying, "The lines of the vessel could not be better in any way."

These plans were redrawn by R. H. Hambidge from deteriorated blueprints in the Ships Plans Collection at Mystic Seaport Museum.

The construction section of this vessel shows the massive size of her structural members and the variety of woods used in her. To date, no sail plan has been found.

Venus   *Drawing on page 229*

The three-masted schooner *Venus* was built in 1893. She was probably designed by Joseph Sauerhoff, master builder for the J. E. Johnson Company at Cambridge, Maryland. She originally served in the pineapple trade out of Baltimore. The *Venus* was twice renamed: first the *Santa Luiza* under the Portugese flag and then the *Edna Bright Hough* when returned to the U.S. flag. She was eventually abandoned at Norfolk in 1938.

These line drawings for the *Venus* were drawn from the builder's half-model and were taken off by J. Kleinschmidt at Mystic Seaport Museum. The half-model is in a private collection. The plans are now in the Ships Plans Collection at Mystic Seaport Museum. No sail plan for this vessel has yet come to light.

The *Venus* was built of oak and yellow pine and had galvanized fastenings.

Yawl boat from the schooner
William J. Stanford   *Drawing on page 230*

This yawl boat is typical of those that served Chesapeake Bay two- and three-masted schooners. She served the small three-masted *William J. Stanford* in the last phase of the schooner's career until her end in 1948. Certainly, this was not the first yawl boat to serve the *Stanford*, which was built in 1868 before powered yawl boats appeared.

The importance of the powered yawl boat often is overlooked. Schooners depended on these boats in calms and in close quarters, and it was the powered yawl boats that allowed the schooners' continued economic viability well into this century.

This boat went on to serve the A. Smith & Sons Shipyard at Curtis Bay as a yard tug. Joe Liener of Whitman, Maryland, took off her lines and recorded her construction details before the hulk was destroyed. She is the only Bay schooner yawl boat to have been so documented.

These lines were retraced for publication by R. H. Hambidge from the collection of the Chesapeake Bay Maritime Museum.

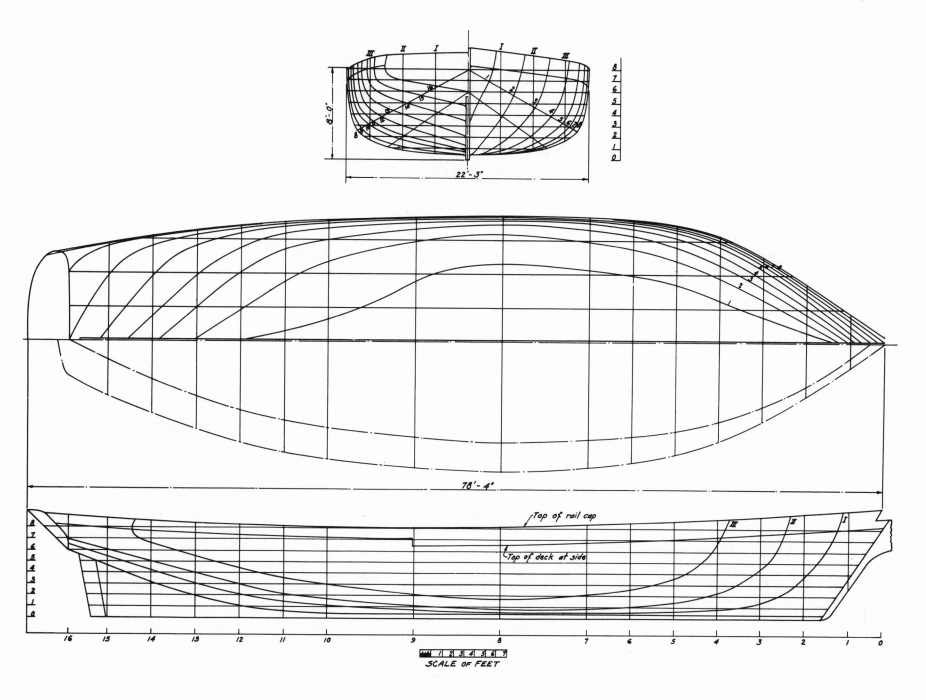

Caradora plan view and inboard profile. (Courtesy of Smithsonian Institution, National Museum of American History, HAMMS Collection)

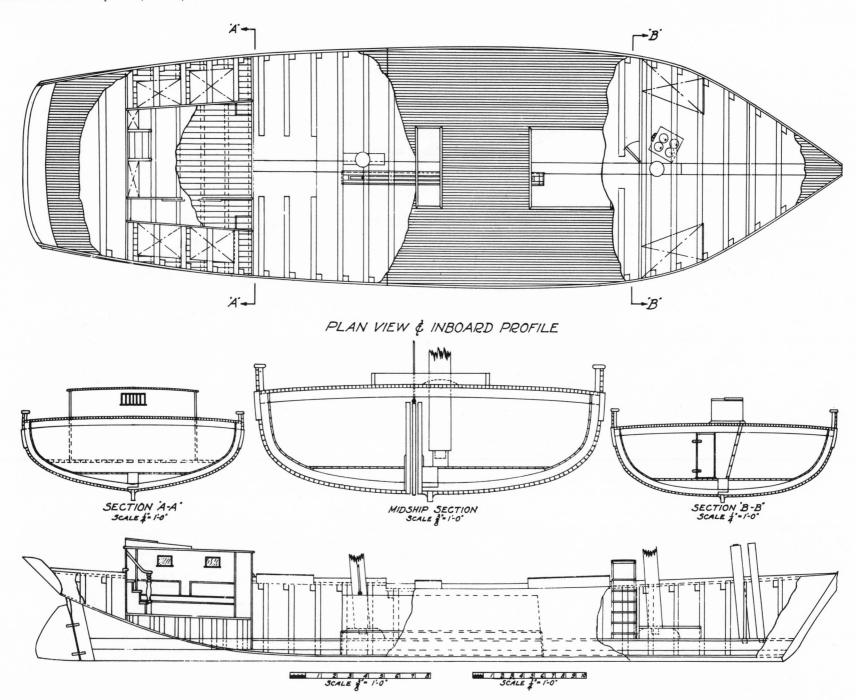

PLAN VIEW & INBOARD PROFILE

SECTION "A-A"
SCALE ¼"=1'-0"

MIDSHIP SECTION
SCALE ⅜"=1'-0"

SECTION "B-B"
SCALE ¼"=1'-0"

SCALE ⅜"=1'-0"

SCALE ¼"=1'-0"

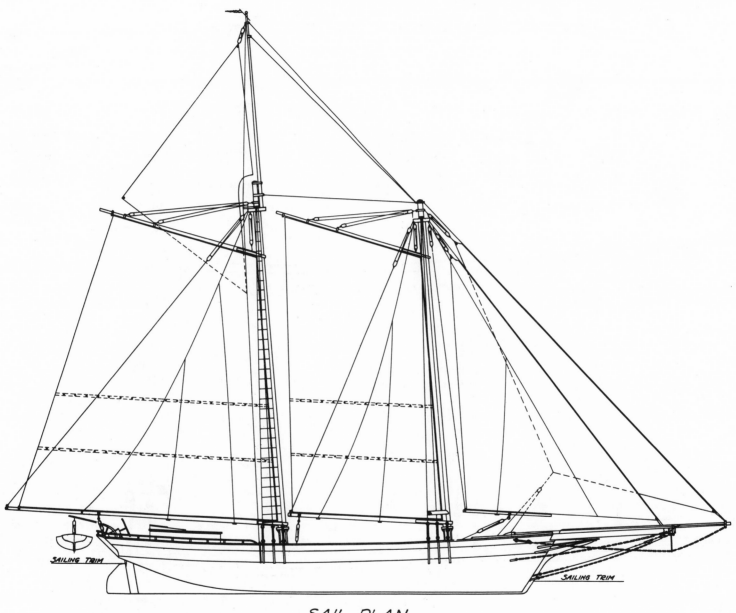

SAIL PLAN

NOTE:-
    This sail plan is only approximate.
Information secured from sail maker

SCALE of FEET

Caradora deck plan and outboard profile. (Courtesy of Smithsonian Institution, National Museum of American History, HAMMS Collection)

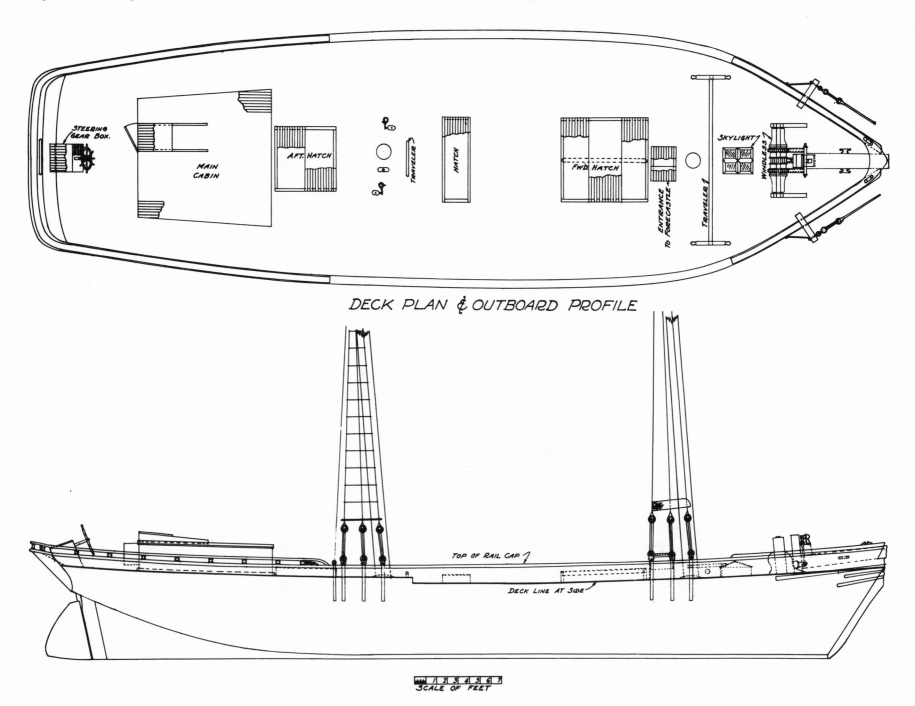

DECK PLAN & OUTBOARD PROFILE

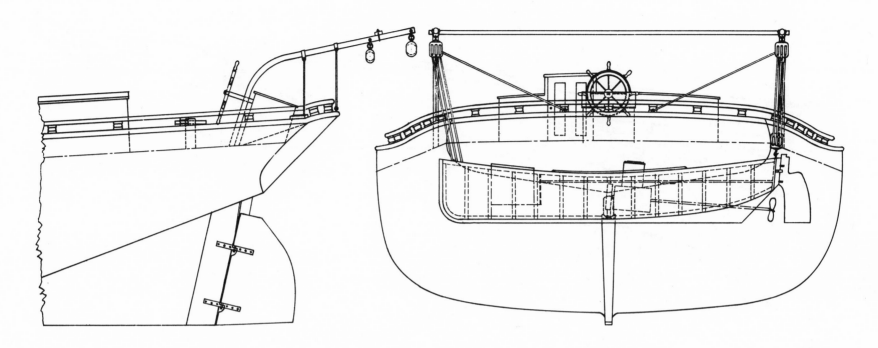

DETAIL OF STERN & YAWL

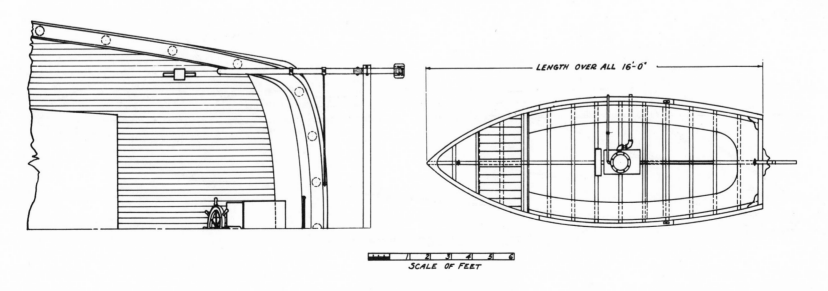

LENGTH OVER ALL 16'-0"

SCALE OF FEET

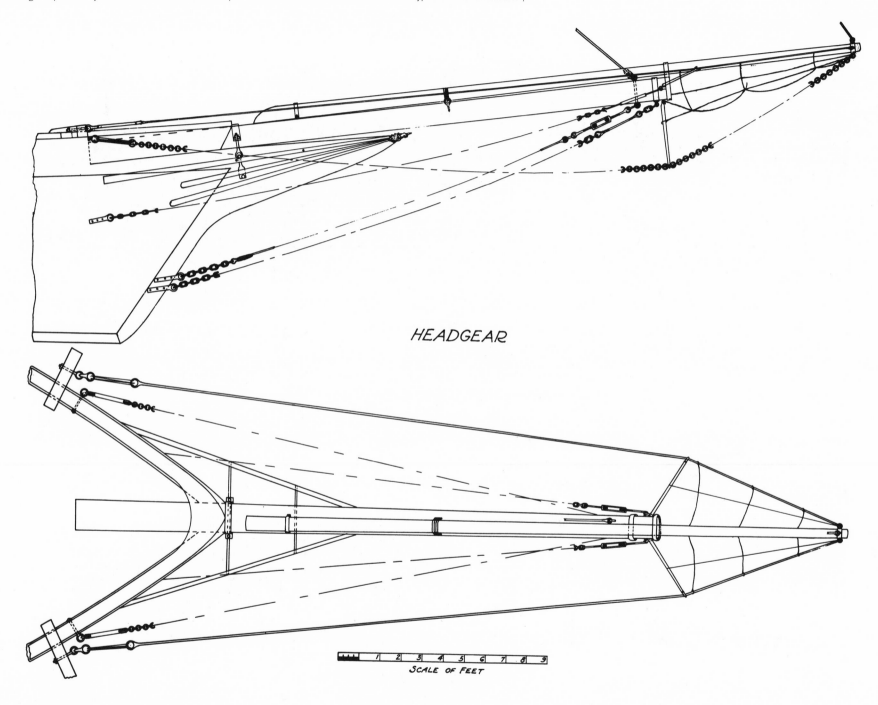

HEADGEAR

SCALE OF FEET

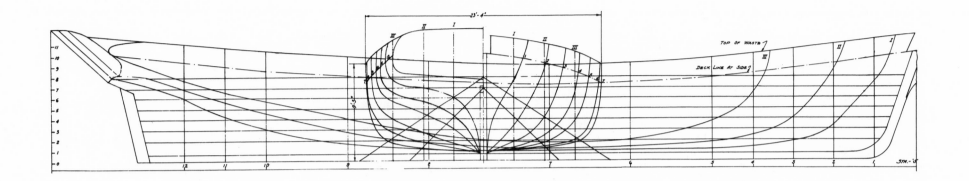

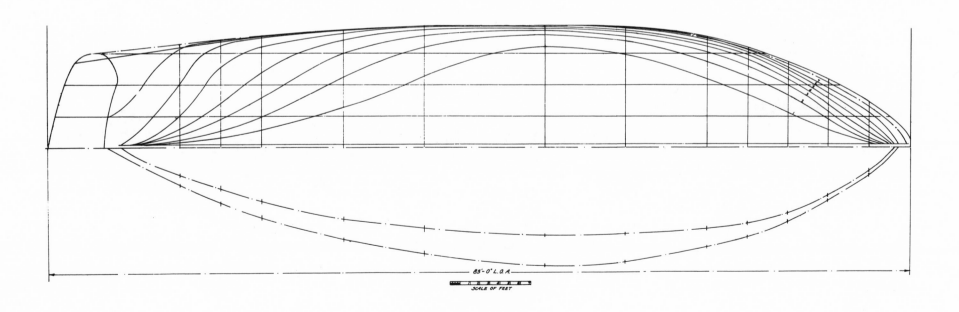

Smith K. Martin deck plan and profile. (Courtesy of Smithsonian Institution, National Museum of American History, HAMMS Collection)

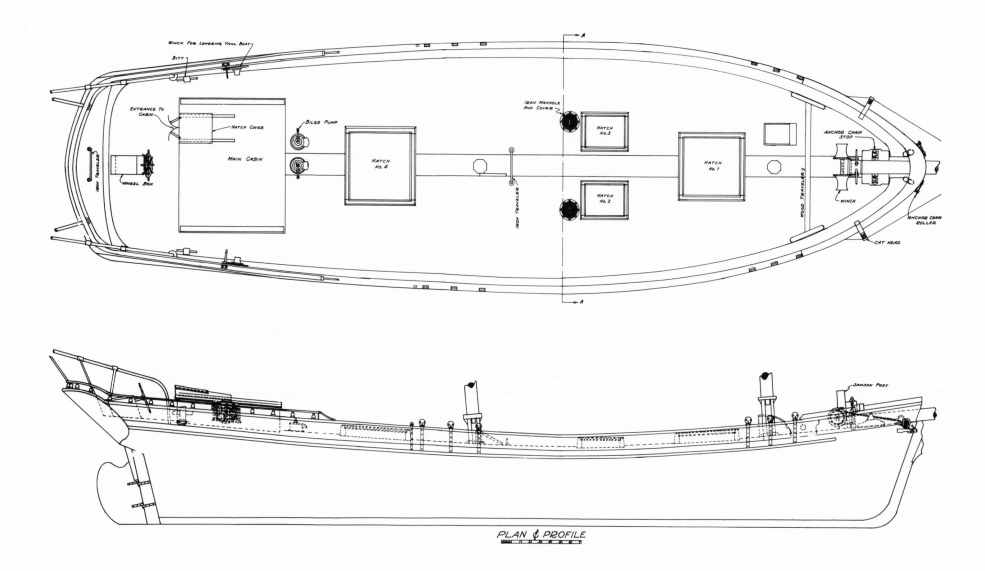

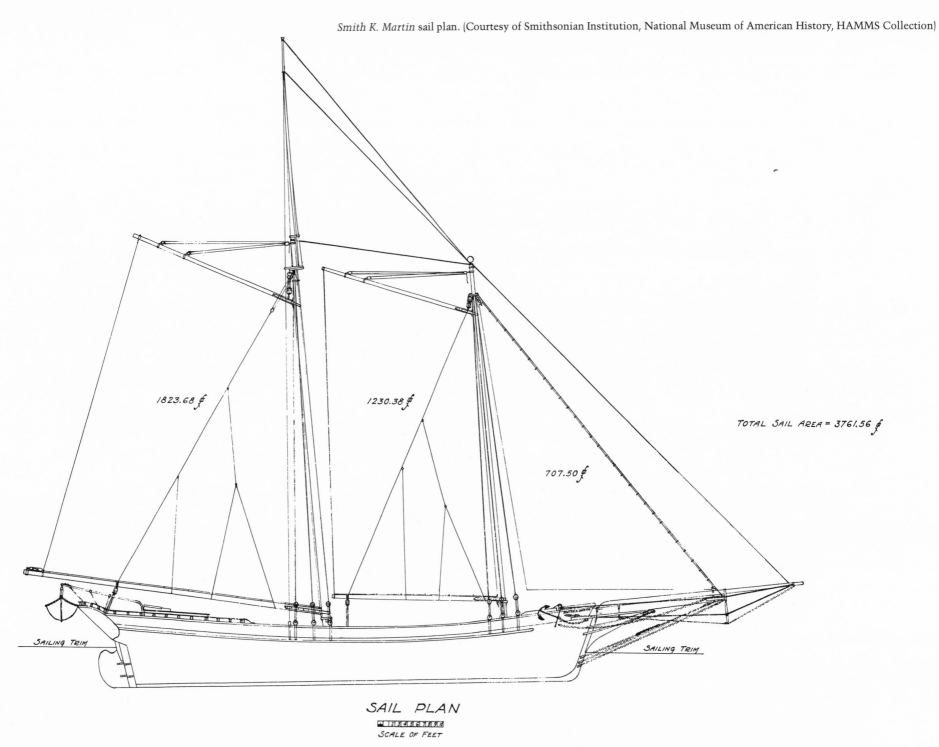

Smith K. Martin sail plan. (Courtesy of Smithsonian Institution, National Museum of American History, HAMMS Collection)

1823.68 ₰

1230.38 ₰

TOTAL SAIL AREA = 3761.56 ₰

707.50 ₰

SAILING TRIM

SAILING TRIM

SAIL PLAN

SCALE OF FEET

Smith K. Martin cross section. (Courtesy of Smithsonian Institution, National Museum of American History, HAMMS Collection)

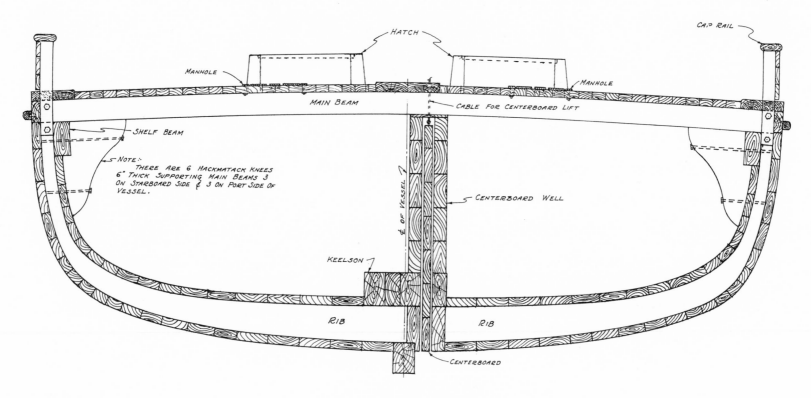

CROSS SECTION

THIS SECTION TAKEN AT "A-A" SEE SHEET No.

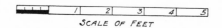

SCALE OF FEET

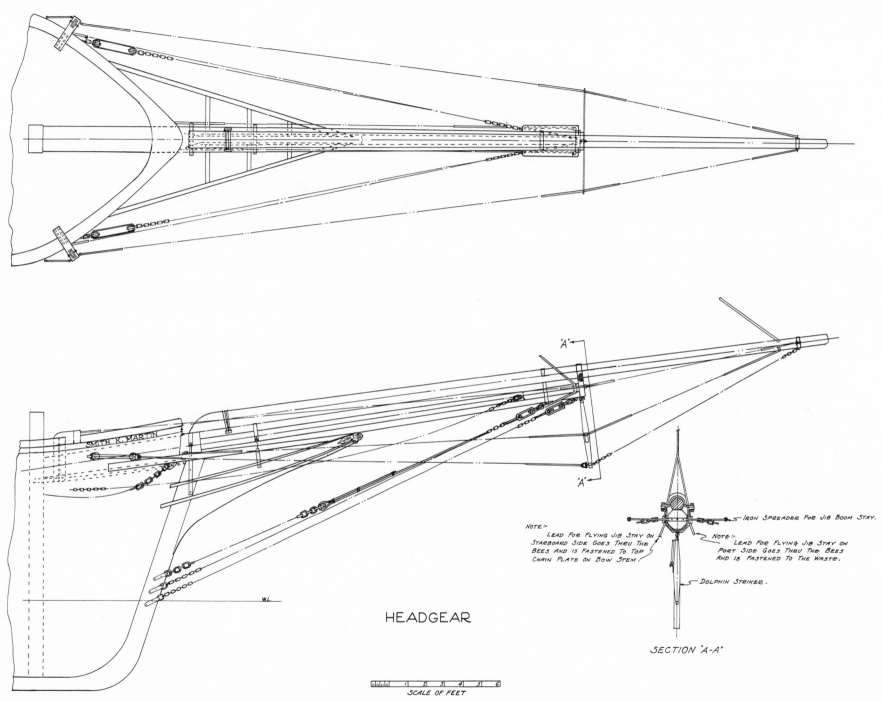

NOTE:-
LEAD FOR FLYING JIB STAY ON
STARBOARD SIDE GOES THRU THE
BEES AND IS FASTENED TO TOP
CHAIN PLATE ON BOW STEM.

IRON SPREADER FOR JIB BOOM STAY.

NOTE:-
LEAD FOR FLYING JIB STAY ON
PORT SIDE GOES THRU THE BEES
AND IS FASTENED TO THE WASTE.

DOLPHIN STRIKER.

HEADGEAR

SECTION "A-A"

SCALE OF FEET

Minnie Mae Kirwan lines. (Courtesy of Smithsonian Institution, National Museum of American History, HAMMS Collection)

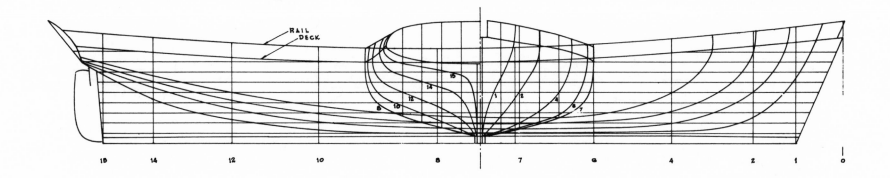

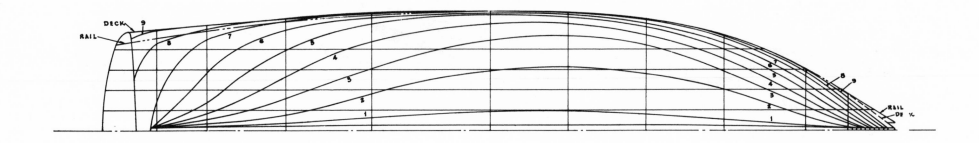

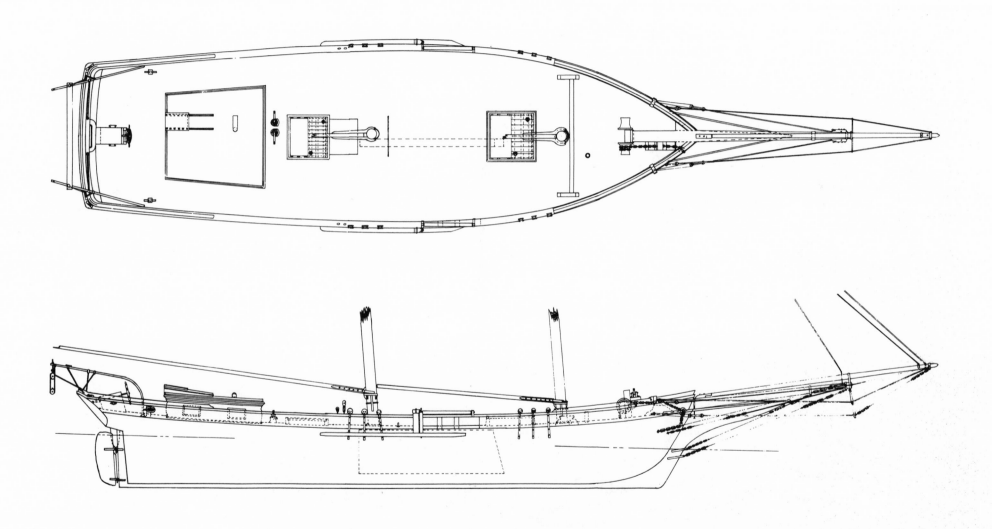

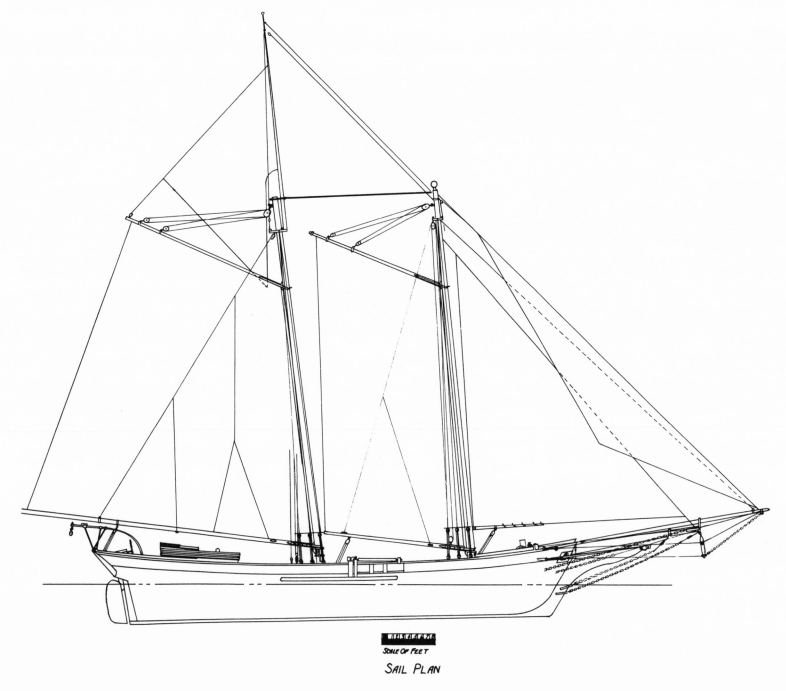

SCALE OF FEET

SAIL PLAN

Kate Darlington lines. (Chesapeake Bay Maritime Museum)

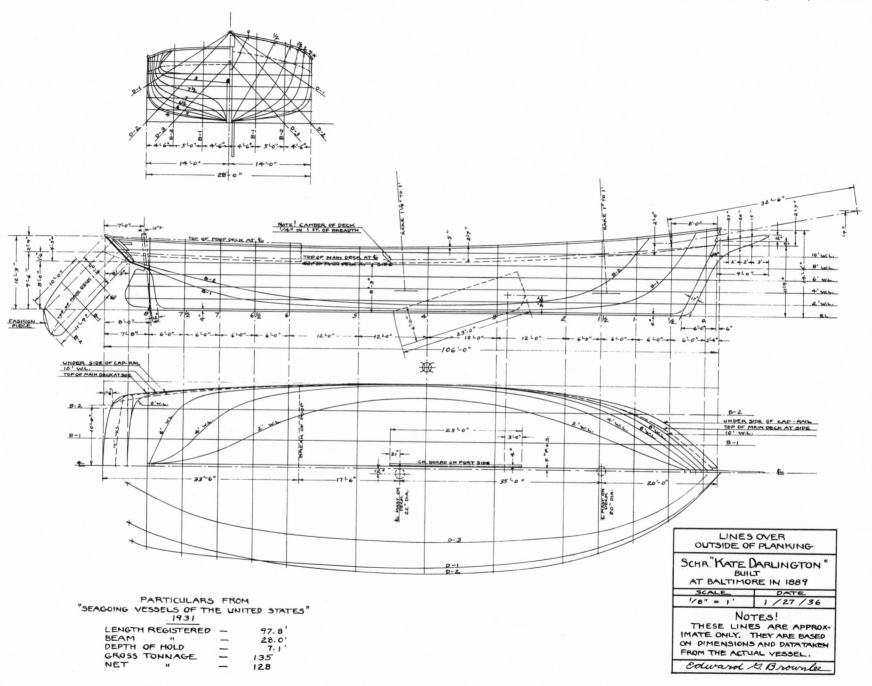

PARTICULARS FROM
"SEAGOING VESSELS OF THE UNITED STATES"
1931

LENGTH REGISTERED —	97.8'
BEAM " —	28.0'
DEPTH OF HOLD —	7.1'
GROSS TONNAGE —	135
NET " —	128

LINES OVER
OUTSIDE OF PLANKING

Schr. "Kate Darlington"
BUILT
AT BALTIMORE IN 1889

SCALE	DATE
1/8" = 1'	1 / 27 / 36

NOTES!
THESE LINES ARE APPROX-
IMATE ONLY. THEY ARE BASED
ON DIMENSIONS AND DATA TAKEN
FROM THE ACTUAL VESSEL.

Edward G. Brownlee

Kate Darlington sail plan. (Chesapeake Bay Maritime Museum)

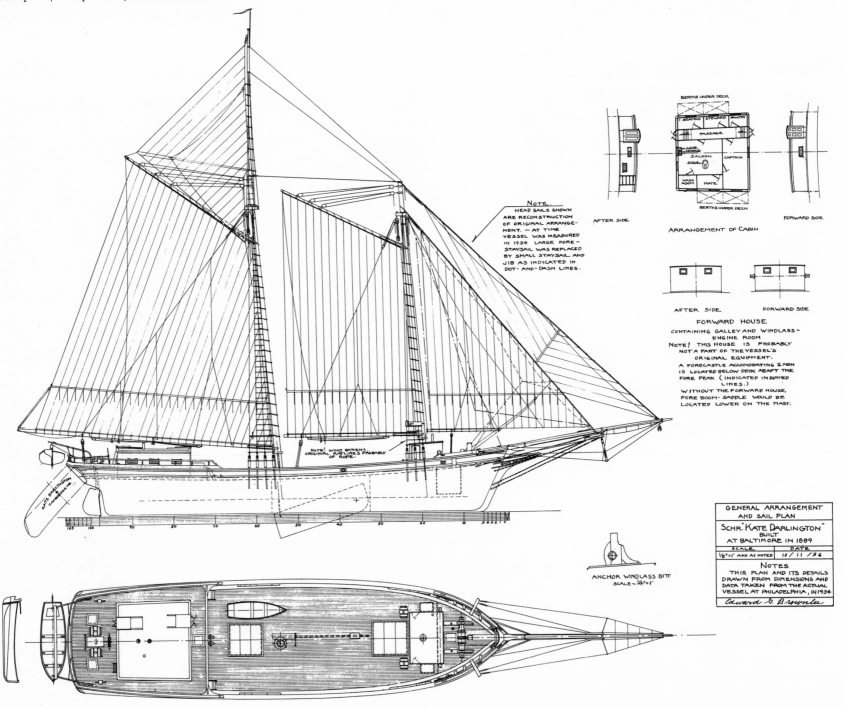

NOTE.
HEAD SAILS SHOWN
ARE RECONSTRUCTION
OF ORIGINAL ARRANGE-
MENT. — AT TIME
VESSEL WAS MEASURED
IN 1934 LARGE FORE-
STAYSAIL WAS REPLACED
BY SMALL STAYSAIL AND
JIB AS INDICATED IN
DOT- AND-DASH LINES.

BERTHS UNDER DECK

SEAMAN | STEWARD | PANTRY
PASSAGE
SALOON | CAPTAIN
WASH ROOM | MATE.

BERTHS UNDER DECK

AFTER SIDE   FORWARD SIDE

ARRANGEMENT OF CABIN

AFTER SIDE   FORWARD SIDE

FORWARD HOUSE
CONTAINING GALLEY AND WINDLASS-
ENGINE ROOM
NOTE! THIS HOUSE IS PROBABLY
NOT A PART OF THE VESSEL'S
ORIGINAL EQUIPMENT.
A FORECASTLE ACCOMODATING 2 MEN
IS LOCATED BELOW DECK ABAFT THE
FORE PEAK (INDICATED IN DOTTED
LINES.)
WITHOUT THE FORWARD HOUSE,
FORE BOOM- SADDLE WOULD BE
LOCATED LOWER ON THE MAST.

NOTE! WOOD BATTENS
ORIGINAL RATLINES PROBABLY
OF ROPE.

ANCHOR WINDLASS BITT
SCALE ~ 1/4"=1'

GENERAL ARRANGEMENT
AND SAIL PLAN
SCHR."KATE DARLINGTON"
BUILT
AT BALTIMORE IN 1889

SCALE	DATE
1/8"=1' AND AS NOTED	10/11/36

NOTES
THIS PLAN AND ITS DETAILS
DRAWN FROM DIMENSIONS AND
DATA TAKEN FROM THE ACTUAL
VESSEL AT PHILADELPHIA, IN 1934

Edward G. Brownlee

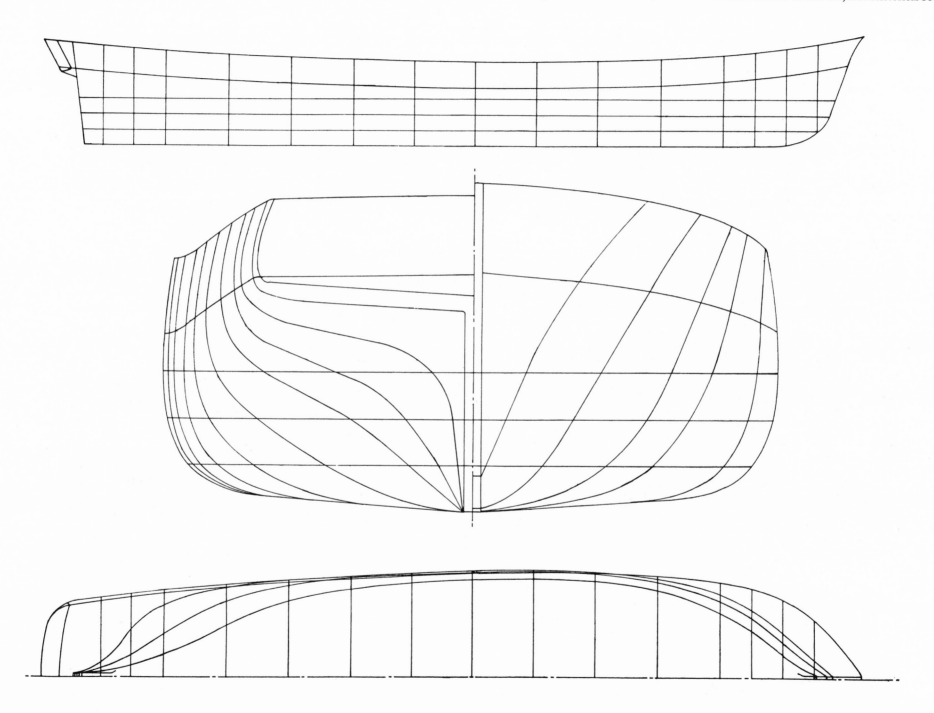

George C. A. Travers lines. (Radcliffe Maritime Museum of the Maryland Historical Society)

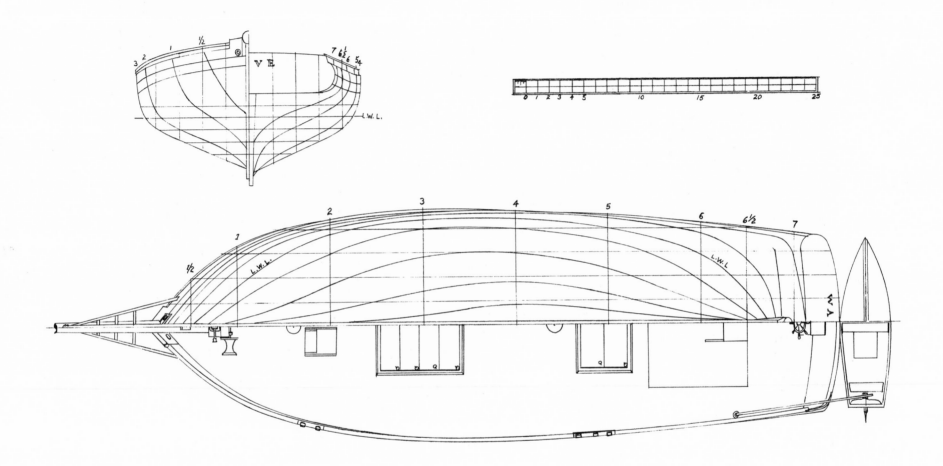

Amanda F. Lewis lines. (Courtesy of Smithsonian Institution, National Museum of American History, HAMMS Collection)

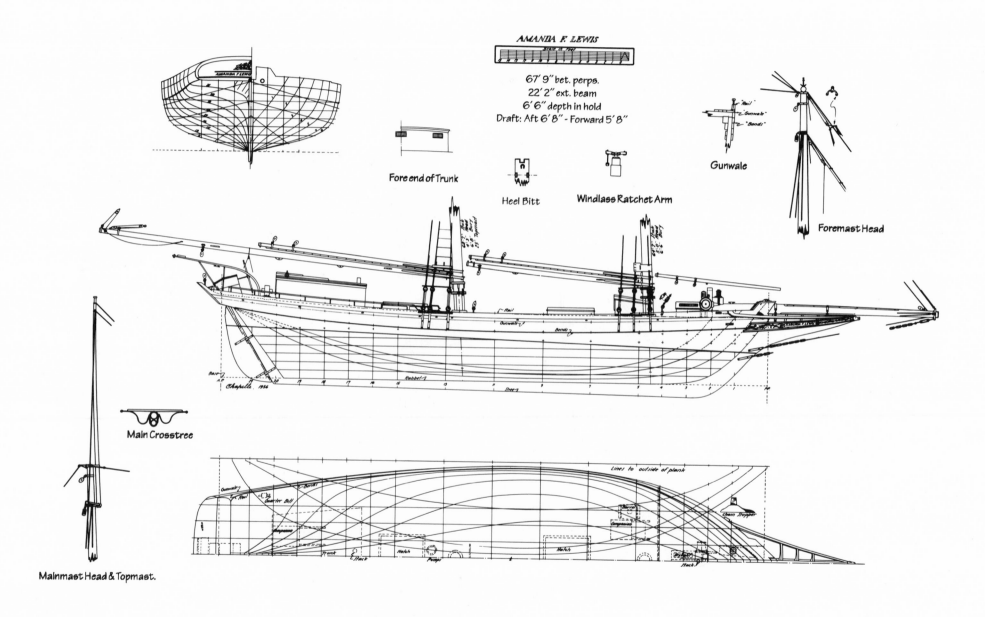

AMANDA F. LEWIS

67′ 9″ bet. perps.
22′ 2″ ext. beam
6′ 6″ depth in hold
Draft: Aft 6′ 8″ - Forward 5′ 8″

Fore end of Trunk

Heel Bitt

Windlass Ratchet Arm

Gunwale

Foremast Head

Main Crosstree

Mainmast Head & Topmast.

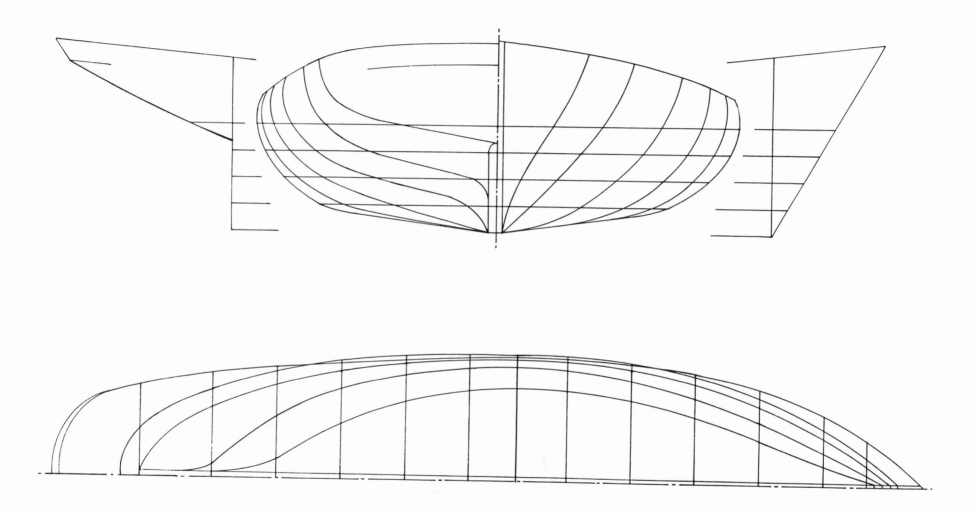

Lizzie Lee sail plan. (Mystic Seaport Museum, Ships Plans Dept.)

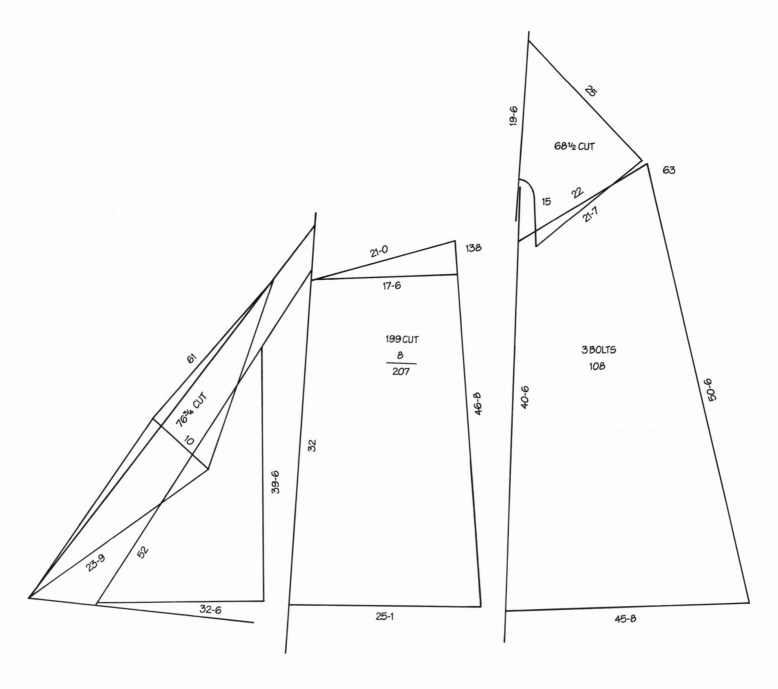

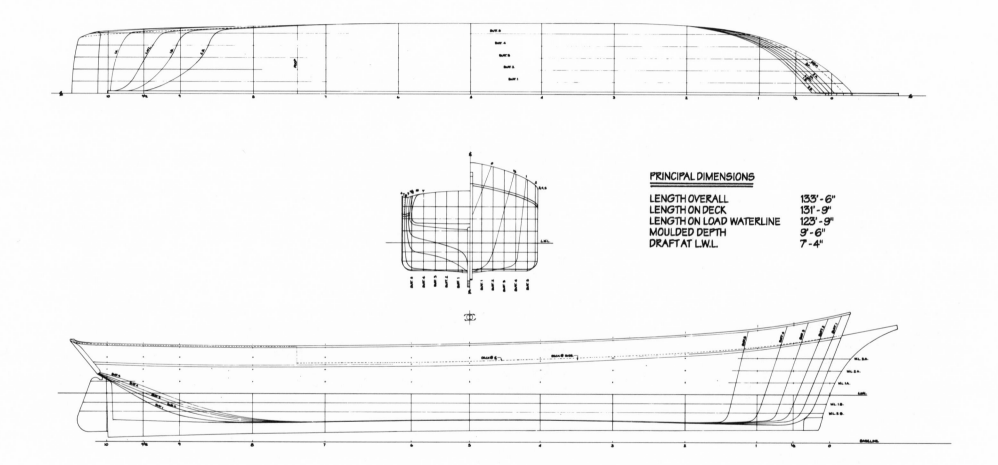

PRINCIPAL DIMENSIONS

LENGTH OVERALL	133'-6"
LENGTH ON DECK	131'-9"
LENGTH ON LOAD WATERLINE	123'-9"
MOULDED DEPTH	9'-6"
DRAFT AT L.W.L.	7'-4"

Victory Chimes (as *Edwin and Maud*) sail plan. (Chesapeake Bay Maritime Museum)

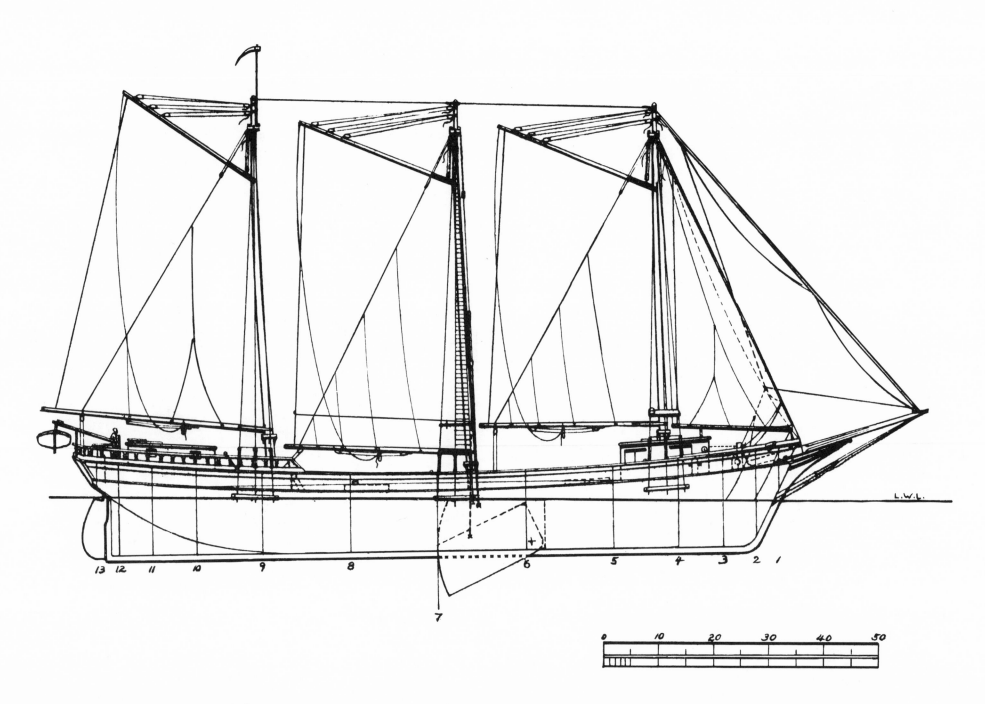

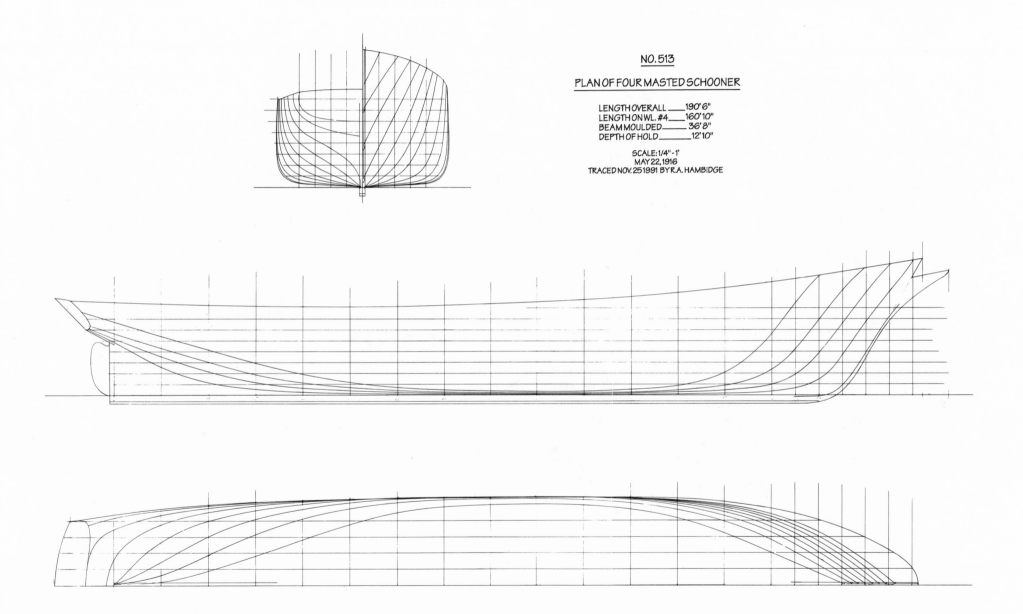

NO. 513

PLAN OF FOUR MASTED SCHOONER

LENGTH OVERALL _____ 190' 6"
LENGTH ON W.L. #4 _____ 160' 10"
BEAM MOULDED _____ 36' 8"
DEPTH OF HOLD _____ 12' 10"

SCALE: 1/4" - 1'
MAY 22, 1916
TRACED NOV. 25 1991 BY R.A. HAMBIDGE

Charles M. Struven cross section. (Mystic Seaport Museum, Ships Plans Dept.)

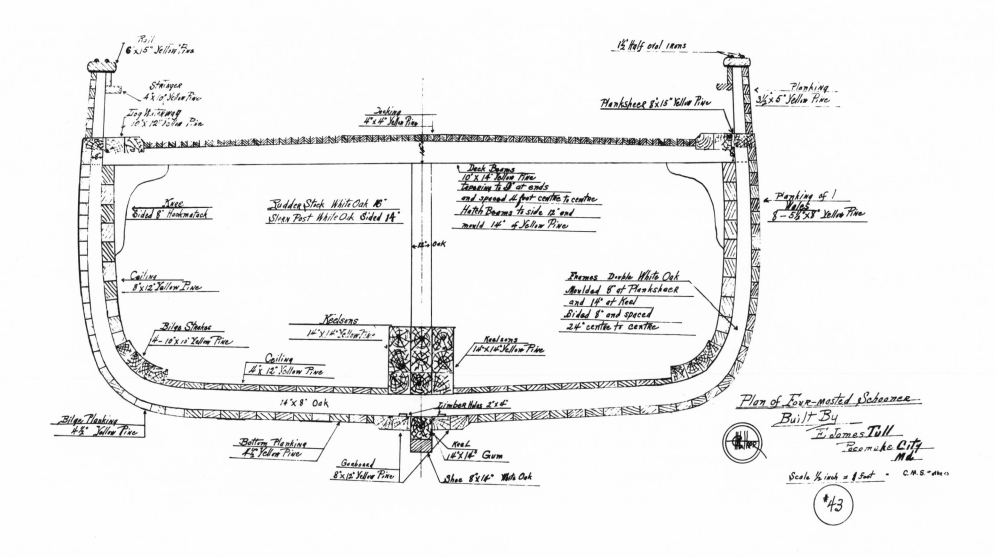

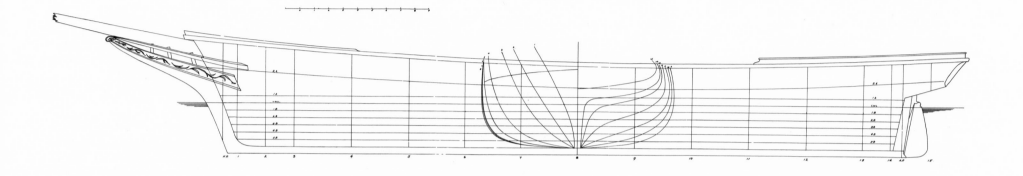

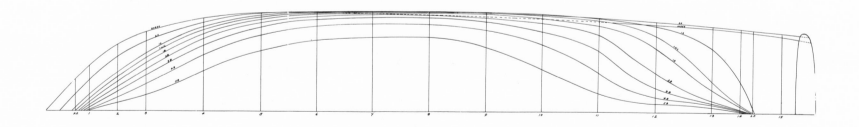

Yawl boat from the schooner *William J. Stanford* lines/construction. (Chesapeake Bay Maritime Museum)

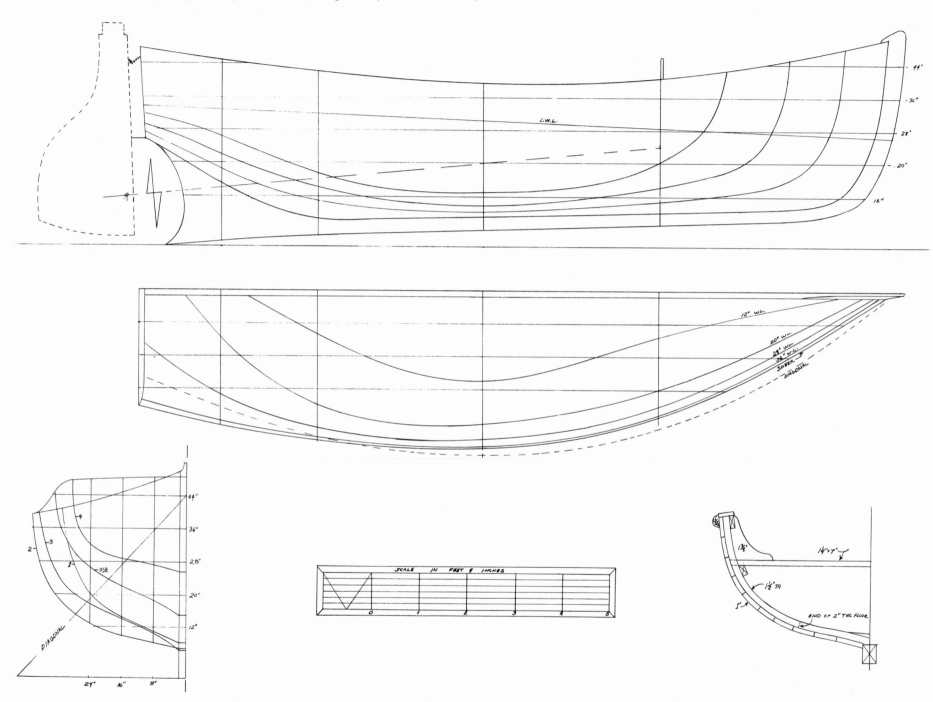

Appendix III – Influence of Economic Trends on Schooner Construction

These graphs were compiled with data taken from the "Report of the Secretary of the Treasury on Commerce and Navigation of the United States, Article 23, Statement showing the Number and Class of Vessels Built and the Tonnage There-of in Each State and Territory," volumes 1840-1892. Fluctuations in numbers shown in these graphs indicate the influence of general economic trends, both national and local. The period of the late 1840s and early 1850s, for example, was characterized by a general growth nationally of business and industry spurred by the discovery of gold and westward expansion.

Regionally, schooner building prospered largely as a result of the opening of the Chesapeake & Ohio Railroad, bringing coal in and carrying oysters to western markets. The so-called Panic of 1857, brought on by overspeculation in railroad construction, is clearly reflected by a sharp decline in schooner construction.

The years of the Civil War and its aftermath show a clear depression in shipbuilding, especially in Virginia where whatever vessels were built were not reported to the federal government. Growth was slow following the war, with Virginia suffering from the adverse effects of Reconstruction and showing less activity than Maryland.

Again, a sharp decline in schooner construction occurred during the Panic of 1873, which was felt nationwide. A turnaround in the local maritime economy ten years later brought a peak in construction driven by the demands of the oyster and coal trades. In 1884, the "Oyster Boom" topped off with its record catch of fifteen million bushels. During the same period, the opening of the Newport News Coal Terminal spurred Bay builders with an increased demand for larger vessels and greater tonnage.

Note the contrast between numbers and tonnage of schooners built as shown in the two graphs for the years 1869-1892. The apparent discrepancy is due to the fact that it might take a dozen smaller vessels to equal the tonnage of a single four-master.

Building fell off rapidly after 1886. Overfishing brought on a swift decline in oyster production and the need for more vessels. At about the same time, large schooner construction shifted to northern shipbuilding centers. To add to the forces at work was

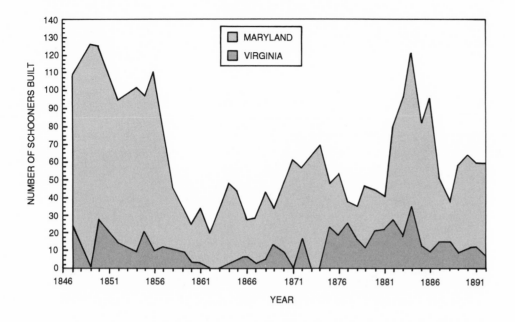

the continued and increasing investment in steam vessels, which took a steady toll in the demand for new schooners.

Sources

Gorton, Carruth & Associates. *Encyclopedia of American Facts and Dates*. 6th ed. New York: Thomas Y. Crowell Corp., 1971.

Hutchins, John G.B. *American Maritime Industries*. Cambridge, Mass.: Harvard University Press, 1941.

Morris, Richard D. *Encyclopedia of American History*. New York: Harper Brothers Publishers, 1961.

Wennersten, John R. *The Oyster Wars of Chesapeake Bay*, Centreville, Md: Tidewater Publishers, 1981.

Yates, Charles C. *Summary of Oyster Bars of Maryland 1906-1912*. Washington, D.C.: U.S. Government Printing Office, 1913.

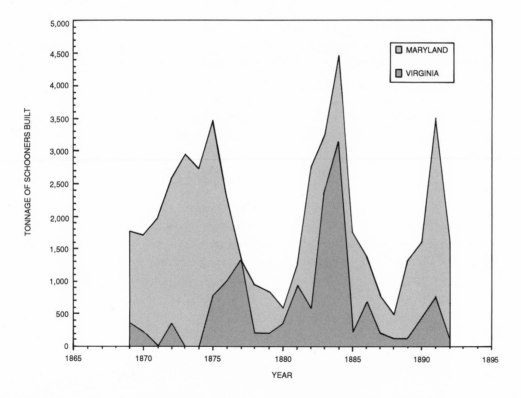

Endnotes

Preface

1. Kenneth F. Brooks, Jr., *Run to the Lee* (New York: W. W. Norton & Co., 1965; Baltimore: Johns Hopkins Paperbacks, 1988), 30.

Chapter 1

1. C. Calvert Evans, interview, Cambridge, October 8, 1988.
2. Earl Brannock, interview, Cambridge, January 18, 1989.
3. Evans, October 8, 1988.
4. Ibid.
5. Ibid.
6. Ibid.
7. Ibid.
8. Ibid.
9. Ibid.
10. D'Arcy Grant, "Drawing Long Bow in Harbor," *The Sunday Sun Magazine*, May 5, 1940.
11. Ibid.
12. D'Arcy Grant, "Her Schooner Capsized, But All Hands Were Saved," *The Sun*, August 21, 1940.
13. D'Arcy Grant, "Schooner Sinking Leaves 2 Captains 'On Beach,'" *Evening Sun*, August 21, 1940.
14. Evans, October 8, 1988.

Chapter 2

1. E. P. Morris, *The Fore-and-Aft Rig in America* (New Haven: Yale University Press, 1927), 174.
2. Ibid., 168.
3. Howard I. Chapelle, *The Search for Speed Under Sail* (New York: W. W. Norton, 1967), 11.
4. M.V. Brewington Papers, research notes (Mystic Seaport Museum, undated and uncatalogued).
5. Cerinda W. Evans, *Some Notes on Shipbuilding in Colonial Virginia* (Williamsburg: Virginia 350th Anniversary Celebration Corporation, 1957), 16-17.
6. Joseph A. Goldenberg, *Shipbuilding in Colonial America* (Charlottesville: University Press of Virginia, 1976; published for The Mariners' Museum, Newport News), 23-24.
7. Robert Greenhalgh Albion, *Rise of New York Port 1815-1860* (New York: Charles Scribner's Sons, South Street Seaport edition, 1939), 81, 177.
8. Arthur Pierce Middleton, *Tobacco Coast: A Maritime History of the Chesapeake Bay in the Colonial Era* (Newport News: The Mariners' Museum, 1953; Baltimore: Maryland Paperback Bookshelf, Johns Hopkins University Press and Maryland State Archives, 1984), 197.
9. Ibid., 251.
10. M.V. Brewington Papers, research notes, undated and uncatalogued.
11. A Contract for Building a Schooner at Annapolis, Maryland 1733, *Carroll-Maccubbin Papers* (Baltimore: Maryland Historical Society).
12. Goldenberg, *Shipbuilding*, 69.
13. Ibid., 62.
14. Ibid., 62.
15. Middleton, *Tobacco Coast*, 254.
16. Charles H. Cramp, "The War Eagle," 16th Annual Meeting, November 19-20, 1908, *Transactions of the Society of Naval Architects and Marine Engineers* (Mystic: Mystic Seaport Museum), 2.
17. Ibid., 3.
18. Howard I. Chapelle, *The National Watercraft Collection* (Washington, D.C.: Smithsonian Institution, 1960), 9.
19. E. P. Morris, *The Fore-and-Aft Rig*, 196, 198.
20. Middleton, *Tobacco Coast*, 89.
21. M. V. Brewington, "The Chesapeake Bay Pilots," Baltimore: *Maryland Historical Magazine* (June 2, 1953), 48; reprinted in Telltales (St. Michaels: Chesapeake Bay Maritime Museum, November 1972), 27.
22. M. V. Brewington, *Chesapeake Bay: A Pictorial Maritime History*, (Cambridge, Md.: Cornell Maritime Press, 1953), 64.
23. Chapelle, *Search for Speed*, 175.
24. Evans, *Notes on Shipbuilding*, 29-30.
25. Chapelle, *Search for Speed*, 62.
26. Ibid., 55, 57.
27. Goldenberg, *Shipbuilding*, 79.
28. Chapelle, *Search for Speed*, 144-45.
29. Goldenberg, *Shipbuilding*, 120.
30. Chapelle, *Search for Speed*, 211-12.
31. Ibid., 213.
32. Ibid., 146-49.

Chapter 3

1. Middleton, *Tobacco Coast*, 198.
2. Ibid., 260-62.
3. Ibid., 269.
4. Jerome R. Garitee, *The Republic's Private Navy: The American Privateering Business as practiced by Baltimore during the War of 1812* (Middletown, Ct.: Wesleyan University Press for Mystic Seaport, 1977), 14.

5. Arthur Pierce Middleton, "Ships and Ship-building in the Chesapeake and Tributaries," in *Chesapeake Bay in the American Revolution*, ed. Ernest M. Eller (Centreville, Md.: Tidewater Publishers, 1981), 106.

6. Ibid., 130.

7. Ernest M. Eller, "Chesapeake Bay in the American Revolution," in *Chesapeake Bay in the American Revolution*, ed. Eller, 30; *Naval Documents of the American Revolution*, vol. 7 (Washington, D.C.: Naval Historical Center, Navy Department), 522.

8. Garitee, *Republic's Private Navy*, 143.

9. Ibid., 17.

10. Howard I. Chapelle, *The Baltimore Clipper: Its Origin and Development* (Marine Research Society, Bonanza Books edition), 16.

11. Middleton, "Ships and Shipbuilding," 131-32.

12. Garitee, *Republic's Private Navy*, 17-18.

13. Ibid., 16.

14. Ibid., 18.

15. Winthrop L. Marvin, *The American Merchant Marine: Its History and Romance from 1620 to 1902* (New York: Charles Scribner's Sons, 1902), 13-14.

16. Chapelle, *Baltimore Clipper*, 34.

17. Ibid., 35.

18. Marvin, *American Merchant Marine*, 13.

19. Chapelle, *Baltimore Clipper*, 18.

20. Ibid., 18-19.

21. Ibid., 115.

22. Chapelle, *Baltimore Clipper*, 3.

23. Ibid., 14.

24. *Niles Weekly Register*, June 23, 1832.

25. Chapelle, *Search for Speed*, 146.

26. Garitee, *Republic's Private Navy*, 27.

27. Ibid., 107.

28. Geoffrey Gilbert, "The Ships of Federalist Baltimore," *Maryland Historical Magazine*, 79, no. 4 (Winter 1984): 314.

29. Garitee, *Republic's Private Navy*, 16.

30. Tina H. Sheller, "Artisans, Manufacturing, and the Rise of a Manufacturing Interest in Revolutionary Baltimore Town," *Maryland Historical Magazine*, 83, no. 1 (Spring 1988): 4.

31. Sheller, "Artisans," 5.

32. Garitee, *Republic's Private Navy*, 25.

33. Howard I. Chapelle, *The History of the American Sailing Navy: The Ships and Their Development* (New York: W. W. Norton & Company, 1949), 145.

34. "Enterprise," *Dictionary of American Naval Fighting Ships* (Washington, D.C.: Ships' Histories Branch, Naval Historical Center, 1959), 355-56.

35. Marvin, *American Merchant Marine*, 109-24.

Chapter 4

1. Garitee, *Republic's Private Navy*, 119, 174-82.

2. Ibid., 30.

3. Ibid., 11.

4. Ibid., 251.

5. John Philips Cranwell & William Bowers Crane, *Men of Marque: A History of Private Armed Vessels out of Baltimore During the War of 1812* (New York: W. W. Norton & Company, 1940), 100.

6. Ibid., 101-102.

7. Garitee, *Republic's Private Navy*, 192.

8. Cranwell & Crane, *Men of Marque*, 104.

9. Ibid.

10. Ibid.

11. Ibid.

12. Ibid.

13. Chapelle, *Baltimore Clipper*, 83.

14. Cranwell & Crane, *Men of Marque*, 106-11.

15. Chapelle, *Baltimore Clipper*, 82.

16. Charles Gordon, Capt. USN, to Secretary of the Navy William Jones, Early Naval Records (Washington, D.C.: U.S. Naval History Center) NA, RG 45, M125, Captain's Letters, 1813, vol. 2, no. 155.

17. Gordon to Jones, ALS, DNA, RG 45, Captain's Letters, 1813, vol. 3, no. 99.

18. Garitee, *Republic's Private Navy*, 128.

19. Gordon to Jones, RG 45, Master Commandant Letters, 16 Feb. 1813.

20. Gordon to Jones, RG 45, Captain's Letters, 20 Mar. 1813.

21. Gordon to Jones, NA, RG 45, M 125, Captain's Letters, 19 May 1813, vol. 3, no. 153.

22. Gordon to Jones, ALS, DNA, RG 45, Captain's Letters, 18 Apr. 1813, vol. 3, no. 9.

23. Gordon to Jones, ALS, DNA, RG 45, Captain's Letters, 30 May 1813.

24. Garitee, *Republic's Private Navy*, 113.

25. Ibid., 241.

26. Ibid., 244.

27. Chapelle, *Search for Speed*, 299.

28. Ibid.

29. Ibid., 300-301.

30. Ibid.

31. Ibid.

32. Ibid., 297.

33. Ibid., 300-301.

34. Ibid., 301.

35. Ibid., 303.

36. "The Amistad Incident: A Summary," Amistad Research Center (New Orleans: Tulane University), 1.

37. Warren Marr II, "Out of Bondage," reprinted by the American Missionary Assn. from the *United Church Herald*, Division of Publication, United Church Board for Homeland Ministries (New York, 1964).

38. Chapelle, *Baltimore Clipper*, 142.

39. Ibid.

40. Ibid., 144.

41. Ibid., 144-45.

42. Ibid., 147.

43. George Coggeshall, *History of American Privateers*, published by the author (New York, 1856); quoted by Evelyn Chisolm in *Pride of Baltimore: Renaissance of the Baltimore Clipper* (Baltimore: Baltimore Operation Sail, Ltd., 1977), 7.

Chapter 5

1. M. Florence Bourne, "Thomas Kemp, Shipbuilder, and His Home, Wades Point," *Maryland Historical Magazine*, 49, no. 3 (September 1954), 278.

2. Ibid., 282.

3. Ibid., 284-287.

4. Robert D. Lambdin, "Early Shipbuilding in Maryland: Autobiography of Robert Dawson Lambdin," John W. Crowley, comp. (St. Michaels: Chesapeake Bay Maritime Museum, 1935).

5. M.V. Brewington, "The Chesapeake Bay Pilots," *Maryland Historical Magazine*, 48, no. 2 (June 2, 1953), 109-33.

6. Ibid.

7. Ibid.

8. Ibid.

9. Ibid.

10. Ibid.

11. Ibid.

12. Ibid.

13. Ibid.

14. Ibid.

15. Ibid.

16. Ibid.

17. Ibid.

18. Howard I. Chapelle, *The National Watercraft Collection* (Washington, D.C.: United States National Museum Bulletin 219, Smithsonian Institution, Government Printing Office, 1960), 51.

19. Ibid., 51.

20. Ibid.

21. Ibid., 52.

22. Chapelle, *Search for Speed*, 260.

23. Howard I. Chapelle, "Pilot Boats II," research notes, undated (St. Michaels: archives, Chesapeake Bay Maritime Museum).

24. Albion, *Rise of New York Port*, 306.

25. Middleton, *Tobacco Coast*, 73, 81.

26. Ibid., 42.

27. Chapelle, *Watercraft*, 43.

28. Maynadier-Sands Letters, 1808-1811 (Annapolis: Maryland State Archives), The Sands Collection, SC 2095, folders 33-36.

29. Maynadier-Sands, folder 33.

30. Ibid.

31. Ibid.

32. Maynadier-Sands, folder 34.

33. Ibid.

34. Maynadier-Sands, folder 35.

35. Joseph Sands, personal papers, (Annapolis: Maryland State Archives), The Sands Collection, SC 2095, folder 47.

36. A. St. Clair Wright with Joy Gary, comp., brochure, *Historic Annapolis* (Annapolis: Historic Annapolis, Inc., 1959), reprint of "Sailing Packet," advertisement, *Maryland Gazette* (date unknown), 15.
37. Joseph Sands, folder 69.
38. *Niles Weekly Register* (Baltimore: June, 1832).
39. Chapelle, *Watercraft*, 43.
40. "History of the Oxford Shipyard," by "The Oldtimer," The Easton *Star Democrat*, November 9, 1934.

Chapter 6

1. Cramp, "The War Eagle": "Whether the 'pungy' was a development of the 'clipper' or that the 'clipper' was a development of the 'pungy' I have never been able to find out, but I believe the development of each was coincident, and that they are the outgrowth of the necessities of the period—each in its own class represented the principle of the survival of the fittest."
2. M.V. Brewington, "The Schooner," Brewington Papers, unpublished manuscript, undated, uncatalogued (Mystic: Mystic Seaport Museum), 2.
3. John Earle, Brewington Papers, notes on pungies, unpublished manuscript, undated, uncatalogued (Mystic: Mystic Seaport Museum), 2.
4. Earle, notes on pungies, unpublished manuscript, use of term "beanie" confirmed by phone with Mr. Earle on Sept. 25, 1991.
5. Eric Steinlein, "In Pursuit of the Pungy," *The Skipper*, April 1965: 37.
6. Earle, notes on pungies, unpublished manuscript, 3-4.
7. Brewington, "The Schooner," 2.
8. Steinlein, "Pursuit of the Pungy," 38.
9. Earle, notes on pungies, 4-5.
10. Steinlein, "Pursuit of the Pungy," 38.
11. Earle, notes on pungies, 2-3.
12. Steinlein, "Pursuit of the Pungy," 38.
13. Chapelle, *Watercraft*, 40.
14. Steinlein, "Pursuit of the Pungy," 39.
15. Charles H. Stevenson, *The Oyster Industry of Maryland* (Washington, D.C.: Government Printing Office, 1894), 239.
16. Robert H. Burgess, *This Was Chesapeake Bay* (Centreville: Tidewater Publishers, 1963), 116.
17. Steinlein, "Pursuit of the Pungy," 39.
18. Ibid.
19. Ibid., 39-40.
20. Ibid., 37.
21. Brewington, "The Schooner," 2-3.
22. John Earle, interview, Easton, Md., June 24, 1989.
23. Chapelle, *Watercraft*, 168.
24. Ibid., 197.
25. Ibid., 78-79.
26. John R. Wennersten, *The Oyster Wars of Chesapeake Bay* (Centreville: Tidewater Publishers, 1981), 17.
27. Ibid., 28-36.
28. Ibid., 89-95.
29. Steinlein, "Pursuit of the Pungy," 38.
30. Earle, 1989.
31. Ibid.
32. Lambdin, "Early Shipbuilding in Maryland," 6.
33. Steinlein, "Pursuit of the Pungy," 38.
34. Ibid.
35. Ibid.
36. Robert H. Burgess, "The Chesapeake Bay Pungy," *The Chesapeake Skipper* (January 1948): 34.
37. Robert H. Burgess, *Chesapeake Sailing Craft: Part I* (Cambridge: Tidewater Publishers, 1975), 58.
38. Burgess, "Chesapeake Bay Pungy," 18, 34, 35.
39. Burgess, *Chesapeake Sailing Craft*, 60.
40. Burgess, *This Was Chesapeake Bay*, 119.
41. Eric Steinlein, "Amanda Lewis Last Of Bay's True Clippers," *The Sun*, March 16, 1938.

Chapter 7

1. Earle, June 24, 1989.
2. Thomas C. Gillmer, *Chesapeake Bay Sloops* (St. Michaels: Chesapeake Bay Maritime Museum, 1982), 28.
3. Ibid., 29.
4. Earle, June 24, 1989.
5. Brewington, "Schooners and Pungys," 3-4.
6. Chapelle, *Watercraft*, 40.
7. Joe Liener, interview, Chesapeake Bay Maritime Museum, October 20, 1988.
8. Ibid.
9. Wennersten, *Oyster Wars*, 11-12.
10. John A. Mellin, "Civil War Privateers in Bay," Annapolis: *The Capital*, May 15, 1986.
11. Royce Gordon Shingleton, *John Taylor Wood: Sea Ghost of the Confederacy* (Athens: The University of Georgia Press).
12. Arthur Thurston, *Tallahassee Skipper* (Nova Scotia: Lescarbot Press, 1981).
13. William T. Hooper, *My Years Before the Mast*, Gladys Ione Hooper, ed., comp. (Dorchester County: date and publisher unknown).
14. James E. Marvil, *Sailing Rams* (Lewes, Del.: Sussex Press, 1974), 39.
15. Harrison Johnson, "Racing Schooners of the Chesapeake," *The Sun*, date unknown, clipping, vertical file, Chesapeake Bay Maritime Museum, St. Michaels.

Chapter 8

1. Stevenson, *Oyster Industry*.
2. Chapelle, *Watercraft*, 189.
3. Chapelle, *Watercraft*, 197; *see also* "Report of Oyster Commission for the State of Maryland" (Annapolis: Maryland State Printer, 1884), 38.
4. Stevenson, *Oyster Industry*, 235.
5. Ibid., 236.
6. Wennersten, *Oyster Wars*, 70.
7. Stevenson, *Oyster Industry*, 236; *see also* Burgess, *Sailing Craft*, 159.
8. Evans, October 8, 1988.
9. Frederick Tilp, "Baltimore: When Oysters Were King," *Maryland Magazine* 20, no. 1 (Autumn, 1987): 70.
10. Wennersten, *Oyster Wars*, 87.
11. Stevenson, *Oyster Industry*, 240.
12. Earl Brannock, January 18, 1989.
13. Arthur L. Van Name, M.D., interview, Urbanna, July 19, 1988.
14. Ibid.
15. Ibid.
16. Ibid.
17. Hooper, *Years Before the Mast*, 47.
18. Ibid.
19. Van Name, July 19, 1988.
20. Ibid.
21. Hooper, *Years Before the Mast*, 13.
22. Ibid., 13-14.
23. Ibid., 16.
24. Ibid., 14.
25. Ibid.
26. Ibid., 16-17.
27. Ibid., 23.
28. Ibid., 23-24.
29. Louis Sayer, "Arcady for Some," *The Rudder*, 26, no. 2 (August 1911): 50.
30. Nelson Barnard, clipping of letter to editors of *The Sun Magazine*, date unknown. May possibly be responding to article in *The Sun Magazine*, May 31, 1964, by H. Osborne Michael, "The Sailing Scow, Vanished Bay Craft," 13.
31. Ibid.
32. Ibid.
33. Porter, May 9, 1989.
34. William Seaford Stevens, interview, Chester, May 16, 1989.
35. Woodrow Aaron, interview, Cambridge, May 6, 1989.
36. Stevens, May 16, 1989.
37. Earl Brannock, January 18, 1989.
38. Sayer, "Arcady for Some," 53-54.
39. Ibid.

Chapter 9

1. Marvil, *Sailing Rams*, 166.
2. Ibid., 168.
3. Harry B. Porter, interview, Annapolis, May 9, 1989.
4. Hooper, *Years Before the Mast*, 60.
5. Porter, May 9, 1989.

6. Stevens, May 16, 1989.
7. Porter, May 9, 1989.
8. Stevens, May 16, 1989.
9. Jim Richardson, interview, Cambridge, April 1990.
10. Frank Henry, "Fertilizer Capital of the World," *The Sun Magazine*, clipping, vertical file, Chesapeake Bay Maritime Museum, St. Michaels, 10.
11. Ibid., 11.
12. Evans, October 8, 1988.
13. Stevens, May 16, 1989.
14. Evans, May 6, 1989.
15. Ibid.
16. Hooper, *Years Before the Mast*, 31-32.
17. Stevens, May 16, 1989.
18. Ibid.
19. Aaron, May 6, 1989.
20. Robert H. Burgess, "Gone, But Not Forgotten!" *The Daily Press* (Newport News, Va.), February 5, 1967, 3.
21. Ibid.
22. Ibid.
23. H. Osborne Michael, "The Chesapeake Bay Schooner *Mary Vickers:* A Bayman Who Sailed on Her Refutes the Idea that These Craft Were Heavy and Slow," *The Sun*, January 26, 1958.
24. Ibid.
25. Ibid.
26. Ibid.
27. Henry Hall, "Report on the Shipbuilding Industry" (Washington: Government Printing Office, 1880), 128-29; *also*, "Ship Building in the United States," quoted by M.V. Brewington, "The Potomac Long-Boat," *American Neptune*, 1 (1941): 159-63.
28. Ibid.
29. Ibid.
30. Robert H. Burgess, "Once This Was Pineapple Time in Our Port," *The Sun Magazine* (April 3, 1966): 28-29.
31. Robert H. Burgess, "The Chesapeake Pineapple Trade," *The Chesapeake Skipper* (April 1949): 6.
32. Burgess, "Pineapple Time," 6.

33. Burgess, "Chesapeake Pineapple Trade," 6.
34. Brannock, January 18, 1989.
35. Burgess, "Pineapple Time," 29.
36. Ibid.
37. G. Terry Sharrer, "The Maryland Tomato," *Maryland Magazine* (Summer 1987): 23.
38. Evans, May 6, 1989.
39. Aaron, May 6, 1989.
40. Evans, May 6, 1989.
41. Aaron, May 6, 1989.
42. Evans, May 6, 1989.
43. Hooper, *My Years Before the Mast*, 25.
44. Ibid.
45. Ibid., 26.
46. Ibid.
47. Ibid.
48. Stevens, May 16, 1989.
49. Brewington, *Chesapeake Bay*, 140.

Chapter 10

1. Lynn Perry, interview, Urbanna, May 25, 1988.
2. Perry, June 21, 1988.
3. Ibid.
4. Stevens, May 16, 1989.
5. Porter, May 9, 1989.
6. Perry, June 21, 1988.
7. Jim Richardson, April 1990.
8. Brannock, January 18, 1989.
9. Hooper, *My Years Before the Mast*, 34.
10. Ibid.
11. Perry, June 21, 1988.
12. George W. Rappleyea, "Navigation With a Yardstick," *Motor Boating* (March 1945).
13. Perry, May 25, 1988.
14. Evans, October 8, 1988.
15. Perry, June 21, 1988.
16. Evans, October 8, 1988.
17. Ibid.
18. Ibid.
19. Frank Henry, "When the Wind Blows," *The Sun*, October 30, 1949.
20. Stevens, May 16, 1989.
21. Evans, October 8, 1988.
22. Brewington, *Chesapeake Bay*, 157.
23. Robert H. Burgess, *This Was Chesapeake Bay*, 132.

24. John Earle, interview, Easton, June 24, 1989; *see also* William Henry Dare, "Improvement in Means for Clewing up Gaff-Topsails" (Whitesboro, New York, specifications forming part of Letters Patent No. 190831, May 15, 1877).
25. Evans, October 8, 1988.
26. Perry, May 25, 1988.
27. Stevens, May 16, 1989.
28. Ibid.
29. Marvil, *Sailing Rams*, 135.
30. Lynn Perry & Arthur Van Name, interview, July 19, 1988.
31. Perry, May 25, 1988.
32. Ibid.
33. Ibid.
34. Ibid.
35. Ibid.
36. Ibid.
37. Ibid.
38. Ibid.

Chapter 11

1. Stevens, May 16, 1989.
2. Ibid.
3. Ibid.
4. Aaron, May 6, 1989.
5. Perry, May 25, 1988.
6. Perry, June 21, 1988.
7. Porter, May 9, 1989.
8. Orlando V. Wooten, "Captain Vernon T. Hopkins," *Salisbury Times*, August 4, 1968.
9. Brannock, January 18, 1989.
10. Stevens, May 16, 1989.
11. Brannock, January 18, 1989.
12. Shirley Brannock, interview, Cambridge, January 18, 1989.
13. Porter, May 9, 1989.
14. Stevens, May 16, 1989.
15. Howard O'Day, "The Ram *Jennie D. Bell*," *The Sun Magazine*, January 12, 1969.
16. Ibid.
17. Ibid.

18. Robert H. Burgess, "A Veteran of the Days When Sail Was King," *The Sun Magazine* (clipping in vertical file, Chesapeake Bay Maritime Museum, date unknown), 20.
19. Marvil, *Sailing Rams*, 140.
20. Shirley Brannock, January 18, 1989.
21. Ibid.
22. Ibid.
23. James F. Waesche, "Baltimore's Ship Chandlers," *Maryland Magazine* (Spring 1987): 24.
24. Ibid.
25. Ibid., 25.
26. D'Arcy Grant, *The Sun Magazine*, June 9, 1940.
27. O'Day, *Jennie D. Bell*.
28. Evans, October 8, 1988.
29. Porter, May 9, 1989.
30. "Logbook Entry," *Logbook* (The Mariners' Museum) (Summer 1991): 14.
31. Marvil, *Sailing Rams*, 96.
32. Porter, May 9, 1989.
33. Robert H. Burgess, *Chesapeake Circle* (Cambridge, Md.: Cornell Maritime Press, 1965), 21.

Chapter 12

1. Robert H. Burgess, "Logwood," *Chesapeake Skipper* (January 1953): 24.
2. Burgess, "Logwood," 60; *also This Was Chesapeake Bay*, 44.
3. Burgess, "Logwood," 61; *This Was Chesapeake Bay*, 44-45.
4. Burgess, "Logwood," 60; *This Was Chesapeake Bay*, 44.
5. W. J. Lewis Parker, *The Great Coal Schooners of New England: 1870-1909* (Mystic: The Marine Historical Association, Inc., vol. II, no. 6, December 10, 1948), 17.
6. Paul C. Morris, *American Sailing Coasters of the North Atlantic* (Chardon, Ohio: Block and Osborn, 1973), 47-49.
7. John Lyman, ed. "Shipbuilding at Alexandria, Virginia," *Log Chips*, 3, no. 3 (November 1952): 27.
8. Parker, *Great Coal Schooners*, 18.
9. Ibid., 19.
10. Ibid., 52.

11. Ibid., 53-54.
12. Ibid., 56.
13. Ibid., 54.
14. Ibid., 60-61.
15. Ibid., 67-68.
16. Ibid., 92.
17. Morris, *Sailing Coasters*, 49.
18. Burgess, *This Was Chesapeake Bay*, 57.
19. Ibid., 54.
20. Joseph C. Jones, Jr., *America's Icemen* (Humble, Texas: Jobeco Books, 1984).
21. Henry Hall, *The Ice Industry of the United States*, H.R. Misc. Doc. 42, 47th Congress, 2nd Session (Washington, D.C.: U.S. Department of the Interior, Census Division, Government Printing Office, 1888).
22. Morris, *Sailing Coasters*, 45.
23. Philip C. Foster Smith, *Crystal Blocks of Yankee Coldness* (Salem: Essex Institute Historical Collections, July, 1961).
24. Helen C. Milius, "Ice Queen," Richmond: *Commonwealth* magazine, 26, no. 12 (December 1959): 42-49.
25. Ibid., 43.
26. Jennie G. Everson, *Tidewater Ice of the Kennebec River* (Freeport: Maine State Museum, 1970).
27. Hall, *The Ice Industry*.
28. Parker, *Great Coal Schooners*, 5.
29. Ibid.
30. Ibid.
31. Everson, *Tidewater Ice*.
32. Morris, *Sailing Coasters*, 47.
33. Jones, *America's Icemen*, 126, 130.
34. Morris, *Sailing Coasters*, 45.
35. Parker, *Great Coal Schooners*, 4.
36. Ibid., 8.
37. Morris, *Sailing Coasters*, 47.
38. Ibid., 52.
39. Ibid., 51.
40. Earle, June 24, 1989.
41. H. Osborne Michael, "The Sailing Scow, Vanished Bay Craft," *The Sun Magazine* (May 31, 1964).
42. H. Osborne Michael & Nelson M. Berg, "The Scow Ella Barnard," letters in "Our Readers Write," *The Sun Magazine*, clipping, date unknown.
43. Brannock, January 18, 1989.

Chapter 13

1. Chapelle, *Watercraft*, 40-41.
2. Ibid., 47.
3. Dorothy R. Brewington, "Wire Rigging," *American Neptune* (1941): 399.
4. Ibid.
5. Morris, *Sailing Coasters*, 83
6. Lyman, ed. "Shipbuilding at Alexandria, Virginia," *Log Chips: The Periodical Publication of Recent Maritime History*, 3, no. 3, (November 1952): 27.
7. Marvil, *Sailing Rams*, 130.
8. Elizabeth Paul Bacon, "Christening a Four-Master," as told to Robert H. Burgess, *The Sun Magazine* (January 19, 1975).
9. Burgess, *Chesapeake Circle*, 20-21.
10. Ibid.
11. Aaron, May 6, 1989.
12. Burgess, *Chesapeake Circle*, 20-21.
13. Burgess, *Chesapeake Sailing Craft*, 262.
14. Burgess, *Chesapeake Circle*, 189.
15. Parker, *The Great Coal Schooners*, 33.
16. Lyman, "*Shipbuilding at Alexandria*," 28
17. Marvil, *Sailing Rams*, 134.
18. Ibid., 131.
19. Harold G. Foss, "Schooner *Sallie C. Marvil*," *Log Chips*, 4, no. 8 (September-December 1959).
20. Ibid.
21. Ibid.
22. Robert H. Burgess, "Baltimore Was Home to Four Masters," *The Sun* (clipping, date unknown)
23. Clarence N. Rogers, "*Anna R. Heidritter, ex-Cohasset*," *The Rudder* (clipping, date unknown), 30.
24. Robert H. I. Goddard, "*Anna R. Heidritter*," *American Neptune*, (1943): 59.
25. Ibid., 60.
26. Ibid., 59.
27. Lewis S. Gannett, "Wooden Ship Program Viewed In Light Of Later Events, *The Nautical Gazette*, 98, no. 9 (February 1920): 299.
28. Ibid.
29. Burgess, *This Was Chesapeake Bay*, 39-42.
30. "Gielow-Designed Schooner," *The Rudder* (June 1918): 280.
31. Cox & Stevens, design no. 210, complete set of plans at Mystic Seaport Museum, Mystic, Connecticut. Dimensions and date would indicate that they were for the *Anandale*. The plans were drawn for the Johnson/ Lightridge Co. of Staten Island, New York. No hull number is given, but there were no other two-decked schooners built on the Chesapeake. The vessel's proposed tonnage and *Anandale*'s registered tonnage come within a few tons of each other; their length within a few feet.
32. Bacon/Burgess, *The Sun Magazine*.
33. Ibid.
34. Lee McCardell, "White Sails in the Sunset" (August 30, 1936), clipping, vertical file, Chesapeake Bay Maritime Museum, St. Michaels.
35. Bacon/Burgess, *The Sun Magazine*.
36. Robert H. I. Goddard, "The Schooner *Lillian E. Kerr*," *American Neptune*, 4, 172.
37. Ibid.
38. Ibid.
39. Ibid., 174.
40. McCardell, "White Sails."
41. Burgess, *Chesapeake Circle*, 98.
42. Marvil, *Sailing Rams*, 125.
43. Ibid.
44. Burgess, *Chesapeake Sailing Craft*, 255.
45. Burgess, *This Was Chesapeake Bay*, 54.
46. Ibid., 45.
47. Parker, *The Great Coal Schooners*, 37.
48. Ibid., 39.
49. Joseph G. O'Keefe, "Coal Schooners: Stages for Drama at Sea," *The Sun Magazine* (October 2, 1977): 31.
50. Burgess, *This Was Chesapeake Bay*, 64.
51. Marvil, *Sailing Rams*, 126.
52. Parker, *The Great Coal Schooners*, 41.

Chapter 14

1. Marvil, *Sailing Rams*, 16.
2. Ibid., 17.
3. Ibid., 166.
4. Ibid., 56.
5. Ann Jensen, "Chesapeake City and the C & D Canal," *Annapolitan* (October 1981): 25.
6. Ibid.
7. Marvil, *Sailing Rams*, 46-48.
8. Ibid., 107.
9. Ibid., 21.
10. Ibid., 21, 30.
11. Ibid., 14.
12. Lyman, "The Chesapeake Bay Ram," *Log Chips*, 2, no. 11 (March 1952): 123.
13. Ibid.
14. Ibid., 124.
15. Howard O'Day, "The Ram *Jennie D. Bell*," *The Sun Magazine*, January 12, 1969: 2.
16. Aaron, May 6, 1989.
17. Frank Henry, "When the Wind Blows," *The Sun*, October 30, 1949.
18. Ibid.
19. "Schooner Sinks In Tangier Sound," *Evening Sun*, September 19, 1955.
20. Marvil, *Sailing Rams*, 19.
21. Ibid., 19, 52.
22. Ibid., 56-58.
23. Ibid., 58-59.
24. Ibid., 63, 241.
25. Ibid., 67.
26. Ibid., 63.
27. Ibid.
28. Ibid., 59.
29. Liener, October 20, 1988.
30. *Historic American Merchant Marine Survey*, field notes (Works Progress Administration Federal Project No. 6, for the Watercraft Collection of the Smithsonian Institution, 1937).
31. Marvil, *Sailing Rams*, 64-65.
32. Ibid.
33. Ibid., 64.
34. Ibid., 44.
35. Burgess, *This Was Chesapeake Bay*, 113.
36. Marvil, *Sailing Rams*, 98.
37. Ibid., 101.

38. "Some New England Three-masters," *American Neptune* 5 (1945): 291.

39. Marvil, *Sailing Rams*, 21.

40. Ibid., 88.

41. Ibid.

42. Howard O'Day, *The Sun Magazine*.

43. Robert H. Burgess, "A Veteran of the Days When Sail Was King," *The Sun Magazine* (clipping, vertical file, Chesapeake Bay Maritime Museum, St. Michaels, date unknown): 20.

44. Burgess, *The Sun Magazine*, 20.

45. Marvil, *Sailing Rams*, 138.

46. Evans, October 8, 1988.

47. Marvil, *Sailing Rams*, 84.

48. Marvil, *Sailing Rams*, 2nd ed. (Lewes, Del.: Sussex Press, 1974), 267.

49. Malcolm Allen, "The Bay's Last Ram Dies on a Mud Flat," *The Sun Magazine*, (August 20, 1967): 15.

Chapter 15

1. Marvil, *Sailing Rams*, 128.

2. Ibid., 188.

3. Burgess, *This Was Chesapeake Bay*, 131.

4. Marvil, *Sailing Rams*, 116.

5. Aaron, May 6, 1989.

6. Porter, May 9, 1989.

7. Evans, October 8, 1988.

8. Arthur Van Name, research notes, interview July 19, 1988.

9. Middleton, *Tobacco Coast*, 43-46.

10. Evans, October 8, 1988.

11. Ibid.

12. Ibid.

13. Stevens, May 16, 1989.

14. Burgess, *This Was Chesapeake Bay*, 105.

15. Porter, May 9, 1989.

16. Ibid.

17. John Frye, "One by One," *Sailing* (March 1975).

18. Brannock, January 18, 1989.

19. Evans, May 6, 1989.

20. Burgess, *Chesapeake Sailing Craft*, 102.

21. Ibid., 106-108.

22. Burgess, *This Was Chesapeake Bay*, 170.

23. Frye, *Sailing*.

24. Burgess, *Chesapeake Circle*, 192.

25. Frye, *Sailing*.

26. Evans, May 6, 1989.

27. Burgess, *Chesapeake Sailing Craft*, 152-53.

28. Evans, May 6, 1989.

29. Frye, *Sailing*.

30. Ibid.

31. Evans, May 6, 1989.

32. Frye, *Sailing*.

33. Evans, May 6, 1989.

34. Ibid.

35. Porter, May 9, 1989.

36. Evans, May 6, 1989.

37. Porter, May 9, 1989.

38. Ibid.

39. Evans, May 6, 1989.

40. Ibid.

41. Ibid.

42. Perry, June 21, 1988.

Chapter 16

1. Burgess, *Chesapeake Sailing Craft*, 94-95.

2. Burgess, *Chesapeake Circle*, 117-18.

3. William B. Crane, "Passengers Sail The Bay Again," *The Sun*, July 13, 1941.

4. Burgess, *Chesapeake Circle*, 192.

5. Evans, October 8, 1988.

6. Burgess, *Chesapeake Circle*, 193.

7. Burgess, *This Was Chesapeake Bay*, 114.

8. Marvil, *Sailing Rams*, 77.

9. Ibid., 67, 68, 106.

10. Lester R. Trott, interview, Annapolis, July 1986.

11. Ibid.

12. Ibid.

13. Lester R. Trott, *A Different Vacation: Cruising the Historic Chesapeake Bay*, brochure, Chesapeake Vacation Cruises, Inc., Annapolis, Md. (1949).

14. Marjorie Dent Candee, "A Three-Master Cruises the Intracoastal Waterway," *Motor Boating* (May 1946): 92.

15. Ibid., 42.

16. Ibid., 44.

17. Trott, July 1986.

18. Maribelle W. Rhodes, "Captain Frederick B. Guild and *Victory Chimes*," *Down East* (May 1973).

19. Ibid.

20. "History of Ram Schooner *Victory Chimes*," (November 1987) information compiled after vessel was sold to Domino's Pizza by Jerry Smith of A. Smith Shipyard, Curtis Bay, Maryland.

21. Ibid.

22. Marvil, *Sailing Rams*, 77.

23. Ibid., 68.

24. "Why Did They Drown?" *Skipper* (October 1955): 62.

25. "Report of Marine Board of Investigation: foundering of the schooner *Levin J. Marvel* off North Beach, Md., 12 August 1955," By order of The Commandant, Vice Adm. A.C. Richmond, U.S. Coast Guard, Baltimore, Md. (January 24, 1956), 2.

26. "Captain's Story," *The Sun*, August 14, 1955.

27. "Marine Board," 3.

28. "Captain's Story," *The Sun*.

29. "Why?" *Skipper*, 59.

30. "Captain's Story," *The Sun*.

31. "Marine Board," 4.

32. "Why?" *Skipper*, 59.

33. "Captain's Story," *The Sun*.

34. "Why?" *Skipper*, 60.

35. Ibid.

36. Ibid.

37. "Captain's Story," *The Sun*.

38. "Why?" *Skipper*, 60.

39. "Marine Board," 5.

40. Ibid., 6.

41. "Captain's Story," *The Sun*.

42. Ibid.

43. "1st Survivor in Bay Mishap Cites Ordeal," Baltimore: *The Sun*, August 14, 1955.

44. "Captain's Story," *The Sun*.

45. Ibid.

46. Ibid.

47. "Why?" *Skipper*, 62.

48. "Marine Board," 1.

49. "Find Last Body From Shipwreck," *The Evening Capital*, August 16, 1955.

50. "Marine Board," 9.

Epilogue

1. Burgess, *Chesapeake Sailing Craft*, 152.

2. Ibid., 71.

3. Ibid., 83.

4. Ibid., 266.

5. Ibid., 257.

6. Burgess, *Chesapeake Circle*, 187.

7. Ibid., 189.

8. H.G. Wells, quoted by Rafe Parker in "A Seafarer's Lament," *Historic Preservation*, (April 1986): 30-31.

9. Melbourne Smith, interview by Ann Jensen, *Pride of Baltimore* building site, Inner Harbor, Baltimore, January, 1977.

10. Thomas C. Gillmer, "The Emergence of *Pride*, A Baltimore Clipper," *WoodenBoat*, no. 14 (January-February 1977), 18.

11. Ibid., 19.

12. Ibid., 21.

13. Armin Elsaesser, *Pride of Baltimore: Final Log*, vol. 5, no. 2, Pride of Baltimore, Inc., (Summer 1986), 10.

14. "Statement of First Mate John 'Sugar' Flanagan," May 21, 1986, *Final Log*, 10.

15. Ibid.

16. Baxter Smith, "Chesapeake Pungy takes 20th century form," *Soundings* (November 1985), section II, 10.

17. Ann Jensen, "Western Union Carries a Message—Work Pays," *National Fisherman* (June 1977): 18-C, 19-C.

18. "Just Passing By," *Commandant's Bulletin 10-86*, U.S. Coast Guard (May 9, 1986): 3.

19. Ibid.

20. Orlando Wooten, "Captain Vernon T. Hopkins," *Salisbury Times*, August 4, 1968; reprinted in Marvil, *Sailing Rams*, 1974 edition, 283.

Glossary

Admiralty. British Navy's management board. Thanks to eighteenth and nineteenth century Admiralty practice of taking lines from captured vessels, we have a record of early Bay pilot and clipper schooners.

Admiralty court. Also "prize court." District court that had jurisdiction over maritime matters, including cases of vessels or property seized by privately armed vessels. *See* Letter-of-marque and Privateer.

Adz. One of oldest shipyard hand tools. Arching blade set at right angle to wooden handle used for rough and fine shaping.

Athwart. Across.

Athwartships. Running across ship from side to side, right angle to centerline.

Bald-headed. Having no topmasts.

Baltimore-built. Early term applied to fast, sharp-built, light-hulled schooners with tall sharply raking masts. Built mainly, but not exclusively, in Baltimore in late eighteenth and early nineteenth centuries. Later called clippers.

Barge. Sloop- or schooner-rigged or unrigged craft of full body and heavy construction used for transporting bulky freight such as coal, lumber, sand, or stone. These vessels were designed to be towed.

Bateau. Planked, hard chine boat with shallow V-bottom. Two-sail vessel known as the skipjack.

Batten. Narrow, thin strip of wood used to "fair," adjust, or straighten lines or surface of hull under construction. Also, used to hold tarps, hatches, or other things in place.

Beanie. Type of pungy, with no overhang aft and rudder hung outboard. Disappeared early in twentieth century.

Beat to windward. To sail, "work," or make progress by alternating tacks in direction from which wind is blowing.

Becket. Short piece of rope with hook at one end and loop at the other used to hold wheel, spar, or other moving gear in a set position.

Bends. Thick strakes of planking (also called wales) on vessel's sides just below waterways.

Billethead. Decorative scroll at end of longhead under bowsprit.

Bilge. Lowest area inside hull of vessel; area from turn of the side to the bottom.

Binnacle. Protective stand or case for compass, positioned to be read easily from helm.

Block. Mechanical device made up of one or more grooved pulleys mounted in casings, fitted with hook or some other means of attaching it. It was used to transmit power or change direction of motion of rope or chain run through it. Large two-masted schooners had fifty or more, each with specific names and purposes.

Block coefficient. Ratio or relationship between a vessel's body volume and a solid rectangle of equal length, breadth, and depth. Derived by dividing gross tonnage by the product of length times breadth, times depth. Varies among types of schooners. A full-built schooner, such as a ram, would have a high block coefficient; a pilot boat or pungy, a low one.

Boat falls. Ropes by which boat is lowered or raised; also davit falls.

Body plan. End view showing curves of sides of vessel's transverse frame lines. Frame lines forward of midships are shown to the right of centerline; lines aft, to the left.

Bolt ropes. Ropes secured around the perimeter of a sail.

Boom. Spar or pole which anchors foot of fore-and-aft sail.

Bowsprit. Large spar projecting from bow of sailing vessel. Supports headsails and foremast by means of headstays.

Boxboarded timber. Crisscross method of loading lumber on deck of schooner, alternating fore-and-aft and athwartships.

Boxboat. Local mid-Atlantic term for plank-built, hard-chine Bay freight boat.

Breeches buoy. Life ring fitted with canvas seat or breeches, suspended from a running block on heavy rope or wire, to remove passengers and crew from vessels in distress.

Brig. Two-masted, square-rigged vessel.

Bugeye. Three-sail, round-bilge workboat, with raking masts and foremast taller than main. Usually carried sharp-headed triangular sails. Called "square-rigged" when carrying gaff-sails. *See* M. V. Brewington's *Chesapeake Bay Log Canoes and Bugeyes.*

Bull's eye. Round or oval block, without sheave as fairhead.

Bulwarks. Extension of side of vessel above weather deck to protect persons and objects on deck from going overboard.

Burdensome. In relation to vessel, meaning to have large cargo capacity.

Buy boat. Vessels engaged in buying and carrying oysters from dredgers to packinghouses. When a captain buys on his own account to resell, it is called a buy boat. When boat is owned by dealer and captain works on commission, referred to as run boat.

Cabin trunk. Part of a cabin extending above deck.

Caprail. Finished rail that tops bulwarks.

Capstan. Vertical shaft or drum used as spindle for winding rope or anchor cable.

Careen. To lay vessel on its side to work on sections of hull beneath waterline.

Carronade. Short cannon used on vessels in close fighting.

Catch. See Ketch.

Cathead. A timber or piece of iron projecting from each side of bow, used in hoisting anchor from water and in supporting it when stowed.

Cavil. Large wooden cleat usually fitted to inside of bulwark stanchions.

Ceiled bulwarks. Bulwarks in which planking is fastened to inner faces or inboard side of stanchions.

Ceiling. Inner planking of a vessel's hull attached to frames.

Centerboard. Movable board of wood or metal, enclosed in watertight casing that can be raised or lowered through a slot in bottom of vessel. Allows vessels to work alternately in deep and shallow water.

Centerboard well. Watertight casing through which centerboard is raised or lowered. Also called centerboard trunk.

Chain plates. Flat pieces of metal attached to vessel's hull where deadeyes and lanyards secure ends of shrouds.

Chandler. Harbor merchants, so-called because they originally supplied ships with candles. Later supplied everything from equipment to clothing to foodstuffs.

Chine. Where bottom and sides of hull meet. Called hard chine when bottom and sides meet in sharp angle. Soft chine refers to curved or round-bottom hull.

Chine-built. Bay term for vessel with sharp intersection of bottom and sides and relatively shallow V-bottom; as in bateaux.

Chunk-built. Vessel in which large sections are fashioned from single large logs or pieces of timber.

Clew. Lower, aftermost corner of fore-and-aft sail.

Clipper. Fast-sailing, sharp-built brigs and schooners with especially fine lines and large rig, which evolved from Virginia pilot boat model. "Clip" was an eighteenth century colloquialism meaning to move swiftly.

Close-hauled. When sails are trimmed for heading as close as possible in direction from which wind is blowing, or "on the wind." A schooner will sail about 4 compass points off the wind; a ram, 5 points. *See* Points of sailing.

Clump schooner. Term used to describe slow, full-built, high-capacity freight schooners of early nineteenth century. Full-built as opposed to moderate- or sharp-built.

Coaster. A vessel designed, equipped, manned, and licensed to engage regularly in coasting trade, coastwise or short sea passages.

Coefficient of fineness. Statistical reckoning referring to form of hull. It relates fineness of line and displacement to hull speed, as in a mathematical comparison of pungies and yachts.

Con. To direct steering of vessel.

Corsair. Pirate or private armed vessel.

Cotton duck. Strong cotton fabric, lighter than canvas, used for light sails.

Course. Lowest squaresail on each mast of a square-rigger. On square topsail schooners, sail hung on lowest yard.

Cutter. (1) Single-masted, fore-and-aft rigged vessel with deeper draft and narrower hull than sloop; served as auxiliary vessels with British Navy and in other services; (2) square-sterned ship's rowing boat.

Cutwater. Timber bolted to foreside of stem for added strength, especially in ornamental curve of clipper bow. A false stem.

Davit falls. See Boat falls.

Davits. Pair of light cranes used to lower and lift yawl boats. Used singly to help lift anchors and other equipment.

Deadeye. Strong, rounded block of hardwood with holes through which lanyards are passed or "rove." Used as blocks to connect shrouds and chain plates.

Deadrise. Relative angle of vessel's hull between keel and waterline or chine. Also called "rise of floor."

Dead water. Eddying water along side of moving vessel particularly beneath her stern. Any still water.

Deadweight. Vessel's lifting or weight-carrying capacity in number of "long tons" (2,240 lbs). Difference between displacement tonnage loaded and displacement tonnage when light.

Deadwood. Knees or other timbers used to strengthen inner hull where keel joins stem and sternposts.

Deck chaser. Early steering gear which had rolling action between two upright stanchions. Also called "walking bedstead."

Diamond screw gear. Type of iron steering gear which replaced early deck chaser.

Displacement. Volume or weight of water displaced by hull of vessel which is equal to weight of that hull. Generally expressed in

long tons (2,240 lbs). Also calculated in terms of cubic feet divided by 35, which is number of cubic feet in a long ton of seawater.

Documented vessels. (1) Registered if engaged in foreign trade; (2) enrolled if in coastal trade; (3) licensed if under 20 tons in coasting trade or fisheries.

Donkey engine. Small steam or internal combustion engine used to haul anchors, set sails, pump water, and raise yawl boats.

Draft. Depth measured from waterline to lowest part of keel. Depth of water necessary to keep vessel afloat.

Drag. Amount by which vessel's draft at stern exceeds that at stem.

Driver. Fifth mast from forward on a six-masted schooner. The fore-and-aft sail set abaft the spanker mast.

Drogher. Heavy, usually clumsy, cargo vessel used for carrying bulk cargo such as lumber or stone. Also "caddy" on the Bay.

Dude cruisers. Term used to describe vessels carrying passengers on vacation cruises.

Dyewood. Also called logwood. Dark, gnarled, heavy wood used to make black and dark blue dyes and certain medicines.

Entrance. Shape of bow and forward part of immersed hull from stem to widest part at waterline. Narrow entrance forms long, slender wedge.

Fathom. Nautical measure for cordage, anchor chains, lead lines; also depth of water at sea. Equal to 6 feet.

Fisherman staysail. Primarily a light air sail set between the masts when wind is abeam or abaft the beam.

Flax. Strong, durable fiber used for early sails. Replaced by cotton which held its shape better.

Floor. Timbers forming bottom interior hull structure running athwartships between frames. May be either flat or have slight rise depending on degree of deadrise.

Floor ribband. Long strip of wood or metal used to hold ends of floor timbers in place during construction.

Fluke. Flat part of anchor which holds in bottom. Also called the palm.

Flush deck. Absence of superstructure or break in vessel's upper or weather deck. A continuous deck.

Flying jib. Light triangular jib set aloft on jib-boom.

Flyers. Letter-of-marque private armed vessels as opposed to "sea wolves," or privateers.

Fore-and-aft. Running from stem to stern or lengthwise, parallel to vessel's keel.

Forecastle, Fo'c'sle. Forward living compartment for crew; usually below, in larger schooners, sometimes in forward deckhouse. Also, raised deck above crew's quarters. Part of deck forward of foremast.

Foremast. Mast closest to stem.

Forepeak. Space aft of stem.

Forestay. Heaviest of standing rigging. Supports foremast. Runs from masthead to stem or knighthead.

Freeboard. Height of vessel's sides from deck to surface of water.

Gaff. Spar to which upper edge of the four-sided sail on schooner or sloop is attached. Outer end is the peak; forward end at the mast, the throat.

Gaffsail. A four-sided sail secured to gaff and forward edge secured to mast.

Gallery. Railed or enclosed platform or balcony over stern on older ships.

Garboard plank. Bottom, often heavier, plank laid next to keel. Line of such planks makes up garboard strake.

Gasket. Small line or canvas strap to secure a sail.

Gnaw hole. Section of planking left out of bow of vessel under construction so that timber and other materials could be fed through to inside of hull.

Grapnel. Also grappling-iron. Clawed anchor used by boarders to hook enemy vessel. Also used for dragging the sea bottom.

Gross tonnage. Measure of internal volume of vessel for registry.

Gunwale. Top planking on vessel's side, capped by a rail. Usually on small craft.

Guy ropes. Ropes rigged to support spar. Any ropes or chains used to steady or guide objects being hoisted or lowered.

Half-model. Longitudinal three-dimensional representation of half of ship's hull used in preliminary vessel design. Often made before a draught or drawing. Dated back to seventeenth century. Not widely used in Chesapeake until 1840s. Earliest were block models, carved from solid block of wood and shaped to represent half of proposed hull. Next came the framed "hawk's nest" or "crow's nest" model which is a plank-and-frame representation formed against a backboard in the shape of the hull profile. Last and most useful type of builder's model to be developed was the lift model. Made from horizontal "lifts" or layers of wood, temporarily fastened together to form a solid block. The block is then shaped into desired hull form. Lines for vessel were taken off model and laid down in mold loft to give builder full-size drawing of hull form.

Halyard. Rope or tackle used to hoist or set sails.

Hard chine. See Chine.

Hatch. Opening in deck of vessel, usually covered.

Hawseholes. Openings in vessel's bow through which anchor cable passes.

Head. Referring to either foremost or uppermost part. The upper edge of a sail. Also toilet space.

Head boats. See Dude cruisers. Reference to fact that passage was sold by the "head."

Head gear. Collection of rigging and hardware supporting bowsprit.

Headrail. Rail or cap to bulwark at vessel's head, or rail extending back from figurehead to bow.

Headsails. Sails forward of foremast such as jibs and staysails.

Heeling. When force of wind against sails causes vessel to lean to one side.

Heeler. A sharp-built, fast-sailing vessel.

Hogging. Tendency of vessel's hull to droop in both bow and stern. Caused by lack of buoyancy in the ends to support their weight.

Hold. Cargo space below deck.

Hull speed. Theoretical speed that hull can reach based on its design. A function of length.

Inside ram. Type of ram with beam less than the 24-foot width of the C & D Canal. Worked primarily in Bay and inland waterways from the Carolinas to Philadelphia.

In irons. When a vessel under sail is unable to move under its own power, as when in the eye of the wind and unable to fall off on either tack.

Jib. Triangular-shaped sail set forward of forestay.

Jibboom. Spar secured to and extending forward from bowsprit.

Jib-headed. General term for all sails of triangular shape. Term "sharp-headed" used on Chesapeake Bay.

Joiner. Ship carpenter skilled in joining wood and doing finer woodwork.

Keel. Backbone of vessel, forming bottom centerline.

Keelson. Internal reinforcing structure running parallel and bolted to the keel, usually on top of floors.

Keen. Sharp or pointed, as bow of "sharp-built" schooner.

Ketch. Also "catch." Two-masted colonial vessel with square sail on one mast and gaffsail on other. Possible ancestor of schooner. Also, modern two-masted vessel with foresail larger than main.

Knighthead. Top of the first timbers either side of the stem. Once carved with knights' heads.

Lanyards. Rope reeved through deadeyes used for setting up rigging.

Lateen sail. Shaped like 45-degree right-angled triangle. In use in Mediterranean as early as twelfth century. Rig is exceptionally good for sailing close-hauled or with wind blowing at right angle to vessel's course.

Launching ways. Smooth inclined tracks which carry vessel to water when it is launched. Made of hardwood.

Lazy jacks. Several small lines used to keep schooner's lowered sails from falling on deck. Keep sail stowed on boom.

Lazy board. Also "reef plank." Plank lashed athwartships between stern davits to facilitate reefing. Also used to support main boom.

Lead. Piece of metal used as sinker on line for sounding or determining depth of water. Lower end cupped for "arming" with tallow to sample bottom.

Lee. Side away from direction of wind. Opposite of "weather."

Letter-of-marque. Document issued by state or national governments authorizing owners of privately armed vessels to seize vessels and property of other countries. Term also used for private armed vessel itself. Referred to those vessels engaged primarily in trade and authorized to seize only those enemy ships encountered on a voyage. *See* privateer.

Lighter. Scow, barge, or other boat used to carry cargo or other materials between vessel and shore. Usually is not powered.

Load waterline. Line to which vessel sinks when loaded.

Loft. Open upper floor of shipyard building. Floor is clear for preparing rigging, laying out molds or sails. Also, process of drawing vessel's lines full-size to establish molds or patterns used in making parts for construction.

Log canoe. Small Bay sailing vessel, usually sharp on both ends, constructed from hollowed logs. Style varies regionally, but usually carries two-sail, leg-of-mutton rig, although other sails are added depending on whether canoe is racing or working.

Logwood. See Dyewood.

Longboat. Undecked centerboard schooner with two fore-and-aft sails and large jib. Built shallow with flat floor, round sides, and sharp bow, it was developed on Bay, principally on Potomac River, to carry cordwood. Also called "wood boat" or "wood drogger."

Long ton. Measure of weight equal to 2,240 lbs.

Loose-footed. Refers to fore-and-aft sail without a boom *or* not laced to a boom.

Lug foresail. Gaffsail without boom.

Lugger. Two- or three-masted vessel carrying lug-rigged sails.

Mainmast. Principal mast. Second and taller mast on two-masted schooner. Also second mast on multimasted schooner and after mast on bugeye.

Mainsail. Usually largest sail, or large gaffsail on main mast of multimasted schooner.

Marlin. Also "marline." Small two-strand hemp rope, usually tarred. Used to serve wire and lashings.

Mast. Wood or metal pole that supports booms, gaffs, yards, and gear for carrying sails.

Masthead. Upper part of mast above standing rigging.

Mate. Second in command on commercial vessel.

Mizzen. Third mast from forward or aftermost mast on three-masted vessel. Sail on third mast.

Mold. Also "mould." Template or pattern made of thin wood used to fashion vessel's frames or other parts.

Mold loft. Large enclosed space where structural lines of vessel are laid down and templates drawn from them.

Monkey rail. Small light rail around stern of vessel, as seen on pungy or bugeye.

Mould. See mold.

Net tonnage. Internal volume less certain exemptions for engine space, fuel tanks, store rooms, crew quarters, subtracted from gross tonnage.

Oakum. Tarred hemp fiber used for caulking vessel's seams.

Oil bag. Canvas bag filled with oakum and "storm oil" (usually fish oil) thrown overboard to the windward and allowed to drag in the sea. Oil seeps out and smooths breaking sea.

Outside ram. Larger type with beam up to 34.5 feet used for coastwise and occasionally oceangoing trade.

Packet. Fast-sailing vessel running on regular schedule to carry mail, passengers, and cargo.

Palm. See Fluke.

Patented rigging. Nonstandard rigging that was protected by government patent.

Patent topsail. Topsail that could be stowed and set from deck. Seen on many late nineteenth century schooners. Especially popular on the Bay.

Peak. After end of gaff or gaffsail. Upper corner of triangular sail. Usually called "head" on a jib.

Peak halyard. Halyard which raises or lowers aft end of gaffsail.

Pilot. Person, possessing "local" knowledge of conditions, qualified or licensed to guide vessels through unfamiliar waters.

Pilot boat. Sharp-built, fast-sailing schooners and sloops used in Virginia and Maryland to transport pilots to inbound vessels to con them into the Bay. Such vessels were used in other areas.

Pinnace. Small lug- or schooner-rigged vessel used as ship's tender.

Point of sailing. Angle of sail in relationship to intended course, i.e. beating, reaching, running. A point is one of 32 divisions on a compass. Used in determining direction of object in relation to compass point. Distance between two points is $11\frac{1}{4}$ degrees.

Preventer. Additional rope or tackle rigged to relieve strain or hold an object in place.

Prismatic coefficient. Method of determining fineness of hull.

Privateer. Privately owned armed vessel commissioned by federal and state governments to seize or destroy an enemy's vessel of war or commerce. *See* Prize. Operated strictly as vessel of war to capture or sink enemy shipping. *See* Letter-of-marque.

Prize. Vessel or property seized by private armed or other vessel under laws of belligerent states.

Privateer-built. Sharp-built schooners and brigs built as blockade runners and privateers.

Pungy. Fast-sailing shoal-draft keel schooner with long, low hull and raking masts was final incarnation of Baltimore clipper. Used as oyster boats and freight schooners on Bay.

Push boat. See Yawl boat.

Quarterdeck. Raised deck or area between mainmast and stern.

Rabbet. Groove cut along edge of ship's timber, such as keel or stem- or sternposts, into which edges or ends of planking are fitted.

Rack of eye. Phrase denoting shipwright's judgment as to rightness of lines or shape of vessel he was building.

Rake. Angle of stem- and sternposts and masts in relation to keel.

Ram. Type of schooner developed by J. M. C. Moore for traversing the C & D Canal. Originally narrow, shoal, wall-sided three-masters.

Ratlines. Small ropes running between shrouds forming ladder for climbing aloft.

Reach. Point of sailing when neither beating to windward nor running before the wind. Close reach is when wind is before the beam; broad reach is with wind aft abeam, but not running.

Reef. To take in part of a sail in order to decrease the area of canvas. Also, the part of a sail taken in by reefing.

Reef plank. See Lazy board.

Reef points. Short pieces of rope set into sail for securing reefed section.

Rig. Particular arrangement of masts and sails that distinguishes a vessel type.

Rigging. Collective term for masts, spars, sails, shrouds, stays, and other equipment.

Rise. Angle at which floor rises from keel to chine.

Rise of floor. See Deadrise.

Rudderhead. Top of rudder stock to which tiller is attached.

Run. Underwater shape of after part of hull from its widest point to stern. A "fine" run tapers aft.

Run boat. See Buy boat.

Saddle. Support for boom or other spar in stowed position. Also block of wood placed vertically between jaws of gaff to facilitate sliding of spar up and down the mast. Also called clapper, tumbler, or tongue.

Sawpit. In colonial shipyards, timbers were spread across trestles or opening of sawpit and cut with large two-man saw.

Schooner. Fore-and-aft rigged vessel with two or more masts and gaffsails.

Schooner barge. Type of seagoing barge usually towed, but fitted with masts and sails.

Scow. Wide, flat-bottomed vessel with square bow and stern, used for freight, as lighter or ferry. Scow schooner carries schooner rig.

Scuppers. Waterway along the side of the weather deck. Openings through which water is carried off deck.

Scuttle. Small opening. Usually covered. Also means to intentionally sink a vessel.

Sea anchor. Also "drag" or drogue. Funnel-shaped canvas bag thrown overboard in storm to keep vessel head or stern to wind and sea.

Sea wolves. Popular name for privateers as distinguished from letter-of-marque vessels. *See* Flyers.

Shallop. Small colonial vessel carrying fore-and-aft rig on one or two masts.

Sharp-built. Vessel designed for speed and built with fine lines, narrow, fine bow, and long run aft.

Sharp-headed. See Jib-headed.

Sharp-rigged. Having jib-headed or triangular sails rather than gaffsails.

Sheer. Line of deck from stem to stern. May be curved or flat.

Sheet. Rope or tackle leading from sail's clew, or from boom near clew, used to take in or ease off sail as needed.

Sheet horse. Traveller to which lower end of sheet tackle is attached.

She-pungy. Pungy with centerboard.

Ship. Type of large, oceangoing sailing vessel, square-rigged with three or more masts.

Ship-rigged. All masts rigged with yards and square sails.

Shoal. Shallow.

Shoal draft. Shallow draft.

Shroud. Rope or wire which is part of standing rigging to support mast in an athwartships position as opposed to a stay that is a fore-and-aft support.

Skeg. Deadwood next to sternpost. *See* Deadwood.

Skids. Parallel pieces of timber used as runners upon which vessel is launched or heavy objects are moved.

Skipjack. Single-masted, hard-chine Bay workboat used for dredging oysters. Carries leg-of-mutton sail and jib.

Slack bilge. Vessel having a very shallow curve to its bilge.

Slick. Large, chisel-like tool.

Sloop. Single-masted fore-and-aft rigged vessel.

Snatch block. Block with opening that allows rope to be placed over roller without having to be run all the way through from an end.

Snow. Type of brig with jack mast aft of main.

Spanker. Fourth mast on four-masted schooner, or the sail set on it.

Spar. Term denoting boom, mast, yard, or other round pole.

Spring stay. Rope or wire stay running between and near the head of the masts.

Spritsail. Similar to gaffsail and carried in same position with spar reaching diagonally from mast to peak.

Square halves. Master's share or one-half of net freight money received, out of which he paid crew's wages, and bought food and provisions.

Square rig. Having square sails set at right angles to vessel's centerline. "Square-rigged" when used to refer to Bay boats may also mean gaff-rigged.

Square-stern bugeye. Another term for "she-pungy" or a pungy with a centerboard, if carrying a schooner rig.

Stanchion. Post or pillar used as support for rail, bulwark, deck, or other structure.

Standing rigging. Collection of shrouds and stays used to support masts, bowsprit, and jibboom.

Stay. Rope or wire that is part of standing rigging which supports mast in fore-and-aft position as opposed to shroud, which is a lateral support.

Staysail. Fore-and-aft triangular sail, not a jib, which is spread from a stay.

Steambox. Box used to apply steam to planks that had to be bent in construction of vessel, as in a bow section.

Steeving bowsprit. The angle above horizontal given a bowsprit. Varies according to size and type of vessel.

Stem. Structural upright timber at bow of vessel. Also to make progress against a wind, tide, or current.

Step. Block, socket, or platform on which mast or stanchion rests. Also, to place mast in its position.

Stocks. Timber frames in which vessel rests when being built.

Storm trysail. Heavy, triangular sail which can be rigged in various positions when needed in storm.

Strake. Line of planking.

Sweep. Long oar with broad blade used to row or steer vessel.

Tack. Direction of vessel's head relative to trim of sails. Starboard tack is with wind over the starboard side. Port tack is with wind over the port side. To change course when sailing by turning a vessel's head into the wind; to go about. Also, lower forward corner of fore-and-aft sail.

Tern schooner. Early term for a three-masted schooner.

Throat halyard. Rope for hoisting throat or upper, forward corner of gaffsail; upper corner next to mast.

Tiller. The helm. An arm, as opposed to wheel, for turning rudder.

Top hamper. Upper rigging of a vessel.

Topmast. Second mast extending from and above lower mast.

Topsail schooner. Fore-and-aft rigged schooner with square sails set on fore-topmast. Sometimes found with square sails set also on main topmast.

Trailboard. Ornamental plank on either side of cutwater.

Tramp schooner. Commercial schooner that carried whatever cargo was available. Had no regularly scheduled run.

Transom. Transverse planking forming stern of square-ended vessel.

Trim. To arrange sails, rigging, or cargo in the best condition for sailing. The difference between draft forward and aft.

Trysail. see Storm trysail.

Trunk. Between decks enclosure for hatchway. Part of cabin extending above deck. Walls of watertight box enclosing centerboard.

Trunk cabin. Cabin whose sides extend above deck.

Tuck. Where planking meets beneath overhang of stern.

Tumble home. Where hull turns inward above waterline.

'Tween decks. Between decks. Deck and area below upper and above lowest deck.

Two-topmast schooner. Schooner with topmast fitted on both fore- and mainmasts.

Waist. Midship or widest part of deck.

Wale strakes. Uppermost strake or row of planking, usually thicker than other planks; bends.

Walking bedstead. See Deck chaser.

Waterway. Two or more wide strakes of deck planking along the edge of the deck at the side of the vessel to carry water off through scuppers or freeing ports.

Weather side. Side toward the direction of wind. *See* Lee.

Weatherly. Capable of sailing close to the wind.

Wheelbox. Housing for steering gear.

Winch head. Top of capstan used for hoisting anchors, yawl boats, and other heavy objects on board vessel.

Windward. Direction from which wind is blowing.

Windlass. Horizontal winch for hauling in anchor.

Wing-and-wing. Also "reading both pages" or "wung-out." Set of sails when vessel is running before wind and one sail is set to each side of vessel.

Wood boat. See Longboat.

Yard. Horizontal spar for carrying head of square sail.

Yawl boat. Small working boat carried on stern davits and lowered to push or pull schooner when there is not enough wind to move her under sail or in tight quarters.

Bibliography

Albion, Robert Greenhalgh with collaboration of Jennie Barnes Pope. *The Rise of the New York Port 1815-1860.* New York: Charles Scribner's Sons, 1939.

Barry, R., and George Barry, Jr. *Cruises Mainly in the Bay of the Chesapeake.* Bryn Mawr, Pa.: Franklin Press, 1909.

Blanchard, Fessenden S. *A Cruising Guide to the Chesapeake.* New York: Dodd, Mead & Co., 1950.

Brewington, M. V. *Chesapeake Bay: A Pictorial Maritime History.* Cambridge, Md.: Cornell Maritime Press, 1953.

Brooks, Kenneth F., Jr. *Run to the Lee.* New York: W. W. Norton & Co., 1965.

Burgess, Robert H. *Chesapeake Circle.* Cambridge, Md.: Cornell Maritime Press, 1965.

———. *Chesapeake Sailing Craft: Part I.* Cambridge, Md.: Tidewater Publishers, 1975.

———. *This Was Chesapeake Bay.* Centreville, Md.: Tidewater Publishers, 1963.

Chapelle, Howard I. *The American Fishing Schooners 1825-1935.* New York: W. W. Norton, 1973.

———. *The Baltimore Clipper: Its Origin and Development.* New York: Bonanza Books, 1930.

———. *History of the American Sailing Navy.* New York: W. W. Norton, 1949.

———. *The History of American Sailing Ships.* New York: W. W. Norton, 1935.

———. *National Watercraft Collection.* Washington, D.C.: United States National Museum Bulletin 219, Smithsonian Institution, Government Printing Office, 1960.

———. *The Search for Speed Under Sail 1700-1855.* New York: W. W. Norton, 1967.

Chatterton, E. Keble. *Fore-and-Aft: The Story of the Fore-and-Aft Rig from the Earliest Times to the Present Day.* Philadelphia: J. B. Lippincott, 1912.

Clancy, Roger. *Ships, Ports, and Pilots.* Jefferson, N.C.: McFarland & Co., 1984.

Coggeshall, George. *History of American Privateers.* New York: by the author, 1856.

Cranwell, John Philips, and William Bowers Crane. *Men of Marque: A History of Private Armed Vessels out of Baltimore During the War of 1812.* New York: W. W. Norton, 1940.

Dozer, Donald M. *A Portrait of the Free State.* Cambridge, Md.: Tidewater Publishers, 1976.

Dudley, William S., ed. *The Naval War of 1812: A Documentary History.* Volume I. Washington, D.C.: Naval Historical Center, Department of the Navy, 1985.

Eller, Ernest M., ed. *Chesapeake Bay in the American Revolution.* Centreville, Md.: Tidewater Publishers, 1981.

Evans, Cerinda W. *Some Notes on Shipbuilding and Shipping in Colonial Virginia.* Williamsburg: The Virginia 350th Anniversary Celebration Corporation, 1957.

Everson, Jennie G. *Tidewater Ice of the Kennebec River.* Freeport, Me.: Maine State Museum, 1970.

Fairburn, William A. *Merchant Sail.* Volume V. Lovell, Me.: Fairburn Marine Educational Foundation, 1955.

Footner, Hulbert. *Rivers of the Eastern Shore: Seventeen Maryland Rivers.* New York: Farrar & Rinehart, 1944. Reprint. Centreville, Md.: Tidewater Publishers, 1964.

Garitee, Jerome R. *The Republic's Private Navy: The American Privateering Business as practiced by Baltimore during the War of 1812.* Middletown, Conn.: Wesleyan University Press for Mystic Seaport, Inc., 1977.

Gillmer, Thomas C., N.A. *Chesapeake Bay Sloops.* St. Michaels, Md.: Chesapeake Bay Maritime Museum, 1982.

Goldenberg, Joseph A. *Shipbuilding in Colonial America.* Charlottesville: University Press of Virginia for The Mariners' Museum, Newport News, Va., 1976.

Hall, Henry. *Report of the Shipbuilding Industry of the United States.* Washington, D.C.: Government Printing Office, 1880.

Hooper, Gladys Ione, ed. *My Years Before the Mast: Memoirs of Chesapeake Bay Waterman William T. Hooper.* Dorchester County Maryland.

Jones, Joseph C., Jr. *America's Icemen.* Humble, Tx.: Jobeco Books, 1984.

Keith, Robert C. *Baltimore Harbor: A Picture History.* Baltimore: Ocean World Publishing Co., 1982.

Laing, Alexander. *American Sail: A Pictorial History.* New York: Dutton, 1961.

Leavitt, John. *Wake of the Coasters.* Middletown, Conn.: Marine Historical Association, Wesleyan University Press, 1970.

MacGregor, David R. *Schooners in Four Centuries.* Annapolis, Md.: Naval Institute Press, 1982.

Marvil, James E. *Sailing Rams.* Lewes, Del.: Sussex Press, 1961, 1974.

Marvin, Winthrop L. *The American Merchant Marine.* New York: Charles Scribner's Sons, 1902.

McEwen, W. A., and A. H. Lewis. *Encyclopedia of Nautical Knowledge.* Centreville, Md.: Cornell Maritime Press, 1953.

Merchant Vessels of the United States. Washington, D.C.: Bureau of Navigation, U.S. Treasury Department. Various editions.

Middleton, Arthur Pierce. *Tobacco Coast: A Maritime History of the Chesapeake Bay in the Colonial Era.* Newport News, Va.: The Mariners' Museum, 1953; Baltimore, Md.: The Johns Hopkins University Press, Baltimore, and The Maryland State Archives, Annapolis; Maryland Paperback Bookshelf edition, 1984.

Morris, Edward P. *The Fore-and-Aft Rig in America.* New Haven, Conn.: Yale University Press, 1927.

Parker, W. J. Lewis. *The Great Coal Schooners of New England: 1870-1909.* Mystic, Conn.: The Marine Historical Association, 1948.

Scharf, John Thomas. *History of Maryland from the Earliest Period to the Present Day.* Baltimore, Md., 1879.

Steinlein, Eric. *Historic American Marine Survey.* Vol. II. Washington, D.C.: Smithsonian Institution, Government Printing Office, 1937.

Stevenson, Charles H. *The Oyster Industry of Maryland.* Washington, D.C.: Government Printing Office, 1894.

Tilp, Fred. *Chesapeake Bay of Yore.* Alexandria, Va.: Chesapeake Bay Foundation, 1982.

Wennersten, John R. *The Oyster Wars of Chesapeake Bay.* Centreville, Md.: Tidewater Publishers, 1981.

Articles and Essays

Bourne, M. Florence. "Thomas Kemp, Shipbuilder." *Maryland Historical Magazine* 49, no. 3 (1954).

Brewington, M.V. "The Chesapeake Bay Pilots." *Maryland Historical Magazine* 48, no. 2 (June 1953).

Gilbert, Geoffrey. "The Ships of Federalist Baltimore." *Maryland Historical Magazine* 79, no. 4 (Winter 1984).

Hall, Henry. "The Ice Industry of the U.S." U.S. Dept. of the Interior. H.R. Misc. Dr. 42. 47th Congress, 2nd Session, 1888.

Lyman, John, ed., *Log Chips* (Chapel Hill, N.C.), vol. 1-4 (1948-59).

Milius, Helen C. "Ice Queen." *Commonwealth Magazine* 26, no. 12 (December 1959).

Niles Weekly Register (1813; July-Nov. 1814; Oct. 1825; April 1831; June-Aug. 1832; July 1833).

Parker, W. J. Lewis, USCG (Ret.). "The East Coast Ice Trade of the U.S." National Maritime Museum Symposium Monograph no. 49, 1891.

Sayer, Louis. "Oystering Aboard the Ella F. Cripps." *The Rudder* (August 1911). Chesapeake Bay Maritime Museum, vertical file.

Sheller, Tina H. "Artisans, Manufacturing, and the Rise of a Manufacturing Interest in Revolutionary Baltimore Town." *Maryland Historical Magazine* 83, no. 1 (Spring 1988).

Smith, Philip C. Foster. "Crystal Blocks of Yankee Coldness." Essex Institute Historical Collections, Salem, Mass., July 1961.

Steinlein, Eric. "In Pursuit of the Pungy." *The Chesapeake Skipper* (April 1965). St. Michaels, Md.: Chesapeake Bay Maritime Museum, vertical file.

____. "Pungy Boats." *WoodenBoat* 45 (April 1984).

Primary Sources

A. Smith & Sons Shipyard, Curtis Bay, Maryland: records and photographs.

Bethel Historical Society, Bethel, Delaware: manuscripts, logs, and photos.

Brannock Maritime Museum, Cambridge, Maryland: manuscripts, library, and photo collection.

Calvert Marine Museum, Solomons Island, Maryland: vertical files and plans.

Cape Ann Historical Society, Gloucester, Massachusetts: photo archives.

Cape May County Historical Society, Cape May Court House, New Jersey: half-model collection.

Chesapeake & Delaware Canal Museum, Chesapeake City, Maryland: photos and historical data.

Chesapeake Bay Maritime Museum, St. Michaels, Maryland; vertical file, manuscripts, photo archives, and plans collection.

Cumberland County Historical Society, Greenwich, New Jersey: photo archives, half-model and manuscript collections.

Enoch Pratt Free Library, Baltimore, Maryland: manuscripts, *The* [Baltimore] *Sun* archives, and vertical files.

Free Library of Philadelphia: photo collections.

Historical Society of Delaware, Wilmington: photo archives.

Lewes Historical Society, Lewes, Delaware: half-model collection of Howard I. Chapelle.

The Mariners' Museum, Newport News, Virginia: manuscript and photo archives, and library.

Maryland Historical Society, Baltimore: "Shipbuilding in Maryland," list compiled by John G. Earle, Manuscript Collection.

Maryland State Archives, Annapolis: manuscript, photo archives, and Sands Collection.

Mystic Seaport Museum, Mystic, Connecticut: photo and manuscript archives, ship plans, and library.

National Archives, Washington, D.C.: photo archives, Customs House records, and Admeasurement Certificates.

Naval Historical Center, Washington Navy Yard, Washington, D.C.: Early Naval Records Center; Captain Charles Gordon, USN, correspondence with Secretary of the Navy Jones.

New Jersey Historic Society, Newark: Wayne Yarnall Maritime Collection.

Peabody Museum, Salem, Massachusetts: library, ship plans, and photo archives.

Peale Museum, Baltimore, Maryland: manuscript and photo archives.

Philadelphia Maritime Museum: manuscript, photo, and plans collections.

Radcliffe Maritime Museum of the Maryland Historical Society, Baltimore: manuscript, plans, and photo collections, and volumes of *Maryland Historical Magazine.*

Smithsonian Institution, Division of Transportation, Museum of American History, Washington, D.C.: *Historic American Merchant Marine Survey* field notes, photo archives, manuscripts, and plans.

Author Interviews

Aaron, Woodrow. Oral history source. Served as crew on several Bay schooners. Cambridge, Maryland. Died 1991.

Brannock, Earl. Oral history source. Former director of Maryland Office of Economic Development; founder of Brannock Maritime Museum, Cambridge, Maryland.

Brannock, Shirley. Oral history source. Chesapeake Bay marine artist. Cambridge, Maryland.

Brownlee, Edward G. Marine engineer, historian, associated with Philadelphia Maritime Museum. Cherry Hill, New Jersey.

Burgess, Robert H. Former director of exhibits, The Mariners' Museum; author and Chesapeake Bay historian. Newport News, Virginia.

Dubois, John. Retired shipbuilder and oysterman, photographer, and collector. Absecon, New Jersey.

Earle, John. Marine engineer, historian, collector, contributed significantly to work of M. V. Brewington. Easton, Maryland. Died 1992.

Evans, C. Calvert. Owner of *Sarah C. Conway* and *Carol Ann*. Primary oral history source. Cambridge, Maryland.

Jackson, Mary. Naval architect.

King, Jack. Oysterman, captain of oyster vessels. Port Norris, New Jersey.

Liener, Joe. Oral history source. Boatbuilder, historian, associated with Chesapeake Bay Maritime Museum. Pot Pie, Maryland.

Marvil, James E., M.D. Author, historian, collector. Lewes, Delaware.

Murphy, Wade. Oysterman, owner of *Rebecca Ruark*. Tilghman, Maryland.

Perry, Lynn. Oral history source. Photographer, chronicler of schooner history and lore. Urbanna, Virginia.

Porter, Harry B. Oral history source. Former skipper of Maryland governors' yachts, *Lady Maryland, Aurora,* and *Independence*; Bay freight captain. Kent Island, Maryland.

Richardson, Jim. Oral history source, seventh-generation boat builder. LeCompte, Maryland.

Smith, Jerry. Collector and photographer. A. Smith & Sons Shipyard. Curtis Bay, Maryland.

Trott, Lester. Former director of tourism, state of Maryland; former publicist for Chesapeake Vacation Cruises; collector of Bay memorabilia. Annapolis, Maryland.

Van Name, Arthur, M.D. Marine artist, photographer, historian; source of information on schooners and oyster industry. Urbanna, Virginia.

Ward, John, Sr. Captain, Bay freight vessels. Deltaville, Virginia.

Whittolz, Charles C. Naval architect, designer of *Mystic Clipper, Young America, Pegasus,* and *Providence*. Redesigned rig of *Western Union*. Silver Spring, Maryland.

Index

Page numbers in italics indicate illustrations.